WORDSWORTH CLASSICS
OF WORLD LITERATURE

General Editor: Tom Griffith

ABRAHAM LINCOLN
Life, Speeches and Lertters

D0064079

ABRAHAM LINCOLN

Life, Speeches and Letters

The Life of Abraham Lincoln
by Henry Ketcham

Speeches and Letters, 1832–1865
selected by Merwin Roe

❖

*with an introduction
by Hugh Griffith*

**WORDSWORTH CLASSICS
OF WORLD LITERATURE**

In loving memory of
MICHAEL TRAYLER
the founder of Wordsworth Editions

I

Readers who are interested in other titles from
Wordsworth Editions are invited to visit our website at
www.wordsworth-editions.com

For our latest list and a full mail order service contact
Bibliophile Books, Unit 5 Datapoint,
South Crescent, London E16 4TL
Tel: +44 0207 515 9222
Fax: +44 0207 538 4115
e-mail: orders@bibliophilebooks.com

This edition published 2009 by Wordsworth Editions Limited
8b East Street, Ware, Hertfordshire SG12 9HJ

ISBN 978 1 84022 631 7

Typeset in Great Britain by Roperford Editorial
Printed and bound by Clays Ltd, St Ives plc

CONTENTS

SPEECHES AND LETTERS

INTRODUCTION

I shall do nothing in malice. What I deal with is too vast for malicious dealing.

Abraham Lincoln was a most unlikely choice for President. True, he was generally liked, patently honest, a sociable man, a great raconteur. But on the surface there was little to suggest unusual ability. He was almost entirely lacking in formal education. His manner was plain and unpolished, sometimes odd enough to be embarrassing to those around him. 'So you're John Sherman,' said the new President on meeting a distinguished senator. 'Let's see if you're as tall as I am. We'll measure.' There were those who found this kind of simplicity endearing. Others were alarmed that such a person should hold the affairs of the country in his hands. Unlike most of his competitors, Lincoln had never been a senator or state governor. His experience of government and matters of state was unusually limited. Nor did it help that his physical appearance was ungainly and awkward. There was no doubting the sincerity and good nature of the man, but it was a pity he could not make a more dignified appearance in public.

At a deeper level, as Americans came to realise almost immediately when they heard of his death, Lincoln had greater natural dignity than anyone. His respect for people was genuine and profound, his capacity for fellow-feeling remarkable. It was typical of him that he was able to wage a relentless war on those who espoused the cause of slave-owning, a practice which he himself found hateful, without feeling any moral indignation whatever against slave-owners themselves. Even in the South it came to be seen that Lincoln was no personal enemy of theirs, that he was in some sense the best friend they could have had. When Alexander Stephens, the Vice-President of the Confederacy, met Lincoln in early 1865, he was told to abandon any hope of entering into negotiations on ending the war. Lincoln made it clear that he still regarded the Confederates as rebels who were liable to be hanged for treason. 'We supposed that would have to be your view,' Stephens replied. 'But, to tell you the truth, we have none of us been much afraid of being hanged with you as President.'

The earnestness of Lincoln's sympathy is perfectly conveyed by words of his own, ending a letter that he wrote in 1862 to one Cuthbert Bullitt, a citizen of Louisiana, one of the Confederate states. 'I shall do nothing in malice. What I deal with is too vast for malicious dealing.' Any politician might express a similar idea and we might or might not believe that it was sincerely meant. Abraham Lincoln, in a unique way, by the very care and precision with which he chooses those exact words, in particular the word 'vast', leaves his reader entirely satisfied that what he says is true.

It was also typical of Lincoln that, for all his earnest desire that peace should come and wounds be allowed to heal, he continued to see with complete clarity during the final stages of the war the crucial point that almost everyone in the North preferred to ignore – that an early end to the fighting, if it could only come through a negotiated settlement with the South, would be a disaster. There must be absolute and unconditional surrender. Anything less would leave the seceding states with some shreds of self-justification, enough to foster a secret hope of reviving their project at a later date.

Lincoln was the ideal President for the greatest crisis in the history of the United States. Very possibly, without him those states might no longer be united, or their unity might be an uneasy muddle and infected with ancient resentment. What Lincoln could offer, in his odd way, was a long vision and matchless patience, together with an unusual passion for clarifying and laying bare the truth. Because of his oddness, and because of his ingenuous faith in the power of logic and reason, he was commonly misunderstood. He was always a more powerful thinker, a more formidable debater, a more obstinate opponent than first appearances suggested. Even those who approved of him often did so without feeling any need to modify their own sense of superiority.

When the Republican party nominated Lincoln as their candidate in 1860, there is every reason to suppose they were largely ignorant of what they were getting. Two of Lincoln's rivals, William Seward and Salmon Chase, were far more notable politicians with much more impressive credentials. But both, when it came to slavery, were very advanced in their views. It was feared that their uncompromising stance might scare off many of the voters in a national contest. Lincoln was more moderate and would be the safer candidate, more willing to compromise – or so it was supposed. But Lincoln, though he liked to say yes if he could, had no fear of saying no if he needed to, and having said it was less likely than anyone on earth to bend his opinion under pressure. Thus, by the happiest of accidents, the right man was chosen because many of those making the choice had an inaccurate picture of who he was.

The slavery question

Abraham Lincoln is a hero to Americans because he abolished slavery. But at the time he lived no one was more aware than Lincoln himself that slavery in the United States was the thorniest and most intractable of questions. That it was wrong, was simple. How to get rid of it, was a problem of hideous complexity.

When the Founding Fathers drew up the Constitution in 1789, they set up a federal system in which power is divided between the central authority and the individual states. The states are only subject to the control of the federal government in certain areas, and retain control over all matters which affect only themselves. Right from the start, this meant there was a distinction between abolishing the importation of slaves from abroad (a federal decision, passed into law on 1 January 1808) and abolishing slave ownership within the borders of each individual state (a question for that state alone). The overriding need at the time was to establish a firm Union of the states and to bind them as closely together as possible, for the strength and security of the new and potentially vulnerable nation. With this in mind, all direct mention of slaves and slavery was omitted from the Constitution, in order not to create any immediate cause of dissension between slave-owning states and states that were free.

It was Lincoln's firm belief, backed up with careful research, that Washington and Jefferson and their companions, without confronting the matter directly, had desired and expected that slavery would eventually become extinct. Before the Union came into existence, Jefferson had tried to pass an Ordinance excluding slavery from all territory that might ever belong to the Congress (as the alliance of states was then called). He failed, but in 1787 an Ordinance was passed imposing such an exclusion on the North-west Territory, an enormous tract of land to the north and west of the Ohio River that was now beginning to be opened up for settlement. This had the momentous effect over time that when, in due course, the states of Ohio, Indiana, Illinois, Michigan and Wisconsin were created, each one was legally barred from becoming a slave state.

The scene was therefore set for a long struggle. Since the federal government had no jurisdiction to decide the matter within the borders of any fully existing state, it would be in the newly acquired lands of the Territories, which were federally governed, that the future survival of slavery would be determined. Up until 1820, new states were generally admitted to the Union in pairs, one slave state together with one free. Then it was the turn of Missouri to be admitted, and the senators of the South won their fight to have slavery permitted in the new state's constitution. The North, it seemed, had lost. But they had won an important concession for the future. In the rest of the territory bought from France in the Louisiana Purchase, slavery would from now on be unlawful north of latitude 36° 30', and lawful south of that line. This was the Missouri Compromise of 1820.

So matters stood for thirty years or so. Slavery was at least contained, though it was very far from being eliminated. In the meantime there was war with Mexico, and on the shakiest of pretexts Texas was annexed by the United States. The Southern leaders were jubilant. Here was a vast new stretch of territory ripe for cultivation by slaves. Shortly after this another immense area of land was taken from Mexico, later to form the new states of California, Arizona and New Mexico. To the horror of those in the North, slavery threatened to spread westwards as far as the Pacific Ocean.

In 1849 the inhabitants of California elected a Convention whose task it was to draw up a state constitution. This Convention – to the surprise of many who thought the place was a wilder-ness peopled only by ruffians – decided unanimously that slavery should be prohibited. Most Americans approved, but to the South the decision was anathema and they blocked the admission of the new state to the Union. After some wrangling they agreed to give way, but only at the price of certain concessions which fed their hope that slave ownership might still be further extended wherever new settlement took place. In both Nebraska and Kansas the same issue arose, in slightly different form. It resolved into a series of interlinked questions. Was it for the federal government to determine whether slavery was permitted in these territories? Alternatively, were the inhabitants of a territory entitled to agree amongst themselves to prohibit slavery? And what then if someone from the South came to a new settlement, bringing his slaves with him? Were they still slaves or did the law recognise them as free? These were the vital matters which dominated all politics during the ten years leading up to the Civil War. North and South had never agreed about slavery, but before 1850 they had managed to rub along together well enough. Times were now different. Each side now found the attitude of the other intolerable.

From our perspective it seems almost incredible that halfway through the nineteenth century the slave states of the South, far from being in retreat, were actually gaining in confidence. Not only was there no shame in their defence of slavery, but a widespread belief existed amongst them that their institutions were superior, and foremost among them the institution of slavery itself. Yet, as Lincoln pointed out on many occasions, theirs was a split view. They boasted that slavery was good. But throughout the South all were united in reviling the slave dealer in their midst: decent folk kept their children well away from his. Surely there was some recognition here, if only a confused one, that the trade was a vile one, that the treating of people as property, the breaking up of families, the prodding and poking of human flesh to test its value, were an assault on humanity.

In all this, however, it is essential to remember that most people in the North were not arguing for outright abolition of slavery throughout the Union. If the old slave states wanted to continue in their ways, that was distressing and wrong, but it was still for them to decide. That was what the Founding Fathers had meant when they set up a federal system of government. There were those – the Abolitionists – who saw slavery as so grievous an injustice that it demanded instant remedy by any means possible, even at the cost of transgressing the Constitution. But they were in the minority. The new party of the North, Lincoln's party of Republicans, were not Abolitionists, though they detested slavery and wanted an end to it. As they saw it, their duty was to oppose any extension of slavery, remaining within the limits of what the Constitution allowed. For Lincoln, the Union, and the Constitution that safeguarded it, came before everything, even ending slavery. Hence the words that he wrote in 1862, replying to the criticisms of Horace Greeley, editor of the *New York Tribune*:

> My paramount object in this struggle is to save the Union. If I could save the Union without freeing any slaves I would do it; and if I could save it by freeing all the slaves I would do it; and if I could save it by freeing some and leaving others alone, I would also do that.

Preparation for the Presidency

Lincoln's great task on becoming President was to save the Union. In this he succeeded, as perhaps very few others could have done. What was it, then, that fitted him so well for that task? He had been moderately successful as a politician, but no more than that: a member of the Illinois state legislature, and later a United States Congressman for a mere two years, between 1847 and 1849. He had opposed the war with Mexico, thereby losing much potential support, together with any chance of re-election. When he went back to his law practice in 1849 there was little reason to expect that any great opportunity in politics still lay ahead of him. For an ambitious man, this was a depressing realisation.

Lincoln stayed out of politics for five years. He may have thought his career had been a failure, but if so that did not sour his outlook. On the contrary, it seems that he now began to form the idea of deepening and enlarging his education. His term in Congress, combined with visits to New England and some of the eastern cities, had brought home to him some of his deficiencies in that area. He studied constantly, reading aloud whenever he needed to impress anything firmly on his mind, and thereby driving his partner to distraction. Lawyers in the circuit courts of Illinois travelled as a group on horseback, eating their meals together and sharing a single room for the night in small inns along their way. While the rest snored, Lincoln would stay up late poring over his books by candlelight. One of his closest companions was a copy of Euclid's *Elements*, which he had first studied as a young trainee lawyer.

Nowadays the idea of reading and re-reading Euclid seems nothing if not bizarre. In Lincoln's day it was not quite so strange. The study of Euclid had been recommended for 2,000 years as one of the best ways to train the mind in logic and clarity of argument. In the age of Thomas Jefferson, it still stood as a powerful symbol of what could be achieved through the human capacity for reasoning. Still, the number of people who ever seriously studied Euclid in Lincoln's day was almost certainly minuscule. Logical precision, clear demonstration of a proposition, the elimination of all vagueness – these seem to have been Lincoln's preoccupations. At the same time, the lawyer's daily round gave him the chance to deepen and extend his study of human nature, a field in which he was already something of a master.

Whatever his feelings may have been about those five years in the wilderness, the Lincoln who returned to politics in 1854 was a stronger man than the one who left Congress in 1849. What brought him back was the urgent need to found a new party which would fight the Democratic party over slavery. In 1854 Stephen Douglas, a Democratic senator from Lincoln's own state of Illinois, had succeeded in getting a bill passed through Congress that allowed the people of Kansas (not yet a state) to choose whether or not to permit slavery. This amounted to a repeal of the Missouri Compromise. There was no longer any guarantee for new territories that slavery would remain outside their borders. It was solely for this purpose that the Republican party was formed, to fight the extension of slavery in the territories.

For the next four years Lincoln directed all his energies to opposing Douglas. Judged by visible results, the victory might have been granted to his opponent. Douglas was four years younger but a more successful and prominent politician than Lincoln. Many regarded him as the natural leader of the Democrats in the North. He had urbanity, wit and charm. On two occasions during this period, 1856 and 1858, the people of Illinois voted to elect one of their senators; each time Lincoln stood and lost to a Democrat. The second time it was Douglas himself who beat him. Lincoln, however, was a clever and wily campaigner who played a long game. During the long and gruelling series of public debates which he held with Douglas in 1858, he secured two vital objectives, at the minor cost (so it seemed to him) of sacrificing his own chance of becoming senator. The first was to expose the latent threat of the slavery question in terms as clear as they were compelling. The second was to ensure, with great cunning, that whatever the result of the senatorial contest, a fatal split would occur in the Democratic party, which would thus be left with no chance whatever of winning the next presidential election in 1860.

In his first speech of his 1858 campaign, Lincoln uttered the most carefully prepared words of his life so far. They spelled out with absolute directness, in a way that no one in public life had yet dared to do, a truth which most Americans would rather go on ignoring:

> 'A house divided against itself cannot stand.' I believe this Government cannot endure permanently half slave and half free. I do not expect the Union to be dissolved – I do not expect the house to fall – but I do expect that it will cease to be divided. It will become all one thing or all the other. Either the opponents of slavery will arrest the further spread of it, and place it where the public mind shall rest in the belief that it is in course of ultimate extinction; or its advocates will push it forward till it shall become lawful alike in all the States, old as well as new – North as well as South.

Before he delivered the speech, Lincoln read it to a group of close supporters. Of the 'house divided' passage, one said it was 'ahead of its time', another called it 'a damned fool utterance'. All except one advised against including it in the speech. The exception was his law partner, William Herndon, who said simply, 'It will make you President.'

Lincoln lost the campaign to become senator. But during the course of it he forced Douglas to give certain answers, on extending slavery into the territories, that he knew would alienate the Democrats of the South, to the point where they would never agree to put Douglas forward for the Presidency. This indeed was what happened. The Democratic party was incapable of agreeing on the choice of their candidate in 1860, thereby making Lincoln's party, the Republicans, certain winners right from the start. It would be wrong to see Lincoln as a political innocent, too honest for schemes or manoeuvring. He gave every impression of positively enjoying the rough and tumble of politics; likewise of having a remarkably sharp nose for popular sentiment. One Illinois political insider described him thus: 'He was one of the shrewdest politicians in the state. Nobody had more experience in that way. Nobody knew better what was passing in the minds of the people. Nobody knew better how to turn things to advantage politically.'

Presidency and the Civil War

By the time Lincoln was sworn in as President on 4 March 1861, seven states of the South had seceded from the Union and a Confederacy had been formed. Others were to join them. Within two months all hope of a peaceful resolution was gone and the nation was at war.

Dark times followed. Militarily, the North was ill-prepared. In the beginning, they had no generals to match those of the South. There was hesitancy, delay, failure to follow up advantages when they were gained. In all this, Lincoln's greatest difficulty was uniting his side in a common purpose. From every side, as long as the war lasted, came advice from those who were convinced they knew how to run the war better than he did. Even before hostilities began, William Seward, a member of his Cabinet, wrote a long letter to Lincoln telling him what he ought to be doing, and virtually requiring him to hand over the direction of policy to someone better qualified. Lincoln replied to this breathtaking advance with the utmost politeness, as was his custom. But Seward was left in no doubt who was in charge, and the episode tells us much about Lincoln's style. He put Seward firmly in his place because this needed to be done, but saw nothing to be gained by causing unnecessary offence. His reward was loyalty. Whatever their individual opinions, his Cabinet remained united; of all Lincoln's achievements, this was one of the most significant.

The pattern was to be repeated many times over. In August 1861 General Fremont issued a proclamation in Missouri, liberating the slaves there and confiscating the property of anyone convicted (by court martial) of aiding the enemy. The measure went far beyond his competence, and invited all manner of unwelcome consequences. Missouri, though a slave state, had not seceded, and Fremont's action was liable to drive the wavering state of Kentucky into the arms of the Confederacy. Lincoln invited Fremont to withdraw his proclamation, by private letter but in the strongest terms: 'Can it be pretended that it is any longer the Government of the United States – any government of constitution and laws –

wherein a general or a president may make permanent rules of property by proclamation?' Rather than submit, Fremont made Lincoln publicly overrule him, more concerned with his own reputation as a lover of freedom than with measures of broad policy.

Maintaining unity amongst the people of the North was an almost impossible task. Had the United States been at war with a foreign power, it would have been much easier. In a civil war feelings run differently. Loyalties are divided and muddled. Inevitably, there are ties of duty and affection connecting some supporters of one side with some of the other. What one person calls treachery, another calls friendship or family honour. Then there is the problem of how far or how strenuously to prosecute the war. Do you hesitate to strike because your enemy was once your friend? In January 1863 a campaign to end the war was begun by a group of Democrats in the North. Lincoln was accused by one Congressman of 'imperial despotism', and there were those who liked to call him 'King Abraham I', in reference to his assumption of special powers. In the latter stages of the war the whole country, by his declaration, was under martial law, and Lincoln was ruthless in repressing any speech or act that might help the enemy. This applied especially to anything that might oppose the Conscription Act.

In Lincoln's own party there were many who had thought he was timid or half-hearted over the question of liberating the slaves. Yet when emancipation did come, plenty of Democrats in the North were less than overjoyed, believing there was no justification for it. For Democrats generally, a weakening of popular support for the war offered their best hope of electoral success in 1864: at their Convention in that year, they demanded 'that immediate efforts be made for a cessation of hostilities'. In the face of all this, Lincoln could only hope that the country as a whole would stay firm. Success in battle was the cure for poor morale, but success in battle was a long time coming. The North was never in any danger of losing to the South, and therein lay part of the problem. Their greatest danger was increasing despondency and a general sense that the cause was not worth the lives that had to be sacrificed in order to win.

Against the growing mood of hopelessness was set the resolve of Lincoln, and it was this which prevailed. Not, of course, that the will of a single person could ever be enough to overcome all opposition. But in a country where transport was slow and inform-ation was spread not on a national level but through localities, people kept themselves remarkably well-informed about national affairs. As a younger politician speaking before crowds in remotest Illinois – as it then was – Lincoln had relied on the fact that his listeners were intelligent and keenly attentive to his arguments. Now, as President, he could rely on his words being regularly reported and read in newspapers by ordinary men and women of the North. Perhaps more important, the soldiers of the armies in the eastern campaign by this time knew him well, and their trust in him was transmitted to families and friends in their various home states. Unlike a modern President, he was not hedged around and pro-tected from personal contact. Farmers and country people came to see him, and all manner of others with requests and appeals.

The strain of these incessant interviews, added to all the other duties, was a great burden, but one that Lincoln could not be persuaded to avoid. It seems that the people at large drew great encouragement from his willingness to give help, and consolation where necessary, to all who asked for it. From political circles in Washington the tone of carping and belittlement remained strong throughout the four years of his Presidency. Further afield, how-ever, the nation as a whole was less blind, more appreciative of Lincoln's strengths. When he told them the war must be fought to its conclusion they were inclined to believe, however reluctantly, that he was right.

Lincoln as speaker and writer

It was hardly likely that Lincoln, with his ill-fitting clothes and general ungainliness, was going to cut a dashing figure as a public speaker. It made no difference. He commanded attention as few men have done before or since, both for what he said and, just as important, for what he was. In debating with Douglas, he would spend much of his time in dry, painstaking argument, leading his audience on a long trail from initial premises to the necessary conclusion. It says much for the underlying mentality of these gatherings that they were willing to follow him, but the success of the tactic depended entirely on the force of Lincoln's intention. After one such speech in 1855, a newspaper editor offered a simple analysis: 'Beyond and above all skill was the overwhelming conviction imposed upon the audience that the speaker himself was charged with an irresistible and inspiring duty to his fellow men.'

Backed by this strength of purpose, Lincoln was never going to be dull. The effect was one of power rather than brilliance, since he was not out to dazzle an audience, only persuade them. All the same, he could transport them when he chose, and on a few famous occasions his words aroused a kind of rapture. Perhaps most remarkable of all was the speech he gave at the first ever national convention of the Republican party, the 'lost speech' – so called because the reporters in the hall became so carried away that all of them failed to take down Lincoln's words in shorthand. We have a brief sketch of the scene: 'the audience arose from their chairs and with pale faces and quivering lips pressed unconsciously towards him.' It was not only the party faithful who could be so affected. When Lincoln spoke at the Cooper Institute in New York in February of 1860, he was facing the intellectual cream of the city. If they expected the kind of over-ornate eloquence that normally came out of the west, they were surprised. We know that Lincoln was ill at ease before the speech, conscious that this was in some sense the stiffest test of his life. 'When he spoke, he was transformed; his eye kindled, his voice rang, his face shone and seemed to light up the whole assembly. For an hour and a half he held his audience in the hollow of his hand.'

That testimony comes from Joseph Choate, a young man when he heard Lincoln but in later life one of the most successful advocates in America. Choate himself became renowned as a brilliant speaker. As for the rhetorical style which produced the effect he describes, it certainly was not that of the frontier show-man: 'It was marvellous to see how this untutored man, by mere self-discipline and the chastening of his own spirit, had outgrown all meretricious arts, and found his way to the grandeur and strength of absolute simplicity.' The committee overseeing the publication of the speech was more specific in its praise:

From the first line to the last, from his premises to his conclusion, he travels with a swift, unerring directness which no logician ever excelled, an argument complete and full, without the affectation of learning, and without the stiffness which usually accompanies dates and details. A single, easy, simple sentence of plain Anglo-Saxon words, contains a chapter of history that, in some instances, has taken days of labor to verify, and which must have cost the author months of investigation to acquire.

It surprised Herndon that Lincoln read few serious books, and seldom finished those he did read. Early in life he immersed himself in the Bible, Shakespeare and *Pilgrim's Progress*. For vitality and directness of expression no better models could be found. General principles of rhetoric – balance, contrast, repetition, rhythm – he may well have worked out for himself. Given a keen ear, a love of words and the clearest of minds, there was no need of anything more.

> Fondly do we hope – fervently do we pray – that this mighty scourge of war may speedily pass away. Yet, if God wills that it continue until all the wealth piled by the bondman's two hundred and fifty years of unrequited toil shall be sunk, and until every drop of blood drawn with the lash shall be paid with another drawn with the sword, as was said three thousand years ago, so still it must be said, 'The judgments of the Lord are true and righteous altogether.'

This is from the Second Inaugural Address, given in March 1865. In his portraits Lincoln has more than a suggestion of an Old Testament prophet – one of the more melancholy ones. His words resound with a similar force. The Bible, Shakespeare and *Pilgrim's Progress* are still available for anyone wanting to learn how to write English. Or they can just go straight to the speeches of Abraham Lincoln.

HUGH GRIFFITH

THE LIFE OF
ABRAHAM LINCOLN

by Henry Ketcham

PREFACE

The question will naturally be raised, Why should there be another *Life of Lincoln*? This may be met by a counter question, Will there ever be a time in the near future when there will *not* be another *Life of Lincoln*? There is always a new class of students and a new enrolment of citizens. Every year many thousands of young people pass from the Grammar to the High School grade of our public schools. Other thousands are growing up into manhood and womanhood. These are of a different constituency from their fathers and grandfathers who remember the civil war and were perhaps in it.

'To the younger generation,' writes Carl Schurz, 'Abraham Lincoln has already become a half mythical figure, which, in the haze of historic distance, grows to more and more heroic proportions, but also loses in distinctness of outline and figure.' The last clause of this remark is painfully true. To the majority of people now living, his outline and figure are dim and vague. There are today professors and presidents of colleges, legislators of prominence, lawyers and judges, literary men, and successful business men, to whom Lincoln is a tradition. It cannot be expected that a person born after the year (say) 1855, could remember Lincoln more than as a name. Such an one's ideas are made up not from his remembrance and appreciation of events as they occurred, but from what he has read and heard about them in subsequent years.

The great mine of information concerning the facts of Lincoln's life is, and probably will always be, the *History* by his secretaries, Nicolay and Hay. This is worthily supplemented by the splendid volumes of Miss Tarbell. There are other biographies of great value. Special mention should be made of the essay by Carl Schurz, which is classic.

The author has consulted freely all the books on the subject he could lay his hands on. In this volume there is no attempt to write a history of the times in which Lincoln lived and worked. Such historical events as have been narrated were selected solely because they illustrated some phase of the character of Lincoln. In this biography the single purpose has been to present the living man with such distinctness of outline that the reader may have a sort of feeling of being acquainted with him. If the reader, finishing this volume, has a vivid realization of Lincoln as a man, the author will be fully repaid.

To achieve this purpose in brief compass, much has been omitted. Some of the material omitted has probably been of a value fully equal to some that has been inserted. This could not well be avoided. But if the reader shall here acquire interest enough in the subject to continue the study of this great, good man, this little book will have served its purpose.

H.K.
Westfield, New Jersey
February 1901

CHAPTER ONE

The Wild West

At the beginning of the twentieth century there is, strictly speaking, no frontier to the United States. At the beginning of the nineteenth century, the larger part of the country was frontier. In any portion of the country today, in the remotest villages and hamlets, on the enormous farms of the Dakotas or the vast ranches of California, one is certain to find some, if not many, of the modern appliances of civilization such as were not dreamed of one hundred years ago. Aladdin himself could not have commanded the glowing terms to write the prospectus of the closing years of the nineteenth century. So, too, it requires an extraordinary effort of the imagination to conceive of the condition of things in the opening years of that century.

The first quarter of the century closed with the year 1825. At that date Lincoln was nearly seventeen years old. The deepest impressions of life are apt to be received very early, and it is certain that the influences which are felt previous to seventeen years of age have much to do with the formation of the character. If, then, we go back to the period named, we can tell with sufficient accuracy what were the circumstances of Lincoln's early life. Though we cannot precisely tell what he had, we can confidently name many things, things which in this day we class as the necessities of life, which he had to do without, for the simple reason that they had not then been invented or discovered.

In the first place, we must bear in mind that he lived in the woods. The West of that day was not wild in the sense of being wicked, criminal, ruffian. Morally, and possibly intellectually, the people of that region would compare with the rest of the country of that day or of this day. There was little schooling and no literary training. But the woodsman has an education of his own. The region was wild in the sense that it was almost uninhabited and untilled. The forests, extending from the mountains in the East to the prairies in the West, were almost unbroken and were the abode of wild birds and wild beasts. Bears, deer, wild-cats, raccoons, wild turkeys, wild pigeons, wild ducks and similar creatures abounded on every hand.

Consider now the sparseness of the population. Kentucky has an area of 40,000 square miles. One year after Lincoln's birth, the total population, white and colored, was 406,511, or an average of ten persons – say less than two families – to the square mile. Indiana has an area of 36,350 square miles. In 1810 its total population was 24,520, or an average of one person to one and one-half square miles; in 1820 it contained 147,173 inhabitants, or about four to the square mile; in 1825 the population was about 245,000, or less than seven to the square mile.

The capital city, Indianapolis, which is today of surpassing beauty, was not built nor thought of when the boy Lincoln moved into the State.

Illinois, with its more than 56,000 square miles of territory, harbored in 1810 only 12,282 people; in 1820, only 55,211, or less than one to the square mile; while in 1825 its population had grown a trifle over 100,000 or less than two to the square mile.

It will thus be seen that up to his youth, Lincoln dwelt only in the wildest of the wild woods, where the animals from the chipmunk to the bear were much more numerous, and probably more at home, than man.

There were few roads of any kind, and certainly none that could be called good. For the mud of Indiana and Illinois is very deep and very tenacious. There were good saddle-horses, a sufficient number of oxen, and carts that were rude and awkward. No locomotives, no bicycles, no automobiles. The first railway in Indiana was constructed in 1847, and it was, to say the least, a very primitive affair. As to carriages, there may have been some, but a good carriage would be only a waste on those roads and in that forest.

The only pen was the goose-quill, and the ink was home-made. Paper was scarce, expensive, and, while of good material, poorly made. Newspapers were unknown in that virgin forest, and books were like angels' visits, few and far between.

There were scythes and sickles, but of a grade that would not be salable today at any price. There were no self-binding harvesters, no mowing machines. There were no sewing or knitting machines, though there were needles of both kinds. In the woods thorns were used for pins.

Guns were flint-locks, tinder-boxes were used until the manufacture of the friction match. Artificial light came chiefly from the open fireplace, though the tallow dip was known and there were some housewives who had time to make them and the disposition to use them. Illumination by means of molded candles, oil, gas, electricity, came later. That was long before the days of the telegraph.

In that locality there were no mills for weaving cotton, linen, or woolen fabrics. All spinning was done by means of the hand loom, and the common fabric of the region was linsey-woolsey, made of linen and woolen mixed, and usually not dyed.

Antiseptics were unknown, and a severe surgical operation was practically certain death to the patient. Nor was there ether, chloroform, or cocaine for the relief of pain.

As to food, wild game was abundant, but the kitchen garden was not developed and there were no importations. No oranges, lemons, bananas. No canned goods. Crusts of rye bread were browned, ground, and boiled; this was coffee. Herbs of the woods were dried and steeped; this was tea. The root of the sassafras furnished a different kind of tea, a substitute for the India and Ceylon teas now popular. Slippery elm bark soaked in cold water sufficed for lemonade. The milk-house, when there was one, was built over a spring when that was possible, and the milk vessels were kept carefully covered to keep out snakes and other creatures that like milk.

Whisky was almost universally used. Indeed, in spite of the constitutional 'sixteen-to-one', it was locally used as the standard of value. The luxury of quinine, which came to be in general use throughout that entire region, was of later date.

These details are few and meager. It is not easy for us, in the midst of the luxuries, comforts, and necessities of a later civilization, to realize the conditions of western life previous to 1825. But the situation must be understood if one is to know the life of the boy Lincoln.

Imagine this boy. Begin at the top and look down him — a long look, for he was tall and gaunt. His cap in winter was of coon-skin, with the tail of the animal hanging down behind. In summer he wore a misshapen straw hat with no hat-band. His shirt was of linsey-woolsey, above described, and was of no color whatever, unless you call it 'the color of dirt'. His breeches were of deer-skin with the hair outside. In dry weather these were what you please, but when wet they hugged the skin with a clammy embrace, and the victim might sigh in vain for sanitary underwear. These breeches were held up by one suspender. The hunting shirt was likewise of deer-skin. The stockings – there weren't any stockings. The shoes were cow-hide, though moccasins made by his mother were substituted in dry weather. There was usually a space of several inches between the breeches and the shoes, exposing a tanned and bluish skin. For about half the year he went barefoot.

There were schools, primitive and inadequate, indeed, as we shall presently see, but 'the little red schoolhouse on the hill', with the stars and stripes floating proudly above it, was not of that day. There were itinerant preachers who went from one locality to another, holding 'revival meetings'. But church buildings were rare and, to say the least, not of artistic design. There were no regular means of travel, and even the 'star route' of the post-office department was slow in reaching those secluded communities.

Into such circumstances and conditions Lincoln was born and grew into manhood.

CHAPTER TWO

The Lincoln Family

When one becomes interested in a boy, one is almost certain to ask, Whose son is he? And when we study the character of a great man, it is natural and right that we should be interested in his family. Where did he come from? Who were his parents? Where did they come from? These questions will engage our attention in this chapter.

But it is well to be on our guard at the outset against the fascinations of any theory of heredity. Every thoughtful observer knows something of the seductions of this subject either from experience or from observation. In every subject of research there is danger of claiming too much in order to magnify the theory. This is emphatically true of this theory. Its devotees note the hits but not the misses. 'It took five generations of cultured clergymen to produce an Emerson.' Undoubtedly; but what of the sixth and seventh generations? 'Darwin's greatness came from his father and grandfather.' Very true; but are there no more Darwins?

If Abraham Lincoln got his remarkable character from parents or grandparents, from whom did he get his physical stature? His father was a little above medium height, being five feet ten and one-half inches. His mother was a little less than medium height, being five feet five inches. Their son was a giant, being no less than six feet four inches. It is not safe to account too closely for his physical, mental, or moral greatness by his descent. The fact is that there are too many unexplored remainders in the factors of heredity to make it possible to apply the laws definitely.

The writer will therefore give a brief account of the Lincoln family simply as a matter of interest, and not as a means of proving or explaining any natural law.

The future president was descended from people of the middle class. There was nothing either in his family or his surroundings to attract the attention even of the closest observer, or to indicate any material difference between him and scores of other boys in the same general locality.

Lincoln is an old English name, and in 1638 a family of the name settled in Hingham, Mass., near Boston. Many years later we find the ancestors of the president living in Berks County, Pa. It is possible that this family came direct from England; but it is probable that they came from Hingham. Both in Hingham and in Berks County there is a frequent recurrence of certain scriptural names, such as Abraham, Mordecai, and Thomas, which seems to be more than a coincidence.

From Berks County certain of the family, who, by the way, were Quakers, moved to Rockingham County, Va. In 1769 Daniel Boone, the adventurous pioneer, opened up what is now the state of Kentucky, but was then a part of Virginia.

About twelve years later, in 1781, Abraham Lincoln, great-grandfather of the president, emigrated from Virginia into Kentucky. People have asked, in a puzzled manner, why did he leave the beautiful Shenandoah valley? One answer may be given: The Ohio valley also is beautiful. During the major portion of the year, from the budding of the leaves in April until they pass away in the blaze of their autumn glory, the entire region is simply bewitching. No hills curve more gracefully, no atmosphere is more soft, no watercourses are more enticing. Into this region came the Virginian family, consisting, besides the parents, of three sons and two daughters.

A year or two later the head of the family was murdered by a skulking Indian, who proceeded to kidnap the youngest son, Thomas. The oldest son, Mordecai, quickly obtained a gun and killed the Indian, thus avenging his father and rescuing his little brother.

This boy Thomas was father of the president. He has been called by some writers shiftless and densely ignorant. But he seems to have been more a creature of circumstances. There were no schools, and he, consequently, did not go to school. There was no steady employment, and consequently he had no steady employment. It is difficult to see how he could have done better. He could shoot and keep the family supplied with wild game. He did odd jobs as opportunity opened and 'just growed'.

But he had force enough to learn to read and write after his marriage. He had the roving disposition which is, and always has been, a trait of pioneers. But this must be interpreted by the fact that he was optimistic rather than pessimistic. He removed to Indiana because, to him, Indiana was the most glorious place in the whole world. He later removed to Illinois because that was more glorious yet.

He certainly showed good taste in the selection of his wives, and what is equally to the purpose, was able to persuade them to share his humble lot. He had an unfailing stock of good nature, was expert in telling a humorous story, was perfectly at home in the woods, a fair carpenter and a good farmer; and in short was as agreeable a companion as one would find in a day's journey. He would not have been at home in a library, but he was at home in the forest.

In 1806 he married Nancy Hanks, a young woman from Virginia, who became the mother of the president. Doubtless there are many women among the obscure who are as true and loyal as she was, but whose life is not brought into publicity. Still, without either comparing or contrasting her with others, we may attest our admiration of this one as a 'woman nobly planned'. In the midst of her household cares, which were neither few nor light, she had the courage to undertake to teach her husband to read and write. She also gave her children a start in learning. Of her the president, nearly half a century after her death, said to Seward, with tears – 'All that I am or hope to be, I owe to my angel mother – blessings on her memory.'

Mr Lincoln himself never manifested much interest in his genealogy. At one time he did give out a brief statement concerning his ancestors because it seemed to be demanded by the exigencies of the campaign. But at another time, when questioned by Mr J. L. Scripps, editor of the Chicago *Tribune*, he answered: 'Why, Scripps, it is a great piece of folly to attempt to make anything out of me or my early life. It can all be condensed into a single sentence, and that sentence you will find in Gray's *Elegy*:

The short and simple annals of the poor.

That's my life, and that's all you or anyone else can make out of it.'

In all this he was neither proud nor depreciative of his people. He was simply modest. Nor did he ever outgrow his sympathy with the common people.

CHAPTER THREE

Early Years

The year 1809 was fruitful in the birth of great men in the Anglo-Saxon race. In that year were born Charles Darwin, scientist, Alfred Tennyson, poet, William E. Gladstone, statesman, and, not least, Abraham Lincoln, liberator.

Thomas Lincoln was left fatherless in early boyhood, and grew up without any schooling or any definite work. For the most part he did odd jobs as they were offered. He called himself a carpenter. But in a day when the outfit of tools numbered only about a half dozen, and when every man was mainly his own carpenter, this trade could not amount to much. Employment was unsteady and pay was small.

Thomas Lincoln, after his marriage to Nancy Hanks, lived in Elizabethtown, Ky., where the first child, Sarah, was born. Shortly after this event he decided to combine farming with his trade of carpentering, and so removed to a farm fourteen miles out, situated in what is now La Rue County, where his wife, on the twelfth day of February, 1809, gave birth to the son who was named Abraham after his grandfather. The child was born in a log cabin of a kind very common in that day and for many years later. It was built four-square and comprised only one room, one window, and a door.

Here they lived for a little more than four years, when the father removed to another farm about fifteen miles further to the north-east.

The occasion of this removal and of the subsequent one, two or three years later, was undoubtedly the uncertainty of land titles in Kentucky in that day. This 'roving disposition' cannot fairly be charged to shiftlessness. In spite of the extraordinary disadvantages of Thomas Lincoln's early life, he lived as well as his neighbors, though that was humble enough, and accumulated a small amount of property in spite of the low rate of compensation.

In the year 1816 Thomas determined to migrate to Indiana. He sold out his farm, receiving for it the equivalent of $300. Of this sum, $20 was in cash and the rest was in whisky – ten barrels – which passed as a kind of currency in that day. He then loaded the bulk of his goods upon a flat boat, floating down the stream called Rolling Fork into Salt Creek, thence into the Ohio River, in fact, to the bottom of that river. The watercourse was obstructed with stumps and snags of divers sorts, and especially with 'sawyers', or trees in the river which, forced by the current, make an up-and-down motion like that of a man sawing wood.

The flat boat became entangled in these obstructions and was upset, and the cargo went to the bottom. By dint of great labor much of this was rescued and the travelers pushed on as far as Thompson's Ferry in Perry County, Indiana. There the cargo was left in the charge of friends, and Lincoln returned for his family and the rest of his goods.

During his father's absence, the boy Abe had his first observation of sorrow. A brother had been born in the cabin and had died in infancy. The little grave was in the wilderness, and before leaving that country forever, the mother, leading her six-year-old boy by the hand, paid a farewell visit to the grave. The child beheld with awe the silent grief of the mother and carried in his memory that scene to his dying day.

The father returned with glowing accounts of the new home. The family and the furniture – to use so dignified a name for such meager possessions – were loaded into a wagon or a cart, and they were soon on the way to their new home.

The traveling was slow, but the weather was fine, the journey prosperous, and they arrived duly at their destination. They pushed northward, or back from the river, about eighteen miles into the woods and settled in Spencer County near to a hamlet named Gentryville. Here they established their home.

The first thing, of course, was to stake off the land, enter the claim, and pay the government fee at the United States Land Office at Vincennes. The amount of land was one quarter section, or one hundred and sixty acres.

The next thing was to erect a cabin. In this case the cabin consisted of what was called a half-faced camp. That is, the structure was entirely open on one of its four sides. This was at the lower side of the roof, and the opening was partly concealed by the hanging of the skins of deer and other wild animals. This open face fully supplied all need of door and window.

The structure was built four square, fourteen feet each way. Posts were set up at the corners, then the sides were made of poles placed as near together as possible. The interstices were filled in with chips and clay, which was called 'chinking'. The fireplace and chimney were built at the back and outside. The chief advantage of this style of domicile is that it provides plenty of fresh air. With one side of the room entirely open, and with a huge fireplace at the other side, the sanitary problem of ventilation was solved.

There were no Brussels carpets, no Persian rugs, no hardwood floors. The bare soil was pounded hard, and that was the floor. There were two beds in the two rear corners of the rooms. The corner position saved both space and labor. Two sides of the bed were composed of parts of the two walls. At the opposite angle a stake, with a forked top, was driven into the ground, and from this to the walls were laid two poles at right angles. This made the frame of the bed. Then 'shakes', or large hand-made shingles, were placed crosswise. Upon these were laid the ticks filled with feathers or corn husks, and the couch was complete. Not stylish, but healthful and comfortable.

The produce of his farm was chiefly corn, though a little wheat was raised for a change of diet. Doubtless there were enough of the staple vegetables which grow easily in that country. Butcher shops were not needed, owing to the abundance of wild game.

The principal portion of the life of the average boy concerns his schooling. As nearly as can be determined the aggregate of young Lincoln's schooling was about one year, and this was divided between five teachers – an average of less than three months to each – and spread out over as many years. The branches taught were 'readin', writin', and cipherin' to the rule of three'. Any young man who happened along with a fair knowledge of the three great R's – 'Readin', 'Ritin', and 'Rithmetic' – was thought fit to set up a school, taking his small pay in cash and boarding around – that is, spending one day or more at a time as the guest of each of his patrons.

There was nothing of special interest in any of these teachers, but their names are preserved simply because the fact that they did teach him is a matter of great interest. The first teacher was Zachariah Riney, a Roman Catholic, from whose schoolroom the Protestants were excluded, or excused, during the opening exercises. Then came Caleb Hazel. These were in Kentucky, and therefore their instruction of Lincoln must have come to an end by the time he was seven years old. When ten years old he studied under one Dorsey, when about fourteen under Crawford, and when sixteen under Swaney.

It can hardly be doubted that his mother's instruction was of more worth than all these put together. A woman who, under such limitations, had energy enough to teach her husband to read and write, was a rare character, and her influence could not be other than invaluable to the bright boy. Charles Lamb classified all literature in two divisions: 'Books that are not books, and books that are books'. It is important that every boy learn to read. But a far more important question is, What use does he make of his ability to read? Does he read 'books that are books'? Let us now see what use Lincoln made of his knowledge of reading.

In those days books were rare and his library was small and select. It consisted at first of three volumes: The Bible, *Aesop's Fables* and *Pilgrim's Progress*. Some time in the 'eighties a prominent magazine published a series of articles written by men of eminence in the various walks of life, under the title of 'Books that have helped me'. The most noticeable fact was that each of these eminent men – men who had read hundreds of books – specified not more than three or four books. Lincoln's first list was of three. They were emphatically books. Day after day he read, pondered and inwardly digested them until they were his own. Better books he could not have found in all the universities of Europe, and we begin to understand where he got his moral vision, his precision of English style, and his shrewd humor.

Later he borrowed from a neighbor, Josiah Crawford, a copy of Weems's *Life of Washington*. In lieu of a bookcase he tucked this, one night, into the chinking of the cabin. A rain-storm came up and soaked the book through and through. By morning it presented a sorry appearance. The damage was done and could not be repaired. Crestfallen the lad carried it back to the owner and, having no money, offered to pay for the mischief in work. Crawford agreed and named seventy-five cents (in labor) as a fair sum.

'Does this pay for the book,' the borrower asked, 'or only for the damage to the book?' Crawford reckoned that the book 'wa'n't of much account to him nor to anyone else.' So Lincoln cheerfully did the work – it was for three days – and owned the book.

Later he had a life of Henry Clay, whom he nearly idolized. His one poet was Burns, whom he knew by heart 'from a to izzard'. Throughout his life he ranked Burns next to Shakespeare.

The hymns which he most loved must have had influence not only on his religious spirit, but also on his literary taste. Those which are mentioned are, 'Am I a soldier of the cross?' 'How tedious and tasteless the hours', 'There is a fountain filled with blood'; and 'Alas, and did my Saviour bleed?' Good hymns every one of them, in that day, or in any day.

Having no slate he did his 'sums' in the sand on the ground, or on a wooden shovel which, after it was covered on both sides, he scraped down so as to erase the work. A note-book is preserved, containing, along with examples in arithmetic, this boyish doggerel.

> Abraham Lincoln
> his hand and pen
> he will be good but
> god knows When.

The penmanship bears a striking resemblance to that in later life.

About a year after Thomas Lincoln's family settled in Indiana, they were followed by some neighbors, Mr and Mrs Sparrow and Dennis Hanks, a child. To these the Lincolns surrendered their camp and built for themselves a cabin, which was slightly more pretentious than the first. It had an attic, and for a stairway there were pegs in the wall up which an active boy could readily climb. There was a stationary table, the legs being driven into the ground, some three-legged stools, and a Dutch oven.

In the year 1818 a mysterious epidemic passed over the region, working havoc with men and cattle. It was called the 'milk-sick'. Just what it was physicians are unable to determine, but it was very destructive. Both Mr and Mrs Sparrow were attacked. They were removed, for better care, to the home of the Lincolns, where they shortly died. By this time Mrs Lincoln was down with the same scourge. There was no doctor to be had, the nearest one being thirty-five miles away. Probably it made no difference. At all events she soon died and the future president passed into his first sorrow.

The widowed husband was undertaker. With his own hands he 'rived' the planks, made the coffin, and buried Nancy Hanks, that remarkable woman. There was no pastor, no funeral service. The grave was marked by a wooden slab, which, long years after, in 1879, was replaced by a stone suitably inscribed.

A traveling preacher known as Parson Elkin had occasionally preached in the neighborhood of the Lincolns in Kentucky. The young boy now put to use his knowledge of writing. He wrote a letter to the parson inviting him to come over and preach the funeral sermon. How he contrived to get the letter to its destination we do not know, but it was done. The kind-hearted preacher cheerfully consented, though it involved a long and hard journey. He came at his earliest convenience, which was some time the next year.

There was no church in which to hold the service. Lincoln never saw a church building of any description until he was grown. But the neighbors to the number of about two hundred assembled under the trees, where the parson delivered the memorial sermon.

Lincoln was nine years old when his mother died, October 5th, 1818. Her lot was hard, her horizon was narrow, her opportunities were restricted, her life was one of toil and poverty. All through her life and after her untimely death, many people would have said that she had had at best but a poor chance in the world. Surely no one would have predicted that her name would come to be known and reverenced from ocean to ocean. But she was faithful, brave, cheerful. She did her duty lovingly. In later years the nation joined with her son in paying honor to the memory of this noble, overworked, uncomplaining woman.

CHAPTER FOUR
In Indiana

The death of his wife had left Thomas Lincoln with the care of three young children: namely, Sarah, about eleven years old, Abe, ten years old, and the foster brother, Dennis (Friend) Hanks, a year or two younger. The father was not able to do woman's work as well as his wife had been able to do man's work, and the condition of the home was pitiable indeed. To the three motherless children and the bereaved father it was a long and dreary winter. When spring came they had the benefits of life in the woods and fields, and so lived through the season until the edge of the following winter. It is not to be wondered at that the father was unwilling to repeat the loneliness of the preceding year.

Early in December, 1819, he returned to Elizabethtown, Ky., and proposed marriage to a widow, Mrs Sally Bush Johnston. The proposal must have been direct, with few preliminaries or none, for the couple were married next morning. The new wife brought him a fortune, in addition to three children of various ages, of sundry articles of household furniture. Parents, children, and goods were shortly after loaded into a wagon drawn by a four-horse team, and in all the style of this frontier four-in-hand, were driven over indescribable roads, through woods and fields, to their Indiana home.

The accession of Sally Bush's furniture made an important improvement in the home. What was more important, she had her husband finish the log cabin by providing window, door, and floor. What was most important of all, she brought the sweet spirit of an almost ideal motherhood into the home, giving to all the children alike a generous portion of mother-love.

The children now numbered six, and not only were they company for one another, but the craving for womanly affection, which is the most persistent hunger of the heart of child or man, was beautifully met. She did not humor them to the point of idleness, but wisely ruled with strictness without imperiousness. She kept them from bad habits and retained their affection to the last. The influence upon the growing lad of two such women as Nancy Hanks and Sally Bush was worth more than that of the best appointed college in all the land.

The boy grew into youth, and he grew very fast. While still in his teens he reached the full stature of his manhood, six feet and four inches. His strength was astonishing, and many stories were told of this and subsequent periods to illustrate his physical prowess, such as: he once lifted up a hencoop weighing six hundred pounds and carried it off bodily; he could lift a full barrel of cider to his mouth and drink from the bung-hole; he could sink an ax-halve deeper into a log than any man in the country.

During the period of his growth into youth he spent much of his time in reading, talking, and, after a fashion, making speeches. He also wrote some. His political writings won great admiration from his neighbors. He occasionally wrote satires which, while not refined, were very stinging. This would not be worth mentioning were it not for the fact that it shows that from boyhood he knew the force of this formidable weapon which later he used with so much skill. The country store furnished the frontier substitute for the club, and there the men were wont to congregate. It is needless to say that young Lincoln was the life of the gatherings, being an expert in the telling of a humorous story and having always a plentiful supply. His speech-making proved so attractive that his father was forced to forbid him to practise it during working hours because the men would always leave their work to listen to him.

During these years he had no regular employment, but did odd jobs wherever he got a chance. At one time, for example, he worked on a ferryboat for the munificent wages of thirty-seven and one half cents a day.

When sixteen years old, Lincoln had his first lesson in oratory. He attended court at Boonville, county seat of Warwick County, and heard a case in which one of the aristocratic Breckenridges of Kentucky was attorney for the defense. The power of his oratory was a revelation to the lad. At its conclusion the awkward, ill-dressed, bashful but enthusiastic young Lincoln pressed forward to offer his congratulations and thanks to the eloquent lawyer, who haughtily brushed by him without accepting the proffered hand. In later years the men met again, this time in Washington City, in the white house. The president reminded Breckenridge of the incident which the latter had no desire to recall.

When about nineteen years old, he made his first voyage down the Ohio and Mississippi rivers. Two incidents are worth recording of this trip. The purpose was to find, in New Orleans, a market for produce, which was simply floated down stream on a flat-boat. There was, of course, a row-boat for tender. The crew consisted of himself and young Gentry, son of his employer.

Near Baton Rouge they had tied up for the night in accordance with the custom of flat-boat navigation. During the night they were awakened by a gang of seven ruffian negroes who had come aboard to loot the stuff. Lincoln shouted 'Who's there?' Receiving no reply he seized a handspike and knocked over the first, second, third, and fourth in turn, when the remaining three took to the woods. The two northerners pursued them a short distance, then returned, loosed their craft and floated safely to their destination.

It was on this trip that Lincoln earned his first dollar, as he in after years related to William H. Seward.

. . . A steamer was going down the river. We have, you know, no wharves on the western streams, and the custom was, if passengers were at any of the landings, they were to go out in a boat, the steamer stopping and taking them on board. . . . Two men with trunks came down to the shore in carriages, and looking at the different boats, singled out mine, and asked, 'Who owns this?' I modestly answered, 'I do.' 'Will you take us and our trunks out to the steamer?' 'Certainly.' . . . The trunks were put in my boat, the passengers seated themselves on them, and I sculled them out to the steamer. They got on board, and I lifted the trunks and put them on the deck. The steamer was about to put on steam again, when I called out: 'You have forgotten to pay me.' Each of them took from his pocket a silver half dollar and threw it on the bottom of my boat. I could scarcely believe my eyes as I picked up the money. You may think it was a very little thing, and in these days it seems to me like a trifle, but it was a most important incident in my life. I could scarcely credit that I, a poor boy, had earned a dollar in less than a day; that by honest work I had earned a dollar. I was a more hopeful and thoughtful boy from that time.

The goods were sold profitably at New Orleans and the return trip was made by steamboat. This was about twenty years after Fulton's first voyage from New York to Albany, which required seven days. Steamboats had been put on the Ohio and Mississippi rivers, but these crafts were of primitive construction – awkward as to shape and slow as to speed. The frequency of boiler explosions was proverbial for many years. The lads, Gentry and Lincoln, returned home duly and the employer was well satisfied with the results of the expedition.

In 1830 the epidemic 'milk-sick' reappeared in Indiana, and Thomas Lincoln had a pardonable desire to get out of the country. Illinois was at that time settling up rapidly and there were glowing accounts of its desirableness. Thomas Lincoln's decision to move on to the new land of promise was reasonable. He sold out and started with his family and household goods to his new destination. The time of year was March, just when the frost is coming out of the ground so that the mud is apparently bottomless. The author will not attempt to describe it, for he has in boyhood seen it many times and knows it to be indescribable. It was Abe's duty to drive the four yoke of oxen, a task which must have strained even his patience.

They settled in Macon County, near Decatur. There the son faithfully worked with his father until the family was fairly settled, then started out in life for himself. For he had now reached the age of twenty-one. As he had passed through the periods of childhood and youth, and was on the threshold of manhood, it is right and fitting to receive at this point the testimony of Sally Bush, his stepmother.

'Abe was a good boy, and I can say what scarcely one woman – a mother – can say in a thousand: Abe never gave me a cross word or look, and never refused, in fact or appearance, to do anything I requested him. I never gave him a cross word in all my life. . . . He was a dutiful son to me always. I think he loved me truly. I had a son John who was raised with Abe. Both were good boys; but I must say, both being now dead, that Abe was the best boy I ever saw, or expect to see.'

These words of praise redound to the honor of the speaker equally with that of her illustrious stepson.

Lincoln came into the estate of manhood morally clean. He had formed no habits that would cause years of struggle to overcome, he had committed no deed that would bring the blush of shame to his cheek, he was as free from vice as from crime. He was not profane, he had never tasted liquor, he was no brawler, he never gambled, he was honest and truthful. On the other hand, he had a genius for making friends, he was the center of every social circle, he was a good talker and a close reasoner. Without a thought of the great responsibilities awaiting him, he had thus far fitted himself well by his faithfulness in such duties as fell to him.

CHAPTER FIVE
Second Journey to New Orleans

The first winter in Illinois, 1830–31, was one of those epochal seasons which come to all communities. It is remembered by 'the oldest inhabitant' to this day for the extraordinary amount of snow that fell. There is little doing in such a community during any winter; but in such a winter as that there was practically nothing doing. Lincoln always held himself ready to accept any opportunity for work, but there was no opening that winter. The only thing he accomplished was what he did every winter and every summer of his life: namely, he made many friends.

When spring opened, Denton Offutt decided to send a cargo of merchandise down to New Orleans. Hearing that Lincoln, John Hanks, and John Johnston were 'likely boys', he employed them to take charge of the enterprise. Their pay was to be fifty cents a day and 'found', and, if the enterprise proved successful, an additional sum of twenty dollars. Lincoln said that none of them had ever seen so much money at one time, and they were glad to accept the offer.

Two events occurred during this trip which are of sufficient interest to bear narration.

The boat with its cargo had been set afloat in the Sangamon River at Springfield. All went well until, at New Salem, they came to a mill dam where, in spite of the fact that the water was high, owing to the spring floods, the boat stuck. Lincoln rolled his trousers 'five feet more or less' up his long, lank legs, waded out to the boat, and got the bow over the dam. Then, without waiting to bail the water out, he bored a hole in the bottom and let it run out. He constructed a machine which lifted and pushed the boat over the obstruction, and thus their voyage was quickly resumed. Many years later, when he was a practising lawyer, he whittled out a model of his invention and had it patented. The model may today be seen in the patent office at Washington. The patent brought him no fortune, but it is an interesting relic.

This incident is of itself entirely unimportant. It is narrated here solely because it illustrates one trait of the man – his ingenuity. He had remarkable fertility in devising ways and means of getting out of unexpected difficulties. When, in 1860, the Ship of State seemed like to run aground hopelessly, it was his determination and ingenuity that averted total wreck. As in his youth he saved the flatboat, so in his mature years he saved the nation.

The other event was that at New Orleans, where he saw with his own eyes some of the horrors of slavery. He never could tolerate a moral wrong. At a time when drinking was almost universal, he was a total abstainer. Though born in a slave state, he had an earnest and growing repugnance to slavery. Still, up to this time he had never seen much of its workings. At this time he saw a slave market – the auctioning off of human beings.

The details of this auction were so coarse and vile that it is impossible to defile these pages with an accurate and faithful description. Lincoln saw it all. He saw a beautiful mulatto girl exhibited like a race-horse, her 'points' dwelt on, one by one, in order, as the auctioneer said, that 'bidders might satisfy themselves whether the article they were offering to buy was sound or not.' One of his companions justly said slavery ran the iron into him then and there. His soul was stirred with a righteous indignation. Turning to the others he exclaimed with a solemn oath: 'Boys, if ever I get a chance to hit that thing [slavery] I'll hit it hard!'

He bided his time. One-third of a century later he had the chance to hit that thing. He redeemed his oath. He hit it hard.

CHAPTER SIX

Desultory Employments

Upon the arrival of the Lincoln family in Illinois, they had the few tools which would be considered almost necessary to every frontiersman: namely, a common ax, broad-ax, hand-saw, whip-saw. The mauls and wedges were of wood and were made by each workman for himself. To this stock of tools may also be added a small supply of nails brought from Indiana, for at that period nails were very expensive and used with the strictest economy. By means of pegs and other devices people managed to get along without them.

When Abraham Lincoln went to New Salem it was (like all frontier towns) a promising place. It grew until it had the enormous population of about one hundred people, housed – or log-cabined – in fifteen primitive structures. The tributary country was not very important in a commercial sense. To this population no less than four general stores – that is, stores containing nearly everything that would be needed in that community – offered their wares.

The town flourished, at least it lived, about through the period that Lincoln dwelt there, after which it disappeared.

Lincoln was ready to take any work that would get him a living. A neighbor advised him to make use of his great strength in the work of a blacksmith. He seriously thought of learning the trade, but was, fortunately for the country, diverted from doing so.

The success of the expedition to New Orleans had won the admiration of his employer, Denton Offutt, and he now offered Lincoln a clerkship in his prospective store. The offer was accepted partly because it gave him some time to read, and it was here that he came to know the two great poets, Burns and Shakespeare.

Offutt's admiration of the young clerk did him credit, but his voluble expression of it was not judicious. He bragged that Lincoln was smart enough to be president, and that he could run faster, jump higher, throw farther, and 'wrastle' better than any man in the country. In the neighborhood there was a gang of rowdies, kind at heart but very rough, known as 'the Clary's Grove boys'. They took the boasting of Offutt as a direct challenge to themselves and eagerly accepted it. So they put up a giant by the name of Jack Armstrong as their champion and arranged a 'wrastling' match. All went indifferently for a while until Lincoln seemed to be getting the better of his antagonist, when the 'boys' crowded in and interfered while Armstrong attempted a foul. Instantly Lincoln was furious. Putting forth all his strength he lifted Jack up and shook him as a terrier shakes a rat. The crowd, in their turn, became angry and set out to mob him. He backed up against a wall and in hot indignation awaited the onset. Armstrong was the first to recover his good sense. Exclaiming, 'Boys, Abe Lincoln's the best fellow that ever broke into the settlement,' he held out his hand to Lincoln who received it with perfect good nature. From that day these boys never lost their admiration for him. He was their hero. From that day, too, he became the permanent umpire, the general peacemaker of the region. His good nature, his self-command, and his manifest fairness placed his decisions beyond question. His popularity was established once for all in the entire community.

There are some anecdotes connected with his work in the store which are worth preserving because they illustrate traits of his character. He once sold a half pound of tea to a customer. The next morning as he was tidying up the store he saw, by the weights which remained in the scales, that he had inadvertently given her four, instead of eight, ounces. He instantly weighed out the balance and carried it to her, not waiting for his breakfast.

At another time when he counted up his cash at night he discovered that he had charged a customer an excess of six and a quarter cents. He closed up the store at once and walked to the home of the customer, and returned the money. It was such things as these, in little matters as well as great, that gave him the nickname of 'honest Abe' which, to his honor be it said, clung to him through life.

One incident illustrates his chivalry. While he was waiting upon some women, a ruffian came into the store using vulgar language. Lincoln asked him to desist, but he became more abusive than ever. After the women had gone, Lincoln took him out of the store, threw him on the ground, rubbed smartweed in his face and eyes until he howled for mercy, and then he gave him a lecture which did him more practical good than a volume of Chesterfield's letters.

Some time after Offutt's store had 'winked out', while Lincoln was looking for employment there came a chance to buy one half interest in a store, the other half being owned by an idle, dissolute fellow named Berry who ultimately drank himself into his grave. Later, another opening came in the following way: the store of one Radford had been wrecked by the horse-play of some ruffians, and the lot was bought by Mr Greene for four hundred dollars. He employed Lincoln to make an invoice of the goods and he in turn offered Greene two hundred and fifty dollars for the bargain and the offer was accepted. But even that was not the last investment. The fourth and only remaining store in the hamlet was owned by one Rutledge. This also was bought out by the firm of Berry & Lincoln. Thus they came to have the monopoly of the mercantile business in the hamlet of New Salem.

Be it known that in all these transactions not a dollar in money changed hands. Men bought with promissory notes and sold for the same consideration. The mercantile venture was not successful. Berry was drinking and loafing, and Lincoln, who did not work as faithfully for himself as for another, was usually reading or telling stories. So when a couple of strangers, Trent by name, offered to buy out the store, the offer was accepted and more promissory notes changed hands. About the time these last notes came due, the Trent brothers disappeared between two days. Then Berry died.

The outcome of the whole series of transactions was that Lincoln was left with an assortment of promissory notes bearing the names of the Herndons, Radford, Greene, Rutledge, Berry, and the Trents. With one exception, which will be duly narrated, his creditors told him to pay when he was able. He promised to put all of his earnings, in excess of modest living expenses, into the payment of these obligations. It was the burden of many years and he always called it 'the national debt'. But he kept his word, paying both principal and the high rate of interest until 1848, or after fifteen years, when a member of Congress, he paid the last cent. He was still 'honest Abe'. This narrative ranks the backwoodsman with Sir Walter Scott and Mark Twain, though no dinners were tendered to him and no glowing eulogies were published from ocean to ocean.

His only further experience in navigation was the piloting of a Cincinnati steamboat, the *Talisman*, up the Sangamon River (during the high water in spring time) to show that that stream was navigable. Nothing came of it however, and Springfield was never made 'the head of navigation'.

It was in the midst of the mercantile experiences above narrated that the Black Hawk war broke out. Black Hawk was chief of the Sac Indians, who, with some neighboring tribes, felt themselves wronged by the whites. Some of them accordingly put on the paint, raised the whoop, and entered the warpath in northern Illinois and southern Wisconsin. The governor called for soldiers, and Lincoln volunteered with the rest.

The election of captain of the company was according to an original method. The two candidates were placed a short distance apart and the men were invited to line up with one or the other according to their preference. When this had been done it was seen that Lincoln had about three quarters of the men. This testimony to his popularity was gratifying. After he became president of the United States he declared that no success that ever came to him gave him so much solid satisfaction.

Lincoln saw almost nothing of the war. His only casualty came after its close. He had been mustered out and his horse was stolen so that he was compelled to walk most of the way home. After the expiration of his term of enlistment he re-enlisted as a private. As he saw no fighting the war was to him almost literally a picnic. But in

1848, when he was in Congress, the friends of General Cass were trying to make political capital out of his alleged military services. This brought from Lincoln a speech which showed that he had not lost the power of satire which he possessed while a lad in Indiana.

Did you know, Mr Speaker, I am a military hero? In the days of the Black Hawk war I fought, bled, and – came away. I was not at Stillman's defeat, but I was about as near it as General Cass was to Hull's surrender; and, like him, I saw the place very soon afterwards. It is quite certain I did not break my sword, for I had none to break, but I bent my musket pretty bad on one occasion. If General Cass went in advance of me picking whortleberries, I guess I surpassed him in charges on the wild onions. If he saw any live fighting Indians, it was more than I did, but I had a good many bloody struggles with the mosquitoes; and although I never fainted from loss of blood, I can truly say I was often very hungry. If ever I should conclude to doff whatever our Democratic friends may suppose there is of black-cockade Federalism about me, and thereupon they shall take me up as their candidate for the Presidency, I protest that they shall not make fun of me, as they have of General Cass, by attempting to write me into a military hero.

In 1833 Lincoln was appointed postmaster at New Salem. To him the chief advantage of this position was the fact that it gave him the means of reading the papers. The principal one of these was the Louisville *Journal*, an exceedingly able paper, for it was in charge of George D. Prentice, one of the ablest editors this country has ever produced. The duties of the post-office were few because the mail was light. The occasional letters which came were usually carried around by the postmaster in his hat. When one asked for his mail, he would gravely remove his hat and search through the package of letters.

This office was discontinued in a short time, but no agent of the government came to close up the accounts. Years afterwards, when Lincoln was in Springfield, the officer suddenly appeared and demanded the balance due to the United States, the amount being seventeen dollars and a few cents. A friend who was by, knowing that Lincoln was short of funds, in order to save him from embarrassment, offered to lend him the needful sum. 'Hold on a minute and let's see how we come out,' said he. He went to his room and returned with an old rag containing money. This he counted out, being the exact sum to a cent. It was all in small denominations of silver and copper, just as it had been received. In all his emergencies of need he had never touched this small fund which he held in trust. To him it was sacred. He was still 'honest Abe'.

In the early thirties, when the state of Illinois was being settled with great rapidity, the demand for surveyors was greater than the supply. John Calhoun, surveyor for the government, was in urgent need of a deputy, and Lincoln was named as a man likely to be able to fit himself for the duties on short notice. He was appointed. He borrowed the necessary book and went to work in dead earnest to learn the science. Day and night he studied until his friends, noticing the wearing effect on his health, became alarmed. But by the end of six weeks, an almost incredibly brief period of time, he was ready for work.

It is certain that his outfit was of the simplest description, and there is a tradition that at first, instead of a surveyor's chain he used a long, straight, wild-grape vine. Those who understand the conditions and requirements of surveying in early days say that this is not improbable. A more important fact is that Lincoln's surveys have never been called in question, which is something that can be said of few frontier surveyors. Though he learned the science in so short a time, yet here, as always, he was thorough.

It was said in the earlier part of this chapter that to the holders of Lincoln's notes who consented to await his ability to pay, there was one exception. One man, when his note fell due, seized horse and instruments, and put a temporary stop to his surveying. But a neighbor bought these in and returned them to Lincoln. He never forgot the kindness of this man, James Short by name, and thirty years later appointed him Indian agent.

At this point may be mentioned an occurrence which took place a year or two later. It was his first romance of love, his engagement to a beautiful girl, Ann Rutledge, and his bereavement. Her untimely death nearly unsettled his mind. He was afflicted with melancholy to such a degree that his friends dared not leave him alone. For years afterwards the thought of her would shake his whole frame with emotion, and he would sit with his face buried in his hands while the tears trickled through. A friend once begged him to try to forget his sorrow. 'I cannot,' he said; 'the thought of the rain and snow on her grave fills me with indescribable grief.'

Somehow, we know not how, the poem 'Oh, why should the spirit of mortal be proud?' was in his mind connected with Ann Rutledge. Possibly it may have been a favorite with her. There was certainly some association, and through his whole life he was fond of it and often repeated it. Nor did he forget her. It was late in life that he said: 'I really and truly loved the girl and think often of her now.' Then, after a pause, 'And I have loved the name of Rutledge to this day.'

This bereavement took much from Lincoln. Did it give him nothing? Patience, earnestness, tenderness, sympathy – these are sometimes the gifts which are sent by the messenger Sorrow. We are justified in believing that this sad event was one of the means of ripening the character of this great man, and that to it was due a measure of his usefulness in his mature years.

CHAPTER SEVEN
Entering Politics

Lincoln's duties at New Salem, as clerk, storekeeper, and post-master, had resulted in an intimate acquaintance with the people of that general locality. His duties as surveyor took him into the outlying districts. His social instincts won for him friends wherever he was known, while his sterling character gave him an influence unusual, both in kind and in measure, for a young man of his years. He had always possessed an interest in public, even national, questions, and his fondness for debate and speech-making increased this interest. Moreover he had lived month by month going from one job to another, and had not yet found his permanent calling.

When this combination of facts is recalled, it is a foregone conclusion that he would sooner or later enter politics. This he did at the age of twenty-three, in 1832.

According to the custom of the day he announced in the spring his candidacy. After this was done the Black Hawk war called him off the ground and he did not get back until about ten days before the election, so that he had almost no time to attend to the canvass. One incident of this campaign is preserved which is interesting, partly because it concerns the first known speech Lincoln ever made in his own behalf, and chiefly because it was an exhibition of his character.

He was speaking at a place called Cappsville when two men in the audience got into a scuffle.

Lincoln proceeded in his speech until it became evident that his friend was getting the worst of the scuffle, when he descended from the platform, seized the antagonist and threw him ten or twelve feet away on the ground, and then remounted the platform and took up his speech where he had left off without a break in the logic.

The methods of electioneering are given by Miss Tarbell in the following words:

> Wherever he saw a crowd of men he joined them, and he never failed to adapt himself to their point of view in asking for votes. If the degree of physical strength was the test for a candidate, he was ready to lift a weight, or wrestle with the countryside champion; if the amount of grain a man could cut would recommend him, he seized the cradle and showed the swath he could cut. (I. 109).

The ten days devoted to the canvass were not enough, and he was defeated. The vote against him was chiefly in the outlying region where he was little known. It must have been gratifying to him that in his own precinct, where he was so well known, he received the almost unanimous vote of all parties. Biographers differ as to the precise number of votes in the New Salem precinct, but by Nicolay and Hay it is given as 277 for, and three against. Of this election Lincoln himself (speaking in the third person) said: 'This was the only time Abraham was ever defeated on the direct vote of the people.'

His next political experience was a candidacy for the legislature 1834. At this time, as before, he announced his own candidacy. But not as before, he at this time made a diligent canvass of the district. When the election came off he was not only successful but he ran ahead of his ticket. He usually did run ahead of his ticket excepting when running for the presidency, and then it was from the nature of the case impossible. Though Lincoln probably did not realize it, this, his first election, put an end forever to his drifting, desultory, frontier life. Up to this point he was always looking for a job. From this time on he was not passing from one thing to another. In this country politics and law are closely allied. This two-fold pursuit, politics for the sake of law, and law for the sake of politics, constituted Lincoln's vocation for the rest of his life.

The capital of Illinois was Vandalia, a village said to be named after the Vandals by innocent citizens who were pleased with the euphony of the word but did not know who the Vandals were. Outwardly the village was crude and forbidding, and many of the Solons were attired in coon-skin caps and other startling apparel. The fashionable clothing, the one which came to be generally adopted as men grew to be 'genteel', was blue jeans. Even 'store clothes', as they came to be called, were as yet comparatively unknown.

But one must not be misled by appearances in a frontier town. The frontier life has a marvelous influence in developing brains. It is as hard for some people in the centers of culture to believe in the possible intelligence of the frontier, as it was in 1776 for the cultured Englishmen to believe in the intelligence of the colonial patriots. In that collection of men at Vandalia were more than a few who afterwards came to have national influence and reputation.

Apart from Lincoln himself, the most prominent member of the legislature was his lifelong antagonist, Stephen A. Douglas. Whatever may be said of this man's political principles, there can be no question as to the shrewdness of his political methods. It is the opinion of the present writer that in the entire history of our political system no man has ever surpassed him in astuteness. Even today all parties are using the methods which he either devised or introduced. The trouble with him was that he was on the wrong side. He did not count sufficiently on the conscience of the nation.

Lincoln was re-elected to the legislature as often as he was willing to be a candidate, and served continuously for eight years. One session is much like another, and in this eight years of legislative experience only two prominent facts will be narrated. One was the removal of the capital to Springfield. To Lincoln was entrusted the difficult task – difficult, because there were almost as many applications for the honor of being the capital city as there were towns and villages in the central part of the state. He was entirely successful, and thenceforward he was inseparably connected with Springfield. It was his home as long as he lived, and there his remains were buried.

The prophetic event of his legislative work was what is known as the Lincoln-Stone protest. This looks today so harmless that it is not easy to understand the situation in 1837. The pro-slavery feeling was running high, an abolitionist was looked on as a monster and a menace to national law and order. It was in that year that the Reverend Elijah P. Lovejoy was murdered – martyred – at Alton, Ill. The legislature had passed pro-slavery resolutions. There were many in the legislature who did not approve of these, but in the condition of public feeling, it was looked on as political suicide to express opposition openly. There was no politic reason why Lincoln should protest. His protest could do no practical good. To him it was solely a matter of conscience. Slavery was wrong, the resolutions were wrong, and to him it became necessary to enter the protest. He succeeded in getting but one man to join him, and he did so because he was about to withdraw from politics and therefore had nothing to lose. Here is the document as it was spread on the journal.

Resolutions upon the subject of domestic slavery having passed both branches of the General Assembly at its present session, the undersigned hereby protest against the passage of the same.

They believe that the institution of slavery is founded on both injustice and bad policy, but that the promulgation of abolition doctrines tends rather to increase than abate its evils.

They believe that the Congress of the United States has no power under the Constitution to interfere with the institution of slavery in the different States.

They believe that the Congress of the United States has the power, under the Constitution, to abolish slavery in the District of Columbia, but that the power ought not to be exercised, unless at the request of the people of the District.

The difference between these opinions and those contained in the above resolutions is their reason for entering this protest.

(Signed) DAN STONE
A. LINCOLN
Representatives from the county of Sangamon

In 1836 Lincoln made an electioneering speech which was fortunately heard by Joshua Speed, and he has given an account of it. Be it remembered that at that time lightning rods were rare and attracted an unreasonable amount of attention. One Forquer, who was Lincoln's opponent, had recently rodded his house – and everyone knew it. This man's speech consisted partly in ridiculing his opponent, his bigness, his awkwardness, his dress, his youth. Lincoln heard him through without interruption and then took the stand and said:

> The gentleman commenced his speech by saying that this young man would have to be taken down, and he was sorry the task devolved upon him. I am not so young in years as I am in the tricks and trades of a politician; but live long or die young, I would rather die now than, like the gentleman, change my politics and simultaneous with the change receive an office worth three thousand dollars a year, and then have to erect a lightning-rod over my house to protect a guilty conscience from an offended God.

It need hardly be said that that speech clung to its victim like a burr. Wherever he went, someone would be found to tell about the guilty conscience and the lightning-rod. The house and its lightning-rod were long a center of interest in Springfield. Visitors to the city were taken to see the house and its lightning-rod, while the story was told with great relish.

Having served eight terms in the legislature, Lincoln in 1842 aspired to Congress. He was, however, defeated at the primary. His neighbors added insult to injury by making him one of the delegates to the convention and instructing him to vote for his successful rival, Baker. This did not interrupt the friendship which united the two for many years, lasting, indeed, until the death of Colonel Baker on the field of battle.

In 1846 he renewed his candidacy, and this time with flattering success. His opponent was a traveling preacher, Peter Cartwright, who was widely known in the state and had not a little persuasive power. In this contest Cartwright's 'arguments' were two: the first, that Lincoln was an atheist, and the second that he was an aristocrat. These 'arguments' were not convincing, and Lincoln was elected by a handsome majority, running far ahead of his ticket. This was, at the time, the height of his ambition, yet he wrote to Mr Speed: 'Being elected to Congress, though I am grateful to our friends for having done it, has not pleased me as much as I expected.'

His one term in Congress was uneventful. Twice his humor bubbled over. Once was when he satirized the claims that Cass was a military hero, in the speech already mentioned. The other time was his introducing the resolutions known as the 'spot resolutions'. The President had sent to Congress an inflammatory, buncombe message, in which he insisted that the war had been begun by Mexico, 'by invading our territory and shedding the blood of our citizens on our own soil'. The resolutions requested from the President the information:

First. Whether the spot on which the blood of our citizens was shed, as in his messages declared, was or was not within the territory of Spain, at least after the treaty of 1819, until the Mexican revolution.
Second. Whether that spot is or is not within the territory which was wrested from Spain by the revolutionary government of Mexico.
Third. Whether the spot is or is not, etc., etc.

It is the recurrence of the word *spot* which gave the name to the resolutions.

Lincoln had now served eight years in the legislature and one term in Congress. He had a good understanding of politics. He was never a time-server, and he had done nothing unwise. He knew how to win votes and he knew what to do with himself when the votes were won. He held the confidence of his constituency. His was a constantly growing popularity. He could do everything but one – he could not dishonor his conscience. His belief that 'slavery was founded on injustice' was the only reason for his protest. He never hesitated to protest against injustice. The Golden Rule had a place in practical politics. The Sermon on the Mount was not an iridescent dream.

CHAPTER EIGHT
Entering the Law

In treating of this topic, it will be necessary to recall certain things already mentioned. One characteristic which distinguished Lincoln all through his life was thoroughness. When he was President a man called on him for a certain favor, and, when asked to state his case, made a great mess of it, for he had not sufficiently pre-pared himself. Then the President gave him some free advice. 'What you need is to be thorough', and he brought his hand down on the table with the crash of a maul – 'to be thorough'. It was his own method. After a successful practise of twenty years he advised a young law student: 'Work, work, work is the main thing.' He spoke out of his own experience.

There is one remarkable passage in his life which is worth re-peating here, since it gives an insight into the thoroughness of this man. The following is quoted from the Rev. J. P. Gulliver, then pastor of the Congregational church in Norwich, Conn. It was a part of a conversation which took place shortly after the Cooper Institute speech in 1860, and was printed in *The Independent* for September 1, 1864.

Oh, yes! 'I read law', as the phrase is; that is, I became a lawyer's clerk in Springfield, and copied tedious documents, and picked up what I could of law in the intervals of other work. But your question reminds me of a bit of education I had, which I am bound in honesty to mention.'

In the course of my law reading I constantly came upon the word *demonstrate*. I thought, at first, that I understood its meaning, but soon became satisfied that I did not. I said to myself, What do I do when I *demonstrate* more than when I *reason* or *prove*? How does *demonstration* differ from any other proof? I consulted Webster's Dictionary. They told of 'certain proof', 'proof beyond the possi-bility of doubt'; but I could form no idea of what sort of proof that was. I thought a great many things were proved beyond the possi-bility of doubt, without recourse to any such extraordinary process of reasoning as I understood *demonstration* to be. I consulted all the dictionaries and books of reference I could find, but with no better results. You might as well have defined *blue* to a blind man. At last I said – Lincoln, you never can make a lawyer if you do not under-stand what *demonstrate* means; and I left my situation in Springfield, went home to my father's house, and stayed there till I could give any proposition in the six books of Euclid at sight. I then found out what *demonstrate* means, and went back to my law studies.

Was there ever a more thorough student?

*　　*　　*

He, like everyone else, had his library within the library. Though he read everything he could lay his hands on, yet there are five books to be mentioned specifically, because from childhood they furnished his intellectual nutriment. These were the Bible, *Aesop's Fables* and *Pilgrim's Progress*, Burns, and Shakespeare. These were his mental food. They entered into the very substance of his thought and imagination. 'Fear the man of one book.' Lincoln had five books, and so thoroughly were they his that he was truly formidable. These did not exclude other reading and study; they made it a thousand times more fruitful. And yet people ask, where did Lincoln get the majesty, the classic simplicity and elegance of his Gettysburg address? The answer is here.

While Lincoln was postmaster, he was a diligent reader of the newspapers, of which the chief was the Louisville *Journal*. It was edited by George D. Prentice, who was, and is, second to no other editor in the entire history of American journalism. The ability of this man to express his thoughts with such power was a mystery to this reader. The editor's mastery of language aroused in Lincoln a burning desire to obtain command of the English tongue. He applied for counsel to a friend, a schoolmaster by the name of Mentor Graham. Graham recommended him to study English grammar, and told him that a copy of one was owned by a man who lived six miles away. Lincoln walked to the house, borrowed the book – 'collared' it, as he expressed it – and at the end of six days had mastered it with his own thoroughness.

The first law book he read was *The Statutes of Indiana*. This was when he was a lad living in that state, and he read the book, not for any special desire to know the subject, but because he was in the habit of reading all that came into his hands.

His next book was Blackstone's *Commentaries*. The accidental way in which he gained possession of, and read, this book is of sufficient interest to narrate in his own words. It was shortly after he got into the grocery business.

One day a man who was migrating to the West drove up in front of my store with a wagon which contained his family and household plunder. He asked me if I would buy an old barrel for which he had no room in his wagon, and which he said contained nothing of special value. I did not want it, but to oblige him I bought it, and paid him, I think, half a dollar for it. Without further examination I put it away in the store and forgot all about it. Some time after, in overhauling things, I came upon the barrel, and emptying it upon the floor to see what it contained, I found at the bottom of the rubbish a complete edition of Blackstone's *Commentaries*. I began to read those famous works, and I had plenty of time; for during the long summer days, when the farmers were busy with their crops, my customers were few and far between. The more I read, the more intensely interested I became. Never in my whole life was my mind so thoroughly absorbed. I read until I devoured them.

All this may have been fatal to the prosperity of the leading store in that hamlet of fifteen log cabins, but it led to something better than the success of the most magnificent store in New York.

It was in 1834 that Lincoln was first elected to the legislature. During the canvass he was brought into the company of Major John T. Stuart, whom he had met in the Black Hawk war. Stuart advised him to enter definitely on the study of the law. He decided to do this. This proved to be quite the most important thing that occurred to him that year.

Stuart further offered to lend him the necessary books. This offer was gladly accepted, and having no means of travel, he walked to and from Springfield, a distance of twenty miles, to get the books and return them. During this tramp he was able to read forty pages of the volume. Thus he read, and we may venture to say mastered, Chitty, Greenleaf, and Story, in addition to Blackstone before mentioned. It was the best foundation that could have been laid for a great lawyer.

During this reading he was getting his bread and butter by the other employments – store-keeping, postmaster, and surveyor. These may not have interfered greatly with the study of the law, but the study of the law certainly interfered with the first of these. He read much out of doors. He would lie on his back in the shade of some tree, with his feet resting part way up the tree, then follow the shadow around from west to east, grinding around with the progress of the sun. When in the house his attitude was to cock his feet high in a chair, thus 'sitting on his shoulder blades', to use a common expression. When in his office he would throw himself on the lounge with his feet high on a chair. These attitudes, bringing his feet up to, and sometimes above, the level with his head, have been characteristic of American students time out of mind. He never outgrew the tendency. Even when President and sitting with his Cabinet, his feet always found some lofty perch.

While he was not reading, he was pondering or memorizing. Thus he took long walks, talking to himself incessantly, until some of his neighbors thought he was going crazy.

He was admitted to the bar in 1837. At that date there was no lawyer nearer to New Salem than those in Springfield, which was twenty miles off. Consequently he had a little amateur practise from his neighbors. He was sometimes appealed to for the purpose of drawing up agreements and other papers. He had no office, and if he chanced to be out of doors would call for writing-materials, a slab of wood for a desk, draw up the paper, and then resume his study.

This same year he became a partner of Stuart, in Springfield. The latter wanted to get into politics, and it was essential that he should have a trustworthy partner. So the firm of Stuart and Lincoln was established in 1837 and lived for four years. In 1841 he entered into partnership with Logan, and this also lasted about four years. In the year 1845 was established the firm of Lincoln and Herndon, which continued until the assassination of the President in 1865.

After a brief period Lincoln himself got deeper into politics, this period culminating with the term in Congress. In this he necessarily neglected the law more or less. But late in 1848, or early in 1849, he returned to the law with renewed vigor and zeal, giving it his undivided attention for six years. It was the repeal of the Missouri Compromise that called him back into the arena of politics. This will be narrated later.

His partnership with Stuart of course necessitated his removal to Springfield. This event, small in itself, gives such a pathetic picture of his poverty, and his cheerful endurance, that it is well worth narrating. It is preserved by Joshua F. Speed, who became, and through life continued, Lincoln's fast friend. The story is given in Speed's words.

He had ridden into town on a borrowed horse, with no earthly property save a pair of saddlebags containing a few clothes. I was a merchant at Springfield, and kept a large country store, embracing dry-goods, groceries, hardware, books, medicines, bed-clothes, mattresses – in fact, everything that the country needed. Lincoln said he wanted to buy the furniture for a single bed. The mattress, blankets, sheets, coverlet, and pillow, according to the figures made by me, would cost seventeen dollars. He said that perhaps was cheap enough; but small as the price was, he was unable to pay it. [Note that at this time he was carrying the debts of the merchants of New Salem.] But if I would credit him until Christmas, and his experiment as a lawyer was a success, he would pay then; saying in the saddest tone, 'If I fail in this, I do not know that I ever can pay you.' As I looked up at him I thought then, and I think now, that I never saw a sadder face.

I said to him: 'You seem to be so much pained at contracting so small a debt, I think I can suggest a plan by which you can avoid the debt, and at the same time attain your end. I have a large room with a double bed upstairs, which you are very welcome to share with me.'

'Where is your room?' said he.

'Upstairs,' said I, pointing to a pair of winding-stairs, which led from the store to my room.

He took his saddle-bags on his arm, went upstairs, set them on the floor, and came down with the most changed expression of countenance. Beaming with pleasure, he exclaimed: 'Well, Speed, I am moved!'

Thus he became established in the profession of the law and a resident of Springfield. It was not a large city, but it was a very active one, though small, and was the capital of the state. Lincoln was there favorably known, because he had been chiefly instrumental in getting the capital moved to that place from Vandalia. His first law partner was very helpful to him, and he had abundant reason all his life to be thankful also for the friendship of Joshua F. Speed.

CHAPTER NINE
On the Circuit

The requirements of the lawyer in that part of the country, at that date, were different from the requirements in any part of the world at the present date. The Hon. Joseph H. Choate, in a lecture at Edinburgh, November 13, 1900, said: 'My professional brethren will ask me how could this rough backwoodsman . . . become a learned and accomplished lawyer? Well, he never did. He never would have earned his salt as a writer for the *Signet*, nor have won a place as advocate in the Court of Session, where the teachings of the profession has reached its highest perfection, and centuries of learning and precedent are involved in the equipment of a lawyer.'

The only means we have of knowing what Lincoln could do is knowing what he did. If his biography teaches anything, it teaches that he never failed to meet the exigencies of any occasion. The study of his life will reveal this fact with increasing emphasis. Many a professional brother looked on Lincoln as 'this rough backwoodsman', unable to 'become a learned and accomplished lawyer', to his own utter discomfiture. We are justified in saying that if he had undertaken the duties of the Scots writer to the *Signet*, he would have done them well, as he did every other duty.

When Douglas was congratulated in advance upon the ease with which he would vanquish his opponent, he replied that he would rather meet any man in the country in that joint debate than Abraham Lincoln. At another time he said: 'Lincoln is one of those peculiar men who perform with admirable skill whatever they undertake.'

Lincoln's professional duties were in the Eighth Judicial Circuit, which then comprised fifteen counties. Some of these counties have since been subdivided, so that the territory of that district was larger than would be indicated by the same number of counties today. It was one hundred and fifty miles long and nearly as wide. There were few railroads, and the best county roads were extremely poor, so that traveling was burdensome. The court and the lawyers traveled from one county seat to another, sometimes horseback, sometimes in buggies or wagons, and sometimes afoot.

The duties of one county being concluded, the entire company would move on to another county. Thus only a small part of his duties were transacted at Springfield.

These periodic sessions of the court were of general interest to the communities in which they were held. There were no theaters, no lyceums for music or lectures, and few other assemblages of any sort, excepting the churches and the agricultural fairs. It thus came about that the court was the center of a greater interest than would now be possible. It was the rostrum of the lecturer and the arena of the debate. Nor were comedies lacking in its multifarious proceedings. The attorney was therefore sure of a general audience, as well as of court and jury.

This peripatetic practise threw the lawyers much into one another's company. There were long evenings to be spent in the country taverns, when sociability was above par. Lincoln's inexhaustible fund of wit and humor, and his matchless array of stories, made him the life of the company. In this number there were many lawyers of real ability. The judge was David Davis, whose culture and legal ability will hardly be questioned by anyone. Judge Davis was almost ludicrously fond of Lincoln. He kept him in his room evenings and was very impatient if Lincoln's talk was interrupted.

There were two qualities in Lincoln's anecdotes: their resistless fun, and their appropriateness. When Lincoln came into court it was usually with a new story, and as he would tell it in low tones the lawyers would crowd about him to the neglect of everything else, and to the great annoyance of the judge. He once called out: 'Mr Lincoln, we can't hold two courts, one up here and one down there. Either yours or mine must adjourn.'

Once Lincoln came into the room late, leaned over the clerk's desk and whispered to him a little story. Thereupon the clerk threw back his head and laughed aloud. The judge thundered out, 'Mr Clerk, you may fine yourself five dollars for contempt of court.' The clerk quietly replied, 'I don't care; the story's worth it.' After adjournment the judge asked him, 'What was that story of Lincoln's?' When it was repeated the judge threw back his head and laughed, and added, 'You may remit the fine.'

A stranger, hearing the fame of Lincoln's stories, attended court and afterward said, 'The stories are good, but I can't see that they help the case any.' An admiring neighbor replied with more zeal and justice than elegance, 'Don't you apply that unction to your soul.' The neighbor was right. Lincoln had not in vain spent the days and nights of his boyhood and youth with Aesop. His stories were as luminous of the point under consideration as were the stories which explained that 'this fable teaches'.

Judge Davis wrote of him that 'he was able to claim the attention of court and jury when the cause was most uninteresting by the *appropriateness* of his anecdotes.' Those who have tried to claim Judge Davis's attention when he did not want to give it, will realize the greatness of praise implied in this concession.

To this may be joined the remark of Leonard Swett, that 'any man who took Lincoln for a simple-minded man would wake up with his back in the ditch.'

As Lincoln would never adopt the methods of his partner Herndon, the latter could not quite grasp the essential greatness of the former, and he uses some patronizing words. We may again quote Judge Davis: 'In all the elements that constitute a great lawyer he had few equals . . . He seized the strong points of a cause and presented them with clearness and great compactness. . . . Generalities and platitudes had no charms for him. An unfailing vein of humor never deserted him.' Then follows the passage already quoted.

Lincoln never could bring himself to charge large fees. Lamon was his limited partner (with the office in Danville and Bloom-ington) for many years. He tells one instance which will illustrate this trait. There was a case of importance for which the fee was fixed in advance at $250, a very moderate fee under the circum-stances. It so happened that the case was not contested and the business required only a short time. The client cheerfully paid the fee as agreed. As he went away Lincoln asked his partner how much he charged. He replied, '$250.' 'Lamon,' he said, 'that is all wrong. Give him back at least half of it.' Lamon protested that it was according to agreement and the client was satisfied. 'That may be, but *I* am not satisfied. This is positively wrong. Go, call him back and return him half the money at least, or I will not receive one cent of it for my share.'

One may imagine the amazement of the client to receive back one half of the fee. But the matter did not end here. The affair had attracted the attention of those near at hand, including the court. Judge Davis was of enormous physical size, and his voice was like a fog horn. The author writes this from vivid remembrance. Once in early youth he quaked in his shoes at the blast of that voice. The conclusion of the incident is given in the words of Lamon.

The judge never could whisper, but in this case he probably did his best. At all events, in attempting to whisper to Mr Lincoln he trumpeted his rebuke in about these words, and in rasping tones that could be heard all over the court room: 'Lincoln, I have been watching you and Lamon. You are impoverishing this bar by your picayune charges of fees, and the lawyers have reason to complain of you. You are now almost as poor as Lazarus, and if you don't make people pay you more for your services, you will die as poor as Job's turkey.'

The event justified the Judge's remarks. It was not unusual for Lincoln's name, as attorney, to be found on one side or the other of every case on the docket. In other words, his practise was as large as that of any lawyer on the circuit, and he had his full proportion of important cases. But he never accumulated a large sum of money. Probably no other successful lawyer in that region had a smaller income. This is a convincing commentary on his charges.

The largest fee he ever received was from the Illinois Central Railroad. The case was tried at Bloomington before the supreme court and was won for the road. Lincoln went to Chicago and presented a bill for $2,000 at the offices of the company. 'Why,' said the official, in real or feigned astonishment, 'this is as much as a first-class lawyer would have charged.'

Lincoln was greatly depressed by this rebuff, and would have let the matter drop then and there had not his neighbors heard of it. They persuaded him to raise the fee to $5,000, and six leading lawyers of the state testified that that sum was a moderate charge. Lincoln sued the road for the larger amount and won his case. It is a matter of interest that at that time the vice-president of the railroad was George B. McClellan.

It was Lincoln's habit always to go to the heart of a case. Quibbles did not interest him. The non-professional public who have attended jury trials will not easily forget the monotonous 'I object' of the attorneys, usually followed by, 'I except to the ruling of the court', and 'The clerk will note the exception.' Lincoln generally met the objections by the placid remark, 'I reckon that's so.' Thus he gave up point after point, apparently giving away his case over and over again, until his associates were brought to the verge of nervous prostration. After giving away six points he would fasten upon the seventh, which was the pivotal point of the case, and would handle that so as to win. This ought to have been satisfactory, but neither Herndon nor his other associates ever got used to it.

Lincoln put his conscience into his legal practise to a greater degree than is common with lawyers. He held (with Blackstone) that law is for the purpose of securing justice, and he would never make use of any technicality for the purpose of thwarting justice. When others maneuvered, he met them by a straightforward dealing. He never did or could take an unfair advantage. On the wrong side of a case, he was worse than useless to his client, and he knew it. He would never take such a case if it could be avoided. His partner Herndon tells how he gave some free and unprofessional advice to one who offered him such a case: 'Yes, there is no reasonable doubt but that I can gain your case for you. I can set a whole neighborhood at loggerheads; I can distress a widowed mother and her six fatherless children, and thereby get for you six hundred dollars, which rightfully belongs, it appears to me, as much to them as it does to you. I shall not take your case, but will give a little advice for nothing. You seem a sprightly, energetic man. I would advise you to try your hand at making six hundred dollars in some other way.'

Sometimes, after having entered on a case, he discovered that his clients had imposed on him. In his indignation he has even left the court room. Once when the Judge sent for him he refused to return. 'Tell the judge my hands are dirty; I came over to wash them.'

The most important law-suit in which Lincoln was ever engaged was the McCormick case. McCormick instituted a suit against one Manny for alleged infringement of patents. McCormick virtually claimed the monopoly of the manufacture of harvesting machines. The suit involved a large sum of money besides incidental considerations. The leading attorney for the plaintiff was the Hon. Reverdy Johnson, one of the foremost, if not the foremost, at the bar in the entire country. It was the opportunity of crossing swords with

Johnson that, more than anything else, stirred Lincoln's interest. With him, for the defense, was associated Edwin M. Stanton.

The case was to be tried at Cincinnati, and all parties were on hand. Lincoln gave an extraordinary amount of care in the preparation of the case. But some little things occurred. Through an open doorway he heard Stanton make some scornful remarks of him – ridiculing his awkward appearance and his dress, particularly, for Lincoln wore a linen duster, soiled and disfigured by perspiration. When the time came for apportioning the speeches, Lincoln, although he was thoroughly prepared and by the customs of the bar it was his right to make the argument, courteously offered the opportunity to Stanton, who promptly accepted. It was a great disappointment to Lincoln to miss thus the opportunity of arguing with Reverdy Johnson. Neither did Stanton know what he missed. Nor did Johnson know what a narrow escape he had.

This chapter will not be complete without making mention of Lincoln's professional kindness to the poor and unfortunate. Those who could find no other friends were sure to find a friend in Lincoln. He would freely give his services to the needy. At that time the negro found it hard to get help, friendship, justice. Though Illinois was a free state, public opinion was such that anyone who undertook the cause of the negro was sure to alienate friends. Lincoln was one of the few who never hesitated at the sacrifice.

A young man, a free negro living in the neighborhood, had been employed as cabin boy on a Mississippi river steamboat. Arriving at New Orleans, he went ashore without a suspicion of what the law was in a slave state. He was arrested for being on the street after dark without a pass, thrown into jail, and fined. Having no money to pay the fine, he was liable to be sold into slavery, when his mother, in her distress, came to Lincoln for help. Lincoln sent to the governor to see if there was no way by which this free negro could be brought home. The governor was sorry that there was not. In a towering wrath Lincoln exclaimed: 'I'll have that negro back soon, or I'll have a twenty years' excitement in Illinois until the governor does have a legal and constitutional right to do something in the premises!'

He had both. He and his partner sent to New Orleans the necessary money by which the boy was released and restored to his mother. The twenty years' excitement came later.

CHAPTER TEN

Social Life and Marriage

Springfield was largely settled by people born and educated in older and more cultured communities. From the first it developed a social life of its own. In the years on both sides of 1840, it maintained as large an amount of such social activity as was possible in a new frontier city. In this life Lincoln was an important factor. The public interest in the man made this necessary, even apart from considerations of his own personal preferences.

We have seen that he was extremely sociable in his tastes. He was fond of being among men. Wherever men were gathered, there Lincoln went, and wherever Lincoln was, men gathered about him. In the intervals of work, at nooning or in the evening, he was always the center of an interested group, and his unparalleled flow of humor, wit, and good nature was the life of the assemblage. This had always been so from childhood. It had become a second nature with him to entertain the crowd, while the crowd came to look upon him as their predestined entertainer.

But Lincoln had been brought up in the open air, on the very frontier, 'far from the madding crowd'. His social experience and his tastes were with men, not ladies. He was not used to the luxuries of civilization – elegant carpets, fine china, fashionable dress. Though he had great dignity and nobility of soul, he did not have that polish of manners which counts for so much with ladies. His ungainly physique accented this lack. He was not, he never could be, what is known as a ladies' man. While his friendly nature responded to all sociability, he was not fond of ladies' society. He was naturally in great demand, and he attended all the social gatherings. But when there, he drifted away from the company of the ladies into that of the men. Nor were the men loath to gather about him.

The ladies liked him, but one of them doubtless spoke the truth, when she declared that their grievance against him was that he monopolized the attention of the men. This was natural to him, it had been confirmed by years of habit, and by the time he was thirty years old it was practically impossible for him to adopt the ways acceptable to ladies.

Into this society in Springfield came a pretty, bright, educated, cultured young lady – Miss Mary Todd. She was of an aristocratic family from Kentucky. It is said that she could trace the family genealogy back many centuries. She may have been haughty – she was said to be so – and she may have been exacting in those little matters which make up so large a measure of what is known as polish of manners. These would be precisely the demands which Lincoln was unable to meet.

It was a foregone conclusion that the two would be thrown much into each other's society, and that the neighbors would connect them in thought. For Lincoln was the most popular man and Miss Todd was the most popular young lady in Springfield. It was simply another case of the attraction of opposites, for in everything except their popularity they were as unlike as they could be.

It is proverbial that the course of true love never did run smooth. If there were ripples and eddies and counter-currents in the course of this love, it was in nowise exceptional. It is only the prominence of the parties that has brought this into the strong light of publicity.

Much has been written that is both unwarranted and unkind. Even the most confidential friends do not realize the limitations of their knowledge on a matter so intimate. When they say they know all about it, they are grievously mistaken. No love story (outside of novels) is ever told truly. In the first place, the parties themselves do not tell all. They may say they do, but there are some things which neither man nor woman ever tells. In the heart of love there is a Holy of Holies into which the most intimate friend is not allowed to look.

And in the second place, even the lovers do not see things alike. If both really understood, there could be no *mis*understanding. It is, then, presumptive for even the confidants, and much more for the general public, to claim to know too much of a lovers' quarrel.

We would gladly pass over this event were it not that certain salient facts are a matter of public record. It is certain that Lincoln became engaged to Miss Todd in the year 1840. It is certain that he broke the engagement on January 1, 1841. It is certain that about that time he had a horrible attack of melancholy. And we have seen that he never outgrew his attachment to his early love, Ann Rutledge. Whether this melancholy was the cause of his breaking the engagement, or was caused by it, we cannot say. Whether the memory of Ann Rutledge had any influence in the matter, we do not know.

Whatever the mental cause of this melancholy, there is no doubt that it had also a physical cause. This was his most violent attack, but by no means his only one. It recurred, with greater or less severity, all through his life. He had been born and had grown up in a climate noted for its malaria. Excepting for the facts that he spent much time in the open air, had abundant exercise, and ate plain food, the laws of sanitation were not thought of. It would be strange if his system were not full of malaria, or, what is only slightly less abominable, of the medicines used to counteract it. In either case he would be subject to depression. An unfortunate occurrence in a love affair, coming at the time of an attack of melancholy, would doubtless bear abundant and bitter fruit.

Certain it is that the engagement was broken, not a little to the chagrin of both parties. But a kind neighbor, Mrs Francis, whose husband was editor of the Springfield *Journal*, interposed with her friendly offices. She invited the two lovers to her house, and they went, each without the knowledge that the other was to be there. Their social converse was thus renewed, and, in the company of a third person, Miss Jayne, they continued to meet at frequent intervals. Among the admirers of Miss Todd were two young men who came to be widely known. These were Douglas and Shields. With the latter only we are concerned now. He was a red-headed little Irishman, with a peppery temper, the whole being set off with an inordinate vanity. He must have had genuine ability in some directions, or else he was wonderfully lucky, for he was an officeholder of some kind or other, in different states of the Union, nearly all his life. It is doubtful if another person can be named who held as many different offices as he; certainly no other man has ever represented so many different states in the senate.

At this particular time, Shields was auditor of the state of Illinois. The finances of the state were in a shocking condition. The state banks were not a success, and the currency was nearly worthless. At the same time, it was the only money current, and it was the money of the state. These being the circumstances, the governor, auditor, and treasurer, issued a circular forbidding the payment of state taxes in this paper currency of the state. This was clearly an outrage upon the taxpayers.

Against this Lincoln protested. Not by serious argument, but by the merciless satire which he knew so well how to use upon occasion. Under the pseudonym of Aunt Rebecca, he wrote a letter to the Springfield *Journal*. The letter was written in the style of Josh Billings, and purported to come from a widow residing in the 'Lost Townships'. It was an attempt to laugh down the unjust measure, and in pursuance of this the writer plied Shields with ridicule. The town was convulsed with laughter, and Shields with fury. The wrath of the little Irishman was funnier than the letter, and the joy of the neighbors increased.

Miss Todd and Miss Jayne entered into the spirit of the fun. Then they wrote a letter in which Aunt Rebecca proposed to soothe his injured feelings by accepting Shields as her husband. This was followed by a doggerel rhyme celebrating the event.

Shields' fury knew no bounds. He went to Francis, the editor of the *Journal*, and demanded the name of the author of the letters. Francis consulted with Lincoln. The latter was unwilling to permit any odium to fall on the ladies, and sent word to Shields that he would hold himself responsible for those letters.

If Shields had not been precisely the kind of a man he was, the matter might have been explained and settled amicably. But no, he must have blood. He sent an insulting and peremptory challenge. When Lincoln became convinced that a duel was necessary, he exercised his right, as the challenged party, of choosing the weapons. He selected 'broadswords of the largest size'. This was another triumph of humor. The midget of an Irishman was to be pitted against the giant of six feet four inches, who possessed the strength of a Hercules, and the weapons were – 'broadswords of the largest size'.

The bloody party repaired to Alton, and thence to an island or sand-bar on the Missouri side of the river. There a reconciliation was effected, honor was satisfied all around, and they returned home in good spirits. For some reason Lincoln was always ashamed of this farce. Why, we do not know. It may have been because he was drawn into a situation in which there was a possibility of his shedding human blood. And he who was too tender-hearted to shoot wild game could not make light of that situation.

The engagement between Lincoln and Miss Todd was renewed, and they were quietly married at the home of the bride's sister, Mrs Edwards, November 4, 1842. Lincoln made a loyal, true, indulgent husband. Mrs Lincoln made a home that was hospitable, cultured, unostentatious. They lived together until the death of the husband, more than twenty-two years later.

They had four children, all boys. Only the eldest, Robert Todd Lincoln, grew to manhood. He has had a career which is, to say the least, creditable to the name he bears. For a few months at the close of the war he was on the staff of General Grant. He was Secretary of War under Garfield and retained the office through the administration of Arthur. Under President Harrison, from 1889 to 1893, he was minister to England. He is a lawyer by profession, residing in Chicago – the city that loved his father – and at the present writing is president of the Pullman Company. In every position he has occupied he has exercised a notably wide influence.

CHAPTER ELEVEN

The Encroachments of Slavery

It is necessary at this point to take a glance at the history of American slavery, in order to understand Lincoln's career. In 1619, or one year before the landing of the *Mayflower* at Plymouth, a Dutch man-of-war landed a cargo of slaves at Jamestown, Virginia. For nearly two centuries after this the slave trade was more or less brisk. The slaves were distributed, though unevenly, over all the colonies. But as time passed, differences appeared. In the North, the public conscience was awake to the injustice of the institution, while in the South it was not. There were many exceptions in both localities, but the public sentiment, the general feeling, was as stated.

There was another difference. Slave labor was more valuable in the South than in the North. This was due to the climate. The negro does not take kindly to the rigors of the North, while in the South the heat, which is excessive to the white man, is precisely suited to the negro. In the course of years, therefore, there came to be comparatively few negroes in the North while large numbers were found in the South.

It is generally conceded that the founders of our government looked forward to a gradual extinction of slavery. In the first draft of the Declaration of Independence, Thomas Jefferson inserted some scathing remarks about the King's part in the slave traffic. But it was felt that such remarks would come with ill grace from colonies that abetted slavery, and the passage was stricken out. It was, however, provided that the slave trade should cease in the year 1808.

The Ordinance of 1787 recognized the difference in sentiment of the two portions of the country on the subject, and was enacted as a compromise. Like several subsequent enactments, it was supposed to set the agitation of the subject for ever at rest. This ordinance provided that slavery should be excluded from the northwestern territory. At that time the Mississippi river formed the western boundary of the country, and the territory thus ordained to be free was that out of which the five states of Ohio, Indiana, Illinois, Michigan, and Wisconsin were subsequently formed. It was not then dreamed that the future acquisition of new territory, or the sudden appreciation of the value of the slave, would reopen the question.

But three facts changed the entire complexion of the subject. It was discovered that the soil and climate of the South were remarkably well adapted to the growth of cotton. Then the development of steam power and machinery in the manufacture of cotton goods created a sudden and enormous demand from Liverpool, Manchester, and other cities in England for American cotton. There remained an obstacle to the supply of this demand. This was the difficulty of separating the cotton fiber from the seed. A negro woman was able to clean about a pound of cotton in a day.

In 1793, Eli Whitney, a graduate of Yale college, was teaching school in Georgia, and boarding with the widow of General Greene. Certain planters were complaining, in the hearing of Mrs Greene, of the difficulty of cleaning cotton, when she declared that the Yankee school teacher could solve the difficulty, that he was so ingenious that there was almost nothing he could not do.

The matter was brought to Whitney's attention, who protested that he knew nothing of the subject – he hardly knew a cotton seed when he saw it. Nevertheless he set to work and invented the cotton gin. By this machine one man, turning a crank, could clean fifty pounds of cotton a day. The effect of this was to put a new face upon the cotton trade. It enabled the planters to meet the rapidly increasing demand for raw cotton.

It had an equal influence on the slavery question. Only negroes can work successfully in the cotton fields. There was a phenomenal increase in the demand for negro labor. And this was fifteen years before the time limit of the slave trade in 1808.

There soon came to be a decided jealousy between the slave-holding and the non-slave-holding portion of the country which continually increased. At the time of the Ordinance of 1787 the two parts of the country were about evenly balanced. Each section kept a vigilant watch of the other section so as to avoid losing the balance of power.

As the country enlarged, this balance was preserved by the admission of free and slave states in turn. Vermont was paired with Kentucky; Tennessee with Ohio; Louisiana with Indiana; and Mississippi with Illinois. In 1836, Michigan and Arkansas were admitted on the same day. This indicates that the jealousy of the two parties was growing more acute.

Then Texas was admitted December 29, 1845, and was not balanced until the admission of Wisconsin in 1848.

We must now go back to the admission of Missouri. It came into the Union as a slave state, but by what is known as the Missouri Compromise of 1820. By this compromise the concession of slavery to Missouri was offset by the enactment that all slavery should be forever excluded from the territory west of that state and north of its southern boundary: namely, the parallel of 36 degrees 30'.

The mutterings of the conflict were heard at the time of the admission of Texas. It was again 'set forever at rest' by what was known as the Wilmot proviso. A year or two later, the discovery of gold in California and the acquisition of New Mexico reopened the whole question. Henry Clay of Kentucky, a slaveholder but opposed to the extension of slavery, was then a member of the House. By a series of compromises – he had a brilliant talent for compromise – he once more set the whole question 'forever at rest'. This rest lasted for four years. But in 1852 Mrs Harriet Beecher Stowe published *Uncle Tom's Cabin*, an event of national importance. To a degree unprecedented, it roused the conscience of those who were opposed to slavery and inflamed the wrath of those who favored it.

The sudden and rude awakening from this rest came in 1854 with the repeal of the Missouri Compromise. The overland travel to California after the year 1848 had given to the intervening territory an importance far in excess of its actual population. It early became desirable to admit into the Union both Kansas and Nebraska; and the question arose whether slavery should be excluded according to the act of 1820. The slave-holding residents of Missouri were hostile to the exclusion of slavery. It was situated just beyond their border, and there is no wonder that they were unable to see any good reason why they could not settle there with their slaves. They had the sympathy of the slave states generally.

On the other hand, the free states were bitterly opposed to extending the slave power. To them it seemed that the slaveholders were planning for a vast empire of slavery, an empire which should include not only the southern half of the United States, but also Mexico, Central America, and possibly a portion of South America. The advocates of slavery certainly presented and maintained an imperious and despotic temper. Feeling was running high on both sides in the early fifties.

A leading cyclopedia concludes a brief article on the Missouri Compromise with the parenthetical reference – 'see Douglas, Stephen A.' The implication contained in these words is fully warranted. The chief event in the life of Douglas is the repeal of the Missouri Compromise. And the history of the Missouri Compromise cannot be written without giving large place to the activity of Douglas. His previous utterances had not led observers, however watchful, to suspect this. In the compromise of 1850 he had spoken with great emphasis: 'In taking leave of this subject, I wish to state that I have determined never to make another speech upon the slavery question. . . . We claim that the compromise is a final settlement. . . . Those who preach peace should not be the first to commence and reopen an old quarrel.'

This was the man who four years later recommenced and reopened this old quarrel of slavery. In the meantime something had occurred. In 1852 he had been the unsuccessful candidate for the Democratic nomination for President, and he had aspirations for the nomination in 1856, when a nomination would have been equivalent to an election. It thus seemed politic for him to make some decided move which would secure to him the loyalty of the slave power.

Upon Stephen A. Douglas rested the responsibility of the repeal of the Missouri Compromise. He was at that time chairman of the Senate committee on Territories. His personal friend and political manager for Illinois, William A. Richardson, held a similar position in the House. The control of the legislation upon this subject was then absolutely in the hands of Senator Douglas, the man who had 'determined never to make another speech on the slavery question'.

It is not within the scope of this book to go into the details of this iniquitous plot, for plot it was. But the following passage may be quoted as exhibiting the method of the bill: 'It being the true intent and meaning of this act not to legislate slavery into any territory or state, nor to exclude it therefrom, but to leave the people thereof perfectly free to form and regulate their domestic institutions in their own way, subject only to the Constitution.' In other words, no state or territory could be surely safe from the intrusion of slavery.

Lincoln had been practising law and had been out of politics for six years. It was this bill which called him back to politics, 'like a fire-bell in the night'.

CHAPTER TWELVE

The Awakening of the Lion

The repeal of the Missouri Compromise caused great excitement throughout the land. The conscience of the anti-slavery portion of the community was shocked, as was also that of the large numbers of people who, though not opposed to slavery in itself, were opposed to its extension. It showed that this institution had a deadening effect upon the moral nature of the people who cherished it. There was no compromise so generous that it would satisfy their greed, there were no promises so solemn that they could be depended on to keep them. They were not content with maintaining slavery in their own territory. It was not enough that they should be allowed to take slaves into a territory consecrated to freedom, nor that all the powers of the law were devoted to recapturing a runaway slave and returning him to renewed horrors. They wanted all the territories which they had promised to let alone. It was a logical, and an altogether probable conclusion that they only waited for the opportunity to invade the northern states and turn them from free-soil into slave territory.

The indignation over this outrage not only flamed from thousands of pulpits, but newspapers and political clubs of all kinds took up the subject on one side or the other. Every moralist became a politician, and every politician discussed the moral bearings of his tenets.

In no locality was this excitement more intense than in Illinois. There were special reasons for this. It is a very long state, stretching nearly five hundred miles from north to south. Now, it is a general law among Americans that migration follows very nearly the parallels of latitude from East to West. For this reason the northern portion of the state was mostly settled by northern people whose sympathies were against slavery; while the southern portion of the state was mostly settled by southern people, whose sympathies were in favor of slavery. The state was nearly evenly divided, and the presence of these two parties kept up a continual friction and intensified the feeling on both sides.

To this general condition must be added the fact that Illinois was the home of Douglas, who was personally and almost solely responsible for the repeal of the Missouri Compromise. In that state he had risen from obscurity to be the most conspicuous man in the United States. His party had a decided majority in the state, and over it he had absolute control. He was their idol. Imperious by nature, shrewd, unscrupulous, a debater of marvelous skill, a master of assemblies, a man who knew not the meaning of the word fail – this was Douglas. But his home was in Chicago, a city in which the anti-slavery sentiment predominated.

When Douglas returned to his state, *his* in more than one sense, it was not as a conquering hero. He did not return direct from Washington, but delayed, visiting various portions of the country.

Possibly this was due to the urgency of business, probably it was in order to give time for the excitement to wear itself out. But this did not result, and his approach was the occasion of a fresh outbreak of feeling in Chicago; the demonstrations of the residents of that city were not a flattering welcome home. Bells were tolled as for public mourning, flags were hung at half mast. Nothing was omitted that might emphasize the general aversion to the man who had done that infamous deed.

A public meeting was planned, at which he was to speak in defense of his course. A large crowd, about five thousand people, gathered. Douglas was surrounded by his own friends, but the major portion of the crowd was intensely hostile to him. When he began to speak the opposition broke out. He was interrupted by questions and comments. These so exasperated him that he completely lost control of himself. He stormed, he shook his fist, he railed. The meeting broke up in confusion. Then came a reaction which greatly profited him. The papers published that he had attempted to speak and had not been allowed to do so, but had been hooted by a turbulent mob. All of which was true. By the time he spoke again the sympathy of the public had swung to his side, and he was sure of a favorable hearing.

This second speech was on the occasion of the state fair at Springfield. Men of all kinds and of every political complexion were present from even the remotest localities in the state. The speech was to be an address to a large audience fairly representative of the entire state.

Lincoln was there. Not merely because Springfield was his home. He doubtless would have been there anyhow. His ability as a politician, his growing fame as a lawyer and a public speaker, his well-known antipathy to slavery, singled him out as the one man who was pre-eminently fitted to answer the speech of Douglas, and he was by a tacit agreement selected for this purpose.

Lincoln himself felt the stirring impulse. It is not uncommon for the call of duty, or opportunity, to come once in a lifetime to the heart of a man with over-mastering power, so that his purposes and powers are roused to an unwonted and transforming degree of activity. It is the flight of the eaglet, the awakening of the lion, the transfiguration of the human spirit. To Lincoln this call now came. He was the same man, but he had reached another stage of development, entered a new experience, exhibiting new powers – or the old powers to such a degree that they were virtually new. It is the purpose of this chapter to note three of his speeches which attest this awakening.

The first of these was delivered at the state fair at Springfield. Douglas had spoken October 3rd, 1854. Lincoln was present, and it was mentioned by Douglas, and was by all understood, that he would reply the following day, October 4th. Douglas was, up to that time, not only the shrewdest politician in the country, but he was acknowledged to be the ablest debater. He was particularly well prepared upon this subject, for to it he had given almost his entire time for nearly a year, and had discussed it in Congress and out, and knew thoroughly the current objections. The occasion was unusual, and this was to be, and doubtless it was, his greatest effort.

The following day came Lincoln's reply. As a matter of fairness, he said at the outset that he did not want to present anything but the truth. If he said anything that was not true, he would be glad to have Douglas correct him at once. Douglas, with customary shrewdness, took advantage of this offer by making frequent interruptions, so as to break the effect of the logic and destroy the flow of thought. Finally Lincoln's patience was exhausted, and he paused in his argument to say: 'Gentlemen, I cannot afford to spend my time in quibbles. I take the responsibility of asserting the truth myself, relieving Judge Douglas from the necessity of his impertinent corrections.' This silenced his opponent, and he spoke without further interruption to the end, his speech being three hours and ten minutes long.

The effect of the speech was wonderful. The scene, as described next day in the Springfield *Journal*, is worth quoting.

Lincoln quivered with feeling and emotion. The whole house was as still as death. He attacked the bill with unusual warmth and energy, and all felt that a man of strength was its enemy, and that he meant to blast it if he could by strong and manly efforts. He was most successful; and the house approved the glorious triumph of truth by loud and long-continued huzzas. . . . Mr Lincoln exhibited Douglas in all the attitudes he could be placed in a friendly debate. He exhibited the bill in all its aspects to show its humbuggery and falsehoods, and when thus torn to rags, cut into slips, held up to the gaze of the vast crowd, a kind of scorn was visible upon the face of the crowd, and upon the lips of the most eloquent speaker. . . . At the conclusion of the speech, every man felt that it was unanswerable — that no human power could overthrow it or trample it under foot. The long and repeated applause evinced the feelings of the crowd, and gave token, too, of the universal assent to Lincoln's whole argument; and every mind present did homage to the man who took captive the heart and broke like a sun over the understanding.

The speech itself, and the manner of its reception, could not other than rouse Douglas to a tempest of wrath. It was a far more severe punishment than to be hooted from the stage, as he had been in Chicago. He was handled as he had never been handled in his life. He took the platform, angrily claimed that he had been abused, and started to reply. But he did not get far. He had no case. He became confused, lost his self-control, hesitated, finally said that he would reply in the evening, and left the stage. That was the end of the incident so far as Douglas was concerned. When the evening came he had disappeared, and there was no reply.

Twelve days later, on October 16, Lincoln had promised to speak in Peoria. To that place Douglas followed, or preceded him. Douglas made his speech in the afternoon, and Lincoln followed in the evening. It was the same line of argument as in the other speech. Lincoln later consented to write it out for publication. We thus have the Springfield and Peoria speech, minus the glow of extemporaneous address, the inspiration of the orator. These are important factors which not even the man himself could reproduce. But we have his own report, which is therefore authentic. The most salient point in his speech is his reply to Douglas's plausible representation that the people of any locality were competent to govern themselves. 'I admit,' said Lincoln, 'that the emigrant to Kansas and Nebraska is competent to govern himself, but I deny his right to govern any other person without that other person's consent.' This is the kernel of the entire question of human slavery.

The result of this speech at Peoria was less dramatic than that at Springfield, but it was no less instructive. Douglas secured from

Lincoln an agreement that neither of them should again speak during that campaign. It was quite evident that he had learned to fear his antagonist and did not wish again to risk meeting him on the rostrum. Lincoln kept the agreement. Douglas did not. Before he got home in Chicago, he stopped off to make another speech.

These speeches were made in 1854. It is now worth while to skip over two years to record another epoch-making speech, one which in spirit and temper belongs here. For it shows to what intensity Lincoln was aroused on this vast and ever-encroaching subject of slavery. This was at the convention which was held in Bloomington for the purpose of organizing the Republican party. The date of the convention was May 29, 1856. The center of interest was Lincoln's speech. The reporters were there in sufficient force, and we would surely have had a verbatim report – except for one thing. The reporters did not report. Let Joseph Medill, of the Chicago *Tribune*, tell why.

It was my journalistic duty, though a delegate to the convention, to make a 'longhand' report of the speeches delivered for the Chicago *Tribune*. I did make a few paragraphs of what Lincoln said in the first eight or ten minutes, but I became so absorbed in his magnetic oratory, that I forgot myself and ceased to take notes, and joined with the convention in cheering and stamping and clapping to the end of his speech.

I well remember that after Lincoln had sat down and calm had succeeded the tempest, I waked out of a sort of hypnotic trance, and then thought of my report for the *Tribune*. There was nothing written but an abbreviated introduction.

It was some sort of satisfaction to find that I had not been 'scooped', as all the newspaper men present had been equally carried away by the excitement caused by the wonderful oration, and had made no report or sketch of the speech.

Mr Herndon, who was Lincoln's law partner, and who knew him so intimately that he might be trusted to keep his coolness during the enthusiasm of the hour, and who had the mechanical habit of taking notes for him, because he was his partner, said: 'I attempted for about fifteen minutes, as was usual with me then, to take notes, but at the end of that time I threw pen and paper away and lived only in the inspiration of the hour.'

There is no doubt that the audience was generally, if not unanimously, affected in the same way. The hearers went home and told about this wonderful speech. Journalists wrote flaming editorials about it. The fame of it went everywhere, but there was no report of it. It therefore came to be known as 'Lincoln's lost speech'.

Precisely forty years afterwards one H. C. Whitney published in one of the magazines an account of it. He says that he made notes of the speech, went home and wrote them out. Why he withheld this report from the public for so many years, especially in view of the general demand for it, does not precisely appear. The report, however, is interesting.

But after the lapse of nearly half a century, it is a matter of minor importance whether Mr Whitney's report be accurate or not. To us the value of the three speeches mentioned in this chapter is found largely in the impression they produced upon the hearers. The three taken together show that Lincoln had waked to a new life. The lion in him was thoroughly roused, he was clothed with a tremendous power, which up to this point had not been suspected by antagonists nor dreamed of by admiring friends. This new and mighty power he held and wielded until his life's end. Thenceforth he was an important factor in national history.

CHAPTER THIRTEEN

Two Things that Lincoln Missed

Lincoln's intimate friends have noted that he seemed to be under the impression that he was a man of destiny. This phrase was a favorite with Napoleon, who often used it of himself. But the two men were so widely different in character and career, that it is with reluctance that one joins their names even for the moment that this phrase is used. Napoleon was eager to sacrifice the whole of Europe to satisfy the claims of his personal ambition; Lincoln was always ready to stand aside and sacrifice himself for the country. The one was selfishness incarnate; the other was a noble example of a man who never hesitated to subordinate his own welfare to the general good, and whose career came to its climax in his martyrdom. Whether the presidency was or was not Lincoln's destiny, it was certainly his destination. Had anything occurred to thrust him to one side in this career, it would have prevented his complete development, and would have been an irreparable calamity to his country and to the world.

Twice in his life he earnestly desired certain offices and failed to get them. Had he succeeded in either case, it is not at all probable that he would ever have become President. One therefore rejoices in the knowledge that he missed them.

After his term in Congress he was, in a measure, out of employment. Political life is like to destroy one's taste for the legitimate practise of the law, as well as to scatter one's clients. Lincoln was not a candidate for re-election. Upon the election of General Taylor it was generally understood that the Democrats would be turned out of office and their places supplied by Whigs. The office of Land Commissioner was expected to go to Illinois. At the solicitation of friends he applied for it, but so fearful was he that he might stand in the way of others, or impede the welfare of the state, that he did not urge his application until too late. The President offered him the governorship of the territory of Oregon, which he declined. Had he been successful in his application, it would have kept him permanently out of the study and practise of the law. It would have kept his residence in Washington so that it would not have been possible for him to hold himself in touch with his neighbors. So far as concerned his illustrious career, it would have side-tracked him. He himself recognized this later, and was glad that he had failed in this, his first and only application for a government appointment.

About six years later he again missed an office to which he aspired. This was in 1854, the year of the speeches at Springfield and Peoria described in the last chapter. Shields, the man of the duel with broadswords, was United States senator. His term of office was about to expire and the legislature would elect his successor. The state of Illinois had been Democratic – both the senators, Shields and Douglas, were Democrats – but owing to the new phases of the slavery question, the anti-slavery men were able to carry the legislature, though by a narrow margin.

Lincoln had been very useful to the party during the campaign and had been elected to the legislature from his own district. He wanted to be senator. He was unquestionably the choice of nearly all the Whigs. Had an election taken place then, he would undoubtedly have been elected.

But a curious obstacle intervened. There was a provision in the constitution of Illinois which disqualified members of the legislature from holding the office of United States senator. Lincoln was therefore not eligible. He could only become so by resigning his seat. There appeared to be no risk in this, for he had a safe majority of 605. It seemed as though he could name his successor. But there are many uncertainties in politics.

The campaign had been one of unusual excitement and it was followed by that apathy which is the common sequel to all excessive activity. The Democrats kept quiet. They put up no candidate. They fostered the impression that they would take no part in the special election. Only one Democrat was casually named as a possible victim to be sacrificed to the triumph of the Whigs. He was not a popular nor an able man, and was not to be feared as a candidate for this office.

But the unusual quietness of the Democrats was the most dangerous sign. They had organized a 'still hunt'. This was an adroit move, but it was perfectly fair. It is not difficult to guess whose shrewdness planned this, seeing that the question was vital to the career of Douglas. The Democratic party preserved their organization. The trusted lieutenants held the rank and file in readiness for action. When the polls were opened on election day, the Democrats were there, and the Whigs were not. At every election precinct appeared Democratic workers to electioneer for the man of their choice. Carriages were provided for the aged, the infirm, and the indifferent who were driven to the polls so that their votes were saved to the party.

The Whigs were completely taken by surprise. It was too late to talk up their candidate. They had no provision and no time to get the absent and indifferent to the polls. The result was disastrous to them. Lincoln's 'safe' majority was wiped out and a Douglas Democrat was chosen to succeed him.

It may be surmised that this did not tend to fill the Whigs with enthusiasm, nor to unite the party. From all over the state there arose grumblings that the Sangamon contingent of the party had been so ignobly outwitted. Lincoln had to bear the brunt of this discontent. This was not unnatural nor unreasonable, for he was the party manager for that district. When the legislature went into joint session Lincoln had manifestly lost some of his prestige. It may be said by way of palliation that the 'still hunt' was then new in politics. And it was the only time that Lincoln was caught napping.

Even with the loss to the Whigs of this seat, the Douglas Democrats were in a minority. Lincoln had a plurality but not a majority. The balance of power was held by five anti-Nebraska Democrats, who would not under any circumstances vote for Lincoln or any other Whig. Their candidate was Lyman Trumbull. After a long and weary deadlock, the Democrats dropped their candidate Shields and took up the governor of the state. The governor has presumably a strong influence with the legislature, and this move of the partisans was a real menace to the anti-slavery men. Lincoln recognized the danger, at once withdrew his candidacy, and persuaded all the anti-slavery men to unite on Trumbull. This was no ordinary conciliation, for upon every subject except the Nebraska question alone, Trumbull was an uncompromising Democrat. The Whig votes gave him the necessary majority. The man who started in with five votes won the prize. Lincoln not only failed to get into the senate, but he was out of the legislature.

In commenting on this defeat of Lincoln for the United States senate, the present writer wishes first of all to disavow all superstitions and all belief in signs. But there is one fact which is worthy of mention, and for which different persons will propose different explanations. It is a fact that in all the history of the United States no person has been elected direct from the senate to the presidency. This is the more interesting because the prominent senator wields a very powerful influence, an influence second only to that of the President himself. When one considers the power of a leading senator, one would suppose that that was the natural stepping-stone to the presidency. But history does not support this supposition. It teaches the opposite.

Many prominent senators have greatly desired to be President, but no one has succeeded unless he first retired from the senate.

Among the more widely known aspirants to the presidency who have been unsuccessful, are Jackson (his first candidacy), Clay, Webster, Douglas, Morton, Seward, Sherman, and Blaine. So many failures may be a mere coincidence. On the other hand there may be a reason for them. They seem to teach that the senate is not the best start for the presidential race, but the worst.

The history of ethics teaches that the most determined hostility against the best is the good, not the bad. So it may be that in the politics of this country, the greatest obstacle to the highest position may be the next highest.

These facts, of course, do not prove that if Lincoln had been elected senator in 1854, or in 1858 when he was the opposing candidate to Douglas, he would therefore have failed of election to the presidency. He may have been an exception. He may have been the only one to break this rule in over a hundred years. But the sequel proved that he was best where he was. He remained among his people. He moused about the state library, enduring criticism but mastering the history of slavery. He kept a watchful eye on the progress of events. He was always alert to seize an opportunity and proclaim in trumpet tones the voice of conscience, the demands of eternal righteousness. But he waited. His hour had not yet come. He bided his time. It was not a listless waiting, it was intensely earnest and active. Far more than he could realize, he was in training for the stupendous responsibilities which should in due time fall upon him. It is fortunate for all that he did not learn to limit his powers to the arena of the senate, which, though great, is limited. He kept near to the people. When his hour struck, he was ready.

For this reason we call his two failures escapes. He did not get the government land office, he did not get the senatorship. He did get the presidency, and that in the crisis of the history of the nation. What is more, when he got that he was thoroughly furnished unto every good work.

CHAPTER FOURTEEN

The Birth of the Republican Party

In the course of history there sometimes arises a man who has a marvelous power of attaching others to himself. He commands a measure of devotion and enthusiasm which it is impossible fully to understand. Such a man was Henry Clay. Under the fascination of his qualities Lincoln lived. From childhood to maturity Clay had been his idol, and Clay's party, the Whig, nearly synonymous with all that was desirable in American politics. It was therefore no easy matter for Lincoln to leave the Whig party. Nothing could accomplish this but the overmastering power of a noble emotion.

From childhood Lincoln had hated slavery. The fact that Kentucky was a slave state had its influence in his father's removal to Indiana. His personal observations upon his journeys down the Mississippi River had given him a keener feeling on the subject. The persistent and ever-increasing outrages of the slave power had intensified his hatred. The time had come when he, and such as he, felt that other party questions were of minor importance, and that everything else should for the time be subordinated to the supreme question of slavery.

There were certain reasons why the Whig party could not accomplish the desired end. Its history had identified it with a different class of subjects. Though Clay himself and a majority of his party were opposed to the extension of slavery, there were still pro-slavery men in its ranks in sufficient numbers to prevent any real efficiency on the slavery question.

On the other hand, while the Democratic party was overwhelmingly pro-slavery, there were anti-slavery Democrats who, from their numbers, ability, and character, were not to be overlooked. The election to the senate of Lyman Trumbull as an anti-Douglas Democrat had crystalized this wing of the party. The fiasco of Lincoln's defeat when the Whigs were in a good plurality caused much discontent in that party. If the anti-slavery men were to be united for efficiency in opposing Douglas, it must be under another organization – a new party must be formed.

In this the newspapers took the initiative. A number of papers editorially called for a convention, which was really a mass meeting, for there were no accredited delegates, and could be none. This met in Decatur on Washington's birthday, 1856. It was a motley assembly, from a political standpoint. It included Whigs, Democrats, free-soilers, abolitionists, and know-nothings. Said Lincoln: 'Of strange, discordant, even hostile elements, we gathered from the four winds.' Politicians were conspicuously absent, for it would imperil their political orthodoxy to be seen there. Lincoln was the principal one who had anything to lose. He was consulted on all measures, and gave freely of his counsel. The proceedings ended with a dinner, at which he made a speech.

He was the most prominent man in the new movement, was popular throughout the state, and was the logical candidate for governor. He would have been highly gratified with the candidacy. But again he put personal desires one side that the general good might not be endangered. He therefore proposed, in his after-dinner speech, for nomination a Democrat who had a record of earnest opposition to the slave power. Refusing the use of his own name, he added: 'But I can suggest a name that will secure not only the old Whig vote, but enough anti-Nebraska Democrats to give us the victory. That man is Colonel William H. Bissell.' Bissell was afterwards regularly nominated and triumphantly elected. The meeting at Decatur called for a convention to be held at Bloomington on the 29th of May.

About the same thing had been going on in some other free states. On the very day of the Decatur meeting there was a notable meeting for the same purpose in Pittsburg. This was attended by E. D. Morgan, governor of New York, Horace Greeley, O. P. Morton, Zach. Chandler, Joshua R. Giddings, and other prominent men. They issued the call for the first national convention of the Republican party to be held in Philadelphia in June.

In May the Illinois convention assembled in Bloomington, and the most conspicuous person there was Lincoln. It was there that he made the amazing speech already described. It was the speech which held even the reporters in such a spell that they could not report it. It is known in history as the 'lost speech', but the fame of it endures to this day.

The Democratic convention met in Cincinnati early in June and nominated James Buchanan to succeed Franklin Pierce. Thus Douglas was for a second time defeated for the nomination.

The Republican convention met a few days later in Philadelphia. At that time John C. Fremont was at the height of his fame. His character was romantic, and the record of his adventures was as fascinating as a novel by Dumas. He had earned the name of 'pathfinder' by crossing the continent. Although unauthorized, he had in California raised a military company which was of material assistance to the naval forces of the United States against a Mexican insurrection. He was an ardent hater of slavery. He was precisely the man, as standard-bearer, to infuse enthusiasm into the new party and to give it a good start in its career. He did this and did it well. The large vote which he polled augured well for the future.

All this we may claim without denying the fact that it was fortunate for the party and for the country that he was not elected. There was no doubt of his sincerity or his patriotism. But he lacked self-control, wariness, patience. He was hot-headed, extreme, egotistical. He never could have carried the burdens of the first administration of the Republican party.

When the election was over, it was found that Buchanan had carried every slave state except Maryland, which went to Fillmore. Fremont had carried every New England state and five other northern states. Buchanan received 174 electoral votes; Fremont, 114; Fillmore, 8. The popular vote was, for Buchanan, 1,838,169; for Fremont, 1,341,264; for Fillmore, 874,534. That was an excellent showing for the new party. It showed that it had come to stay, and gave a reasonable hope of victory at the next presidential election.

Lincoln was at the head of the electoral ticket of the state of Illinois. He usually was on the ticket. He playfully called himself one of the electors that seldom elected anybody. In Illinois the honors of the election were evenly divided between the two parties. Buchanan carried the state by a handsome majority, but Bissell was elected governor by a good majority. Lincoln had faithfully canvassed the state and made nearly fifty speeches. One paragraph from a speech made in Galena should be quoted. The slave party had raised the cry of sectionalism, and had charged that the Republicans purposed to destroy the Union. Lincoln said: 'But the Union, in any event, will not be dissolved. We don't want to dissolve it, and if you attempt it we won't let you. With the purse and sword, the army, the navy, and the treasury in our hands and at our command, you could not do it. This government would be very weak indeed if a majority with a disciplined army and navy and a well-filled treasury could not preserve itself, when attacked by an unarmed, undisciplined minority. All this talk about the dissolution of the Union is humbug, nothing but folly. We do not want to dissolve the Union; you shall not.' ·

These words were prophetic of the condition of the country and of his own policy four or five years later. But he apparently did not apprehend that an unscrupulous administration might steal the army and the munitions of war, scatter the navy, and empty the treasury.

On the 10th of December Lincoln spoke at a Republican banquet in Chicago. It was after the election, after Buchanan's supercilious message to Congress. The purpose of the speech was to forecast the future of the young party. The following quotations may be read with interest.

He [Buchanan, in his message to Congress] says the people did it. He forgets that the 'people', as he complacently calls only those who voted for Buchanan, are in a minority of the whole people by about four hundred thousand votes. . . . All of us who did not vote for Mr Buchanan, taken together, are a majority of four hundred thousand. But in the late contest we were divided between Fremont and Fillmore. Can we not come together for the future? Let everyone who really believes, and is resolved, that free society is not and shall not be a failure, and who can conscientiously declare that in the past contest he has done only what he thought best, let every such one have charity to believe that every other one can say as much. Let bygones be bygones; let past differences as nothing be; and with steady eye on the real issue, let us re-inaugurate the good old 'central ideas' of the republic. We can do it. The human heart is with us; God is with us. We shall again be able to declare, not that 'all states as states are equal', nor yet that 'all citizens as citizens are equal', but to renew the broader, better declaration, including these and much more, that 'all men are created equal'.

It was upon the wisdom of this plan that, four years later, he held the foes of slavery united, while the foes of freedom were divided among themselves. It was this that carried the party to its first victory and made him President.

CHAPTER FIFTEEN

The Battle of the Giants

The admiring friends of Douglas had given him the nickname of 'the little giant'. To this he was fairly entitled. Physically he was very little. Intellectually he was a giant. He was in 1858 perhaps the most prominent man in the United States. He was the unquestioned leader of the dominant party. He had been so long in public life that he was familiar with every public question, while upon the burning question of slavery he was the leader.

Lincoln was a giant physically, and it soon became evident that he was no less intellectually. These two men soon were to come together in a series of joint debates. It was manifest that this would be a battle of intellectual giants. No other such debates have ever occurred in the history of the country.

Events led up to this rapidly and with the certainty of fate. In 1854 Lincoln had been candidate for the senate to succeed Shields, but his party had been outwitted and he was compelled to substitute Trumbull. In 1856 he was the logical candidate for governor, but he was of opinion that the cause would be better served permanently by placing an anti-slavery Democrat in nomination. This was done and Bissell was elected. Now in 1858 the senatorial term of Douglas was about to expire and a successor would be chosen. Douglas was the candidate of his own party. The Republicans turned naturally and spontaneously to Lincoln, for it would be no light task to defeat so strong an opponent.

The Republican convention met in Springfield on the 16th of June. Lincoln was by acclamation nominated 'as the first and only choice' of the Republican party for United States senator. The above time-honored phrase was used sincerely on that occasion. There was great enthusiasm, absolute unanimity.

On the evening of the following day he addressed the convention in a speech which has become historic. His opening words were.

If we could first know where we are and whither we are tending, we could better judge what to do and how to do it. We are now far into the fifth year since a policy was initiated, with the avowed object and confident promise of putting an end to the slavery agitation. Under the operation of that policy, that agitation has not only not ceased, but has constantly augmented. In my opinion it will not cease until a crisis shall have been reached and passed. 'A house divided against itself cannot stand.' I believe this government cannot endure permanently half slave and half free. I do not expect the Union to be dissolved – I do not expect the house to fall – but I do expect it will cease to be divided. It will become all one thing or all the other. Either the opponents of slavery will arrest the further spread of it, and place it where the public mind shall rest in the belief that it is in the course of ultimate extinction; or its advocates will push it forward till it shall become alike lawful in all the states, old as well as new, North as well as South.

This speech came quickly to be known as 'the house-divided-against-itself speech'. By that name it is still known. Concluding he said: 'Our cause, then, must be entrusted to and conducted by its own undoubted friends, those whose hands are free, whose hearts are in the work, who do care for the result. . . . The result is not doubtful. We shall not fail. If we stand firm we shall not fail. Wise counsels may accelerate or mistakes delay it, but sooner or later the victory is sure to come.' This was a strong speech, delivered before an audience of men of unusual ability, delegates who represented all parts of the state. It was in no wise a harangue. It was entirely thoughtful and strictly logical. The effect of it was to intensify the enthusiasm, and to spread it all through the state. It was a speech that Douglas could not ignore, though he might misrepresent it. This he did by raising the charge of sectionalism against his adversary.

About three weeks later, on the 9th of July, Douglas made an elaborate speech in Chicago. Lincoln was in the audience. It was unofficially arranged that he should reply. He did so the following evening. A week later a similar thing occurred in Springfield. Douglas made a speech in the afternoon to which Lincoln replied in the evening. Shortly after this Lincoln wrote Douglas a letter proposing a series of joint discussions, or challenging him to a series of joint debates. Douglas replied in a patronizing and irritating tone, asked for a slight advantage in his own favor, but he accepted the proposal. He did not do it in a very gracious manner, but he did it. They arranged for seven discussions in towns, the locations being scattered fairly over the entire territory of the state.

If Illinois had before been 'the cynosure of neighboring eyes', much more was it so now. Lincoln was by no means the most prominent anti-slavery man, but he was the only man in a position to beard his rival. The proposed debates excited not only the interest of the state and the neighboring states, but from the East and the South all minds were turned to this tournament. It was not a local discussion; it was a national and critical question that was at issue. The interest was no less eager in New York, Washington, and Charleston than in Indianapolis, Milwaukee, and St Louis.

The two men had been neighbors for many years. They were together members of the legislature, first in Vandalia and then in Springfield. They had frequently met socially in Springfield. Both paid marked attentions to the same young lady. Both had served in Washington City. Douglas was for most of his life an officeholder, so that in one way or another Lincoln would be brought into association with him. But though they met so frequently it is not probable that, before this time, either recognized in the other his supreme antagonist. After the repeal of the Missouri Compromise Lincoln had, as already related, discussed Douglas with great plainness of speech. This had been twice repeated in this year. But these were, comparatively speaking, mere incidents. The great contest was to be in the debates.

In the outset, Douglas had the advantage of prestige. Nothing succeeds like success. Douglas had all his life had nothing but success. He twice had missed the nomination for presidency, but he was still the most formidable man in the senate. He was very popular in his own state. He was everywhere greeted by large crowds, with bands of music and other demonstrations. He always traveled in a special car and often in a special train, which was freely placed at his disposal by the Illinois Central Railway. Lincoln traveled by accommodation train, freight train, or wagon, as best he could. As both the men were every day speaking independently between the debates, this question of transportation was serious. The inconveniences of travel made a great drain upon the nervous force and the health. One day when the freight train bearing Lincoln was side-tracked to let his rival's special train roll by, he good-humoredly remarked that Douglas 'did not smell any royalty in this car'.

Another fact which gave Douglas the advantage was the friendship and sympathy of Horace Greeley and others, who had much influence with the party of Lincoln. Douglas had broken with Buchanan's administration on a question relating to Kansas. The iniquity of the powers at Washington went so far that even Douglas rebelled. This led Greeley and others to think that Douglas had in him the making of a good Republican if he was only treated with sufficient consideration. Accordingly, all of that influence was bitterly thrown in opposition to Lincoln.

The methods of the two men were as diverse as their bodily appearance. Douglas was a master of what the ancient Greeks would have called 'making the worse appear the better reason'. He was able to misstate his antagonist's position so shrewdly as to deceive the very elect. And with equal skill he could escape from the real meaning of his own statements. Lincoln's characterization is apt: 'Judge Douglas is playing cuttlefish — a small species of fish that has no mode of defending himself when pursued except by throwing out a black fluid which makes the water so dark the enemy cannot see it, and thus it escapes.'

Lincoln's method was to hold the discussion down to the point at issue with clear and forcible statement. He arraigned the iniquity of slavery as an offense against God. He made the phrase 'all men' of the Declaration of Independence include the black as well as the white. Said he: 'There is no reason in the world why the negro is not entitled to all the natural rights enumerated in the Declaration of Independence — the right to life, liberty, and the pursuit of happiness. . . . In the right to eat the bread, without the leave of anybody else, which his own hand earns, he is my equal, and the equal of Judge Douglas, and the equal of every living man.' He quoted Jefferson's remark, 'I tremble for my country when I remember that God is just.' Mercilessly he analyzed Douglas's speeches and exposed his sophistry.

The forensic ability of the two men is suggestively indicated by the remark of a lady who heard them speak, and afterward said: 'I can recall only one fact of the debates, that I felt so sorry for Lincoln while Douglas was speaking, and then *so* sorry for Douglas while Lincoln was speaking.'

These debates occupied seven different evenings of three hours each. The speeches were afterwards published in book form and had a wide circulation. These speeches, numbering twenty-one in all, filled a large volume. It is not the purpose of this chapter to give an outline of the debates, it is only to give a general idea of their result. But out of them came one prominent fact, which so influenced the careers of the two men that it must be briefly recorded. This went by the name of 'the Freeport doctrine'.

In the first debate Douglas had asked Lincoln a series of questions. The villainy of these questions was in the innuendo. They began, 'I desire to know whether Lincoln stands today, as he did in 1854, in favor of', etc. Douglas then quoted from the platform of a convention which Lincoln had not attended, and with which he had nothing to do. Lincoln denied these insinuations, and said that he had never favored those doctrines; but the trick succeeded, and the impression was made that Douglas had cornered him. The questions, to all intents and purposes, were a forgery. This forgery was quickly exposed by a Chicago paper, and the result was not helpful to Douglas. It was made manifest that he was not conducting the debates in a fair and manly way.

Further than this, the fact that these questions had been asked gave Lincoln, in turn, the right to ask questions of Douglas. This right he used. For the next debate, which was to be at Freeport, he prepared, among others, the following question: 'Can the people of a United States territory, in any lawful way, against the wish of any citizen of the United States, exclude slavery from its limits prior to the formation of a state constitution?' If this were answered 'No', it would alienate the citizens of Illinois. If it were answered 'Yes', it would alienate the Democrats of the South.

On the way to Freeport he met a number of friends and took counsel of them. When he read question number two, the one above quoted, his friends earnestly and unanimously advised him not to put that question. 'If you do,' said they, 'you never can be senator.' To which Lincoln replied: 'Gentlemen, I am killing larger game. If Douglas answers, he can never be President, and the battle of 1860 is worth a hundred of this.'

It is not probable that Lincoln expected to be in 1860 the nominee of the Republican party. But he did see the danger of the election of Douglas to the presidency. He was willing to surrender the senatorial election to save the country from a Douglas administration. The sacrifice was made. The prediction proved true. Lincoln lost the senatorship, Douglas lost the presidency.

The popular verdict, as shown in the election, was in favor of Lincoln. The Republicans polled 125,430 votes; the Douglas Democrats, 121,609, and the Buchanan Democrats, 5,071. But the apportionment of the legislative districts was such that Douglas had a majority on the joint ballot of the legislature. He received 54 votes to 46 for Lincoln. This secured his re-election to the senate.

The popular verdict outside the state of Illinois was in favor of Lincoln. The Republican party circulated the volume containing the full report of the speeches. It does not appear that the Democrats did so. This forces the conclusion that the intellectual and moral victory was on the side of Lincoln.

There is a pathetic sequel to this. The campaign had been very arduous on Lincoln. Douglas had made 130 speeches in 100 days, not counting Sundays. Lincoln had made probably about the same number. These were not brief addresses from a railway car, but fully elaborated speeches. The labors commenced early in July and continued through the heat of the summer. With Lincoln the inadequate means of travel added to the draft upon his strength. At the end of all came the triumphant election of his rival. Add to this the fact that the next day he received a letter from the Republican committee saying that their funds would not meet the bills, and asking for an additional contribution. The rest is best told in Lincoln's own words.

Yours of the 15th is just received. I wrote you the same day. As to the pecuniary matter, I am willing to pay according to my ability, but I am the poorest hand living to get others to pay. I have been on expense so long without earning anything that I am absolutely without money now for even household purposes. Still, if you can put up $250 for me towards discharging the debt of the committee, I will allow it when you and I settle the private matter between us. This, with what I have already paid, and with an outstanding note of mine, will exceed my subscription of $500. This, too, is exclusive of my ordinary expenses during the campaign, all which, being added to my loss of time and business, bears pretty heavily on one no better off in world's goods than I; but as I had the post of honor, it is not for me to be over-nice. You are feeling badly – 'And this, too, shall pass away.' Never fear.

CHAPTER SIXTEEN
Growing Audacity of the Slave Power

So closely is the life of Lincoln intertwined with the growth of the slave power that it will be necessary at this point to give a brief space to the latter. It was the persistent, the ever-increasing, the imperious demands of this power that called Lincoln to his post of duty. The feeling upon the subject had reached a high degree of tension at the period we are now considering. To understand this fully, we must go back and come once again down through the period already treated. There are three salient points of development.

The first of these is the fugitive slave law. At the adoption of the Constitution it was arranged that there should be no specific approval of slavery. For this reason the word 'slave' does not appear in that document. But the idea is there, and the phrase, 'person held to service or labor', fully covers the subject. Slaves were a valuable property. The public opinion approved of the institution. To set up one part of the territory as a refuge for escaped slaves would be an infringement of this right of property, and would cause unceasing friction between the various parts of the country.

In 1793, which happens to be the year of the invention of the cotton gin, the fugitive slave law was passed. This was for the purpose of enacting measures by which escaped slaves might be recaptured. This law continued in force to 1850. As the years passed, the operation of this law produced results not dreamed of in the outset. There came to be free states, communities in which the very toleration of slavery was an abomination. The conscience of these communities abhorred the institution. Though these people were content to leave slavery unmolested in the slave states, they were angered at having the horrors of slave-hunting thrust upon them. In other words, they were unable to reside in any locality, no matter how stringent the laws were in behalf of freedom, where they were not liable to be invaded, their very homes entered, by the institution of slavery in its most cruel forms.

This aroused a bitter antagonism in the North. Societies were formed to assist fugitive slaves to escape to Canada. Men living at convenient distances along the route were in communication with one another. The fugitives were passed secretly and with great skill along this line. These societies were known as the Underground Railway. The appropriateness of this name is obvious. The men themselves who secreted the fugitive slaves were said to keep stations on that railway.

This organized endeavor to assist the fugitives was met by an increased imperiousness on the part of the slave power. Slavery is imperious in its nature. It almost inevitably cultivates that disposition in those who wield the power. So that the case was rendered more exasperating by the passage, in 1850, of another fugitive slave law. Nothing could have been devised more surely adapted to inflame the moral sense of those communities that were, in feeling or conscience, opposed to slavery, than this law of 1850. This was a re-enactment of the law of 1793, but with more stringent and cruel regulations. The concealment or assisting of a fugitive was highly penal. Any home might be invaded and searched. No hearth was safe from intrusion. The negro could not testify in his own behalf. It was practically impossible to counteract the oath or affidavit of the pretended master, and a premium was practically put upon perjury. The pursuit of slaves became a regular business, and its operation was often indescribably horrible. These cruelties were emphasized chiefly in the presence of those who were known to be averse to slavery in any form, and they could not escape from the revolting scenes.

The culmination of this was in what is known as the Dred Scott decision. Dred Scott was a slave in Missouri. He was by his master taken to Fort Snelling, now in the state of Minnesota, then in the territory of Wisconsin. This was free soil, and the slave was, at least while there, free. With the consent of his former master he married a free woman who had formerly been a slave. Two children were born to them. The master returned to Missouri, bringing the negroes. He here claimed that they, being on slave soil, were restored to the condition of slavery.

Scott sued for his freedom and won his case. It was, however, appealed to the Supreme Court of the United States. The first opinion of the court was written by Judge Nelson. This treated of this specific case only. Had this opinion issued as the finding of the court, it would not have aroused general attention.

But the court was then dominated by the slave sentiment, and the opportunity of laying down general principles on the subject of slavery could not be resisted. The decision was written by Chief Justice Taney, and reaches its climax in the declaration that the negro 'had no rights which the white man was bound to respect'. Professor T. W. Dwight says that much injustice was done to Chief Justice Taney by the erroneous statement that he had himself affirmed that the negro 'had no rights which the white man was bound to respect'. But while this may be satisfactory to the legal mind, to the lay mind, to the average citizen, it is a distinction without a difference, or, at best, with a very slight difference. The Judge was giving what, in his opinion, was the law of the land. It was his opinion, nay, it was his decision. Nor was it the unanimous ruling of the court. Two justices dissented. The words quoted are picturesque, and are well suited to a battle-cry. On every side, with ominous emphasis in the North, one heard that the negro had no rights which the white man was bound to respect. This was, until 1860, the last and greatest exhibition of audacity on the part of the slave power.

There was another exhibition of the spirit of slavery which deserves special mention. This is the history of the settlement of Kansas. That remarkable episode, lasting from 1854 to 1861, requires a volume, not a paragraph, for its narration. It is almost impossible for the imagination of those who live in an orderly, law-abiding community, to conceive that such a condition of affairs ever existed in any portion of the United States. The story of 'bleeding Kansas' will long remain an example of the proverb that truth is stranger than fiction.

The repeal of the Missouri Compromise, in 1854, opened up to this free territory the possibility of coming into the Union as a slave state. It was to be left to the actual settlers to decide this question. This principle was condensed into the phrase 'squatter sovereignty'. The only resource left to those who wished Kansas to come in as a free state was to settle it with an anti-slavery population.

With this purpose in view, societies were formed in anti-slavery communities, extending as far east as the Atlantic coast, to assist emigrants. From Iowa, Illinois, Ohio, Massachusetts, and elsewhere, emigrants poured into Kansas. But the slave party had the advantage of geographical location. The slave state of Missouri was only just across the river. It was able, at short notice and with little expense, to pour out its population in large numbers. This it did. Many went from Missouri as actual settlers. By far the larger part went only temporarily and for the purpose of creating a disturbance. These were popularly called 'border ruffians'. Their excesses of ruffianism are not easily described. They went into the territory for the purpose of driving out all the settlers who had come in under the emigrant aid societies. Murder was common. At the elections, they practised intimidation and every form of election fraud then known. Every election was contested, and both parties always claimed the victory. The parties elected two separate legislatures, adopted two constitutions, established two capitals. For several years, civil war and anarchy prevailed.

There is no doubt, either reasonable or unreasonable – there is no doubt whatever that the anti-slavery men had a vast majority of actual settlers. The territorial governors were appointed by Presidents Pierce and Buchanan. These were uniformly pro-slavery and extremely partisan. But every governor quickly came to side with the free-state men, or else resigned to get out of the way.

The pro-slavery men, after the farce of a pretended vote, declared the Lecompton constitution adopted. The governor at that time was Walker, of Mississippi, who had been appointed as a sure friend of the interests of slavery. But even he revolted at so gross an outrage, and made a personal visit to Washington to protest against it. It was at this point, too, that Senator Douglas broke with the administration.

In spite of the overwhelming majority of anti-slavery settlers in the state, Kansas was not admitted to the Union until after the inauguration of Abraham Lincoln.

So unscrupulous, imperious, grasping was the slave power. Whom the gods wish to destroy, they first make mad. The slave power had reached the reckless point of madness and was rushing to its own destruction. These three manifestations – the fugitive-slave law, the Dred Scott decision, and the anarchy in Kansas – though they were revolting in the extreme and indescribably painful, hastened the end.

CHAPTER SEVENTEEN

The Backwoodsman at the Center of Eastern Culture

Lincoln's modesty made it impossible for him to be ambitious. He appreciated honors, and he desired them up to a certain point. But they did not, in his way of looking at them, seem to belong to him. He was slow to realize that he was of more than ordinary importance to the community.

At the first Republican convention in 1856, when Fremont was nominated for President, 111 votes were cast for Lincoln as the nominee for vice-president. The fact was published in the papers. When he saw the item it did not enter his head that he was the man. He said 'there was a celebrated man of that name in Massachusetts; doubtless it was he.'

In 1858, when he asked Douglas the fatal question at Freeport, he was simply killing off Douglas's aspirations for the presidency. It was with no thought of being himself the successful rival.

Douglas had twice been a candidate for nomination before the Democratic convention. Had it not been for this question he would have been elected at the next following presidential election.

As late as the early part of 1860, Lincoln vaguely desired the nomination for the vice-presidency. He would have been glad to be the running-mate of Seward, nothing more. Even this honor he thought to be beyond his reach, so slowly did he come to realize the growth of his fame.

The reports of the Lincoln-Douglas debates had produced a profound sensation in the West. They were printed in large numbers and scattered broadcast as campaign literature. Some Eastern men, also, had been alert to observe these events. William Cullen Bryant, the scholarly editor of the New York *Evening Post*, had shown keen interest in the debates.

Even after the election Lincoln did not cease the vigor of his criticisms. It will be remembered that before the formal debate Lincoln voluntarily went to Chicago to hear Douglas and to answer him. He followed him to Springfield and did the same thing. He now, after the election of 1858, followed him to Ohio and answered his speeches in Columbus and Cincinnati.

The Reverend Henry Ward Beecher, who was always watchful of the development of the anti-slavery sentiment, now invited Lincoln to lecture in Plymouth Church, Brooklyn. The invitation was accepted with the provision that the lecture might be a political speech.

J. G. Holland, who doubtless knew whereof he wrote, declares that it was a great misfortune that Lincoln was introduced to the country as a rail-splitter. Americans have no prejudice against humble beginnings, they are proud of self-made men, but there is nothing in the ability to split rails which necessarily qualifies one for the demands of statesmanship. Some of his ardent friends, far more zealous than judicious, had expressed so much glory over Abe the rail-splitter, that it left the impression that he was little more than a rail-splitter who could talk volubly and tell funny stories. This naturally alienated the finest culture east of the Alleghanies. 'It took years for the country to learn that Mr Lincoln was not a boor. It took years for them to unlearn what an unwise and boyish introduction of a great man to the public had taught them. It took years for them to comprehend the fact that in Mr Lincoln the country had the wisest, truest, gentlest, noblest, most sagacious President who had occupied the chair of state since Washington retired from it.'

When he reached New York he found that there had been a change of plan, and he was to speak in Cooper Institute, New

York, instead of Beecher's church. He took the utmost care in revising his speech, for he felt that he was on new ground and must not do less than his best.

But though he made the most perfect intellectual preparation, the esthetic element of his personal appearance was sadly neglected. He was angular and loose-jointed – he could not help that. He had provided himself, or had been provided, with a brand-new suit of clothes, whether of good material or poor we cannot say, whether well-fitting or ill-fitting we do not know, though we may easily guess. But we do know that it had been crowded into a small carpet-bag and came out a mass of wrinkles. And during the speech the collar or lapel annoyed both speaker and audience by persisting in rising up unbidden.

These details are mentioned to show the difficulty of the task before the orator. In the audience and on the platform were many of the most brilliant and scholarly men of the metropolis. There were also large numbers who had come chiefly to hear the westerner tell a lot of funny stories. The orator was introduced by Bryant.

The speech was strictly intellectual from beginning to end. Though Lincoln was not known in New York, Douglas was. So he fittingly took his start from a quotation of Douglas. The speech cannot be epitomized, but its general drift may be divined from its opening and closing sentences.

The quotation from Douglas was that which had been uttered at Columbus a few months before: 'Our fathers, when they framed the government under which we live, understood this question (the question of slavery) just as well, and even better, than we do now.' To this proposition the orator assented. That raised the inquiry, What was their understanding of the question? This was a historical question, and could be answered only by honest and painstaking research.

Continuing, the speaker said:

Does the proper division of local from Federal authority, or any-thing in the Constitution, forbid our Federal government to control as to slavery in our Federal territories? Upon this Senator Douglas holds the affirmative and the Republicans the negative. This affirmation and denial form an issue, and this issue – this question – is precisely what the text declares our fathers under-stood 'better than we'.

I defy anyone to show that any living man in the whole world ever did, prior to the beginning of the present century (and I might almost say prior to the beginning of the last half of the present century), declare that in his understanding any proper division of local from Federal authority, or any part of the Constitution, forbade the Federal government to control as to slavery in the Federal territories. To those who now so declare, I give, not only 'our fathers who framed the government under which we live', but with them all other living men within the century in which it was framed, among whom to search, and they shall not be able to find the evidence of a single man agreeing with them.

One paragraph is quoted for the aptness of its illustration:

But you will not abide the election of a Republican President! In that supposed event, you say you will destroy the Union; and then you say, the great crime of having destroyed it will be upon us! That is cool. A highwayman holds a pistol to my ear, and mutters through his teeth, 'Stand and deliver, or I shall kill you, and then you will be a murderer!' To be sure, what the robber demanded of me – my money – was my own, and I had a clear right to keep it; but it was no more my own than my vote is my own; and the threat of death to me to extort my money, and the threat of destruction to the Union to extort my vote, can scarcely be distinguished in principle.

The speech reached its climax in its closing paragraph:

Wrong as we think slavery is, we can yet afford to let it alone where it is, because that so much is due to the necessity arising from its actual presence in the nation; but can we, while our votes will prevent it, allow it to spread into the national territories, and to overrun us here in the free states? If our sense of duty forbids this, then let us stand by our duty, fearlessly and effectively. Let us be diverted by none of those sophistical contrivances wherewith we are so industriously plied and belabored – contrivances such as groping for some middle ground between the right and the wrong, vain as the search for a man who would be neither a living man nor a dead man; such as a policy of 'don't care' on a question about which all true men do care; such as Union appeals to beseech all true Union men to yield to Disunionists; reversing the divine rule, and calling, not the sinners, but the righteous, to repentance; such as invocations to Washington, imploring men to unsay what Washington said, and undo what Washington did.

Neither let us be slandered from our duty by false accusations against us, nor frightened from it by menaces of destruction to the government, nor of dungeons to ourselves. Let us have faith that right makes might, and in that faith, let us, to the end, dare to do our duty as we understand it.

This speech placed Lincoln in the line of the presidency. Not only was it received with unbounded enthusiasm by the mass of the people, but it was a revelation to the more intellectual and cultivated. Lincoln afterwards told of a professor of rhetoric at Yale College who was present. He made an abstract of the speech and the next day presented it to the class as a model of cogency and finish. This professor followed Lincoln to Meriden to hear him again. The *Tribune* gave to the speech unstinted praise, declaring that 'no man ever before made such an impression on his first appeal to a New York audience.'

The greatest compliment, because the most deliberate, was that of the committee who prepared the speech for general distribution. Their preface is sufficiently explicit.

No one who has not actually attempted to verify its details can understand the patient research and historical labors which it embodies. The history of our earlier politics is scattered through numerous journals, statutes, pamphlets, and letters; and these are defective in completeness and accuracy of statement, and in indices and tables of contents. Neither can anyone who has not traveled over this precise ground appreciate the accuracy of every trivial detail, or the self-denying impartiality with which Mr Lincoln has turned from the testimony of 'the fathers' on the general question of slavery, to present the single question which he discusses. From the first line to the last, from his premises to his conclusion, he travels with a swift, unerring directness which no logician ever excelled, an argument complete and full, without the affectation of learning, and without the stiffness which usually accompanies dates and details. A single, easy, simple sentence of plain Anglo-Saxon words, contains a chapter of history that, in some instances, has taken days of labor to verify, and which must have cost the author months of investigation to acquire.

Surely Mr Bryant and Mr Beecher and the rest had every reason for gratification that they had introduced this man of humble beginnings to so brilliant a New York audience.

Lincoln went to Exeter, N.H., to visit his son who was in Phillips Academy preparing for Harvard College. Both going and returning he made several speeches, all of which were received with more than ordinary favor. By the time he returned home he was no longer an unknown man. He was looked on with marked favor in all that portion of the country which lies north of Mason and Dixon's line.

CHAPTER EIGHTEEN

The Nomination of 1860

The subject of this chapter is the Republican convention that nominated Lincoln for the presidency. But for an intelligent narration of this, it is necessary to give a brief account of at least one of the three other important political conventions that were held that year. That one was the regular Democratic convention at Charleston. And certain other facts also must be narrated.

Leaven was working in two respects. The first is that the plan of secession and of setting up a Southern nation founded upon slavery, was not a sudden or impromptu thought. The evidence is conclusive that the plan had been maturing for years. Recent events had shown that slavery had reached the limit of its development so far as concerned the territory of the United States. The plan to annex Cuba as a garden for the culture of slavery, had failed. California had been admitted as a free state. Slavery had been excluded from Kansas, although that territory had for two years been denied admission to the sisterhood of states.

As the slave power was not content with any limitation what-ever, its leaders now looked for an opportunity to break up this present government and start a new one. At the time (December, 1860) South Carolina passed the ordinance of secession, to be narrated later, certain things were said which may be quoted here. These utterances exposed the spirit that animated the slave power long before Lincoln's election, long before he was even known in politics.

Parker said that the movement of secession had been 'gradually culminating for *a long series of years*'.

Inglis endorsed the remark and added, 'Most of us have had this matter under consideration for the last twenty years.'

Keitt said, 'I have been engaged in this movement *ever since I entered political life.*'

Rhett said, 'The secession of South Carolina was not the event of a day. It is not anything produced by Mr Lincoln's election, or by the non-execution of the fugitive slave law. It is a matter which has been gathering head *for thirty years*. The election of Lincoln and Hamlin was the last straw on the back of the camel. But it was not the only one. The back was nearly broken before.'

The other important fact was the result of Lincoln's Freeport question. The answer of Douglas was: 'I answer *emphatically* . . . that in my opinion the people of a territory can, by lawful means, exclude slavery from its limits prior to the formation of a state constitution.' This answer satisfied the Democrats of Illinois and secured his election to the senate, as Lincoln predicted that it would. But it angered the southern leaders beyond all reason – as Lincoln knew it would.

When, therefore, the Democratic convention met in Charleston, the first purpose of the southern leaders was to defeat Douglas. In their judgment he was not orthodox on slavery. He was far the strongest candidate before the convention, but he was not strong enough to secure the two-thirds vote which under the rules of that party were necessary to a choice. After fifty-seven ballots, and a corresponding amount of debating, the feeling of antagonism rising continually higher, the crisis came. The south-ern delegates withdrew from the convention and appointed a convention of their own to be held in Richmond. This was done with the full knowledge that, if it accomplished anything, it would accomplish the defeat of the party. It was probably done for this very purpose − to defeat the party − so as to give an excuse, more or less plausible, for carrying out the matured plan of secession, claiming to be injured or alarmed at the ascendancy of the Republican party.

Up to this point, at least, Lincoln had no aspirations for the presidency. But he did aspire to the United States senate. He accepted his defeat by Douglas in 1858 as only temporary. He knew there would be another senatorial election in four years. When asked how he felt about this defeat, he turned it into a joke, and said that he felt 'like the boy who had stubbed his toe, too badly to laugh, and he was too big to cry'.

He had thought of being nominated as vice-president with Seward as President, which would have given him, if elected, a place in the senate. He was glad of any possible prominence in the Chicago convention, which was still in the future. For that would help his senatorial aspirations when the time came. But as to anything higher, he declared, 'I must in all candor say that I do not think myself fit for the presidency.' And he was an honest man. With the senate still in view, he added, 'I am not in a position where it would hurt me much not to be nominated [for president] on the national ticket; but I am where it would hurt some for me not to get the Illinois delegates.'

Thus, at the beginning of the year 1860, Lincoln was in no sense in the race for the presidential nomination. About that time a list of twenty-one names of possible candidates was published in New York; Lincoln's name was not on the list. A list of thirty-five was published in Philadelphia. Lincoln's name was not on that list. After the speech at Cooper Institute the *Evening Post* mentioned Lincoln's name along with others. That was the only case in the East.

In Illinois his candidacy developed in February and came to a head at the Republican state convention at Decatur. Lincoln's name had been prominent in the preceding local conventions, and the enthusiasm was growing. Decatur was very near to the place where Thomas Lincoln had first settled when he came into the state. When Abraham Lincoln came into this convention he was greeted with an outburst of enthusiasm. After order had been restored, the chairman, Governor Oglesby, announced that an old-time Macon County Democrat desired to make a contribution to the convention. The offer being accepted, a banner was borne up the hall upon two old fence rails. The whole was gaily decorated and the inscription was:

ABRAHAM LINCOLN

The Rail Candidate
for President in 1860

Two rails from a lot of 3,000 made in
1830 by Thos. Hanks and Abe Lincoln –
whose father was the first pioneer
of Macon County.

This incident was the means of enlarging the soubriquet 'Honest Abe' to 'Honest Old Abe, the Rail-splitter'. The enthusiasm over the rails spread far and wide. That he had split rails, and that he even had done it well, was no test of his statesmanship. But it was a reminder of his humble origin, and it attached him to the common people, between whom and himself there had always been a warm feeling of mutual sympathy.

The Democratic convention had, after the bolt of the extreme southerners, adjourned to Baltimore, where they duly nominated Douglas. What anyone could have done for the purpose of restoring harmony in the party, he did. But the breach was too wide for even that astute politician to bridge over. Lincoln grasped the situation. It was what he had planned two years before, and he confidently expected just this breach. 'Douglas never can be President,' he had said. He fully understood the relentless bitterness of the slave power, and he well knew that whatever Douglas might do for the northern Democrats, he had lost all influence with the southern branch of that party. So Lincoln told his 'little story' and serenely awaited the result.

The second Republican national convention met in Chicago, May 16, 1860. A temporary wooden structure, called a wigwam, had been built for the purpose. It was, for those days, a very large building, and would accommodate about ten thousand people.

The man who was, far and away, the most prominent candidate for the nomination, was William H. Seward, of New York. He had the benefit of thirty years of experience in political life. He was a man of wide learning, fine culture, unequaled as a diplomatist; he was a patriot, a statesman, and loyal to the principles of the Republican party. He had a plurality of the delegates by a wide margin, though not a majority. It seemed a foregone conclusion that he would be nominated. Horace Greeley, who was determinedly opposed to him, gave up the contest and telegraphed to his paper that Seward would be nominated. The opposition, he said, could not unite on any one man.

The next most prominent name was Lincoln. He had the full delegation of Illinois, who, at Decatur, had been instructed to vote for him as 'the first and only choice' of the state. He had many votes, too, from the neighboring states.

In addition to these two candidates before the convention, there were half a dozen others, all 'favorite sons' of their own states, but who at no time developed any great strength.

The only point against Seward was his inability to carry certain doubtful states. If the split in the Democratic party had not occurred, and if the election were to be carried according to the experience of 1856, it would be necessary for the Republicans to carry certain states which they had at that time failed to carry. The most available states were Pennsylvania, New Jersey, Indiana, and Illinois. Under favorable circumstances, these could be carried. Seward's long public career had inevitably caused antagonisms, and these necessary states he could not carry. The question with his opponents then was, Who is most likely to carry these states? Lincoln's popularity in three of the four states named singled him out as the rival of Seward. It then became only a question whether the opposition to Seward could or could not unite in the support of Lincoln.

At this point there came in a political ruse which has been often used in later years. Seward's friends had taken to Chicago a small army of claquers, numbering nearly or quite two thousand. These were distributed through the audience and were apparently under orders to shout whenever Seward's name was mentioned. This gave the appearance of spontaneous applause and seemed to arouse great enthusiasm for the candidate.

Lincoln's friends soon came to understand the situation and planned to beat their rivals at their own game. They sent out into the country and secured two men with phenomenal voices. It was said, with playful exaggeration, that these two men could shout so as to be heard across Lake Michigan. They were made captains of two stentorian bands of followers. These were placed on opposite sides of the auditorium and were instructed to raise the shout at a preconcerted signal and keep it up as long as desired. The plan worked.

Leonard Swett describes the result.

Caleb B. Smith of Indiana then seconded the nomination of Lincoln, and the West came to his rescue. No mortal before ever saw such a scene. The idea of us Hoosiers and Suckers being out-screamed would have been as bad to them as the loss of their man. Five thousand people at once leaped to their seats, women not wanting in the number, and the wild yell made soft vesper breathings of all that had preceded. No language can describe it. A thousand steam-whistles, ten acres of hotel gongs, a tribe of Comanches headed by a choice vanguard from pandemonium, might have mingled in the scene unnoticed.

A dramatic scene had occurred at the adoption of the platform. When the first resolution was read, Joshua E. Giddings, an old-time abolitionist of the extreme type, moved as an amendment to incorporate the words from the Declaration of Independence which announce the right of all men to 'life, liberty, and the pursuit of happiness'. The hostility to this amendment was not so much owing to an objection to the phrase, as to its being intro-duced upon the motion of so extreme a partisan as Giddings. The new party was made up of men of various old parties, and it was important that the moderate Democrats should not be antagonized by the extreme abolitionists. The motion was lost by a decided vote, and the old man, almost broken-hearted, left the hall amid the protestations of his associates.

There then came to his rescue a young man, about thirty-six years of age, who was then not widely known, but who since has more than once decidedly influenced Republican conventions at a critical stage of the proceedings. It was George William Curtis. When the second resolution was under consideration he presented the amendment of Giddings in a form slightly modi-fied. He then urged it in an impassioned speech, and by his torrent of eloquence carried the enthusiasm of the convention with him. 'I have to ask this convention,' he concluded, 'whether they are prepared to go upon the record before the country as voting down the words of the Declaration of Independence. . . . I rise simply to ask gentlemen to think well before, upon the free prairies of the West, in the summer of 1860, they dare to wince and quail before the assertion of the men of Philadelphia in 1776 – before they dare to shrink from repeating the words that these great men enunciated.'

The amendment was adopted in a storm of applause. Giddings, overjoyed at the result, returned to the hall. He threw his arms about Curtis and, with deep emotion, exclaimed – 'God bless you, my boy! You have saved the Republican party. God bless you!'

The candidates in those days were simply announced without speeches of glorification. Mr Evarts of New York named Seward, and Mr Judd of Illinois named Lincoln. The names of half a dozen 'favorite sons' were offered by their states, the most important being Bates of Missouri. After the seconding of the nominations the convention proceeded to the ballot. There were 465 votes, and 233 were necessary for a choice.

On the first ballot Seward received 173½, and Lincoln, 102. The rest were scattering. On the second ballot Seward received 184½, and Lincoln, 181. Seward was still ahead, but Lincoln had made by far the greater gain. On the third ballot Seward received 180, and Lincoln 231½. But this ballot was not announced. The delegates kept tally during the progress of the vote. When it became evident that Lincoln was about elected, while the feeling of expectancy was at the highest degree of tension, an Ohio delegate mounted his chair and announced a change of four Ohio votes from Chase to Lincoln. There was instantly a break. On every side delegates announced a change of vote to Lincoln. The result was evident to everyone, and after a moment's pause, the crowd went mad with joy. One spectator has recorded the event.

The scene which followed baffles all human description. After an instant's silence, which seemed to be required to enable the assembly to take in the full force of the announcement, the wildest and mightiest yell (for it can be called by no other name) burst forth from ten thousand voices which were ever heard from mortal throats. This strange and tremendous demonstration, accompanied with leaping up and down, tossing hats, handkerchiefs, and canes recklessly into the air, with the waving of flags, and with every other conceivable mode of exultant and unbridled joy, continued steadily and without pause for perhaps ten minutes.

It then began to rise and fall in slow and billowing bursts, and for perhaps the next five minutes, these stupendous waves of uncontrollable excitement, now rising into the deepest and fiercest shouts, and then sinking, like the ground swell of the ocean, into hoarse and lessening murmurs, rolled through the multitude. Every now and then it would seem as though the physical power of the assembly was exhausted, when all at once a new hurricane would break out, more prolonged and terrific than anything before. If sheer exhaustion had not prevented, we don't know but the applause would have continued to this hour.

During all this time Lincoln remained at Springfield, where he was in telegraphic communication with his friends at Chicago, though not by private wire. At the time of his nomination he had gone from his office to that of the Sangamon *Journal*. A messenger boy came rushing up to him, carrying a telegram and exclaiming, 'You are nominated.' The friends who were present joyously shook his hands and uttered their eager congratulations. Lincoln thanked them for their good wishes, and said 'There is a little woman on Eighth Street who will be glad to hear this, and I guess I'll go up and carry her the news.' Pocketing the telegram he walked home.

At the wigwam, the news spread quickly. A man had been stationed on the roof as picket. He shouted, 'Hallelujah! Abe Lincoln is nominated. Fire the cannon!' The frenzy of joy spread to the immense throng of citizens outside the wigwam, then through the city, then through the state, then through the neighboring states. At Washington that night someone asked, 'Who is this man Lincoln, anyhow?' Douglas replied, 'There won't be a tar barrel left in Illinois tonight.' With unprecedented enthusiasm the Republican party started on this campaign which led to its first victory in the election of Abraham Lincoln of Illinois, and Hannibal Hamlin of Maine.

CHAPTER NINETEEN

The Election

There are two things which made the campaign of 1860 para-doxical, so to speak. One was that the nomination was equivalent to an election, unless unforeseen difficulties should arise. The other was that this election might be used by the extreme Southern Democrats as an excuse for precipitating war. They threatened this.

After the nomination the committee of the convention duly called on Lincoln to give him the formal notification. This committee included some names that were at that time, and still more so later, widely known. Among them were three from Massachusetts: Ashmun, then Governor, and chairman of the Chicago convention, Bowles, editor of the Springfield *Republican*, and Boutwell. There were also Gideon Welles, Carl Schurz, Francis P. Blair, and W. M. Evarts. The chairman of this committee notified Lincoln in a brief speech, to which he responded with equal brevity. Even these few words impressed his hearers with a sense of dignity and manliness which they were only too glad to perceive. Said Mr Boutwell: 'Why, sir, they told me he was a rough diamond. Nothing could have been in better taste than that speech.'

One who had opposed Lincoln in the convention said: 'We might have done a more daring thing [than nominate him], but we certainly could not have done a better thing.' Carl Schurz evidently shared this feeling.

Judge Kelly of Pennsylvania was a very tall man and was proud of the fact. During the brief ceremony he and Lincoln had been measuring each other with the eye. At the conclusion of the ceremony, the President-elect demanded: 'What's your height?'

'Six feet three. What is yours, Mr Lincoln?'

'Six feet four.'

'Then,' said the judge, 'Pennsylvania bows to Illinois. My dear man, for many years my heart has been aching for a President I could *look up to*, and I've found him at last in the land where we thought there were none but *little* giants.'

The general feeling of the committee was that the convention had made no mistake. This feeling quickly spread throughout the entire party. Some of Seward's friends wanted him to run on an independent ticket. It is to his credit that he scouted the idea. The Democrats, at least the opponents of Lincoln, were divided into three camps, The first was the regular party, headed by Douglas. The second was the bolting party of fire-eaters, who nominated Breckinridge. The third was the party that nominated Bell and Everett. This was wittily called the Kangaroo ticket, because the tail was the most important part. Lincoln's popular vote at the November election was about forty per cent, of the total. It was plain that if his supporters held together and his opponents were divided, he could readily get a plurality. There were attempts on the part of the opponents of Lincoln to run fusion tickets in New York, New Jersey, and Pennsylvania, so as to divert the electoral votes from him; but these came to nothing more than that New Jersey diverted three of her seven electoral votes.

A curious feature of the campaign was that all four candidates declared emphatically for the Union. Breckinridge, who was the candidate of the Southern disunionists, wrote; 'The Constitution and the equality of the states, these are symbols of everlasting union.' Lincoln himself could hardly have used stronger language. Some people were doubtless deceived by these protestations, but not Douglas. He declared: 'I do not believe that every Breckinridge man is a disunionist, but I do believe that every disunionist in America is a Breckinridge man.' During the period of nearly six months between nomination and election, Lincoln continued simple, patient, wise. He was gratified by the nomination. He was not elated, for he was not an ambitious man. On the contrary, he felt the burden of responsibility. He was a far-seeing statesman, and no man more distinctly realized the coming tragedy. He felt the call of duty, not to triumph but to sacrifice. This was the cause of his seriousness and gravity of demeanor.

There was no unnecessary change in his simple manners and unpretentious method of living. Friends and neighbors came, and he was glad to see them. He answered the door-bell himself and accompanied visitors to the door. Some of his friends, desiring to save his strength in these little matters, procured a negro valet, Thomas by name. But Abraham continued to do most of the duties that by right belonged to Thomas.

Someone sent him a silk hat, that he might go to Washington with head-gear equal to the occasion. A farmer's wife knit him a pair of yarn stockings. Hundreds of such attentions, kind in intent, grotesque in appearance, he received with that kindness which is the soul of courtesy. There was a woman at whose modest farmhouse he had once dined on a bowl of bread and milk, because he had arrived after everything else had been eaten up. She came into Springfield to renew her apologies and to remind him that he had said that that repast was 'good enough for the President'. While he commanded the respect of Bryant, Schurz, Boutwell, and such, he was at the same time the idol of the plain people, whom he always loved. He once said he thought the Lord particularly loved plain people, for he had made so many of them.

Shortly after his nomination he was present at a party in Chicago. A little girl approached timidly. He asked, encouragingly, if he could do anything for her. She replied that she wanted his name. He looked about and said, 'But here are other little girls – they will feel badly if I give my name only to you.' She said there were eight of them in all. 'Then,' said he, 'get me eight sheets of paper, and a pen and ink, and I will see what I can do for you.' The materials were brought, and in the crowded drawing-room he sat down, wrote a sentence and his name on each sheet of paper. Thus he made eight little girls happy.

The campaign was one of great excitement. His letter of acceptance was of the briefest description and simply announced his adherence to the platform. For the rest, his previous utterances in the debates with Douglas, the Cooper Institute speech, and other addresses, were in print, and he was content to stand by the record. He showed his wisdom in his refusing to be diverted, or to allow his party to be diverted, from the one important question of preventing the further extension of slavery. The public were not permitted to lose sight of the fact that this was the real issue. The Chicago wigwam was copied in many cities: temporary wooden structures were erected for Republican meetings. These did good service as rallying centers.

Then the campaign biographers began to appear. It was said that by June he had had no less than fifty-two applications to write his biography. One such book was written by W. D. Howells, not so famous in literature then as now. Lincoln furnished a sketch of his life, an 'autobiography' so called. This contains only about five hundred words. Its brevity is an indication of its modesty.

Nor was there any lack of eulogistic music. Among the writers of campaign songs were J. G. Whittier and E. C. Stedman.

The parading contingent of the party was represented by the 'Wide-Awakes'. The uniform was as effective as simple. It consisted of a cadet cap and a cape, both made of oil-cloth, and a torch. The first company was organized in Hartford. It had escorted Lincoln from the hotel to the hall and back again when he spoke in that city in February after his Cooper Institute speech. The idea of this uniformed company of cadets captivated the public fancy. Bands of Wide-Awakes were organized in every community in the North. At the frequent political rallies they poured in by thousands and tens of thousands, a very picturesque sight. The original band in Hartford obtained the identical maul with which Lincoln had split those rails in 1830. It is now in the collection of the Connecticut Historical Society, in Hartford.

Though Lincoln had much to cheer him, he had also his share of annoyances. One of his discouragements was so serious, and at this day it appears so amazing, that it is given nearly in full. A careful canvas had been made of the voters of Springfield, and the intention of each voter had been recorded. Lincoln had the book containing this record. He asked his friend Mr Bateman, the State Superintendent of Public Instruction, to look through the book with him. They noted particularly those who might be considered leaders of public morals: clergymen, officers, or prominent members of the churches.

When the memorandum was tabulated, after some minutes of silence, he turned a sad face to Mr Bateman, and said: 'Here are twenty-three ministers, of different denominations, and all of them are against me but three; and here are a great many prominent members of the churches, a very large majority of whom are against me. Mr Bateman, I am not a Christian – God knows I would be one – but I have carefully read the Bible, and I do not so understand this book.' He drew from his pocket a New Testament. 'These men well know that I am for freedom in the territories, freedom everywhere as far as the Constitution and laws will permit, and that my opponents are for slavery. They know this, and yet, with this book in their hands, in the light of which human bondage cannot live a moment, they are going to vote against me. I do not understand it at all.'

After a long pause, he added with tears: 'I know there is a God, and that He hates injustice and slavery. I see the storm coming, and I know that His hand is in it. If He has a place and work for me – and I think He has – I believe I am ready. I am nothing, but truth is everything. I know I am right because I know that liberty is right, for Christ teaches it, and Christ is God. I have told them that a house divided against itself cannot stand, and Christ and reason say the same; and they will find it so. Douglas doesn't care whether slavery is voted up or voted down, but God cares, and humanity cares, and I care; and with God's help I shall not fail. I may not see the end; but it will come and I shall be vindicated; and these men will find that they have not read their Bibles aright.'

After another pause: 'Doesn't it appear strange that men can ignore the moral aspects of this contest? A revelation could not make it plainer to me that slavery or the government must be destroyed. The future would be something awful, as I look at it, but for this rock [the Testament which he was holding] on which I stand – especially with the knowledge of how these ministers are going to vote. It seems as if God had borne with this thing [slavery] until the very teachers of religion had come to defend it from the Bible, and to claim for it a divine character and sanction; and now the cup of iniquity is full, and the vials of wrath will be poured out.'

Lincoln did not wear his heart upon his sleeve. On the subject of religion, he was reticent to a degree. Peter Cartwright had called him an atheist. There was a wide, if not general, impression, that he was not a religious man. This did him great injustice. It is for this reason that his remarks to Mr Bateman are here quoted at length. From his early boyhood, from before the time when he was at great pains to have a memorial sermon for his mother, he was profoundly, intensely religious. He did no injustice to any other man, he did not do justice to himself.

The election occurred on the sixth day of November. The vote was as follows: Lincoln received 1,866,452 popular votes, and one hundred and eighty electoral votes. Douglas received 1,375,157 popular votes, and twelve electoral votes. Breckinridge received 847,953 popular votes, and seventy-two electoral votes. Bell received 590,631 popular votes, and thirty-nine electoral votes.

Lincoln carried all the free states, excepting that in New Jersey the electoral vote was divided, he receiving four out of seven. In the fifteen slave states he received no electoral vote. In ten states not one person had voted for him.

Of the 303 electoral votes he had received 180, while the aggregate of all against him numbered 123, giving him an absolute majority of 57. The electoral vote was duly counted in the joint session of the two houses of Congress February 13, 1861, and it was officially announced that Abraham Lincoln, having received a majority of the votes of the presidential electors, was duly elected President of the United States for four years, beginning March 4, 1861.

One circumstance is added which may be of interest to the reader. This was published, after his death, by his personal friend, Noah Brooks. It is given in Lincoln's own words.

It was just after my election, in 1860, when the news had been coming in thick and fast all day, and there had been a great 'Hurrah boys!' so that I was well tired out and went home to rest, throwing myself upon a lounge in my chamber. Opposite to where I lay was a bureau with a swinging glass upon it; and looking in that glass, I saw myself reflected nearly at full length; but my face, I noticed, had two separate and distinct images, the tip of the nose of the one being about three inches from the tip of the other. I was a little bothered, perhaps startled, and got up and looked in the glass, but the illusion vanished. On lying down again, I saw it a second time, plainer, if possible, than before; and then I noticed that one of the faces was a little paler – say five shades – than the other. I got up, and the thing melted away, and I went off, and, in the excitement of the hour, forgot all about it – nearly, but not quite, for the thing would once in a while come up, and give me a little pang as though something uncomfortable had happened. When I went home, I told my wife about it, and a few days after I tried the experiment again, when, sure enough, the thing came back again; but I never succeeded in bringing the ghost back after that, though I once tried very industriously to show it to my wife, who was worried about it somewhat. She thought it was 'a sign' that I was to be elected to a second term of office, and that the paleness of one of the faces was an omen that I should not see life through the last term.

The incident is of no interest excepting in so far as everything about Lincoln is of interest. The phenomenon is an optical illusion not uncommon. One image – the 'paler', or more indistinct, one – is reflected from the surface of the glass, while the other is reflected from the silvered back of the glass. Though Lincoln understood that it was an optical illusion, yet the thought of it evidently weighed on him. Otherwise he would not have repeated the experiment several times, nor would he have told of it to different persons.

CHAPTER TWENTY
Four Long Months

Four months would not ordinarily be considered a long period of time. But when one is compelled to see the working of a vast amount of mischief, powerless to prevent it, and knowing one's self to be the chief victim of it all, the time is long. Such was the fate of Lincoln. The election was not the end of a life of toil and struggle, it was the beginning of a new career of sorrow. The period of four months between the election and inauguration could not be devoted to rest or to the pleasant plans for a prosperous term of service. There developed a plan for the disruption of the government. The excuse was Lincoln's election. But he was for four months only a private citizen. He had no power. He could only watch the growing mischief and realize that he was the ultimate victim. Buchanan, who was then President, had a genius for doing the most unwise thing. He was a northern man with southern principles, and this may have unfitted him to see things in their true relations. He certainly was putty in the hands of those who wished to destroy the Union, and his vacill-ation precisely accomplished what they wished. Had he possessed the firmness and spirit of John A. Dix, who ordered – 'If any man attempts to haul down the American flag, shoot him on the spot'; had he had a modicum of the patriotism of Andrew Jackson; had he had a tithe of the wisdom and manliness of Lincoln, secession would have been nipped in the bud and vast treasures of money and irreparable waste of human blood would have been spared. Whatever the reason may have been – incapacity, obliquity of moral and political vision, or absolute championship of the cause of disruption – certain it is that the southern fire-eaters could not have found a tool more perfectly suited to their purpose than James Buchanan. He was the center of one of the most astonishing political cabals of all history.

Lincoln did not pass indiscriminate condemnation upon all men of southern sympathies. At the time of which we are now writing, and consistently up to the end of his life, he made a marked distinction between the rank and file of the Confederates on the one hand, and those leaders who, on the other hand, had, while in the service of the United States government, sought to accomplish its destruction. The first were revolutionists; they were so regarded generally in Europe, and he believed they were sincere; he regarded them as having the spirit of revolutionists. For the second, who held office under, drew pay from, and were under solemn oath to support, the government, while they were using the vantage of their official position to violate the Constitution and disrupt that government, there is but one word, and that a strong one – traitors. This was Lincoln's judgment of the men.

Let us now briefly describe the situation. Jefferson Davis, though not a member of Buchanan's cabinet, was probably the most influential of the Southerners in Washington. He had been Secretary of War under Pierce, and it was he who inaugurated the policy of stripping the North for the purpose of strengthening the military defenses of the South. This policy was vigorously pursued under his successor.

The only person to call a halt to the treasonable proceedings was General Winfield Scott. He was residing in New York City, and on October 29th addressed a letter to President Buchanan containing his views upon the situation. A day or two later he added supplementary considerations addressed to the Secretary of War. He set forth, with much clearness and force, the necessity of garrisoning the southern forts before they should be lost. His letter had its faults, but it accomplished one thing: it showed that there was one high official who was in earnest in the discharge of his duties, and with whom it was not safe to trifle.

President Buchanan sent in his annual message to Congress December 3, 1860. In his discussion of the subject of slavery, he recommended that it be extended to the territories – the very thing that the people had just voted should not be done. Concerning secession, he said for substance that the government had the power to suppress revolt, but that it could not use that power in reference to South Carolina, the state then under consideration. The secessionists had apparently tied the hands of the executive effectually.

Now observe what was going on in the cabinet. Lewis Cass had been Secretary of State, but resigned in indignation over the inaction of the President when he failed to succor the forts in Charleston Harbor. He was succeeded by Jeremiah S. Black, who, as attorney-general, had given to Buchanan an opinion that the Federal government had no power to coerce a seceding state.

Howell Cobb, Secretary of the Treasury, having wasted the funds and destroyed the credit of the government, resigned and left an empty treasury.

John B. Floyd, Secretary of War, was not the least active. He carried out fully the plan which Jefferson Davis had begun to operate several years before. The northern arsenals were stripped of the arms and ammunition which were sent South for storage or use. The number of regular troops was small, but the few soldiers there were, he scattered in distant places, so that they should be out of reach. They were not to be available for the use of the government until the conspirators should have time to complete their work. It was Floyd whom an emotional Virginian later eulogized. With quite as much truth as poetry he declared that the Secretary of War 'thwarted, objected, resisted, and forbade' the efforts of General Scott. This same admirer of Floyd further declared that, if Scott's plans had been adopted and his measures executed, the conspiracy would have been defeated and it would have been impossible to form the Southern Confederacy.

Not worse, perhaps, but more flagrant, was the action of the Secretary of the Interior, Thompson of Mississippi. With the advice and consent of Buchanan, he left his post at Washington to visit North Carolina and help on the work of secession, and then returned and resumed his official prerogatives under the government he had sworn to sustain. This is so grave a matter that a passage from the diary of Mr Clingman is here inserted, quoted by Nicolay and Hay.

About the middle of December (1860) I had occasion to see the Secretary of the Interior on some official business. On my entering the room, Mr Thompson said to me, 'Clingman, I am glad you have called, for I intended presently to go up to the senate to see you. I have been appointed a commissioner by the state of Mississippi to go down to North Carolina to get your state to secede.' . . . I said to him, 'I did not know you had resigned.' He answered, 'Oh, no! I have not resigned.' 'Then,' I replied, 'I suppose you resign in the morning.' 'No,' he answered, 'I do not intend to resign, for Mr Buchanan wished us all to hold on, and go out with him on the 4th of March.' 'But,' said I, 'does Mr Buchanan know for what purpose you are going to North Carolina?' 'Certainly,' he said, 'he knows my object.'

In the meanwhile, Isaac Toucey, the Secretary of the Navy, had been prevailed on to put the navy out of reach. The armed vessels were sent to the ends of the earth. At the critical period, only two were available to the government. What was going on in Congress? That body was very busy doing nothing. Both senate and house raised committees for the purpose of devising means of compromise. But every measure of concession was promptly voted down by the body that had appointed the committees. In the senate the slave power was in full control. In the house the slave power was not in majority, but they enjoyed this advantage that they were able to work together, while the constituency of the free states were usually divided among themselves. And in joint session the extreme pro-slavery men were always able to prevent anything from being accomplished. This was all they wished. They had sufficient pledges from the President that nothing would be done before the 4th of March, and it was their belief that by that time the new power would have so good a start that it could treat with the United States on equal terms. On January 7, 1861, Senator Yulee, of Florida, wrote: 'By remaining in our places until the 4th of March, it is thought we can keep the hands of Mr Buchanan tied, and disable the Republicans from effecting any legislation which will strengthen the hands of the incoming administration.'

On December 14, thirty of the southern senators and representatives had issued a circular to their constituents. They said that the argument was exhausted, that all hope of relief was extinguished, that the Republicans would grant nothing satisfactory, and that the honor, safety, and independence of the Southern people required the organization of a Southern Confederacy.

South Carolina was the first to act. Six days later that state passed the ordinance of secession.

Upon this, one of the extreme traitors was forced out of the cabinet. Floyd, the mischievous Secretary of War, was displaced by Holt, a loyal man. Floyd, however, had done nearly, if not quite, all the mischief he could have done. Stanton had already replaced Black as Attorney-General.

The conspirators then held a caucus. It is supposed that this caucus was held in one of the rooms of the Capitol. At all events it was held in the city of Washington. It was composed of the extreme southern congressmen. It decided to recommend immediate secession, the formation of the Southern Confederacy, and, not least, that the congressmen should remain in their seats to keep the President's hands tied. The committee to carry out these plans consisted of Jefferson Davis, Slidell, and Mallory. By the first day of February, seven states had passed ordinances of secession.

This is about what was going on during the four months Lincoln was waiting for the appointed time when he should enter upon his duties. It was not unlike looking upon a house he was shortly to occupy, and seeing vandals applying the torch and axe of destruction, while he was not permitted to go to the rescue, all the while knowing that he would be held accountable for the preservation of the structure. So Lincoln saw this work of destruction going on at Washington. It was plain that the mischief ought to be, and could be, stopped. But Buchanan would not stop it, and Lincoln was, until March 4th, a private citizen and could do nothing. The bitterest part of it was that all the burden would fall on him. As soon as he should become President it would be his duty to save the government which these men were now openly destroying.

Miss Tarbell has recorded a conversation between Lincoln and his friend Judge Gillespie, which took place in Springfield early in January, in which the former expressed his feelings upon the situation.

'Gillespie,' said he, 'I would willingly take out of my life a period in years equal to the two months which intervene between now and the inauguration, to take the oath of office now.'

'Why?'

'Because every hour adds to the difficulties I am called upon to meet and the present administration does nothing to check the tendency towards dissolution. I, who have been called to meet this awful responsibility, am compelled to remain here, doing nothing to avert it or lessen its force when it comes to me. . . . Every day adds to the situation and makes the outlook more gloomy. Secession is being fostered rather than repressed. . . . I have read, upon my knees, the story of Gethsemane, where the Son of God prayed in vain that the cup of bitterness might pass from him. I am in the garden of Gethsemane now, and my cup of bitterness is full to overflowing.' (Tarbell, *Life of Lincoln*, II., 406)

It was indeed hard to keep his patience and self-control. He was importuned for expressions of his views, for messages conciliatory to the South, for some kind of a proclamation which might quiet the public feeling. But he saw clearly that anything he might say at that time, no matter how wise or conciliatory, would surely be misused as fuel to add to the flames. While therefore he talked and wrote freely to his friends, he made no public announcement. He merely referred to his record. His opinions had been fully expressed in the debates with Douglas and in other speeches. There were four important points as to his future policy. The Union should be preserved, the Constitution should be upheld, and the fugitive slave law (being a law) should be enforced, but slavery should not be extended. These fully covered all the necessary points of the subject, and beyond these he would not go. He who would control others must first control himself. It is hard to imagine a more severe test than this imposed on Lincoln during this period of waiting. He made his preparations in silence, and not an injudicious word escaped him. He left his home for Washington the 11th day of February, but though he made several speeches on the way, he did not outline his policy until he read his inaugural address on the 4th of March.

CHAPTER TWENTY-ONE
Journey to Washington

The long period of waiting approached its end. Most of the states
and cities lying between Springfield and Washington invited him
officially to visit them on his way to the capital. It was decided that
he should accept as many as possible of these invitations. This would
involve a zigzag route and require considerable time. The invitation
of Massachusetts he declined on account of the pressure of time.
Maryland was conspicuous by its omission of courtesy. Two private
citizens of Baltimore invited him to dinner. That was all.

The presidential party consisted of about a dozen, all told. They
were to leave Springfield February 11, and to consume about two
weeks on the way. It was a dreary morning, partly drizzling, and
partly snowing. A large crowd of neighbors had assembled at the
dingy railway station to bid him good-by. The process of handshaking was interrupted by the arrival of the train. After the party
had entered the car, the President reappeared on the rear platform.
He raised his hand to speak, but did not utter a word until the
solemn silence became painful. Then, with great tenderness and
seriousness, he spoke as follows.

> 'My friends, no one, not in my situation, can appreciate my feeling
> of sadness at this parting. To this place, and the kindness of these
> people, I owe everything. Here I have lived a quarter of a century,
> and have passed from a young to an old man. Here my children
> have been born, and one is buried. I now leave, not knowing when
> or whether ever I may return, with a task before me greater than
> that which rested upon Washington. Without the assistance of that
> Divine Being who ever attended him, I cannot succeed. With that
> assistance, I cannot fail. Trusting in Him who can go with me, and
> remain with you, and be everywhere for good, let us confidently
> hope that all will yet be well. To His care commending you, as I
> hope in your prayers you will commend me, I bid you an affection-
> ate farewell.'

The speech was telegraphed, with substantial accuracy all over
the country, and was read with loving sympathy by millions of

loyal citizens. The words above given are the report as revised by Lincoln himself, and first published in the *Century* for December, 1887.

The party was in charge of Colonel Ward Hill Lamon, afterwards Marshal of the District of Columbia. He was a trained athlete, a Hercules in strength, a man who knew not what fear was, and, with an enthusiasm akin to religious zeal, he was devoted to his chief soul and body. In the words of a later Marshal, he 'worshiped every bone in his body'.

A few friends had accompanied the presidential party to Indianapolis, where the first stop was made. After the address of welcome by Governor Morton and the response, after the speech to the legislature, after the reception and the handshaking, they were left in quiet in the Bates House. These friends then took Lamon into a room, locked the door, and in the most solemn and impressive manner laid upon him the responsibilities of guarding Lincoln's person until they should reach Washington. The scene was concluded by Dubois with a mixture of solemnity and playfulness, who said: 'Now, Lamon, we intrust the sacred life of Mr Lincoln to your keeping; and if you don't protect it, never return to Illinois, for we will murder you on sight.'

Neither the exhortation nor the threat were in the least needed by Lamon, who was thoroughly alert. But it is of interest in this, that it indicates that there was a widespread feeling that this journey was fraught with unusual dangers.

Of course Lincoln made many brief speeches. These were closely scanned in the hope of finding some premonition of his inaugural. But not one such word escaped him. He complained that though he had in his day done much hard work, this was the hardest work he had ever done – to keep speaking without saying anything. It was not quite true that he did not say anything, for the speeches were thoughtful and full of interest. But he did not anticipate his inaugural, and to that the popular curiosity was alive. He did not say the things that were uppermost in his mind.

At Indianapolis he asked pregnant questions.

What, then, is 'coercion'? What is 'invasion'? . . . If the United States should merely hold and retake its own forts and other property [in South Carolina that had seceded], and collect the duties on foreign importations, or even withhold the mails from places where they were habitually violated, would any, or all, of these things be 'invasion' or 'coercion'? . . . Upon what principle, what rightful principle, may a state, being no more than one-fiftieth part of the nation in soil and population, break up the nation, and then coerce a proportionally larger subdivision of itself in the most arbitrary way? What mysterious right to play tyrant is conferred on a district of country, with its people, by merely calling it a state? Fellow-citizens, I am not asserting anything. I am merely asking questions for you to consider.'

At Trenton, New Jersey, historic in the annals of the revolutionary war, he spoke with simple candor of the influence upon his life of Weems's *Life of Washington*, one of the first books he ever read. The audience broke into cheers, loud and long, when he appealed to them to stand by him in the discharge of his patriotic duty.

I shall endeavor to take the ground I deem most just to the North, the East, the West, the South, and the whole country. I take it, I hope, in good temper; certainly with no malice towards any section. I shall do all that may be in my power to promote a peaceful settlement of all our difficulties. The man does not live who is more devoted to peace than I am, none who would do more to preserve it; but it may be necessary to put the foot down firmly. And if I do my duty and do right, you will sustain me, will you not?

At Philadelphia he spoke in Independence Hall on Washington's Birthday, and raised a flag.

Our friends had provided a magnificent flag of our country. They had arranged it so that I was given the honor of raising it to the head of its staff. And when it went up, I was pleased that it went to its place by the strength of my own feeble arm. When, according to the arrangement, the cord was pulled, and it flaunted gloriously to the wind without an accident, in the bright glowing sunshine of the morning, I could not help hoping that there was in the entire success of that beautiful ceremony at least something of an omen of what is to come.

On this very day, President Buchanan, in Washington City, was apologizing for permitting the American flag to be carried at the head of a procession that was marching to celebrate the birthday of George Washington!

It was at Philadelphia that matters became more exciting. At that place they were informed of a plot to assassinate the President as he passed through Baltimore. This information came to them from a variety of sources entirely independent, and the various stories so nearly agreed in substance that they could not be disregarded. Most important of these informants was Allan Pinkerton of Chicago, one of the most famous detectives in the world. He had been personally with his assistants in Baltimore and knew the details of the plot. But Lincoln was neither suspicious nor timid, and was therefore disinclined to pay heed to the warnings of Pinkerton.

At about this time the son of William H. Seward met Lincoln with confidential communications from his father. This gave other evidences of this plot, gathered by some detectives from New York City. These two sets of detectives had worked on the case; each party entirely ignorant of the other. Both got specific evidence of the plot.

It was remembered, too, that since leaving Springfield ten days before, they had had at least two escapes. The track had been tampered with in a manifest attempt to wreck the train. A hand grenade had been found in one of the cars. It is not likely that this deadly machine was taken on the train merely for fun.

The members of the party were deeply concerned about the Baltimore revelations. But it was hard to get Lincoln to take them seriously. With difficulty was he persuaded to follow Pinkerton's plan and enter Washington secretly. He consented to do this really out of consideration for the judgment of others, not that he shared their apprehension. On one thing, however, Lincoln was firm. He had made certain appointments for speaking *en route* which he would not abandon. His promise had been given and would be kept. One was the flag-raising at Philadelphia, narrated above, and the other was to address the legislature at Harrisburg. 'Both these appointments,' said he, 'I will keep *if it costs me my life*.' These words suggest that he may have realized more of the danger than he was willing to show.

There are also intimations of the same thing which will be noticed by the careful reader of the speeches at Philadelphia and

Harrisburg. In declining to give a hint of the details of his proposed policy, he said: 'It were useless for me to speak of details of plans now; I shall speak officially next Monday week, *if ever*. If I should not speak then, it were useless for me to do so now.'

Again: 'If this country cannot be saved without giving up that principle — I was about to say that I would rather be *assassinated on this spot* than surrender it.'

And finally: 'I may have said something indiscreet. But I have said nothing but what I am willing to live by, and, if it be the pleasure of Almighty God, *die by*.'

These veiled references would pass unnoticed by the crowd, but they would be perfectly intelligible to those who knew of the warnings that had just been received. Lincoln was not in the habit of using such phrases, and the fact that he used them at this particular time can hardly be explained as a mere coincidence. He took in the situation, and — except for keeping the engagements already made — he submitted meekly to Pinkerton's plans.

An incident occurred at Harrisburg which made a great stir in the little party. This was nothing less than the loss of the manuscript of the inaugural address. This precious document the President himself had carried in a satchel. This satchel he had given to his son Robert to hold. When Robert was asked for it, it was missing. He '*thought* he had given it to a waiter — or somebody.' This was one of the rare occasions on which Lincoln lost control of his temper, and for about one minute he addressed the careless young man with great plainness of speech.

For obvious reasons it was not judicious to say much about this loss. The President applied to Lamon for help. 'Lamon,' he whispered, 'I have lost my certificate of moral character written by myself. Bob has lost my gripsack containing my inaugural address. I want you to help me find it.'

Lamon, who knew Lincoln intimately, said that he never saw him so much annoyed, nor, for the time, so angry. If the address were to be published prematurely, it might be made the occasion of a vast amount of mischief. Then, too, it was the product of much painstaking thought and he had no duplicate copy.

Lincoln and Lamon instituted a search for the missing satchel and were directed to the baggage-room of the hotel. Here they spied a satchel that looked like the lost one. Lincoln tried the key.

It fitted. With great joy he opened it, and he found within – one bottle of whisky, one soiled shirt, and several paper collars. So quickly from the sublime to the ridiculous.

A little later the right satchel was found, and was not again entrusted to Robert. The President kept it in his own hands. After the nervous strain was over, the humor of the situation grew on the President, and it reminded him of a little story.

A man had saved up his earnings until they reached the sum of fifteen hundred dollars. This was deposited for safekeeping in a bank. The bank failed and the man received as his share, ten per cent, or one hundred and fifty dollars. This he deposited in another bank. The second bank also failed and the poor fellow again received ten per cent, or fifteen dollars. When this remnant of his fortune was paid over to him, he held it in his hand, looking at it thoughtfully. Finally he said: 'Now, I've got you reduced to a portable shape, so I'll put you in my pocket.' Suiting the action to the word, Lincoln took his 'certificate of moral character' from the satchel and carefully put it in the inside pocket of his vest. No further mishap came to that document.

The journey from Harrisburg to Washington was accomplished as planned, with the assistance of certain officials of the railway and telegraph companies. First all the wires leading out of Harrisburg were cut, so that, if Lincoln's departure were discovered, the news could not be communicated by telegraph. Then, after the reception, Lincoln, attended by Lamon, left the hotel by a side door and was driven to the railway station. Here they found waiting a special train consisting of one baggage car and one passenger car. The track was for the time kept entirely clear for this train. Arriving at Philadelphia they stopped outside the station, where Pinkerton met them with a closed carriage in readiness. They were driven rapidly across the city to the Washington train which had been detained a few minutes for 'a sick passenger and one attendant'. They entered the rear door of the sleeping car. The 'sick passenger' went to his berth at once and the attendant gave the tickets to the conductor who did not even see the 'sick passenger', and who did not dream of what a precious life he was carrying. They arrived at six o'clock in the morning at Washington City, where they were met by Seward and Washburn and taken to Willard's Hotel.

The rest of the party came on schedule time. At Baltimore there was a large crowd in waiting, but no disturbance. The news of the President's arrival had been telegraphed over the country, and the band of assassins were for the time helpless. Their intended victim had escaped. There was no reason why they should create a disturbance.

Lincoln always regretted this 'secret passage'. He later came to discount heavily the revelations of a professional spy. Long after, he said: 'I did not then, nor do I now, believe I should have been assassinated had I gone through Baltimore as first contemplated, but I thought it wise to run no risk where no risk was necessary.'

It is positively asserted by Lamon, who knew whereof he spake, that there was no time, from the moment of leaving Springfield to his death, when Lincoln was free from danger of murder. Yet he never could be prevailed on to accept precautions. What were the reasons for his apparent carelessness?

It is almost certain that he realized, more than he would have his friends know, that he was surrounded by dangers. He probably realized this more keenly than they did. They could locate specific dangers, but no man ever better understood the murderous spirit which underlay much of the hatred towards this man who had never harmed a human being. He felt that an escape from one danger might be simply running into another more deadly. It was like dodging bullets on the field of battle. He, better than they, realized that the unseen dangers were greater than those which they thought they had discovered. The only way, then, was to go straight ahead as if unmindful of all dangers.

Then, too, though Lincoln could understand dangers in the abstract, his mind did not seem to be able to individualize them. He knew full well that many persons wanted to kill him, but when it came to the point of the murder being done by X, or Y, or Z, he did not believe it possible that they would do such a thing.

These explanations are suggested. There may be others. But these two conflicting and paradoxical facts must be kept in mind. All through his public life he was oppressed with the belief that he would not live to see the end of the national crisis. On the other hand, not all the importunities of his most devoted friends could persuade him to guard himself. In the light of what we now know, it is wonderful that he escaped these plots for more than four years. Had he been more cautious, he might not have escaped so long. At the same time, as we shall presently see, had he heeded the last caution of his devoted friend, he would not have been shot in 1865.

CHAPTER TWENTY-TWO

The Inauguration

Beautiful for situation and beautiful in construction is the Washington City of today. But it was not so in Lincoln's day. The proper decoration of the city did not begin until Grant's administration. In 1861 it was comparatively a small city. Its population numbered only about 65,000. The magnificent modern residences had not been built. The houses were few, low, not handsome, with hideous spaces of unimproved land lying between. The streets were not paved with asphalt. Some were paved with cobble stones, and some consisted of plain aboriginal mud. The dome of the Capitol was but half finished when Lincoln saw it for the first time, and the huge derrick which surmounted it was painfully suggestive of the gallows. The approach was not a well-kept lawn, but a meadow of grass, ragged and ill-cared for.

Washington society was then, as always, composed of people of education and social culture, but it was not such as would kindle the enthusiasm of the patriot. From the time whereof the memory of man runneth not to the contrary, it had been dominated by the slave power. The District of Columbia is situated in a slave state. The politics of South Carolina and Mississippi had always been aggressive, and the social leadership had been the same. J. G. Holland estimated that not more than one in five of the people in Washington in the winter of 1860–61 were glad to have Lincoln come. He was not far from right. Lamon called the city 'a focus of political intrigue and corruption'.

For many years, specifically since 1848, the slave power had been masterful in Washington, while its despotic temper had grown continually more assertive. The intellectual and moral atmosphere became increasingly repulsive to those who believed in freedom, and such people would not therefore choose that city as a place of residence.

The departments were of course filled with employees in sympathy with slavery. Pierce had been made President in 1853. The Missouri Compromise had been repealed in 1854. Buchanan came into office in 1857. The crowning act of his administration was supporting the Kansas infamy in 1859. From these indications it is easy to estimate the political status of Washington society when Lincoln entered the city February 23, 1861. Many thousands of his friends poured in from all quarters north of Mason and Dixon's line to attend the ceremonies of the inaugural. But these were transients, and foreign to the prevailing sentiment of the city.

Every official courtesy, however, was shown to the President-elect. The outgoing President and cabinet received him politely. He had many supporters and some personal friends in both houses of Congress. These received him with enthusiasm, while his opponents were not uncivil. The members of the Supreme Court greeted him with a measure of cordiality. Both Douglas and Breckinridge, the defeated candidates at the late election, called on him. The so-called Peace Conference had brought together many men of local influence, who seized the opportunity of making his acquaintance. So the few days passed busily as the time for inauguration approached.

Of course anxiety and even excitement were not unknown. One instance is enough to relate here. Arrangements were about concluded for the cabinet appointments. The most important selection was for the Secretary of State. This position had been tendered to Seward months before and had by him been accepted. The subsequent selections had been made in view of the fact that Seward was to fill this position. On Saturday, March 2nd, while only a few hours remained before the inaugural, Seward suddenly withdrew his promised acceptance. This utterly upset the balancings on which Lincoln had so carefully worked for the last four months, and was fitted to cause consternation. Lincoln's comment was: 'I can't afford to have Seward take the first trick.' So he sent him an urgent personal note on the morning of March 4th, requesting him to withdraw this refusal. Seward acceded to this and the matter was arranged satisfactorily.

The morning of the day of the inauguration was clear, mild, beautiful. The military display gave a bright and showy appearance to the scene. General Scott had used the utmost care to have the arrangements for the defense of the President perfect. There were guards about the carriage, guards about the Capitol, a flying battery upon a commanding hill. Besides this, sharpshooters were posted on the roofs of the houses along the route of travel, with injunctions to watch narrowly the windows opposite and fire upon the first manifestation of disorder. One cannot resist the temptation to speculate upon the excitement that would have developed had a mischievous boy set off a large fire-cracker at a critical moment!

Shortly after twelve o'clock, noon, Buchanan called to escort his successor to the Capitol. The retiring President and the President-elect rode side by side through the streets. Reaching the grounds of the Capitol they found an improvised board tunnel through which they walked arm in arm to the building. This tunnel had been constructed to guard against assassination, of which there had recently been many threats. They passed through the senate chamber and through the building to the large platform which had been erected at the east front. The procession was headed by the justices of the Supreme Court clothed in cap and gown.

The platform was densely packed, but in the number there were four men of especial interest. When Lincoln had first been nominated for the senate, at Springfield, June 16, 1858, he made the speech which came to be known as 'the house-divided-against-itself speech'. One remarkable paragraph is here quoted.

We cannot absolutely know that all these exact adaptations are the result of preconcert. But when we see a lot of framed timbers, different portions of which we know have been gotten out at different times and places and by different workmen – Stephen, Franklin, Roger, and James, for instance – and when we see these timbers joined together, and see they exactly make the frame of a house or a mill, all the tenons and mortices exactly fitting, and all the lengths and proportions of the different pieces exactly adapted to their respective places, and not a piece too many or too few – not omitting even scaffolding – or, if a single piece be lacking, we see the place in the frame exactly fitted and prepared yet to bring the piece in – in such a case, we find it impossible not to believe that Stephen and Franklin and Roger and James all understood one another from the beginning, and all worked upon a common plan or draft drawn up before the first blow was struck.

The manifest reference here is to the co-workers for the extension of slavery: namely, Stephen A. Douglas, Franklin Pierce, Roger B. Taney, and James Buchanan. One of this number, Franklin, had fallen into welcome oblivion; James had escorted Lincoln to the platform; Stephen stood immediately behind him, alert to show him any courtesy; and Roger, as Chief Justice, was about to administer the oath of office. It was a rare case of poetic justice.

Lincoln was introduced to the vast audience by his former neighbor, E. D. Baker, at this time senator from Oregon. In one hand Lincoln had his silk hat, and as he looked about for a place to put it, his old antagonist, Douglas, took it. To a lady he whispered: 'If I can't be President, I can at least hold the President's hat.'

The inaugural address had been submitted confidentially to a few trusted friends for criticism. The only criticisms of importance were those of Seward. By these Lincoln was guided but not governed. A perusal of the documents will show that, while Seward's suggestions were unquestionably good, Lincoln's finished product was far better. This is specifically true of the closing paragraph, which has been widely admired for its great beauty. From the remarkable address we quote only two passages. In the first he meets the charge that he would involve the country in war. It is as follows.

I shall take care, as the Constitution itself expressly enjoins upon me, that the laws of the Union shall be faithfully executed in all the states. Doing this, which I deem to be only a simple duty on my part, I shall perfectly perform it, so far as is practicable, unless my rightful masters, the American people, shall withhold the requisition, or in some authoritative manner direct the contrary. I trust this will not be regarded as a menace, but only as the declared purpose of the Union that it will constitutionally defend and maintain itself.

In doing this, there need be no bloodshed or violence, and there shall be none unless it is forced upon the national authority. *The*

power confided to me will be used to hold, occupy, and possess the prop-
erty and places belonging to the government, and collect the duties and
imposts. But beyond what may be necessary for these objects there
will be no invasion, no using of force against or among the people
anywhere.

Concerning the clause above italicised there was a general ques-
tioning – Does he mean what he says? In due time they learned
that he meant what he said, and all of it.

The address concluded as follows.

In your hands, my dissatisfied fellow-countrymen, and not in
mine, is the momentous issue of civil war. The government will not
assail you. You can have no conflict without being yourselves the
aggressors. You have no oath registered in Heaven to destroy the
government, while I shall have the most solemn one to 'preserve,
protect, and defend' it.

I am loath to close. We are not enemies, but friends. We must not
be enemies. Though passion may have strained, it must not break,
our bonds of affection. The mystic cords of memory, stretching
from every battlefield and patriot grave to every living heart and
hearthstone all over this broad land, will yet swell the chorus of the
Union, when again touched, as surely they will be, by the better
angels of our nature.

The address was listened to closely throughout. Immediately
upon its conclusion the speaker was sworn into office by Chief
Justice Taney whose name is connected with the famous Dred
Scott decision. James Buchanan was now a private citizen and the
pioneer rail-splitter was at the head of the United States.

In all the thousands of people there assembled, there was no one
who listened more intently than Stephen A. Douglas. At the
conclusion he warmly grasped the President hand's, congratulated
him upon the inaugural, and pledged him that he would stand by
him and support him in upholding the Constitution and enforcing
the laws. The nobler part of the nature of the 'little giant' came to
the surface. The clearness, the gentleness, the magnanimity, the
manliness expressed in this inaugural address of his old rival, won
him over at last, and he pledged him here his fealty. For a few
months, while the storm was brewing, Douglas was inactive, so

that his influence counted on the side of the hostile party, the party
to which he had always belonged. But when war actually broke
out, he hastened to stand by the President, and right nobly did he
redeem his promise which he had given. Had he lived, there are
few men whose influence would have been more weighty in the
cause of the Union. An untimely death cut him off at the beginning of this patriotic activity. His last public act was to address to
the legislature of Illinois a masterly plea for the support of the war
for the Union. He died in Chicago on the 3rd of June, 1861.

CHAPTER TWENTY-THREE

Lincoln His Own President

Had the question been asked early in 1861, Who will be the real
force of the Republican administration? almost every unprejudiced
observer would have answered promptly, Seward. He was a man
of unusual intellectual powers, of the best education, and of the
finest culture. In regard to the moral aspects of politics, he was on
the right side. He had a career of brilliant success extending over
thirty years of practical experience. He had been governor of the
Empire State, and one of the leading members of the United States
senate. He was the most accomplished diplomatist of the day.

In marked contrast was the President-elect. He had, in his
encounters with Douglas, shown himself a master of debate. But
his actual experience of administration was practically nil. He had
served a few years in a frontier legislature and one term in the
lower house of Congress. Only this and nothing more. His record
as representative may be summarized as follows:

1 comic speech on General Cass.

1 set of humorous resolutions, known as the spot resolutions.

1 bill in reference to slavery in the District of Columbia, which
bill failed to pass.

There was thus no comparison between the careers of the two
men. Seward's friends, and Seward himself, assumed as a self-
evident truth, that 'where Seward sits is the head of the table.'
Lincoln did not assent to this proposition.

He considered himself President and head of the cabinet. How the matter came out will appear later in the chapter.

The selection of a cabinet was a difficult and delicate task. It must be remembered that Lincoln confronted a solid South, backed by a divided North. It has already been said that in fifteen states he received not a single electoral vote, and in ten of these not a single popular vote. That was the solid South.

The divided condition of the North may be inferred from the following letter, written by ex-President Franklin Pierce to Jefferson Davis under date of January 6, 1860.

If, through the madness of Northern abolitionists, that dire calamity [the disruption of the Union] must come, the fighting will not be along Mason and Dixon's line merely. It will be *within our own borders, in our own streets*, between the two classes of citizens to whom I have referred. Those who defy law, and scout constitutional obligation, will, if we ever reach the arbitrament of arms, find occupation enough at home.

It is plain that unless Lincoln could, in a large measure, unite the various classes of the North, his utter failure would be a foregone conclusion. He saw this with perfect clearness. His first move was in the selection of his cabinet. These selections were taken not only from the various geographical divisions of the country, but also from the divers political divisions of the party. It was not his purpose to have the secretaries simply echoes of himself, but able and representative men of various types of political opinion. At the outset this did not meet the approval of his friends. Later, its wisdom was apparent. In the more than a hundred years of cabinets in the history of the United States there has never been an abler or a purer cabinet than this.

As guesses, more or less accurate, were made as to what the cabinet would be, many 'leading citizens' felt called on to labor with the President and show him the error of his ways. As late as March 2nd there was an outbreak against Chase. A self-appointed committee, large in numbers and respectable in position, called on Lincoln to protest vigorously. He heard them with undivided attention. When they were through he replied. In voice of sorrow and disappointment, he said, in substance: 'I had written out my choice and selection of members for the cabinet after most careful and deliberate consideration; and now you are here to tell me I must break the slate and begin the thing all over again. I don't like your list as well as mine. I had hoped to have Mr Seward as Secretary of State and Mr Chase as Secretary of the Treasury. But of course I can't expect to have things just as I want them. . . . This being the case, gentlemen, how would it do for us to agree to a change like this? To appoint Mr Chase Secretary of the Treasury, and offer the State department to Mr Dayton of New Jersey?

'Mr Dayton is an old Whig, like Mr Seward and myself. Besides, he is from New Jersey, which is next door to New York. Then Mr Seward can go to England, where his genius will find wonderful scope in keeping Europe straight about our troubles.'

The 'committee' were astounded. They saw their mistake in meddling in matters they did not understand. They were glad enough to back out of the awkward situation. Mr Lincoln 'took *that* trick'.

The names sent on March 5th were: for Secretary of State, William H. Seward, of New York; for Secretary of the Treasury, Salmon P. Chase, of Ohio; for Secretary of War, Simon Cameron, of Pennsylvania; for Secretary of the Navy, Gideon Welles, of Connecticut; for Secretary of the Interior, Caleb B. Smith, of Indiana; for Attorney-General, Edward Bates, of Missouri; for Postmaster-General, Montgomery Blair, of Maryland.

All these names were confirmed by the senate the next day, March 6th. Of the variety of the selection he said, 'I need them all. They enjoy the confidence of their several states and sections, and they will strengthen the administration. The times are too grave and perilous for ambitious schemes and rivalries.' To all who were associated with him in the government, he said, 'Let us forget ourselves and join hands, like brothers, to save the republic. If we succeed, there will be glory enough for all.' He playfully spoke of this cabinet as his happy family.

The only one who withdrew early from this number, was Cameron. He was accused of various forms of corruption, especially of giving fat government contracts to his friends. Whether these charges were true or not, we cannot say. But in the following January he resigned and was succeeded by Edwin M. Stanton, a lifelong Democrat, one who had accepted office under Buchanan.

Probably no person was more amazed at this choice than Stanton himself. But he patriotically accepted the call of duty. With unspeakable loyalty and devotion he served his chief and his country to the end.

As has already been indicated, Seward cheerfully assumed that he was the government, while Lincoln's duties were to consist largely in signing such papers as he instructed him to sign. As difficulties grew fast and thick, he wrote home, 'These cares fall chiefly on me.' Mr Welles wrote that confidence and mutual frankness existed among all the members of the cabinet, 'with the exception of Mr Seward, who had, or affected, a mysterious knowledge which he was not prepared to impart.' He went so far as to meddle with the affairs of his associates. He did not entirely approve of the cabinet meetings and served notice that he would attend only upon special summons of the President.

This condition reached its climax on the first day of April, an appropriate date. Seward addressed on that day a document entitled, 'Some Thoughts for the President's Consideration, April 1, 1861'.

Henry Watterson said that Seward could not have spoken more explicitly and hardly more offensively if he had simply said: 'Mr Lincoln, you are a failure as President, but turn over the direction of affairs exclusively to me, and all shall be well and all be forgiven.' This statement gives a fair and truthful idea of Seward's letter. It is not likely that its amazing assurance has ever been equaled in any nation by 'thoughts' addressed by an inferior officer to his chief. The paper itself is here omitted from lack of space, but its tenor can be guessed from the character of the reply, which is given in full.

Executive Mansion, April 1, 1861
HON. W. H. SEWARD,
MY DEAR SIR: Since parting with you I have been considering your paper dated this day, and entitled 'Some Thoughts for the President's Consideration'. The first proposition in it is, 'First, We are at the end of a month's administration, and yet without a policy either domestic or foreign.'

At the beginning of that month, in the inaugural, I said, 'The power confided to me will be used to hold, occupy, and possess the property and places belonging to the Government, and to collect the duties and imposts.' This had your distinct approval at the time; and, taken in connection with the order I immediately gave General Scott, directing him to employ every means in his power to strengthen and hold the forts, comprises the exact domestic policy you now urge, with the single exception that it does not propose to abandon Fort Sumter.

Again, I do not perceive how the reinforcement of Fort Sumter would be done on a slavery or party issue, while that of Fort Pickens would be on a more national and patriotic one.

The news received yesterday in regard to St Domingo certainly brings a new item within the range of our foreign policy; but up to that time we have been preparing circulars and instructions to ministers and the like, all in perfect harmony, without even a suggestion that we had no foreign policy.'

Upon your closing propositions that 'whatever policy we adopt, there must be an energetic prosecution of it. For this purpose it must be somebody's business to pursue and direct it incessantly. Either the President must do it himself, and be all the while active in it, or devolve it on some member of his cabinet. Once adopted, debates on it must end, and all agree and abide.' I remark that if this must be done, I must do it. When a general line of policy is adopted, I apprehend there is no danger of its being changed without good reason or continuing to be a subject of unnecessary debate; still, upon points arising in its progress I wish, and suppose, I am entitled to have the advice of all the cabinet.

Your ob't serv't,

A. LINCOLN

The courtesy, the convincing logic, the spirit of forbearance shown in this letter, were characteristic of the man at the helm. It need hardly be said that Seward never again tried the experiment of patronizing his chief. He saw a great light. He suddenly realized that these cares did not fall chiefly on him.

So far as is known, neither gentleman ever made any reference to this correspondence. The result was worth while. It bound Seward to his President with hoops of steel. For four long, weary, trying years he served his chief with a loyal devotion which did credit to both men. Thus the hallucination that he was premier was forever dispelled. The *Public Man* wrote: 'There can be no doubt of it any longer. This man from Illinois is not in the hands of Mr Seward.'

There was surely no doubt of it. Lincoln was President. In the councils, the place where Lincoln sat was the head of the table. Seward was his secretary. And a good secretary he was, as well as a true man.

CHAPTER TWENTY-FOUR

Fort Sumter

The events connected with the fall of Fort Sumter were so dramatic that that name is in memory linked with, and stands for, the opening of the war. The fort was not a large military structure. The number of men defending it was not great. But the events connected with it were great. It stood as the representative of great principles and facts. The firing on it marked an epoch in the same sense as Caesar's crossing the Rubicon. It is vitally connected with events that precede and follow.

Wendell Phillips says that when Charles Sumner entered the senate, free speech could hardly be said to exist there. To him, as much as to any man, was due the breaking of the chain that fettered free speech. On all important subjects he spoke his mind eloquently and in words that were not ambiguous. In August, 1852, he made a speech – the more accurate phrase would be, he delivered an oration – under the title, 'Freedom National, Slavery Sectional'. It may easily be guessed that this highly incensed the slave power and the fire-eaters never outgrew their hatred of the Massachusetts senator.

In May, 1856, he delivered an excoriating address upon 'the Crime against Kansas'. This greatly angered the southern congressmen. After the senate had adjourned, Sumner was seated at his desk writing. Preston S. Brooks, of South Carolina, approached from the rear and with a heavy cane began to beat Sumner on the head. He was not only defenseless, but, though a powerful man in body, was to a certain extent held down by his desk, and it was only as he wrenched the desk from the floor that he was able to rise. The beating had been terrible and Sumner suffered from it, often with the most excruciating pains, until the day of his death. This ruffian attack was by a large portion of the North looked on as an exhibition of southern chivalry, so called, and not entirely without reason as the sequel showed. Congress censured Brooks *by a divided vote*. He resigned but was re-elected by his constituents with great enthusiasm. Thus his act was by them adopted as representative of their spirit and temper. This was his 'vindication'.

South Carolina was the first state to secede, and since Fort Sumter commanded Charleston Harbor, it instantly became the focus of national interest. The Secretary of War, Floyd, had so dispersed the little army of the United States that it was impossible to command the few hundred men necessary adequately to garrison the United States forts. As matters in and about Charleston grew threatening, Major Anderson, who was in command of the twin forts, Moultrie and Sumter, decided to abandon the former and do his utmost to defend the latter. The removal was successfully accomplished in the night, and when the fact was discovered it was greeted by the South Carolinians with a howl of baffled wrath. Buchanan had endeavored to send provisions. The steamer, *Star of the West*, had gone there for that purpose, but had been fired on by the South Carolinians and forced to abandon the attempt.

When Lincoln took the government at Washington, it may well be believed that he found matters in a condition decidedly chaotic. His task was many-sided, a greater task than that of Washington as he had justly said. First, of the fifteen slave states seven had seceded. It was his purpose to hold the remaining eight, or as many of them as possible. Of this number, Delaware and Maryland could have been held by force. Kentucky and Missouri, though slave states, remained in the Union. The Union party in Tennessee, under the lead of Andrew Johnson, made a strong fight against secession, but failed to prevent the ordinance.

The next task of Lincoln was to unite the North as far as possible. The difficulty of doing this has already been set forth. On the other hand there was in the North a sentiment that had been overlooked. It was devotion to the flag. Benjamin F. Butler, though an ardent Democrat, had cautioned his southern brethren that while they might count on a large pro-slavery vote in the North, war was a different matter. The moment you fire on the flag, he said, you unite the North; and if war comes, slavery goes.

Not the least task of the President was in dealing with foreign nations. The sympathies of these, especially England and France, were ardently with the South. They would eagerly grasp at the slightest excuse for acknowledging the Southern Confederacy as an independent nation. It was a delicate and difficult matter so to guide affairs that the desired excuse for this could not be found.

The tactics of the southerners were exceedingly exasperating. They kept 'envoys' in Washington to treat with the government. Of course these were not officially received. Lincoln sent them a copy of his inaugural address as containing a sufficient answer to their questions. But they stayed on, trying to spy out the secrets of the government, trying to get some sort of a pledge of conciliation from the administration, or, what would equally serve the purpose, to exasperate the administration into some unguarded word or act. Their attempts were a flat failure.

Lincoln held steadily to the two promises of his inaugural. First, that he would hold the United States forts, and second, that he would not be the aggressor. 'In your hands, my dissatisfied fellow-countrymen, and not in mine, is the momentous issue of civil war. The government will not assail you. You can have no conflict without being yourselves the aggressors. You have no oath registered in heaven to destroy the government; while I have the most solemn one to "preserve, protect, and defend" it.'

To this plan he adhered. It there was to be war it must be begun by the enemies of the country, and the government would patiently bear outrages rather than do a thing which could be tortured into an appearance of 'invading the South' or being an aggressor of any sort.

Meanwhile, Major Anderson was beleaguered in Fort Sumter. He had a handful of men, 76 combatants and 128 all told. He had insufficient ammunition and was nearly out of provisions. Lincoln at last concluded to 'send bread to Sumter' – surely not a hostile act. Owing to complications which he inherited from Buchanan's administration he had given to Governor Pickens, of South Carolina, a promise that he would not attempt to relieve Sumter without first giving him notice. He now sent him notice that there would be an attempt to provision Sumter, peaceably if possible, or otherwise by force.

All this while the southerners were busy perfecting their fortifications, which were now overwhelmingly better, both in number and in completeness of appointment, than the one fort held by the United States that rightfully controlled the entire harbor. General Beauregard was in command of the military forces. He sent to Major Anderson a summons to surrender. The latter replied that if he received from Washington no further direction, and if he was not succored by the 15th of the month, April, he would surrender on honorable terms. It is characteristic of the southern general that he intercepted Major Anderson's mail before notifying him of hostilities. It is characteristic of Lincoln that he sent notice to Governor Pickens of the intended provision of the fort.

On Friday, April 12th, 1861, at 3:30 p.m., General Beauregard gave notice to Major Anderson that he would open fire on Fort Sumter in one hour. Promptly at the minute the first gun was fired and the war had begun. Batteries from various points poured shot and shell into Sumter until nightfall caused a respite.

The little garrison sat up half the night after the attack, as they had done the preceding night, and with their six needles, all they had, made cartridges out of old blankets, old clothing, and whatever else they could lay hands on. These one hundred and twenty-eight men made all the defense that could be made under the circumstances.

The next day the officers' quarters were set on fire either by an exploding shell or by hot shot. The men fought the flames gallantly, but the wind was unfavorable. Then the water tanks were destroyed. As the flames approached the magazine, the powder had to be removed. As the flames approached the places where the powder was newly stored, it had to be thrown into the sea to prevent explosion. In the mean time the stars and stripes were floating gloriously. The flag pole had been struck seven times on Friday. It was struck three times the next day. The tenth shot did the work, the pole broke and the flag fell to the ground at one o'clock Saturday afternoon. An officer and some men seized the flag, rigged up a jury-mast on the parapet, and soon it was flying again.

But ammunition was gone, the fire was not extinguished, and there was no hope of relief. Negotiations were opened and terms of surrender were arranged by eight o'clock that evening. The next day, Sunday, April 14th, the garrison saluted the flag as it was lowered, and then marched out, prisoners of war. Sumter had fallen.

Beauregard was a military man, Lincoln was a statesman. The general got the fort, the President got nearly everything else. The war was on and it had been begun by the South. The administration had not invaded or threatened invasion, but the South had fired on the flag. Dearly they paid for this crime.

The effect of the fall of Sumter was amazing. In the South it was hailed with ecstatic delight, especially in Charleston. There was a popular demonstration at Montgomery, Ala., the provisional seat of the Confederate government. L. P. Walker, Confederate Secretary of War, made a speech and, among other things, said that 'while no man could tell where the war would end, he would prophesy that the flag which now flaunts the breeze here, would float over the dome of the old Capitol at Washington before the end of May,' and that 'it might eventually float over Fanueil Hall itself.' The Confederate government raised a loan of eight millions of dollars and Jefferson Davis issued letters of marque to all persons who might desire to aid the South and at the same time enrich themselves by depredations upon the commerce of the United States.

The effect upon the North was different. There was a perfect storm of indignation against the people who had presumed to fire on the flag. Butler's prediction proved to be nearly correct. This did unite the North in defense of the flag. Butler was a conspicuous example of this effect. Though a Breckinridge Democrat, he promptly offered his services for the defense of the country, and throughout the war he had the distinction of being hated by the South with a more cordial hatred than any other Union general.

It was recollected throughout the North that Lincoln had been conciliatory to a fault towards the South. Conciliation had failed because that was not what the South wanted. They wanted war and by them was war made. This put an end forever to all talk of concession and compromise. Douglas was one of the many whose voice called in trumpet tones to the defense of the flag.

At the date of the fall of Sumter, Lincoln had been in office less than six weeks. In addition to routine work, to attending to extraordinary calls in great numbers, he had accomplished certain very important things: He had the loyal devotion of a cabinet noted for its ability and diversity. He had the enthusiastic confidence of the doubtful minds of the North. He had made it impossible for the European monarchies to recognize the South as a nation. So far as our country was concerned, he might ask for anything, and he would get what he asked. These were no mean achievements. The far-seeing statesman had played for this and had won.

Beauregard got the fort, but Lincoln got the game. In his own words, 'he took *that* trick'.

CHAPTER TWENTY-FIVE

The Outburst of Patriotism

The fall of Sumter caused an outburst of patriotism through the entire North such as is not witnessed many times in a century. On Sunday morning, April 14th, it was known that terms of surrender had been arranged. On that day and on many succeeding Sundays the voices from a thousand pulpits sounded with the certainty of the bugle, the call to the defense of the flag. Editors echoed the call. Such newspapers as were suspected of secession tendencies were compelled to hoist the American flag. For the time at least, enthusiasm and patriotism ran very high. Those who were decidedly in sympathy with the South remained quiet, and those who were of a doubtful mind were swept along with the tide of popular feeling. The flag had been fired on. That one fact unified the North.

On that same evening Senator Douglas arranged for a private interview with President Lincoln. For two hours these men, rivals and antagonists of many years, were in confidential conversation. What passed between them no man knows, but the result of the conference was quickly made public. Douglas came out of the room as determined a 'war Democrat' as could be found between the oceans. He himself prepared a telegram which was everywhere

published, declaring that he would sustain the President in defending the constitution.

Lincoln had prepared his call for 75,000 volunteer troops. Douglas
thought the number should have been 200,000. So it should, and so
doubtless it would, had it not been for certain iniquities of Buchanan's mal-administration. There were no arms, accouterments,
clothing. Floyd had well-nigh stripped the northern arsenals. Lincoln could not begin warlike preparations on any great scale because
that was certain to precipitate the war which he so earnestly strove
to avoid.

Further, the 75,000 was about five times the number of soldiers
then in the army of the United States. Though the number of
volunteers was small, their proportion to the regular army was large.

That night Lincoln's call and Douglas's endorsement were sent
over the wires. Next morning the two documents were published
in every daily paper north of Mason and Dixon's line.

The call for volunteer soldiers was in the South greeted with a
howl of derision. They knew how the arsenals had been stripped.
They had also for years been quietly buying up arms not only from
the North, but also from various European nations. They had for
many years been preparing for just this event, and now that it came
they were fully equipped. During the first months of the war the
administration could not wisely make public how very poorly the
soldiers were armed, for this would only discourage the defenders
of the Union and cheer the enemy.

This call for troops met with prompt response. The various
governors of the northern states offered many times their quota.
The first in the field was Massachusetts. This was due to the
foresight of ex-Governor Banks. He had for years kept the state
militia up to a high degree of efficiency. When rallied upon this he
explained that it was to defend the country against a rebellion of
the slaveholders which was sure to come.

The call for volunteers was published on the morning of April
15th. By ten o'clock the 6th Massachusetts began to rendezvous.
In less than thirty-six hours the regiment was ready and off for
Washington. They were everywhere cheered with much enthusiasm. In New York they were guests of the Astor House, whose
patriotic proprietor would receive no compensation from the
defenders of the flag.

The reception in Baltimore was of a very different sort. Some ruffians of that city had planned to assassinate Lincoln in February, and now they in large numbers prepared to attack the soldiers who were hastening to the defense of the national capital. Here was the first bloodshed of the war. The casualties were four killed and thirty-six wounded. When the regiment reached Washington City, the march from the railway station was very solemn. Behind the marching soldiers followed the stretchers bearing the wounded. The dead had been left behind. Governor Andrew's despatch to Mayor Brown – 'Send them home tenderly' – elicited the sympathy of millions of hearts.

The mayor of Baltimore and the governor of Maryland sent a deputation to Lincoln to ask that no more troops be brought through that city. The President made no promise, but he said he was anxious to avoid all friction and he would do the best he could. He added playfully that if he granted that, they would be back next day to ask that no troops be sent around Baltimore.

That was exactly what occurred. The committee were back the next day protesting against permitting any troops to cross the state of Maryland. Lincoln replied that, as they couldn't march around the state, nor tunnel under it, nor fly over it, he guessed they would have to march across it.

It was arranged that for the time being the troops should be brought to Annapolis and transported thence to Washington by water. This was one of the many remarkable instances of forbearance on the part of the government. There was a great clamor on the part of the North for vengeance upon Baltimore for its crime, and a demand for sterner measures in future. But the President was determined to show all the conciliation it was possible to show, both in this case and in a hundred others.

These actions bore good fruit. It secured to him the confidence of the people to a degree that could not have been foreseen. On the 22nd of July, 1861, Mr Crittenden, of Kentucky, offered the following resolution.

Resolved by the House of Representatives of the United States, That the present deplorable civil war has been forced upon the country by the disunionists of the Southern States, now in arms against the Constitutional Government and in arms around the capital:

That in this national emergency, Congress, banishing all feelings of mere passion or resentment, will recollect only its duty to the whole country;

That this war is not waged on their part in any spirit of oppression, or for any purpose of conquest or subjugation, or purpose of over-throwing or interfering with the rights or established institutions of those states, but to defend and maintain the *supremacy* of the Constitution, and to preserve the Union with all the dignity, equality, and rights of the several states unimpaired; and that, as soon as these objects are accomplished, the war ought to cease.

This resolution was passed with only two dissenting votes. Lincoln's patience, forbearance, conciliation had accomplished this marvel.

Very early in the war the question of slavery confronted the generals. In the month of May, only about two months after the inauguration, Generals Butler and McClellan confronted the subject, and their methods of dealing with it were as widely different as well could be. When Butler was in charge of Fortress Monroe three negroes fled to that place for refuge. They said that Colonel Mallory had set them to work upon the rebel fortifications. A flag of truce was sent in from the rebel lines demanding the return of the negroes. Butler replied: 'I shall retain the negroes as *contraband of war*. You were using them upon your batteries; it is merely a question whether they shall be used for or against us.' From that time the word *contraband* was used in common speech to indicate an escaped slave.

It was on the 26th day of the same month that McClellan issued to the slaveholders a proclamation in which are found these words: 'Not only will we abstain from all interference with your slaves, but we will, on the contrary, with an iron hand crush any attempt at insurrection on their part.' It is plain that McClellan's 'we' did not include his brother-general at Fortress Monroe. Further comment on his attitude is reserved to a later chapter.

The early victims of the war caused deep and profound sympathy. The country was not yet used to carnage. The expectancy of a people not experienced in war was at high tension, and these deaths, which would at any time have produced a profound impression, were emphatically impressive at that time.

One of the very first martyrs of the war was Elmer E. Ellsworth. He was young, handsome, impetuous. At Chicago he had organized among the firemen a company of Zouaves with their spectacular dress and drill. These Zouaves had been giving exhibition drills in many northern cities and aroused no little interest. One result was the formation of similar companies at various places. The fascinating Zouave drill became quite popular.

In 1861 Ellsworth was employed in the office of Lincoln and Herndon in Springfield. When the President-elect journeyed to Washington Ellsworth, to whom Lincoln was deeply attached, made one of the party. At the outbreak of hostilities he was commissioned as colonel to raise a regiment in New York. On the south bank of the Potomac, directly opposite Washington, was Alexandria. The keeper of the Mansion House, in that place, had run up a secession flag on the mast at the top of the hotel. This flag floated day after day in full sight of Lincoln and Ellsworth and the others.

Ellsworth led an advance upon Alexandria on the evening of May 23rd. The rebels escaped. The next morning as usual, the secession flag floated tauntingly from the Mansion House. Ellsworth's blood was up and he resolved to take down that flag and hoist the stars and stripes with his own hand. Taking with him two soldiers he accomplished his purpose.

Returning by a spiral stairway, he carried the rebel flag in his hand. The proprietor of the hotel came out from a place of concealment, placed his double-barreled shot-gun nearly against Ellsworth's body and fired. The assassin was instantly shot down by private Brownell, but Ellsworth was dead. The rebel flag was dyed in the blood of his heart. Underneath his uniform was found a gold medal with the inscription, *non solum nobis, sed pro patria* – 'not for ourselves only but for our country'.

The body was removed to Washington City, where it lay in state in the East room until burial. The President, amid all the cares of that busy period, found time to sit many hours beside the body of his friend, and at the burial he appeared as chief mourner.

This murder fired the northern imagination to a degree. The picture of Ellsworth's handsome face was everywhere familiar. It is an easy guess that hundreds, not to say thousands, of babies were named for him within the next few months, and to this day the name Elmer, starting from him, has not ceased to be a favorite.

A little more than two weeks later, on the 10th of June, the first real battle of the war was fought. This was at Big Bethel, Va., near Fortress Monroe. The loss was not great as compared with later battles, being only eighteen killed and fifty-three wounded. But among the killed was Major Theodore Winthrop, a young man barely thirty-three years of age. He was the author of several successful books, and gave promise of a brilliant literary career. He was a true patriot and a gallant soldier. His death was the source of sorrow and anger to many thousands of readers of *Cecil Dreeme*.

It was two months later that General Lyon fell at Wilson's Creek, Mo. He had been conspicuous for his services to the country before this time. The battle was bitterly contested, and Lyon showed himself a veritable hero in personal courage and gallantry. After three wounds he was still fighting on, leading personally a bayonet charge when he was shot for the fourth time, fell from his horse, and died immediately. It was the gallant death of a brave soldier, that touches the heart and fires the imagination.

These deaths, and such as these, occurring at the beginning of the war, taught the country the painful truth that the cost of war is deeper than can possibly be reckoned. The dollars of money expended, and the lists of the numbers killed, wounded, and missing, do not fully express the profound sorrow, the irreparable loss.

CHAPTER TWENTY-SIX
The War Here to Stay

Lincoln was a man of great sagacity. Few statesmen have had keener insight, or more true and sane foresight. While cordially recognizing this, it is not necessary to claim for him infallibility. He had his disappointments.

The morning after the evacuation of Fort Sumter he issued his call for 75,000 volunteers to serve for three months. We have seen that one reason why the number was so small was that this was the largest number that could possibly be clothed, armed, and officered at short notice. Subsequent experience showed that the brief enlistment of three months was an utterly inadequate period for so serious an insurrection. Did Lincoln really think the rebellion could be put down in three months? Why did he not save infinite trouble by calling for five-year enlistments at the beginning?

For one thing, he had at that time no legal power to call for a longer period of enlistment. Then he desired to continue the conciliatory policy as long as possible, so as to avoid alienating the undecided in both the North and the South. Had the first call been for 500,000 for three years, it would have looked as if he intended and desired a long and bloody war, and this would have antagonized large numbers of persons. But it is probable that neither he nor the community at large suspected the seriousness of the war. The wars in which the men then living had had experience were very slight. In comparison with what followed, they were mere skirmishes. How should they foresee that they were standing on the brink of one of the longest, the costliest, the bloodiest, and the most eventful wars of all history?

Virginia was dragooned into secession. She declined to participate in the Charleston Convention. Though a slave state, the public feeling was by a decided majority in favor of remaining in the Union. But after the fall of Sumter she was manipulated by skilful politicians, appealed to and cajoled on the side of prejudice and sectional feeling, and on April 17th passed the ordinance of secession. It was a blunder and a more costly blunder she could not have made. For four years her soil was the theater of a bitterly contested war, and her beautiful valleys were drenched with human blood.

Back and forth, over and over again, fought the two armies, literally sweeping the face of the country with the besom of destruction. The oldest of her soldiers of legal age were fifty-five years of age when the war closed. The youngest were twelve years of age when the war opened. Older men and younger boys were in the war, ay, and were killed on the field of battle. As the scourge of war passed over that state from south to north, from north to south, for four years, many an ancient and proud family was simply exterminated, root and branch. Of some of the noblest and best families, there is today not a trace and scarcely a memory.

All this could not have been foreseen by these Virginians, nor by the people of the North, nor by the clear-eyed President himself. Even the most cautious and conservative thought the war would be of brief duration. They were soon to receive a rude shock and learn that 'war is hell', and that *this* war was here to stay. This revelation came with the first great battle of the war, which was fought July 21, 1861, at Bull Run, a location not more than twenty-five or thirty miles from Washington.

Certain disabilities of our soldiers should be borne in mind. Most of them were fresh from farm, factory, or store, and had no military training even in the militia. A large number were just reaching the expiration of their term of enlistment and were homesick and eager to get out of the service. The generals were not accustomed to handling large bodies of men. To add to the difficulty, the officers and men were entirely unacquainted with one another. Nevertheless most of them were ambitious to see a little of real war before they went back to the industries of peace. They saw far more than they desired.

It was supposed by the administration and its friends that one crushing blow would destroy the insurrection, and that this blow was to be dealt in this coming battle. The troops went to the front as to a picnic. The people who thronged Washington, politicians, merchants, students, professional men, and ladies as well, had the same eagerness to see a battle that in later days they have to witness a regatta or a game of football. The civilians, men and women, followed the army in large numbers. They saw all they looked for and more.

The battle was carefully planned, and except for delay in getting started, it was fought out very much as planned. It is not the scope of this book to enter into the details of this or any battle. But thus much may be said in a general way. The Confederates were all the day receiving a steady stream of fresh reinforcements. The Federals, on the other hand, had been on their feet since two o'clock in the morning. By three o'clock in the afternoon, after eleven hours of activity and five hours of fighting in the heat of a July day in Virginia, these men were tired, thirsty, hungry – worn out. Then came the disastrous panic and the demoralization. A large portion of the army started in a race for Washington, the civilians in the lead.

The disaster was terrible, but there is nothing to gain by magnifying it. Some of the oldest and best armies in the world have been broken into confusion quite as badly as this army of raw recruits. They did not so far lose heart that they were not able to make a gallant stand at Centerville and successfully check the pursuit of the enemy. It was said that Washington was at the mercy of the Confederates, but it is more likely that they had so felt the valor of the foe that they were unfit to pursue the retreating army. It was a hard battle on both sides. No one ever accused the Confederates of cowardice, and they surely wanted to capture Washington City. That they did not do so is ample proof that the battle was not a picnic to them. It had been boasted that one southern man could whip five northern men. This catchy phrase fell into disuse.

It was natural and politic for the Confederates to magnify their victory. This was done without stint by Jeff Davis who was present as a spectator. He telegraphed the following.

Night has closed upon a hard-fought field. Our forces were victorious. The enemy was routed and fled precipitately, abandoning a large amount of arms, ammunition, knapsacks, and baggage. The ground was strewed for miles with those killed, and the farmhouses and the ground around were filled with wounded. Our force was fifteen thousand; that of the enemy estimated at thirty-five thousand.

That account is sufficiently accurate except as to figures. Jeff Davis never could be trusted in such circumstances to give figures with any approach to accuracy. Lossing estimates that the Federal forces were 13,000, and the Confederates about 27,000. This is certainly nearer the truth than the boast of Jeff Davis. But a fact not less important than the numbers was that the Confederate reinforcements were fresh, while the Federal forces were nearly exhausted from marching half the night before the fighting began.

Although the victorious forces were effectively checked at Centerville, those who fled in absolute rout and uncontrollable panic were enough to give the occasion a lasting place in history. The citizens who had gone to see the battle had not enjoyed their trip. The soldiers who had thought that this war was a sort of picnic had learned that the foe was formidable. The administration that had expected to crush the insurrection by one decisive blow became vaguely conscious of the fact that the war was here to stay months and years.

It is a curious trait of human nature that people are not willing to accept a defeat simply. The mind insists on explaining the particular causes of that specific defeat. Amusing instances of this are seen in all games: football, regattas, oratorical contests. Also in elections; the defeated have a dozen reasons to explain why the favorite candidate was not elected as he should have been. This trait came out somewhat clamorously after the battle of Bull Run. A large number of plausible explanations were urged on Mr Lincoln, who finally brought the subject to a conclusion by the remark: 'I see. We whipped the enemy and then ran away from him!'

The effect of the battle of Bull Run on the South was greatly to encourage them and add to their enthusiasm. The effect on the North was to deepen their determination to save the flag, to open their eyes to the fact that the southern power was strong, and with renewed zeal and determination they girded themselves for the conflict. But the great burden fell on Lincoln. He was disappointed that the insurrection was not and could not be crushed by one decisive blow. There was need of more time, more men, more money, more blood. These thoughts and the relative duties were to him, with his peculiar temperament, a severer trial than they could have been to perhaps any other man living. He would not shrink from doing his full duty, though it was so hard.

It made an old man of him. The night before he decided to send bread to Sumter he slept not a wink. That was one of very many nights when he did not sleep, and there were many mornings when he tasted no food. But weak, fasting, worn, aging as he was, he was always at his post of duty. The most casual observer could see the inroads which these mental cares made upon his giant body. It was about a year later than this that an old neighbor and friend, Noah Brooks of Chicago, went to Washington to live, and he has vividly described the change in the appearance of the President. In *Harper's Monthly* for July, 1865, he writes:

Though the intellectual man had greatly grown meantime, few persons would recognize the hearty, blithesome, genial, and wiry Abraham Lincoln of earlier days in the sixteenth President of the United States, with his stooping figure, dull eyes, careworn face, and languid frame. The old clear laugh never came back; the even temper was sometimes disturbed; and his natural charity for all was often turned into unwonted suspicion of the motives of men, whose selfishness caused him so much wear of mind.'

Again, the same writer said in *Scribner's Monthly* for February, 1878:

There was [in 1862] over his face an expression of sadness, and a faraway look in the eyes, which were utterly unlike the Lincoln of other days. . . . I confess that I was so pained that I could almost have shed tears. . . . By and by, when I knew him better, his face was often full of mirth and enjoyment; and even when he was pensive or gloomy, his features were lighted up very much as a clouded alabaster vase might be softly illuminated by a light within.

He still used his epigram and was still reminded of 'a little story', when he wished to point a moral or adorn a tale. But they were superficial indeed who thought they saw in him only, or chiefly, the jester. Once when he was reproved for reading from a humorous book he said with passionate earnestness that the humor was his safety valve. If it were not for the relief he would die. It was true. But he lived on, not because he wanted to live, for he would rather have died. But it was God's will, and his country needed him.

CHAPTER TWENTY-SEVEN

The Darkest Hour of the War

There were so many dark hours in that war, and those hours were so dark, that it is difficult to specify one as the darkest hour. Perhaps a dozen observers would mention a dozen different times. But Lincoln himself spoke of the complication known as the Trent affair as the darkest hour. From his standpoint it was surely so. It was so because he felt the ground of public confidence slipping out from under him as at no other time. The majority of the North were with him in sentiment for the most part. A goodly number were with him all the time – except this. This time, Charles

Sumner, the Chairman of the Senate Committee on Foreign Relations, was in agreement with him, but beyond that, everybody was against him, North and South, and all Europe as well. Upon him fell the task of turning the very turbulent current of public sentiment into the channel of duty and wisdom.

The facts of the affair were simple. Two men, Mason and Slidell, both ex-senators of the United States, had started, with their secretaries and families, to England and France as emissaries of the Confederate government. These countries had already recognized the Confederates as belligerents, and the mission of these men was to secure the recognition of the Confederate government as a nation. They succeeded in running the blockade at Charleston and put in at Havana. There they were received with much ostentation. They took passage on the British mail steamer *Trent* to St Thomas, intending to take the packet thence to England.

Captain Wilkes, commanding a war vessel of the United States, was in the neighborhood and learned of these proceedings and plans. He stopped the British vessel on the high seas and by force took the two men and their secretaries. They were confined in Fort Warren, Boston Harbor.

This capture set the entire North ablaze with enthusiasm. Seward was in favor of it. Stanton, who a few weeks later was appointed Secretary of War, applauded the act. Welles, Secretary of the Navy, wrote a congratulatory letter upon the 'great public service'. The people of Boston tendered a banquet to the hero of the hour. When Congress assembled about a month later, it gave him a vote of thanks. This wave of public enthusiasm swept the country from ocean to ocean. The southern sympathies of England and France had been so pronounced that this whole country seemed to unite in hilarious triumph over this capture, and regarded it as a slap in the face to England's pride. The fact that the complications threatened war with that nation only added fuel to the flames.

The excitement ran highest among the soldiers. Camp life had become monotonous, no decisive victories had raised their courage and enthusiasm. They were tired. They were exasperated with England's policy. They wanted to fight England.

The feeling upon the other side of the question ran equally high in the South, in England, and in France. As soon as the matter could receive official attention, the British minister at Washington was instructed to demand the instant release of the four men with a suitable apology. He was to wait seven days for an answer, and if the demand was not met by that time, he was to break off diplomatic relations with the United States. This of course meant war.

Sumner seems to have been the only other one who said, 'We shall have to give them up.' Lincoln, when he heard of the capture, declared that they would prove to be white elephants on our hands. 'We shall have to give them up,' he too said. But the difficulty was to lead the excited nation to see the need of this as he saw it. He declared that 'we fought Great Britain for doing just what Captain Wilkes has done. If Great Britain protests against this act and demands their release, we must adhere to our principles of 1812. We must give up these prisoners. Besides, one war at a time.' He again said that it was 'the bitterest pill he ever swallowed. But England's triumph will not last long. After this war is over we shall call her to account for the damage she has done us in our hour of trouble.'

The policy of the government with regard to this matter was not settled in the cabinet meeting until the day after Christmas. Public enthusiasm by that time had had six weeks in which to cool down. In that time the sober second judgment had illuminated many minds, and the general public was ready to see and hear reason. The outline of the reply of the United States was directed by Lincoln, but he instructed Seward to choose his own method of arguing the case. The reply was set forth in a very able and convincing paper. It reaffirmed our adhesion to the doctrine of 1812, said that Captain Wilkes had not done in an orderly way that which he did, promised that the prisoners would be cheerfully set at liberty, but declined to make any apology.

At this late date we are able to look somewhat behind the scenes, and we now know that the Queen and the Prince Consort were very deeply concerned over the possibility of a war with us. They had only the kindest feelings for us, and just then they felt especially grateful for the many courtesies which had been shown to the Prince of Wales upon his recent visit to this country. They were glad to get through with the incident peaceably and pleasantly.

Seward's reply was accepted as fully satisfactory. The English concurred, the Americans concurred, and the danger was over. There was then something of a revulsion of feeling. The feeling between our government and that of England was more cordial than before, and the same is true of the feeling between the two peoples. The South and their sympathizers were bitterly disappointed. The wise management of our President had turned one of the greatest dangers into a most valuable success. There was never again a likelihood that England would form an alliance with the Southern Confederacy.

The result was most fortunate for us and unfortunate for the southern emissaries. They were no longer heroes, they were 'gentlemen of eminence', but not public functionaries. They were like other travelers, nothing more. They were not received at either court. They could only 'linger around the back doors' of the courts where they expected to be received in triumph, and bear as best they could the studied neglect with which they were treated. The affair, so ominous at one time, became most useful in its practical results to our cause. Lord Palmerston, the British premier, got the four prisoners, but Lincoln won the game.

This is a convenient place to speak of the personal griefs of the President. From his earliest years on, he was wonderfully affected by the presence of death. Very few people have had this peculiar feeling of heart-break with such overwhelming power. The death of his infant brother in Kentucky, the death of his mother in Indiana, impressed him and clouded his mind in a degree entirely unusual. We have seen that in Springfield the death of Ann Rutledge wellnigh unseated his reason. From these he never recovered.

The horror of war was that it meant death, death, death! He, whose heart was tender to a fault, was literally surrounded by death. The first victim of the war, Colonel Ellsworth, was a personal friend, and his murder was a personal affliction. There were others that came near to him. Colonel E. D. Baker, an old friend and neighbor of Lincoln, the man who had introduced him at his inaugural, was killed at Ball's Bluff October 21, 1861. Baker's personal courage made him conspicuous and marked him out as a special target for the enemy's aim. While gallantly leading a charge, he fell, pierced almost simultaneously by four bullets. It fell upon Lincoln like the death of a brother. He was consumed with grief.

The following February his two boys, Willie and Tad, were taken ill. Lincoln's fondness for children was well known. This general love of children was a passion in regard to his own sons. In this sickness he not only shared the duties of night-watching with the nurse, but at frequent intervals he would slip away from callers, and even from cabinet meetings, to visit briefly the little sufferers. Willie died on February 20th, and for several days before his death he was delirious. His father was with him almost constantly.

This is one of the few instances when he could be said to neglect public business. For a few days before, and for a longer period after, Willie's death, he was completely dejected. Though he was a devout Christian, in spirit and temper, his ideas of personal immortality were not at that time sufficiently clear to give him the sustaining help which he needed under his affliction.

J. G. Holland records a pathetic scene. This was communicated to him by a lady whose name is not given. She had gone to Washington to persuade the President to have hospitals for our soldiers located in the North. He was skeptical of the plan and was slow to approve it. His hesitation was the occasion of much anxiety to her. When he finally granted the petition, she thanked him with great earnestness and said she was sure he would be happy that he had done it. He sat with his face in his hands and groaned: 'Happy? I shall never be happy again!'

Below all his play of wit and humor, there was an undercurrent of agony. So great were his kindness, gentleness, tenderness of heart, that he could not live in this cruel world, especially in the period when the times were so much out of joint, without being a man of sorrows. The present writer never saw Lincoln's face but twice, once in life and once in death. Both times it seemed to him, and as he remembers it after the lapse of more than a third of a century, it still seems to him, the saddest face his eyes have ever looked upon.

CHAPTER TWENTY-EIGHT

Lincoln and Fremont

In a community like that of the United States, where free press and free speech prevail, where every native-born boy is a possible President, some undesirable results are inevitable. The successful men become egotistic, and it is a common, well-nigh universal, practise for all sorts and conditions of men to speak harshly of the authorities. In the loafers on the street corners, in the illiterate that use the country store as their club, in the very halls of Congress, are heard the most unsparing criticisms and denunciations of the administration. These unwarranted comments fell thick and fast on Lincoln, because he was at the post of responsibility in a critical period, a time of general unrest. Self-appointed committees of business men, politicians, clergymen, editors, and what not, were continually telling him what to do and how to do it. Not a few of even the generals caught the infection.

It is not possible nor desirable to tell of Lincoln's relations with many of the eminent men with whom he dealt. But a few will be selected – Fremont, McClellan, Greeley, and Grant – in order to explain some of the difficulties which were continually rising up before him, and by showing how he dealt with them to illustrate certain phases of his character. This chapter will treat of Fremont.

At the outbreak of the war he was the most conspicuous military man in the North. He had earned the gratitude of the country for distinguished services in California, and he was deservedly popular among the Republicans for his leadership of the party in 1856. He was at the best period of life, being forty-eight years of age. His abilities were marked, and he possessed in an unusual degree the soldierly quality of inspiring enthusiasm. If he could turn all his powers into the channel of military efficiency, he would be the man of the age. He had the public confidence, and he had such an opportunity as comes to few men.

At the opening of the war he was in Paris and was at once summoned home. He arrived in this country about the first of July and was by the President appointed Major-General in the regular army. On the 3rd of July he was assigned to the Western department with headquarters at St Louis. This department included the state of Illinois and extended as far west as the Rocky Mountains.

At that time the condition of affairs in Missouri was distressful and extremely threatening. The state of Missouri covers a very large territory, 69,415 square miles, and it was imperfectly provided with railroads and other means of communication. Private bands of marauders and plunderers were numerous and did a great amount of damage among law-abiding citizens.

There were also several insurgent armies of no mean dimensions
threatening the state from the south-west. There were good
soldiers and officers there in defense of the Union, but they were
untried, insufficiently armed and accoutered, unprovided with
means of transportation, and, above all, they were in need of a
commanding general of sagacity, daring, and personal resources.
Fremont seemed to be just the man for the important post at that
critical hour.

Generals Lyon, Hunter, and others, were sore pressed in Missouri. They needed the presence of their commander and they
needed him at once. Fremont was ordered to proceed to his post
immediately. This order he did not obey. He could never brook
authority, and he was not in the habit of rendering good reasons
for his acts of disobedience. Though he was aware that the need of
his presence was urgent, he dallied about Washington a long time
and then proceeded west with leisure, arriving in St Louis nearly
three weeks later than he should have done. These three weeks
were under the circumstances time enough for an incalculable
amount of damage, enough to make all the difference between
success and failure. It was long enough to insure the death (on
August 10th) of that brave soldier, General Lyon, and long enough
to account for many other disasters.

One of the most annoying things with which the subordinate
generals had to contend, was that about this time the term of
service of the men who had enlisted for three months was beginning to expire. Many of these re-enlisted, and many did not. It was
not possible to plan an expedition of any sort when it was probable
that a large portion of the command would be out of service
before it was completed. There was need of a master hand at
organizing and inspiring loyalty.

Though Fremont had so unaccountably delayed, yet when he
came he was received with confidence and enthusiasm. Lincoln
gave to him, as he did to all his generals, very nearly a *carte blanche*.
His instructions were general, and the commander was left to
work out the details in his own way. All that he required was that
something should be done successfully in the prosecution of the
war. The country was not a judge of military plans; it was a judge
of military success and failure. They expected, and they had a
right to expect, that Fremont should do something more than

keep up a dress parade. Lincoln laid on him this responsibility in perfect confidence.

The first thing Fremont accomplished in Missouri was to quarrel with his best friends, the Blair family. This is important chiefly as a thermometer – it indicated his inability to hold the confidence of intelligent and influential men after he had it. About this time Lincoln wrote to General Hunter a personal letter which showed well how things were likely to go –

> MY DEAR SIR: General Fremont needs assistance which it is difficult to give him. He is losing the confidence of men near him, whose support any man in his position must have to be successful. His cardinal mistake is that he isolates himself and allows no one to see him; and by which he does not know what is going on in the very matter he is dealing with. He needs to have by his side a man of large experience. Will you not, for me, take that place?

It was Louis XV who exclaimed, '*L'etat? C'est moi!*' 'The state? *I'm* the state!' The next move of Fremont can be compared only with that spirit of the French emperor. It was no less than a proclamation of emancipation. This was a civic act, while Fremont was an officer of military, not civil, authority. The act was unauthorized, the President was not even consulted. Even had it been a wise move, Fremont would have been without justification because it was entirely outside of his prerogatives. Even had he been the wisest man, he was not an autocrat and could not have thus transcended his powers.

But this act was calculated to do much mischief. The duty of the hour was to save the Union. Fremont's part in that duty was to drive the rebels out of Missouri. Missouri was a slave state. It had not seceded, and it was important that it should not do so. The same was true of Kentucky and Maryland. It is easy to see, upon reading Fremont's proclamation, that it is the work not of a soldier, but of a politician, and a bungling politician at that.

When this came to the knowledge of the President he took prompt measures to counteract it in a way that would accomplish the greatest good with the least harm. He wrote to the general:

> Allow me, therefore, to ask that you will, as of your own motion, modify that paragraph so as to conform to the first and fourth

sections of the act of Congress entitled, 'An act to confiscate property used for insurrectionary purposes', approved August 6, 1861,
and a copy of which act I herewith send you. This letter is written
in a spirit of caution, and not of censure.

But Fremont was willing to override both President and Congress, and declined to make the necessary modifications. This
placed him, with such influence as he had, in direct antagonism to
the administration. That which ought to have been done by
Fremont had to be done by Lincoln, upon whom was thrown the
onus of whatever was objectionable in the matter. It did give him
trouble. It alienated many of the extreme abolitionists, including
even his old neighbor and friend, Oscar H. Browning. They
seemed to think that Lincoln was now championing slavery. His
enemies needed no alienation, but they made adroit use of this to
stir up and increase discontent.

So matters grew no better with Fremont, but much worse for
three months. The words of Nicolay and Hay are none too strong:
'He had frittered away his opportunity for usefulness and fame;
such an opportunity, indeed, as rarely comes.'

On October 21st, the President sent by special messenger the
following letter to General Curtis at St Louis:

DEAR SIR: On receipt of this, with the accompanying enclosures,
you will take safe, certain, and suitable measures to have the
inclosure addressed to Major-General Fremont delivered to him
with all reasonable despatch, subject to these conditions only, that
if, when General Fremont shall be reached by the messenger –
yourself or anyone sent by you – he shall then have, in personal
command, fought and won a battle, or shall then be in the immediate presence of the enemy in expectation of a battle, it is not to be
delivered but held for further orders.

The inclosure mentioned was an order relieving General Fremont and placing Hunter temporarily in command. It is plain that
the President expected that there would be difficulties, in the way
of delivering the order – that Fremont himself might prevent its
delivery. General Curtis, who undertook its delivery, evidently
expected the same thing, for he employed three different messen-
gers who took three separate methods of trying to reach Fremont.

The one who succeeded in delivering the order did so only because of his successful disguise, and when it was accomplished Fremont's words and manner showed that he had expected to head off any such order. This incident reveals the peril which would have fallen to American institutions had he been more successful in his aspirations to the presidency.

Fremont had one more chance. He was placed in command of a corps in Virginia. There he disobeyed orders in a most atrocious manner, and by so doing permitted Jackson and his army to escape. He was superseded by Pope, but declining to serve under a junior officer, resigned. And that was the end of Fremont as a public man. The fact that he had ceased to be a force in American life was emphasized in 1864. The extreme abolitionists nominated him as candidate for the presidency in opposition to Lincoln. But his following was so slight that he withdrew from the race and retired permanently to private life.

Yet he was a man of splendid abilities of a certain sort. Had he practised guerrilla warfare, had he had absolute and irresponsible command of a small body of picked men with freedom to raid or do anything else he pleased, he would have been indeed formidable. The terror which the rebel guerrilla general, Morgan, spread over wide territory would easily have been surpassed by Fremont. But guerrilla warfare was not permissible on the side of the government. The aim of the Confederates was destruction; the aim of the administration was construction. It is always easier and more spectacular to destroy than to construct.

One trouble with Fremont was his narrowness of view. He could not work with others. If he wanted a thing in his particular department, it did not concern him that it might injure the cause as a whole. Another trouble was his conceit. He wanted to be 'the whole thing', President, Congress, general, and judiciary. Had Lincoln not possessed the patience of Job, he could not have borne with him even so long. The kindness of the President's letter, above quoted, is eloquent testimony to his magnanimity.

CHAPTER TWENTY-NINE
Lincoln and McClellan

McClellan was a very different man from Fremont. Though he was as nearly as possible opposite in his characteristics, still it was not easier to get along with him. He was a man of brilliant talents, fine culture, and charming personality. Graduating from West Point in 1846, he went almost immediately into the Mexican War, where he earned his captaincy. He later wrote a manual of arms for use in the United States army. He visited Europe as a member of the commission of officers to gather military information.

His greatest genius was in engineering, a line in which he had no superior. He went to Illinois in 1857 as chief engineer of the Central Railroad, the following year he became vice-president, and the year after that president of the St Louis and Cincinnati Railway. At the outbreak of the war this captain was by the governor of Ohio commissioned as major-general, and a few days later he received from Lincoln the commission of major-general in the United States army.

He was sent to West Virginia with orders to drive out the rebels. This he achieved in a brief time, and for it he received the thanks of Congress. He was, after the disaster at Bull Run, called to Washington and placed in command of that portion of the Army of the Potomac whose specific duty was the defense of the capital. He was rapidly promoted from one position to another until age and infirmity compelled the retirement of that grand old warrior, Winfield Scott, whereupon he was made general-in-chief of the United States army. All this occurred in less than four months. Four months ago, this young man of thirty-five years was an ex-captain. Today he is general-in-chief, not of the largest army, but probably of the most intelligent army, the world has ever seen. He would be almost more than human if such a sudden turn of the wheel of fortune did not also turn his head.

It was Lincoln's habit to let his generals do their work in their own ways, only insisting that they should accomplish visible and tangible results. This method he followed with McClellan, developing it with great patience under trying circumstances. On this point there is no better witness than McClellan himself. To his wife he wrote, 'They give me my way in everything, full swing and unbounded confidence.' Later he expressed contempt for the President who 'showed him too much deference'. He was a universal favorite, he became known as 'the young Napoleon', he had the confidence of the country and the loyal devotion of the army, and the unqualified support of the administration. Of him great things were expected, and reasonably so. In the power of inspiring confidence and enthusiasm he was second only to Napoleon.

As an organizer and drill-master he was superb. The army after Bull Run was as demoralized as an army could be. The recruits soon began to arrive from the North, every day bringing thousands of such into Washington. These required care and they must be put into shape for effective service. This difficult task he accomplished in a way that fully met the public expectation and reflected great credit upon himself.

In defense he was a terrible fighter. That is to say, when he fought at all – for he fought only in defense – he fought well. A distinguished Confederate soldier said, 'There was no Union general whom we so much dreaded as McClellan. He had, as we thought, no equal.' And they declared they could always tell when McClellan was in command by the way the men fought.

An illustrious comment on this is the splendid fighting at Antietam. That was one of the greatest battles and one of the most magnificent victories of the war. It showed McClellan at his best.

We know what the Army of the Potomac was previous to the accession of McClellan. Let us see what it was after his removal. 'McClellan was retired,' says the Honorable Hugh McCulloch, 'and what happened to the Army of the Potomac? Terrible slaughter under Burnside at Fredericksburg; crushing defeat at Chancellorsville under Hooker.' All this shows that McClellan narrowly missed the fame of being one of the greatest generals in history. But let us glance at another page in the ledger.

His first act, when in command at Cincinnati, was to enter into an agreement with General Buckner that the state of Kentucky should be treated as neutral territory. That agreement put that state into the position of a foreign country, like England or China, when the very purpose of the war was to insist that the United

States was one nation. This act was a usurpation of authority, and further, it was diametrically wrong even had he possessed the authority.

His next notable act, one which has already been mentioned, was to issue a proclamation in defense of slavery, promising to assist the rebels to put down any attempt at insurrection by the slaves. This was wrong. His duty was to conquer the enemy. It was no more his duty to defend slavery than it was Fremont's to emancipate the slaves.

The next development of McClellan was the hallucination, from which he never freed himself, that the enemy's numbers were from five to ten times as great as they really were. 'I am here,' he wrote August 16, 1861, 'in a terrible place; the enemy have from three to four times my force. The President, the old general, cannot or will not see the true state of affairs.' At that time the 'true state of affairs' was that the enemy had from one-third to one-half his force. That is a fair specimen of the exaggeration of his fears. That is, McClellan's estimate was from six to twelve times too much.

At Yorktown he faced the Confederate Magruder, who commanded 11,000 all told. Of this number, 6,000 were spread along a line of thirteen miles of defense across the peninsula, leaving 5,000 for battle. McClellan's imagination, or fears, magnified this into an enormous army. With his 58,000 effective troops he industriously prepared for defense, and when the engineering work was accomplished thought he had done a great act in defending his army. All the while he was calling lustily for reinforcements from Washington. When Magruder was ready he retired with his little army and McClellan's opportunity was gone.

At Antietam he won a brilliant victory, but he failed to follow it up. There was a chance to annihilate the Confederate army and end the war. To do that was nearly as important as it had been to win the victory. To be sure his troops were worn, but as compared with the shattered condition of the enemy, his army was ready for dress parade. So the enemy was allowed to cross the Potomac at leisure, reform, reorganize, and the war was needlessly prolonged. It was this neglect which, more than any other one thing, undermined the general confidence in McClellan.

Later, at second Bull Run he left Pope to suffer. It was clearly his duty to reinforce Pope, but he only said that Pope had got himself into the fix and he must get out as he could. He seemed to forget that there never was a time when he was not calling for reinforcements himself. This wanton neglect was unsoldierly, inhuman. He also forgot that this method of punishing Pope inflicted severe punishment on the nation.

His chronic call for reinforcements, were it not so serious, would make the motive of a comic opera. When he was in Washington, he wanted all the troops called in for the defense of the city. When he was in Virginia, he thought the troops which were left for the defense of the city ought to be sent to reinforce him – the city was safe enough! He telegraphed to Governor Denison of Ohio to pay no attention to Rosecrans' request for troops. He thought that 20,000, with what could be raised in Kentucky and Tennessee, was enough for the Mississippi Valley, while he needed 273,000. When he was insisting that Washington should be stripped in order to furnish him with 50,000 additional men, the President asked what had become of his more than 160,000; and in his detailed reply he gave the item of 38,500 absent on leave. Here was nearly the number of 50,000 which he asked for, if he would only call them in.

Incidentally to all this were persistent discourtesies to the President. He would sit silent in the cabinet meetings pretending to have secrets of great importance. Instead of calling on the President to report, he made it necessary for the President to call on him. At other times he would keep the President waiting while he affected to be busy with subordinates. Once indeed he left the President waiting while he went to bed. All this Lincoln bore with his accustomed patience. He playfully said, when remonstrated with, that he would gladly hold McClellan's horse if he would only win the battles. This he failed to do. And when he was finally relieved, he had worn out the patience not only of the President, but of his army, and of the entire country. One writer of the day said with much bitterness, but with substantial truth, that 'McClellan, with greater means at his command than Alexander, Caesar, Napoleon, or Wellington, has lost more men and means in his disasters than they in their victories.'

What were the defects of this remarkable man? In the first place, he believed in slavery. At this late day it is difficult to realize the devotion which some men had for slavery as a 'divine institution', before which they could kneel down and pray, as if it was the very ark of God. McClellan was one such. And it is not improbable that he early had more than a suspicion that slavery was the real cause of all the trouble. This would in part account for his hesitation.

Then there was a bitter personal hatred between him and Stanton. This led him to resent all suggestions and orders emanating from the War Department. It also made him suspicious of Stanton's associates, including the President.

Then he seemed to lack the nerve for a pitched battle. He could do everything up to the point of action, but he could not act. This lack of nerve is a more common fact in men in all walks of life than is usually recognized. He was unconquerable in defense, he did not know the word *aggressive*. Had he possessed some of the nerve of Sheridan, Hooker, Sherman, or any one of a hundred others, he would have been one of the four great generals of history. But he could not be persuaded or forced to attack. His men might die of fever, but not in battle. So far as he was concerned, the Army of the Potomac might have been reorganizing, changing its base, and perfecting its defenses against the enemy, to this day.

A fatal defect was the endeavor to combine the military and the political. Few men have succeeded in this. There were Alexander, Caesar, Napoleon – but all came to an untimely end; the first met an early death in a foreign land, the second was assassinated, the third died a prisoner in exile. McClellan and Fremont, with all their splendid talents, made the fatal mistake. They forgot that for the time they were only military men. Grant was not a politician until after his military duties were ended.

The conclusion of the relations between Lincoln and McClellan was not generally known until recently made public by Lincoln's intimate friend Lamon. McClellan was nominated in 1864 for President by the Democrats. As election day approached it became increasingly clear that McClellan had no chance whatever of being elected. But Lincoln wanted something more than, and different from, a re-election. His desires were for the welfare of the distracted country. He wanted peace, reconstruction, prosperity. A few days before election he sent a remarkable proposition through a common friend, Francis P. Blair, to McClellan. Mr Blair was in hearty sympathy with the plan.

This proposition set forth the hopelessness of McClellan's chances for the presidency, which he knew perfectly well. It was then suggested that McClellan withdraw from the contest and let the President be chosen by a united North, which would bring the war to a speedy close and stop the slaughter of men on both sides. The compensations for this concession were to be: McClellan was to be promoted immediately to be General of the Army, his father-in-law Marcy was to be appointed major-general, and a suitable recognition of the Democratic party would be made in other appointments.

At first blush McClellan was in favor of the arrangement. It is probable that if left to himself he would have acceded. The imagination can hardly grasp the fame that would have come to 'little Mac', and the blessings that would have come to the reunited country, had this wise plan of Lincoln been accepted. But McClellan consulted with friends who advised against it. The matter was dropped – and that was the end of the history of McClellan. He had thrown away his last chance of success and fame. All that followed may be written in one brief sentence: On election day he resigned from the army and was overwhelmingly defeated at the polls.

CHAPTER THIRTY
Lincoln and Greeley

Much of the mischief of the world is the work of people who mean well. Not the least of the annoyances thrust on Lincoln came from people who ought to have known better. The fact that such mischief-makers are complacent, as if they were doing what was brilliant, and useful, adds to the vexation.

One of the most prominent citizens of the United States at the time of the civil war was Horace Greeley. He was a man of ardent convictions, of unimpeachable honesty, and an editorial writer of the first rank. He did a vast amount of good. He also did a vast amount of mischief which may be considered to offset a part of the good he accomplished.

His intellectual ability made it impossible for him to be any-where a nonentity. He was always prominent. His paper, the New York *Tribune*, was in many respects the ablest newspaper of the day. Large numbers of intelligent Republicans took the utterances of the *Tribune* as gospel truth.

It is not safe for any man to have an excess of influence. It is not surprising that the wide influence which Greeley acquired made him egotistic. He apparently came to believe that he had a mort-gage on the Republican party, and through that upon the country. His editorial became dictatorial. He looked upon Lincoln as a protégé of his own who required direction. This he was willing to give – mildly but firmly. All this was true of many other good men and good Republicans. But it was emphatically true of Greeley.

If there is anything worse than a military man who plumes himself upon his statesmanship, it is the civilian who affects to understand military matters better than the generals, the war department, and the commander-in-chief. This was Greeley. He placed his military policy in the form of a war-cry – 'On to Richmond!' – at the head of his editorial page, and with a pen of marvelous power rung the changes on it.

This is but one sample of the man's proneness to interfere in other matters. With all the infallibility of an editor he was ever ready to tell what the President ought to do as a sensible and patriotic man. *He* would have saved the country by electing Douglas, by per-mitting peaceable secession, by persuading the French ambassador to intervene, by conference and argument with the Confederate emissaries, and by assuming personal control of the administration. At a later date he went so far as to propose to force Lincoln's resignation. He did not seem to realize that Lincoln could be most effective if allowed to do his work in his own way. He did not grasp the truth that he could be of the highest value to the administration only as he helped and encouraged, and that his obstructions oper-ated only to diminish the efficiency of the government. If Greeley had put the same degree of force into encouraging the adminis-tration that he put into hindering its work, he would have merited the gratitude of his generation.

He was singularly lacking in the willingness to do this, or in the ability to recognize its importance. Like hundreds of others he persisted in expounding the duties of the executive, but his patronizing advice was more harmful in proportion to the incis-iveness of his literary ability. This impertinence of Greeley's critic-ism reached its climax in an open letter to Lincoln. This letter is, in part, quoted here. It shows something of the unspeakable annoy-ances that were thrust upon the already overburdened President, from those who ought to have delighted in holding up his hands, those of whom better things might have been expected. The reply shows the patience with which Lincoln received these criticisms. It further shows the skill with which he could meet the famous editor on his own ground; for he also could wield a trenchant pen.

Greeley's letter is very long and it is not necessary to give it in full. But the headings, which are given below, are quite sufficient to show that the brilliant editor dipped his pen in gall in order that he might add bitterness to the man whose life was already filled to the brim with the bitter sorrows, trials, and disappointments of a distracted nation. The letter is published on the editorial page of the New York *Tribune* of August 20, 1862.

THE PRAYER OF TWENTY MILLIONS

To ABRAHAM LINCOLN, *President of the United States*

DEAR SIR: I do not intrude to tell you – for you must know already – that a great proportion of those who triumphed in your election, and of all who desire the unqualified suppression of the Rebellion now desolating our country, are sorely disappointed and deeply pained by the policy you seem to be pursuing with regard to the slaves of the Rebels. I write only to set succinctly and unmistakably before you what we require, what we think we have a right to expect, and of what we complain.

1. We require of you, as the first servant of the Republic, charged especially and preeminently with this duty, that you EXECUTE THE LAWS. . . .

2. We think you are strangely and disastrously remiss in the dis-charge of your official and imperative duty with regard to the emancipating provisions of the new Confiscation Act. . . .

3. We think you are unduly influenced by the counsels, the repre-sentations, the menaces, of certain fossil politicians hailing from the Border States. . . .

4. We think the timid counsels of such a crisis calculated to prove perilous and probably disastrous. . . .

5. We complain that the Union cause has suffered and is now suffering immensely, from mistaken deference to Rebel Slavery. Had you, Sir, in your Inaugural Address, unmistakably given notice that, in case the Rebellion already commenced were persisted in, and your efforts to preserve the Union and enforce the laws should be resisted by armed force, you *would recognize no loyal person as rightfully held in Slavery by a traitor*, we believe that the Rebellion would have received a staggering, if not fatal blow. . . .

6. We complain that the Confiscation Act which you approved is habitually disregarded by your Generals, and that no word of rebuke for them from you has yet reached the public ear. . . .

7. Let me call your attention to the recent tragedy in New Orleans, whereof the facts are obtained entirely through Pro-Slavery channels. . . .

8. On the face of this wide earth, Mr President, there is not one disinterested, determined, intelligent champion of the Union Cause who does not feel that all attempts to put down the Rebellion and at the same time uphold its inciting cause are preposterous and futile – that the Rebellion, if crushed out tomorrow, would be renewed within a year if Slavery were left in full vigor – that the army of officers who remain to this day devoted to Slavery can at best be but half way loyal to the Union – and that every hour of deference to Slavery is an hour of added and deepened peril to the Union. . . .

9. I close as I began with the statement that what an immense majority of the Loyal Millions of your countrymen require of you is a frank, declared, unqualified, ungrudging execution of the laws of the land, more especially of the Confiscation Act. . . . As one of the millions who would gladly have avoided this struggle at any sacrifice but that of Principle and Honor, but who now feel that the triumph of the Union is indispensable not only to the existence of our country, but to the well-being of mankind, I entreat you to render a hearty and unequivocal obedience to the law of the land.

Yours,

HORACE GREELEY

NEW YORK, August 19, 1862

Those who are familiar with the eccentricities of this able editor will not be slow to believe that, had Lincoln, previous to the writing of that letter, done the very things he called for, Greeley would not improbably have been among the first to attack him with his caustic criticism. Lincoln was not ignorant of this. But he seized this opportunity to address a far wider constituency than that represented in the subscription list of the *Tribune*. His reply was published in the Washington *Star*. He puts the matter so temperately and plainly that the most obtuse could not fail to see the reasonableness of it. As to Greeley, we do not hear from him again, and may assume that he was silenced if not convinced. The reply was as follows.

Executive Mansion, Washington
August 22, 1862
HON. HORACE GREELEY,
DEAR SIR: I have just read yours of the 19th, addressed to myself through the New York *Tribune*. If there be in it any statements, or assumptions of fact, which I may know to be erroneous, I do not, now and here, controvert them. If there be in it any inferences which I may believe to be falsely drawn, I do not, now and here, argue against them. If there be perceptible in it an impatient and dictatorial tone, I waive it in deference to an old friend, whose heart I have always supposed to be right. As to the policy I 'seem to be pursuing', as you say, I have not meant to leave anyone in doubt. I would save the Union. I would save it the shortest way under the Constitution. The sooner the national authority can be restored, the nearer the Union will be 'the Union as it was'. If there be those who would not save the Union unless they could at the same time save slavery, I do not agree with them. If there be those who would not save the Union unless they could at the same time destroy slavery, I do not agree with them. My paramount object in this struggle is to save the Union, and is not either to save or to destroy slavery. If I could save the Union without freeing any slave, I would do it; if I could save it by freeing all the slaves, I would do it; and if I could save it by freeing some and leaving others alone, I would also do that. What I do about slavery and the colored race, I do because I believe it helps to save the Union: and what I forbear, I forbear because I do not believe it would help to save the Union. I shall do less whenever I shall believe what I am doing hurts the cause, and I shall do more whenever I shall believe doing more will help the cause. I shall try to correct errors when shown to be errors,

and I shall adopt new views so fast as they shall appear to be true views. I have here stated my purpose according to my view of official duty; and I intend no modification of my oft expressed personal wish that all men everywhere could be free.

Yours,

A. LINCOLN

Not the least interesting fact connected with this subject is that at this very time Lincoln had the Emancipation Proclamation in mind. But not even the exasperating teasing that is fairly represented by Greeley's letter caused him to put forth that proclamation prematurely. It is no slight mark of greatness that he was able under so great pressure to bide his time.

This was not the last of Greeley's efforts to control the President or run the machine. In 1864 he was earnestly opposed to his renomination but finally submitted to the inevitable.

In July of that year, 1864, two prominent Confederates, Clay of Alabama, and Thompson of Mississippi, managed to use Greeley for their purposes. They communicated with him from Canada, professing to have authority to arrange for terms of peace, and they asked for a safe-conduct to Washington. Greeley fell into the trap but Lincoln did not. There is little doubt that their real scheme was to foment discontent and secure division throughout the North on the eve of the presidential election. Lincoln wrote to Greeley as follows: 'If you can find any person, anywhere, professing to have authority from Jefferson Davis, in writing, embracing the restoration of the Union and the abandonment of slavery, whatever else it embraces, say to him that he may come to me with you.'

Under date of July 18, he wrote the following.

To WHOM IT MAY CONCERN

Any proposition which embraces the restoration of peace, the integrity of the whole Union, and the abandonment of slavery, and which comes by and with an authority that can control the armies now at war with the United States, will be received and considered by the Executive government of the United States, and will be met on liberal terms on substantial and collateral points; and the bearer or bearers thereof shall have safe-conduct both ways.

ABRAHAM LINCOLN

Greeley met these 'commissioners' at Niagara, but it turned out that they had no authority whatever from the Confederate government. The whole affair was therefore a mere fiasco. But Greeley, who had been completely duped, was full of wrath, and persistently misrepresented, not to say maligned, the President. According to Noah Brooks, the President said of the affair: 'Well, it's hardly fair to say that this won't amount to anything. It will shut up Greeley, and satisfy the people who are clamoring for peace. That's something, anyhow.'

The President was too hopeful. It did not accomplish quite that, for Greeley was very persistent; but it did prevent a serious division of the North.

CHAPTER THIRTY-ONE

Emancipation

The institution of slavery was always and only hateful to the earnest and honest nature of Lincoln. He detested it with all the energy of his soul. He would, as he said, gladly have swept it from the face of the earth. Not even the extreme abolitionists, Garrison, Wendell Phillips, Whittier, abominated slavery with more intensity than Lincoln. But he did not show his hostility in the same way. He had a wider scope of vision than they. He had, and they had not, an appreciative historical knowledge of slavery in this country. He knew that it was tolerated by the Constitution and laws enacted within the provisions of the Constitution, though he believed that the later expansion of slavery was contrary to the spirit and intent of the men who framed the Constitution. And he believed that slaveholders had legal rights which should be respected by all orderly citizens. His sympathy with the slave did not cripple his consideration for the slave-owner who had inherited his property in that form, and under a constitution and laws which he did not originate and for which he was not responsible.

He would destroy slavery root and branch, but he would do it in a manner conformable to the Constitution, not in violation of it. He would exterminate it, but he would not so do it as to impoverish law-abiding citizens whose property was in slaves. He would eliminate slavery, but not in a way to destroy the country, for that would entail more mischief than benefit. To use a figure, he would throw Jonah overboard, but he would not upset the ship in the act.

Large numbers of people have a limited scope of knowledge. Such overlooked the real benefits of our civilization, and did not realize that wrecking the constitution would simply destroy the good that had thus far been achieved, and uproot the seeds of promise of usefulness for the centuries to come. They wanted slavery destroyed at once, violently, regardless of the disastrous consequences. On the other hand, Lincoln wanted it destroyed, but by a sure and rational process. He wished — and from this he never swerved — to do also two things: first, to compensate the owners of the slaves, and second to provide for the future of the slaves themselves. Of course, the extreme radicals could not realize that he was more intensely opposed to slavery than themselves.

Let us now glance at his record. We have already seen (in Chapter 5) how he revolted from the first view of the horrors of the institution, and the youthful vow which he there recorded will not readily be forgotten. That was in 1831 when he was twenty-two years of age.

Six years later, or in 1837, when he was a youthful member of the Illinois legislature, he persuaded Stone to join him in a protest against slavery. There was positively nothing to be gained by this protest, either personally or in behalf of the slave. The only possible reason for it was that he believed that slavery was wrong and could not rest until he had openly expressed that belief.

> A timely utterance gave that thought relief,
> And I again am strong.

When he was in Congress, in 1846, the famous Wilmot Proviso came up. This was to provide 'that, as an express and fundamental condition to the acquisition of any territory from the republic of Mexico by the United States . . . neither slavery nor involuntary servitude shall ever exist in any part of the said territory.' By reason of amendments, this subject came before the house very many times, and Lincoln said afterwards that he had voted for the proviso in one form or another forty-two times.

On the 16th day of January, 1849, he introduced into Congress a bill for the emancipation of slavery in the District of Columbia. This was a wise and reasonable bill. It gave justice to all, and at the same time gathered all the fruits of emancipation in the best possible way. The bill did not pass, there was no hope at the time that it would pass. But it compelled a reasonable discussion of the subject and had a certain amount of educational influence.

It is interesting that, thirteen years later, April 10, 1862, he had the privilege of fixing his presidential signature to a bill similar to his own. Congress had moved up to his position. When he signed the bill, he said: 'Little did I dream, in 1849, when I proposed to abolish slavery in this capital, and could scarcely get a hearing for the proposition, that it would be so soon accomplished.'

After the expiration of his term in Congress he left political life, as he supposed, for ever. He went into the practise of the law in earnest, and was so engaged at the time of the repeal of the Missouri Compromise which called him back to the arena of politics.

In the early part of the war there were certain attempts at emancipation which Lincoln held in check for the reason that the time for them had not arrived. 'There's a tide in the affairs of men.' It is of prime importance that this tide be taken at the flood. So far as emancipation was concerned, this came in slower than the eagerness of Generals Fremont and Hunter. But it was coming, and in the meantime Lincoln was doing what he could to help matters on. The difficulty was that if the Union was destroyed it would be the death-blow to the cause of emancipation. At the same time not a few loyal men were slaveholders. To alienate these by premature action would be disastrous. The only wise plan of action was to wait patiently until a sufficient number of these could be depended on in the emergency of emancipation. This was what Lincoln was doing.

The first part of the year 1862 was very trying. The North had expected to march rapidly and triumphantly into Richmond. This had not been accomplished, but on the contrary disaster had followed disaster in battle, and after many months the two armies were encamped facing each other and almost in sight of Washington, while the soldiers from the North were rapidly sickening and dying in the Southern camps. Small wonder if there was an impatient clamor.

A serious result of this delay was the danger arising from European sources. The monarchies of Europe had no sympathy with American freedom. They became impatient with the reports of 'no progress' in the war, and at this time some of them were watching for a pretext to recognize the Southern Confederacy. This came vividly to the knowledge of Carl Schurz, minister to Spain. By permission of the President he returned to this country – this was late in January, 1862 – to lay the matter personally before him. With the help of Schurz, Lincoln proceeded to develop the sentiment for emancipation. By his request Schurz went to New York to address a meeting of the Emancipation Society on March 6th. It need not be said that the speaker delivered a most able and eloquent plea upon 'Emancipation as a Peace Measure'. Lincoln also made a marked contribution to the meeting. He telegraphed to Schurz the text of his message to Congress recommending emancipation in the District of Columbia – which resulted in the law already mentioned – and this message of Lincoln was read to the meeting. The effect of it, following the speech of Schurz, was overwhelming. It was quite enough to satisfy the most sanguine expectations. This was not a coincidence, it was a plan. Lincoln's hand in *the whole matter* was not seen nor suspected for many years after. It gave a marked impetus to the sentiment of emancipation.

To the loyal slaveholders of the border states he made a proposal of compensated emancipation. To his great disappointment they rejected this. It was very foolish on their part, and he cautioned them that they might find worse trouble.

All this time, while holding back the eager spirits of the abolitionists, he was preparing for his final stroke. But it was of capital importance that this should not be premature. McClellan's failure to take Richmond and his persistent delay, hastened the result. The community at large became impatient beyond all bounds. There came about a feeling that something radical must be done, and that quickly. But it was still necessary that he should be patient. As the bravest fireman is the last to leave the burning structure, so the wise statesman must hold himself in check until the success of so important a measure is assured beyond a doubt.

An event which occurred later may be narrated here because it illustrates the feeling which Lincoln always had in regard to slavery. The item was written out by the President himself and given to the newspapers for publication under the heading,

THE PRESIDENT'S LAST, SHORTEST, AND BEST SPEECH

On Thursday of last week, two ladies from Tennessee came before the President, asking the release of their husbands, held as prisoners of war at Johnson's Island. They were put off until Friday, when they came again, and were again put off until Saturday. At each of the interviews one of the ladies urged that her husband was a religious man. On Saturday, when the President ordered the release of the prisoners, he said to this lady: You say your husband is a religious man; tell him when you meet him that I say I am not much of a judge of religion, but that, in my opinion, the religion that sets men to rebel and fight against their government because, as they think, that government does not sufficiently help *some* men to eat their bread in the sweat of *other* men's faces, is not the sort of religion upon which people can get to heaven.

As the dreadful summer of 1862 advanced, Lincoln noted surely that the time was at hand when emancipation would be the master stroke. In discussing the possibilities of this measure he seemed to take the opposite side. This was a fixed habit with him. He drew out the thoughts of other people. He was enabled to see the subject from all sides. Even after his mind was made up to do a certain thing, he would still argue against it. But in any other sense than this he took counsel of no one upon the emancipation measure. The work was his work. He presented his tentative proclamation to the cabinet on the 22nd of July, 1862. The rest of the story is best told in Lincoln's own words –

It had got to be midsummer, 1862. Things had gone on from bad to worse, until I felt that we had reached the end of our rope on the plan of operations we had been pursuing; that we had about played our last card, and must change our tactics or lose the game. I now determined upon the adoption of the emancipation policy; and without consultation with, or knowledge of, the cabinet, I prepared the original draft of the proclamation, and after much anxious thought called a cabinet meeting upon the subject. . . . I said to the cabinet that I had resolved upon this step, and had not called them together to ask their advice, but to lay the subject-matter of a proclamation before them, suggestions as to which would be in order after they had heard it read.

The members of the cabinet offered various suggestions, but none which Lincoln had not fully anticipated. Seward approved the measure but thought the time not opportune. There had been so many reverses in the war, that he feared the effect. 'It may be viewed,' he said, 'as the last measure of an exhausted government, a cry for help; the government stretching forth its hands to Ethiopia, instead of Ethiopia stretching forth her hands to the government.' He then suggested that the proclamation be not issued until it could be given to the country supported by military successes. This seemed to Lincoln a wise suggestion, and he acted on it. The document was laid away for the time.

It was not until September 17th that the looked-for success came. The Confederate army had crossed the Potomac with the intention of invading the North. They were met and completely defeated in the battle of Antietam. Lincoln said of it: 'When Lee came over the river, I made a resolution that if McClellan drove him back I would send the proclamation after him. The battle of Antietam was fought Wednesday, and until Saturday I could not find out whether we had gained a victory or lost a battle. It was then too late to issue the proclamation that day; and the fact is I fixed it up a little Sunday, and Monday I let them have it.'

This was the preliminary proclamation and was issued September 22nd. The supplementary document, the real proclamation of emancipation, was issued January 1, 1863. As the latter covers substantially the ground of the former, it is not necessary to repeat both and only the second one is given.

EMANCIPATION PROCLAMATION

Whereas, on the twenty-second day of September, in the year of our Lord one thousand eight hundred and sixty-two, a proclamation was issued by the President of the United States, containing, among other things, the following, to wit –

That on the first day of January in the year of our Lord one thousand eight hundred and sixty-three, all persons held as slaves within any state, or designated part of a state, the people whereof shall then be in rebellion against the United States, shall be then, thenceforward and forever free, and the Executive Government of the United States, including the military and naval authority thereof, will recognize and maintain the freedom of such persons, and will do no act or acts to repress such persons, or any of them, in any efforts they may make for their actual freedom.

That the Executive will, on the first day of January aforesaid by proclamation, designate the states and part of states, if any, in which the people thereof respectively shall then be in rebellion against the United States; and the fact that any state, or the people thereof, shall on that day be in good faith represented in the Congress of the United States by members chosen thereto at elections wherein a majority of the qualified voters of such state shall have participated, shall, in the absence of strong countervailing testimony, be deemed conclusive evidence that such state and the people thereof are not then in rebellion against the United States –

Now, therefore, I, Abraham Lincoln, President of the United States, by virtue of the power in me vested as commander-in-chief of the army and navy of the United States, in time of actual armed rebellion against the authority of, and government of, the United States, and as a fit and necessary war measure for suppressing said rebellion, do, on this first day of January, in the year of our Lord one thousand eight hundred and sixty-three, and in accordance with my purpose so to do, publicly proclaimed for the full period of one hundred days from the day first above mentioned, order, and designate, as the states and parts of states wherein the people thereof respectively are this day in rebellion against the United States [here follows the list].

And by virtue of the power and for the purpose aforesaid, I do order and declare that all persons held as slaves within said desig-nated states and parts of states, are and henceforward shall be free; and that the executive government of the United States, including the military and naval authorities thereof, will recognize and main-tain the freedom of said persons.

And I hereby enjoin upon the people so declared to be free, to abstain from all violence, unless in necessary self-defense, and I recommend to them, that in all cases, when allowed, they labor faithfully for reasonable wages.

And I further declare and make known that such persons of suitable condition will be received into the armed service of the United States to garrison forts, positions, stations, and other places, and to man vessels of all sorts in said service.

And upon this act, sincerely believed to be an act of justice, warranted by the Constitution, upon military necessity, I invoke the considerate judgment of mankind and the gracious favor of almighty God.

In Testimony whereof, I have hereunto set my name and caused the seal of the United States to be affixed.

Done at the city of Washington, this first day of January, in the year of our Lord one thousand eight hundred and sixty-three, and of the Independence of the United States of America the eighty-seventh.

ABRAHAM LINCOLN

By the President:
WILLIAM H. SEWARD, Secretary of State

So he fulfilled his youthful vow. He had hit that thing, and he had hit it hard! From that blow the cursed institution of slavery will not recover in a thousand years.

CHAPTER THIRTY-TWO

Discouragements

The middle period of the war was gloomy and discouraging. Though the Confederates made no substantial progress they certainly held their own. Time is an important factor in all history, and the fact that the Confederates at least gained time counted heavily against the Union. There were no decisive victories gained by the Federal troops. Antietam, to be sure, was won, but the fruits of the victory were lost. For many months the two armies continued facing each other, and for the most part they were much nearer Washington than Richmond.

Meantime the summer, fall, winter were passing by and there was no tangible evidence that the government would ever be able to maintain its authority. All this time the Army of the Potomac was magnificent in numbers, equipment, intelligence. In every respect but one they were decidedly superior to the enemy. The one thing they needed was leadership. The South had generals of the first grade. The generalship of the North had not yet fully developed.

Lincoln held on to McClellan as long as it was possible to do so. He never resented the personal discourtesies. He never wearied of the fruitless task of urging him on. He never refused to let him have his own way provided he could show a reason for it. But his persistent inactivity wore out the patience of the country and finally of the army itself. With the exception of northern Democrats with southern sympathies, who from the first were sure of only one thing, namely, that the war was a failure, the clamor for the removal of McClellan was well-nigh unanimous. To this clamor Lincoln yielded only when it became manifestly foolish longer to resist it.

A succeeding question was no less important: Who shall take his place? There was in the East no general whose record would entitle him to this position of honor and responsibility. In all the country there was at that time no one whose successes were so conspicuous as to point him out as the coming man. But there were generals who had done good service, and just at that time Burnside was at the height of his success. He was accordingly appointed. His record was good. He was an unusually handsome man, of soldierly bearing, and possessed many valuable qualities. He was warmly welcomed by the country at large and by his own army, who thanked God and took courage.

His first battle as commander of the Army of the Potomac was fought at Fredericksburg on the 15th of December and resulted in his being repulsed with terrible slaughter. It is possible, in this as in every other battle, that had certain things been a little different – had it been possible to fight the battle three weeks earlier – he would have won a glorious victory. But these thoughts do not bring to life the men who were slain in battle, nor do they quiet the clamor of the country. Burnside showed a certain persistence when, in disregard of the unanimous judgment of his generals, he tried to force a march through the heavy roads of Virginia, as sticky as glue, and give battle again. But he got stuck in the mud and the plan was given up, the only casualty being the death of a large number of mules that were killed trying to draw wagons through the bottomless mud. After this one battle, it was plain that Burnside was not the coming general.

The next experiment was with Hooker, a valiant and able man, whose warlike qualities are suggested by his well-earned soubriquet of 'fighting Joe Hooker'. He had his limitations, as will presently appear. But upon appointing him to the command Lincoln wrote him a personal letter. This letter is here reproduced because it is a perfect illustration of the kindly patience of the man who had need of so much patience.

Executive Mansion, Washington, D.C.
January 26, 1863
MAJOR-GENERAL HOOKER,
GENERAL: I have placed you at the head of the Army of the Potomac. Of course I have done this upon what appears to me to be sufficient reasons, and yet I think it best for you to know that there are some things in regard to which I am not satisfied with you. I believe you to be a brave and skilful soldier, which of course I like. I also believe that you do not mix politics with your profession, in which you are right. You have confidence in yourself, which is a valuable, if not indispensable, quality. You are ambitious, which, within reason, does good rather than harm; but I think that during General Burnside's command of the army you have taken counsel of your ambition and thwarted him as much as you could, in which you did a great wrong to the country, and to a most meritorious and honorable brother officer. I have heard, in such a way as to believe it, of your recently saying that both the army and the government needed a dictator. Of course it was not for this, but in spite of it, that I have given you the command. Only those generals who gain success can be dictators. What I now ask of you is military success, and I will risk the dictatorship. The government will support you to the utmost of its ability, which is neither more nor less than it has done and will do for all commanders. I much fear that the spirit you have aimed to infuse into the army, of criticising their commander and withholding confidence from him, will now turn upon you. I shall assist you as far as I can to put it down. Neither you, nor Napoleon, if he were alive again, could get any good out of an army

while such a spirit prevails in it. And now, beware of rashness. Beware of rashness, but, with energy and sleepless vigilance, go forward and give us victories.

Yours, very truly,

A. LINCOLN

The first effect of this letter was to subdue the fractious spirit of the fighter. He said, 'That is just such a letter as a father might write to a son. It is a beautiful letter, and although I think he was harder on me than I deserved, I will say that I love the man who wrote it.'

But later his conceit took possession of him. According to Noah Brooks he said to some friends: 'I suppose you have seen this letter or a copy of it?' They had. 'After I have been to Richmond I shall have the letter published in the newspapers. It will be amusing.' When this was told Lincoln he took the good-natured view of it and only said, 'Poor Hooker! I am afraid he is incorrigible.'

It was in January, 1863, that Hooker took command of the army. Three months later he had it in shape for the campaign, and Lincoln went down to see the review. It was indeed a magnificent army, an inspiring sight. But it was noticed by many that Lincoln's face had not the joyous radiancy of hope which it had formerly worn; it was positively haggard. It was plain that he did not share his general's easy confidence. He could not forget that he had more than once seen an army magnificent before battle, and shattered after battle. He spent a week there, talking with the generals, shaking hands with 'the boys'. Many a private soldier of that day carries to this day as a sacred memory the earnest sound of the President's voice, 'God bless you!'

Then came Chancellorsville with its sickening consequences. When the news came to Washington, the President, with streaming eyes, could only exclaim: 'My God, my God! what will the country say?'

The next we hear of Hooker, he had not entered Richmond nor had he found the amusement of publishing the President's fatherly letter. He was chasing Lee in a northerly direction – towards Philadelphia or New York. He became angry with Halleck who refused him something and summarily resigned. It was not, for the country, an opportune time for changing generals, but perhaps it was as well. It certainly shows that while Lincoln took him as the best material at hand, while he counseled, encouraged, and bore with him, yet his diagnosis of Hooker's foibles was correct, and his fears, not his hopes, were realized.

He was succeeded by George C. Meade, 'four-eyed George', as he was playfully called by his loyal soldiers, in allusion to his eyeglasses. It was only a few days later that the great battle of Gettysburg was fought under Meade, and a brilliant victory was achieved. But here, as at Antietam, the triumph was bitterly marred by the disappointment that followed. The victorious army let the defeated army get away. The excuses were about the same as at Antietam – the troops were tired. Of course they were tired. But it may be assumed that the defeated army was also tired. It surely makes one army quite as tired to suffer defeat as it makes the other to achieve victory. It was again a golden opportunity to destroy Lee's army and end the war.

Perhaps Meade had achieved enough for one man in winning Gettysburg. It would not be strange if the three days' battle had left him with nerves unstrung. The fact remains that he did not pursue and annihilate the defeated army. They were permitted to recross the Potomac without molestation, to re-enter what may be called their own territory, to reorganize, rest, re-equip, and in due time to reappear as formidable as ever. It is plain that the hero of Gettysburg was not the man destined to crush the rebellion.

Here were three men, Burnside, Hooker, and Meade, all good men and gallant soldiers. But not one of them was able successfully to command so large an army, or to do the thing most needed – capture Richmond. The future hero had not yet won the attention of the country.

In the meantime affairs were very dark for the administration, and up to the summer of 1863 had been growing darker and darker. Some splendid military success had been accomplished in the West, but the West is at best a vague term even to this day, and it has always seemed so remote from the capital, especially as compared to the limited theater of war in Virginia where the Confederate army was almost within sight of the capital, that these western victories did not have as much influence as they should have had.

And there were signal reverses in the West, too. Both Louisville and Cincinnati were seriously threatened, and the battle of
Chickamauga was another field of slaughter, even though it was
shortly redeemed by Chattanooga. But the attention of the
country was necessarily focussed chiefly on the limited territory
that lay between Washington and Richmond. In that region
nothing permanent or decisive had been accomplished in the
period of more than two years, and it is small wonder that the
President became haggard in appearance.

He did what he could. He had thus far held the divided North,
and prevented a European alliance with the Confederates. He now
used, one by one, the most extreme measures. He suspended the
writ of *habeas corpus*, declared or authorized martial law, authorized
the confiscation of the property of those who were providing aid
and comfort for the enemy, called for troops by conscription when
volunteers ceased, and enlisted negro troops. Any person who
studies the character of Abraham Lincoln will realize that these
measures, or most of them, came from him with great reluctance.
He was not a man who would readily or lightly take up such
means. They meant that the country was pressed, hard pressed.
They were extreme measures, not congenial to his accustomed
lines of thought. They were as necessities.

But what Lincoln looked for, longed for, was the man who
could use skillfully and successfully, the great Army of the Potomac.
He had not yet been discovered.

CHAPTER THIRTY-THREE

New Hopes

The outlook from Washington during the first half of the year 1863
was as discouraging as could well be borne. There had been no real
advance since the beginning of the war. Young men, loyal and
enthusiastic, had gone into the army by hundreds of thousands.
Large numbers of these, the flower of the northern youth, had been
slain or wounded, and far larger numbers had died of exposure in
the swamps of Virginia. There was still no progress. Washington

had been defended, but there was hardly a day when the Confederates were not within menacing distance of the capital.

After the bloody disaster at Chancellorsville matters grew even worse. Lee first defeated Hooker in battle and then he out-maneuvered him. He cleverly eluded him, and before Hooker was aware of what was going on, he was on his way, with eighty thousand men, towards Philadelphia and had nearly a week's start of the Union army. The Confederates had always thought that if they could carry the war into the northern states they would fight to better advantage. Jeff Davis had threatened the torch, but it is not likely that such subordinates as General Lee shared his destructive and barbarous ambition. Still, Lee had a magnificent army, and its presence in Pennsylvania was fitted to inspire terror. It was also fitted to rouse the martial spirit of the northern soldiers, as afterwards appeared.

As soon as the situation was known, Hooker started in hot pursuit. After he had crossed the Potomac going north, he made certain requests of the War Department which were refused, and he, angry at the refusal, promptly sent in his resignation. Whether his requests were reasonable is one question; whether it was patriotic in him to resign on the eve of what was certain to be a great and decisive battle is another question. But his resignation was accepted and Meade was appointed to the command. He accepted the responsibility with a modest and soldierly spirit and quit himself like a man. It is one of the rare cases in all history in which an army has on the eve of battle made a change of generals without disaster. That is surely highly to the credit of General Meade. Lee's objective point was not known. He might capture Harrisburg or Philadelphia, or both. He would probably desire to cut off all communication with Washington. The only thing to do was to overtake him and force a battle. He himself realized this and was fully decided not to give battle but fight only on the defensive. Curiously enough, Meade also decided not to attack, but to fight on the defensive. Nevertheless, 'the best laid schemes o' mice an' men gang aft agley.'

The result was Gettysburg, and the battle was not fought in accordance with the plan of either commander. Uncontrollable events forced the battle then and there. This battlefield was some distance to the north, that is to say, in advance of Pipe Creek, the location selected by Meade. But a conflict between a considerable force on each side opened the famous battle on July 1st. A retreat, or withdrawal, to Pipe Creek would have been disastrous. The first clash was between Heth's division on the Confederate side, and Buford and Reynolds on the Union side. Rarely have soldiers been more eager for the fray than were those of the Union army at this time, especially the sons of Pennsylvania. 'Up and at 'em' was the universal feeling. It was hardly possible to hold them back. The generals felt that it was not wise to hold them back. Thus, as one division after another, on both sides, came up to the help of their comrades, Gettysburg was accepted as the battlefield. It was selected by neither commander, it was thrust upon them by the fortunes of war, it was selected by the God of battles.

Almost the first victim on the Union side was that talented and brave soldier, the general in command, Reynolds. His place was later in the day – that is, about four o'clock in the afternoon – filled, and well filled, by General Hancock.

The scope of this volume does not permit the description of this great battle, and only some of the results may be given. The evening of July 1st closed in with the Union army holding out, but with the advantages, such as they were, on the Confederate side. The second day the fight was fiercely renewed and closed with no special advantage on either side. On the third day it was still undecided until in the afternoon when the climax came in Pickett's famous charge. This was the very flower of the Confederate army, and the hazard of the charge was taken by General Lee against the earnest advice of Longstreet. They were repulsed and routed, and that decided the battle. Lee's army was turned back, the attempted invasion was a failure, and it became manifest that even Lee could not fight to advantage on northern soil.

Gettysburg was the greatest battle ever fought on the western hemisphere, and it will easily rank as one of the great battles of either hemisphere. The number of troops was about 80,000 on each side. In the beginning the Confederates decidedly outnumbered the Federals, because the latter were more scattered and it took time to bring them up. In the latter part, the numbers were more nearly evenly divided, though nearly one-fourth of Meade's men were not in the battle at any time.

The total loss of killed, wounded, and missing, was on the Confederate side over 31,000; on the Union side, about 23,000.

The Confederates lost seventeen generals, and the Federals twenty. When we consider this loss of generals, bearing in mind that on the Union side they were mostly those on whom Meade would naturally lean, it is hardly to be wondered at that he so far lost his nerve as to be unwilling to pursue the retreating enemy or hazard another battle. He could not realize that the enemy had suffered much more than he had, and that, despite his losses, he was in a condition to destroy that army. Not all that Lincoln could say availed to persuade him to renew the attack upon the retreating foe. When Lee reached the Potomac he found the river so swollen as to be impassable. He could only wait for the waters to subside or for time to improvise a pontoon bridge.

When, after waiting for ten days, Meade was aroused to make the attack, he was just one day too late. Lee had got his army safely into Virginia, and the war was not over. Lincoln could only say, 'Providence has twice [the other reference is to Antietam] delivered the Army of Northern Virginia into our hands, and with such opportunities lost we ought scarcely to hope for a third chance.'

Lincoln wrote a letter to Meade. He also wrote him a second letter – or was it the first? – which he did not send. We quote from this because it really expressed the President's mind, and because the fact that he did not send it only shows how reluctant he was to wound another's feelings even when deserved.

Again, my dear general, I do not believe you appreciate the magnitude of the misfortune involved in Lee's escape. He was within your easy grasp, and to have closed upon him would, in connection with our other late successes, have ended the war. As it is, the war will be prolonged indefinitely. If you could not safely attack Lee last Monday, how can you possibly do so south of the river, when you can take with you very few more than two-thirds of the force you then had in hand? It would be unreasonable to expect, and I do not expect, that you can now effect much. Your golden opportunity is gone, and I am distressed immeasurably because of it. I beg you will not consider this a prosecution or persecution of yourself. As you had learned that I was dissatisfied, I thought it best to kindly tell you why.

While not overlooking Meade's omission, as this letter shows, he appreciated the full value of the victory that checked Lee's advance, and thanked the general heartily for that.

On the same afternoon of July 3rd, almost at the very minute that Pickett was making his charge, there was in progress, a thousand miles to the west, an event of almost equal importance. Just outside the fortifications of Vicksburg, under an oak tree, General Grant had met the Confederate general, Pemberton, to negotiate terms of surrender. The siege of Vicksburg was a great triumph, and its capitulation was of scarcely less importance than the victory at Gettysburg. Vicksburg commanded the Mississippi River and was supposed to be impregnable. Surely few cities were situated more favorably to resist either attack or siege. But Admiral Porter got his gunboats below the city, running the batteries in the night, and Grant's investment was complete. The Confederate cause was hopeless, their men nearly starved.

Grant's *plan* was to make a final attack (if necessary) on the 6th or 7th day of July; but some time previous to this he had predicted that the garrison would surrender on the fourth. General Pemberton tried his utmost to avoid this very thing. When it became apparent that he could not hold out much longer, he opened negotiations on the morning of July 3rd for the specific purpose of forestalling the possibility of surrender on the next day, Independence Day. In his report to the Confederate government he claims to have chosen the 4th of July for surrender, because he thought that he could secure better terms on that day. But his pompous word has little weight, and all the evidence points the other way. When on the morning of the 3rd of July he opened negotiations, he could not possibly have foreseen that it would take twenty-four hours to arrange the terms.

It was, then, on the 4th of July that Grant occupied Vicksburg. The account by Nicolay and Hay ends with the following beautiful reflection: 'It is not the least of the glories gained by the Army of the Tennessee in this wonderful campaign that not a single cheer went up from the Union ranks, not a single word that could offend their beaten foes.'

The loss to the Union army in killed, wounded, and missing, was about 9,000. The Confederate loss was nearly 50,000. To be sure many of the paroled were compelled to re-enlist according to the policy of the Confederate government. But even so their parole was a good thing for the cause of the Union. They were so thoroughly disaffected that their release did, for the time, more harm than good to the southern cause. Then it left Grant's army free.

The sequel to this victory came ten months later in Sherman's march to the sea: not less thrilling in its conception and dramatic in its execution than any battle or siege. Much fighting, skilful generalship, long patience were required before this crowning act could be done, but it came in due time and was one of the finishing blows to the Confederacy, and it came as a logical result of the colossal victory at Vicksburg.

There were some eddies and counter-currents to the main drift of affairs. About the time that Lee and his beaten army were making good their escape, terrific riots broke out in New York City in resisting the draft. As is usual in mob rule the very worst elements of human or devilish depravity came to the top and were most in evidence. For several days there was indeed a reign of terror. The fury of the mob was directed particularly against the negroes. They were murdered. Their orphan asylum was burnt. But the government quickly suppressed the riot with a firm hand. The feeling was general throughout the country that we were now on the way to a successful issue of the war. The end was almost in sight. Gettysburg and Vicksburg, July 3 and 4, 1863, had inspired new hopes never to be quenched.

On the 15th day of July the President issued a thanksgiving proclamation, designating August 6th as the day. Later in the year he issued another thanksgiving proclamation, designating the last Thursday in November. Previous to that time, certain states, and not a few individuals, were in the habit of observing a thanksgiving day in November. Indeed the custom, in a desultory way, dates back to Plymouth Colony. But these irregular and uncertain observances never took on the semblance of a national holiday. *That* dates from the proclamation issued October 3rd, 1863. From that day to this, every President has every year followed that example.

Lincoln was invited to attend a public meeting appointed for August 26th at his own city of Springfield, the object of which was to concert measures for the maintenance of the Union. The pressure of public duties did not permit him to leave Washington, but he wrote a characteristic letter, a part of which refers to some of the events touched on in this chapter. A few sentences of this letter are here given.

The Father of Waters again goes unvexed to the sea. Thanks to the great Northwest for it; nor yet wholly to them. Three hundred miles up they met New England, Empire, Keystone, and Jersey, hewing their way right and left. The sunny South, too, in more colors than one, also lent a helping hand. On the spot, their part of the history was jotted down in black and white. The job was a great national one, and let none be slighted who bore an honorable part in it. And while those who have cleared the great river may well be proud, even that is not all. It is hard to say that anything has been more bravely and well done than at Antietam, Murfreesboro, Gettysburg, and on many fields of less note. Nor must Uncle Sam's web-feet be forgotten. At all the watery margins they have been present, not only on the deep sea, the broad bay, and the rapid river, but also up the narrow, muddy bayou, and wherever the ground was a little damp, they have been and made their tracks. Thanks to all. For the great republic — for the principle it lives by and keeps alive — for man's vast future — thanks to all.

Peace does not appear so distant as it did. I hope it will come soon and come to stay; and so come as to be worth the keeping in all future time. It will then have been proved that among freemen there can be no successful appeal from the ballot to the bullet, and that they who take such appeal are sure to lose their case and pay the cost. And there will be some black men who can remember that with silent tongue and clenched teeth and steady eye and well-poised bayonet they have helped mankind on to this great consummation; while I fear there will be some white ones unable to forget that with malignant heart and deceitful speech they have striven to hinder it.

It is plain that after July 4, 1863, the final result was no longer doubtful. So Lincoln felt it. There were indeed some who continued to cry that the war was a failure, but in such cases the wish was only father to the thought.

CHAPTER THIRTY-FOUR
Lincoln and Grant

The great army of R. E. Lee operated, through the whole period of
the four years of the war, almost within sight of Washington City.
It is not in the least strange that eastern men, many of whom had
hardly crossed the Alleghanies, should think that the operations in
Virginia were about all the war there was, and that the fighting
in the West was of subordinate importance. Lincoln could not fall
into this error. Not only had he a singularly broad vision, but he
was himself a western man. He fully appreciated the magnitude of
the operations in that vast territory lying between the Alleghanies
on the east and the western boundary of Missouri on the west. He
also clearly understood the importance of keeping open the Mississippi River throughout its entire length.

At the very time the Army of the Potomac was apparently doing
nothing – winning no victories, destroying no armies, making no
permanent advances – there was a man in the West who was building up for himself a remarkable reputation. He was all the while
winning victories, destroying armies, making advances. He was
always active, he was always successful. The instant one thing was
accomplished he turned his energies to a new task. This was Grant.

He was a graduate of West Point, had seen service in the
Mexican War, and ultimately rose to the grade of captain. At the
outbreak of the war he was in business with his father in Galena,
Illinois. When the President called for the 75,000 men, Grant
proceeded at once to make himself useful by drilling volunteer
troops. He was by the governor of Illinois commissioned as
colonel, and was soon promoted. His first service was in Missouri.
When stationed at Cairo he seized Paducah on his own responsibility. This stroke possibly saved Kentucky for the Union, for the
legislature, which had up to that time been wavering, declared at
once in favor of the Union.

He was then ordered to break up a Confederate force at Belmont,
a few miles below Cairo. He started at once on his expedition, and
though the enemy was largely reinforced before his arrival, he was
entirely successful and returned with victory, not excuses.

Then came Forts Henry and Donaldson. The latter attracted unusual attention because it was the most important Union victory up to that time, and because of his epigrammatic reply to the offer of surrender. When asked what terms he would allow, his reply was, 'Unconditional surrender'. As these initials happened to fit the initials of his name, he was for a long time called 'Unconditional Surrender Grant'. So he passed promptly from one task to another, from one victory to another. And Lincoln kept watch of him. He began to think that Grant was the man for the army.

It has been said that Lincoln, while he gave general directions to his soldiers, and freely offered suggestions, left them to work out the military details in their own way. This is so well illustrated in his letter to Grant that, for this reason, as well as for the intrinsic interest of the letter, it is here given in full.

MY DEAR GENERAL – I do not remember that you and I ever met personally. I write this now as a grateful acknowledgment for the almost inestimable service you have done the country. I wish to say a word further. When you first reached the vicinity of Vicksburg, I thought you should do what you finally did – march the troops across the neck, run the batteries with the transports, and thus go below; and I never had any faith, except a general hope that you knew better than I, that the Yazoo Pass expedition and the like could succeed. When you got below and took Port Gibson, Grand Gulf, and vicinity, I thought you should go down the river and join General Banks; and when you turned northward, east of the Big Black, I thought it was a mistake. I now wish to make the personal acknowledgment that you were right and I was wrong.

There was surely no call for this confession, no reason for the letter, except the bigness of the heart of the writer. Like the letter to Hooker, it was just such a letter as a father might write a son. It was the production of a high grade of manliness.

Prominence always brings envy, fault-finding, hostility. From this Grant did not escape. The more brilliant and uniform his successes, the more clamorous a certain class of people became. The more strictly he attended to his soldierly duties, the more busily certain people tried to interfere – to tell him how to do, or how not to do. In their self-appointed censorship they even besieged the President and made life a burden to him. With wit and unfailing good nature, he turned their criticisms. When they argued that Grant could not possibly be a good soldier, he replied, 'I like him; he fights.'

When they charged him with drunkenness, Lincoln jocularly proposed that they ascertain the brand of the whisky he drank and buy up a large amount of the same sort to send to his other generals, so that they might win victories like him!

Grant's important victories in the West came in rapid and brilliant succession. Forts Henry and Donaldson were captured in February, 1862. The battle of Shiloh, or Pittsburg Landing, was fought in April of the same year. Vicksburg surrendered July 4th, 1863. And the battle of Chattanooga took place in November of that year.

Grant was always sparing of words and his reports were puzzling to the administration. He always reported, and that promptly. But his reports were of the briefest description and in such marked contrast to those of all other officers known to the government, that they were a mystery to those familiar with certain others. Lincoln said that Grant could do anything except write a report. He concluded to send a trusty messenger to see what manner of man this victorious general was. Charles A. Dana, Assistant-Secretary of War, was chosen for this purpose. His investigation was satisfactory, fully so. Lincoln's confidence in, and hopes for, this rising warrior were fully justified.

It was after the capitulation of Vicksburg that Grant grasped the fact that he was the man destined to end the war. After the battle of Chattanooga public opinion generally pointed to him as the general who was to lead our armies to ultimate victory. In February, 1864, Congress passed an act creating the office of Lieutenant General. The President approved that act on Washington's birthday, and nominated Grant for that office. The senate confirmed this nomination on March 2nd, and Grant was ordered to report at Washington.

With his usual promptness he started at once for Washington, arriving there the 8th of March. The laconic conversation which took place between the President and the general has been reported about as follows –

'What do you want me to do?'

'To take Richmond. Can you do it?'

'Yes, if you furnish me troops enough.'

That evening there was a levée at the White House which he attended. The crowd were very eager to see him, and he was persuaded to mount a sofa, which he did blushing, so that they might have a glimpse of him, but he could not be prevailed on to make a speech. On parting that evening with the President, he said, 'This is the warmest campaign I have witnessed during the war.'

That evening Lincoln informed him that he would on the next day formally present his commission with a brief speech – four sentences in all. He suggested that Grant reply in a speech suitable to be given out to the country in the hope of reviving confidence and courage. The formality of the presentation occurred the next day, but the general disappointed the President as to the speech. He accepted the commission with remarks of soldier-like brevity.

It is fitting here to say of General Meade that as he had accepted his promotion to the command of the Army of the Potomac with dignified humility, so he accepted his being superseded with loyal obedience. In both cases he was a model of a patriot and a soldier.

As soon as he received his commission Grant visited his future army – the Army of the Potomac. Upon his return Mrs Lincoln planned to give a dinner in his honor. But this was not to his taste. He said, 'Mrs Lincoln must excuse me. I must be in Tennessee at a given time.'

'But,' replied the President, 'we can't excuse you. Mrs Lincoln's dinner without you would be *Hamlet* with Hamlet left out.'

'I appreciate the honor Mrs Lincoln would do me,' he said, 'but time is very important now – and really – Mr Lincoln – I have had enough of this show business.'

Mr Lincoln was disappointed in losing the guest for dinner, but he was delighted with the spirit of his new general.

Grant made his trip to the West. How he appreciated the value of time is shown by the fact that he had his final conference with his successor, General Sherman, who was also his warm friend, on the railway train en route to Cincinnati. He had asked Sherman to accompany him so far for the purpose of saving time.

On March 17th General Grant assumed command of the armies of the United States with headquarters in the field. He was evidently in earnest. As Lincoln had cordially offered help and encouragement to all the other generals, so he did to Grant. The difference between one general and another was not in Lincoln's offer of help, or refusal to give it, but there was a difference in the way in which his offers were received. The following correspondence tells the story of the way he held himself alert to render assistance.

Executive Mansion
Washington, April 30, 1864
LIEUT.-GENERAL GRANT:
Not expecting to see you again before the spring campaign opens, I wish to express in this way my entire satisfaction with what you have done up to this time, so far as I understand it. The particulars of your plan I neither know nor seek to know. You are vigilant and self-reliant; and, pleased with this, I wish not to obtrude any constraints or restraints upon you. While I am very anxious that any great disaster or capture of our men in great numbers shall be avoided, I know these points will be less likely to escape your attention than they would be mine. If there is anything wanting which is within my power to give, do not fail to let me know it. And now, with a brave army and a just cause, may God sustain you.

> Yours very truly,
> A. LINCOLN

Headquarters Armies of the United States,
Culpepper Court-House, May 1, 1864
THE PRESIDENT:
Your very kind letter of yesterday is just received. The confidence you express for the future and satisfaction with the past in my military administration is acknowledged with pride. It will be my earnest endeavor that you and the country shall not be disappointed. From my first entrance into the volunteer service of the country to the present day, I have never had cause of complaint – have never expressed or implied a complaint against the Administration, or the Secretary of War, for throwing any embarrassment in the way of my vigorously prosecuting what appeared to me my duty. Indeed since the promotion which placed me in command of all the armies, and in view of the great responsibility and importance of success, I have been astonished at the readiness with which

everything asked for has been yielded, without even an explanation being asked. Should my success be less than I desire and expect, the least I can say is, the fault is not with you.

Very truly, your obedient servant,

U. S. GRANT, *Lieut-General*

There is just here a subject on which there is a curious difference of opinion between Grant and John Hay. Grant says that, on his last visit to Washington before taking the field, the President had become acquainted with the fact that a general movement had been ordered all along the line, and *seemed* [italics ours] to think it a new feature in war. He explained this plan to the President who was greatly interested and said, 'Oh, yes! I see that. As we say out West, if a man can't skin, he must hold a leg while somebody else does.'

There is, at the same time, documentary evidence that Lincoln had been continually urging this precise plan on all his generals. Mr Hay therefore distrusts the accuracy of General Grant's memory. To the present writer, there is no mystery in the matter. The full truth is large enough to include the statement of Grant as well as that of Nicolay and Hay. Mr Hay is certainly right in claiming that Lincoln from the first desired such a concerted movement all along the line; for, even though not all could fight at the same time, those not fighting could help otherwise. This was the force of the western proverb, 'Those not skinning can hold a leg', which he quoted to all his generals from Buell to Grant.

When therefore Grant explained precisely this plan to Lincoln, the latter refrained from the natural utterance – 'That is exactly what I have been trying to get our generals to do all these years.' In courtesy to Grant he did not claim to have originated the plan, but simply preserved a polite silence. He followed eagerly as the general reiterated his own ideas, and the exclamation, 'Oh, yes! I see that', would mean more to Lincoln than Grant could possibly have guessed. He did see it, he had seen it a long time.

It will be remembered that Lincoln had, for the sake of comprehending the significance of one word, mastered Euclid after he became a lawyer. There is here another evidence of the same thoroughness and force of will. During the months when the Union armies were accomplishing nothing, he procured the necessary books and set himself, in the midst of all his administrative cares, to the task of learning the science of war. That he achieved more than ordinary success will now surprise no one who is familiar with his character. His military sagacity is attested by so high an authority as General Sherman. Other generals have expressed their surprise and gratification at his knowledge and penetration in military affairs. But never at any time did he lord it over his generals. He did make suggestions. He did ask McClellan why one plan was better than another. He did ask some awkward questions of Meade. But it was his uniform policy to give his generals all possible help, looking only for results, and leaving details unreservedly in their hands. This is the testimony of McClellan and Grant, and the testimony of the two generals, so widely different in character and method, should be and is conclusive. Grant says that Lincoln expressly assured him that he preferred not to know his purposes – he desired only to learn what means he needed to carry them out, and promised to furnish these to the full extent of his power.

Side by side these two men labored, each in his own department, until the war was ended and their work was done. Though so different, they were actuated by the same spirit. Not even the southern generals themselves had deeper sympathy with, or greater tenderness for, the mass of the Confederate soldiers. It was the same magnanimity in Lincoln and Grant that sent the conquered army, after their final defeat, back to the industries of peace that they might be able to provide against their sore needs.

When that madman assassinated the President, the conspiracy included also the murder of the general. This failed only by reason of Grant's unexpected absence from Washington City on the night of the crime.

CHAPTER THIRTY-FIVE
Literary Characteristics

The duties of the President of the United States include the writing of state papers that are considerable both in number and in volume. Many of the Presidents, from Washington down, have been men of great ability, and almost all of them have had sufficient academic training or intellectual environments in their early years. These state papers have frequently been such as to compare favorably with those of the ablest statesmen of Europe. With every new election of President the people wait in expectancy for the inaugural address and the messages to Congress. These are naturally measured by the standard of what has preceded – not of all that has preceded, for the inferior ones are forgotten, but of the best. This is no light test for any man.

Lincoln's schooling was so slight as to be almost nil. He did not grow up in a literary atmosphere. But in the matter of his official utterances he must be compared with the ablest geniuses and most cultured scholars that have preceded him, and not merely with his early associates. He is to be measured with Washington, the Adamses, Jefferson, and not with the denizens of Gentryville or New Salem.

Perhaps the best study of his keenness of literary criticism will be found in his correction of Seward's letter of instruction to Charles Francis Adams, minister to England, under date of May 21, 1861. Seward was a brilliant scholar, a polished writer, a trained diplomatist. If any person were able to compose a satisfactory letter for the critical conditions of that period, he was the one American most likely to do it. He drafted the letter and submitted it to Lincoln for suggestions and corrections. The original manuscript with Lincoln's interlineations, is still preserved, and facsimiles, or copies, are given in various larger volumes of Lincoln's biography. This document is very instructive. In every case Lincoln's suggestion is a marked improvement on the original. It shows that he had the better command of precise English. Lowell himself could not have improved his criticisms. It shows, too, that he had a firmer grasp of the subject. Had Seward's paper gone without these corrections, it is almost certain that diplomatic relations with England would have been broken off. In literary matters Lincoln was plainly the master and Seward was the pupil.

The power which Lincoln possessed of fitting language to thought is marked. It made him the matchless story-teller, and gave sublimity to his graver addresses. His thoroughness and accuracy were a source of wonder and delight to scholars. He had a masterful grasp of great subjects. He was able to look at events from all sides, so as to appreciate how they would appear to different grades of intelligence, different classes of people, different sections of the country. More than once this many-sidedness of his mind saved the country from ruin. Wit and humor are usually joined with their opposite, pathos, and it is therefore not surprising that, being eminent in one, he should possess all three characteristics. In his conversation his humor predominated, in his public speeches pure reasoning often rose to pathos.

If the author were to select a few of his speeches or papers fitted to give the best example of his literary qualities, and at the same time present an evidence of the progress of his doctrine along political lines, he would name the following: The House-divided-against-itself speech, delivered at Springfield June 16, 1858. The underlying thought of this was that the battle between freedom and slavery was sure to be a fight to the finish.

Next is the Cooper Institute speech, Feb. 12, 1860. The argument in this is that, in the thought and intent of the founders of our government, the Union was permanent and paramount, while slavery was temporary and secondary.

Next was his inaugural, March 4, 1861. This warned the country against sectional war. It declared temperately but firmly, that he would perform the duties which his oath of office required of him, but he would *not* begin a war: if war came the aggressors must be those of the other side.

The next was the Emancipation Proclamation, September 22, 1862, and January 1, 1863. This was not a general and complete emancipation of all slaves, it was primarily a military device, a war measure, freeing the slaves of those who were in actual and armed rebellion at the time. It was intended to weaken the belligerent powers of the rebels, and a notice of the plan was furnished more than three months in advance, giving ample time to all who wished to do so, to submit to the laws of their country and save that portion of their property that was invested in slaves.

Then came the second inaugural, March 4, 1865. There was in this little to discuss, for he had no new policy to proclaim, he was simply to continue the policy of the past four years, of which the country had shown its approval by re-electing him. The end of the war was almost in sight, it would soon be finished. But in this address there breathes an intangible spirit which gives it marvelous grandeur. Isaiah was a prophet who was also a statesman. Lincoln – we say it with reverence – was a statesman who was also a prophet. He had foresight. He had *in*sight. He saw the hand of God shaping events, he saw the spirit of God in events. Such is his spiritual elevation of thought, such his tenderness of yearning, that there is no one but Isaiah to whom we may fittingly compare him, in the manly piety of his closing paragraph.

> Fondly do we hope, fervently do we pray, that this mighty scourge of war may speedily pass away. Yet, if God wills that it continue until all the wealth piled by the bondman's two hundred and fifty years of unrequited toil shall be sunk, and until every drop of blood drawn with the lash shall be paid by another drawn with the sword, as was said three thousand years ago, so still it must be said, 'The judgments of the Lord are true and righteous altogether.' With malice toward none, with charity for all, with firmness in the right, as God gives us to see the right, let us strive to finish the work we are in; to bind up the nation's wounds; to care for him who shall have borne the battle, and for his widow, and his orphan; to do all which may achieve and cherish a just and lasting peace among ourselves and with all nations.

The study of these five speeches, or papers, will give the salient points of his political philosophy, and incidentally of his intellectual development. These are not enough to show the man Lincoln, but they do give a true idea of the great statesman. They show a symmetrical and wonderful growth. Great as was the House-divided-against-itself speech, there is yet a wide difference between that and the second inaugural: and the seven years intervening accomplished this growth of mind and of spirit only because they were years of great stress.

Outside of this list is the address at the dedication of Gettysburg cemetery, November 19, 1863. This was not intended for an oration. Edward Everett was the orator of the occasion. Lincoln's part was to pronounce the formal words of dedication. It was a busy time – all times were busy with him, but this was unusually busy – and he wrote it on a sheet of foolscap paper in such odd moments as he could command. In form it is prose, but in effect it is a poem. Many of its sentences are rhythmical. The occasion lifted him into a higher realm of thought. The hearers were impressed by his unusual gravity and solemnity of manner quite as much, perhaps, as by the words themselves. They were awed, many were moved to tears. The speech is given in full.

GETTYSBURG ADDRESS

Fourscore and seven years ago, our fathers brought forth on this continent a new nation, conceived in liberty and dedicated to the proposition that all men are created equal. Now we are engaged in a great civil war, testing whether that nation, or any nation so conceived and so dedicated, can long endure. We are met on a great battlefield of that war. We have come to dedicate a portion of that field as a final resting-place for those who here gave their lives that that nation might live. It is altogether fitting and proper that we should do this. But in a larger sense, we cannot dedicate, we cannot consecrate, we cannot hallow this ground. The brave men, living and dead, who struggled here, have consecrated it far above our poor power to add or detract. The world will little note, nor long remember, what we say here, but it can never forget what they did here. It is for us, the living, rather to be dedicated here to the unfinished work which they who fought here have thus far so nobly advanced. It is rather for us to be here dedicated to the great task remaining before us, – that from these honored dead we take increased devotion to that cause for which they gave the last full measure of devotion – that we here highly resolve that these dead shall not have died in vain – that this nation, under God, shall have a new birth of freedom – and that government of the people, by the people, for the people, shall not perish from the earth.

The effect of this speech was not immediate. Colonel Lamon was on the platform when it was delivered and he says very decidedly that Everett, Seward, himself, and Lincoln were all of opinion that the speech was a failure. He adds: 'I state it as a fact, and without fear of contradiction, that this famous Gettysburg speech was not regarded by the audience to whom it was addressed, or by the press or people of the United States, as a production of extraordinary merit, nor was it commented on as such until after the death of the author.'

A search through the files of the leading New York dailies for several days immediately following the date of the speech, seems to confirm Lamon's remark – all except the last clause above quoted. These papers give editorial praise to the oration of Everett, they comment favorably on a speech by Beecher (who had just returned from England), but they make no mention of Lincoln's speech. It is true that a day or two later Everett wrote him a letter of congratulation upon his success. But this may have been merely generous courtesy – as much as to say, 'Don't feel badly over it, it was a much better speech than you think!' Or, on the other hand, it may have been the result of his sober second thought, the speech having had time to soak in.

But the silence of the great daily papers confirms Lamon up to a certain point. At the very first the speech was not appreciated. But after a few days the public awoke to the fact that Lincoln's 'few remarks' were immeasurably superior to Everett's brilliant and learned oration. The author distinctly remembers that it was compared to the oration of Pericles in memory of the Athenian dead; that it was currently said that there had been no memorial oration from that date to Lincoln's speech of equal power. This comparison with Pericles is certainly high praise, but is it not true? The two orations are very different: Lincoln's was less than three hundred words long, that of Pericles near three thousand. Pericles gloried in war, Lincoln mourned over the necessity of war and yearned after peace. But both orators alike appreciated the glory of sacrifice for one's country. And it is safe to predict that this Gettysburg address, brief, hastily prepared, underestimated by its author, will last as long as the republic shall last, as long as English speech shall endure.

CHAPTER THIRTY-SIX
Second Election

It was Lincoln's lifelong habit to keep himself close to the plain people. He loved them. He declared that the Lord must love them or he would not have made so many of them. Out of them he came, to them he belonged. In youth he was the perennial peacemaker and umpire of disputes in his rural neighborhood. When he was President the same people instinctively turned to him for help. The servants called him Old Abe – from them a term of affection, not of indignity. The soldiers called him Father Abraham. He was glad to receive renowned politicians and prominent business men at the White House; he was more glad to see the plain people. When a farmer neighbor addressed him as 'Mister President', he said, 'Call me Lincoln.' The friendship of these people rested him.

Then, too, he had a profound realization of their importance to the national prosperity. It was their instincts that constituted the national conscience. It was their votes that had elected him. It was their muskets that had defended the capital. It was on their loyalty that he counted for the ultimate triumph of the Union cause. As his administrative policy progressed it was his concern not to outstrip them so far as to lose their support. In other words, he was to lead them, not run away from them. His confidence in them was on the whole well founded, though there were times when the ground seemed to be slipping out from under him.

The middle portion of 1864 was one such period of discouragement. The material for volunteer soldiers was about exhausted, and it was becoming more and more necessary to depend upon the draft, and that measure caused much friction. The war had been long, costly, sorrowful. Grant was before Petersburg, Farragut at Mobile, and Sherman at Atlanta. The two first had no promise of immediate success, and as to the third it was a question whether he was not caught in his own trap. This prolongation of the war had a bad effect on the northern public.

Lincoln, shrewdly and fairly, analyzed the factions of loyal people as follows.

We are in civil war. In such cases there always is a main question; but in this case that question is a perplexing compound – Union and slavery. It thus becomes a question not of two sides merely, but of at least four sides, even among those who are for the Union, saying nothing of those who are against it. Thus –

Those who are for the Union with, but not without, slavery;

Those for it without, but not with;

Those for it with or without, but prefer it with; and

Those for it with or without, but prefer it without.

Among these again is a subdivision of those who are for gradual, but not for immediate, and those who are for immediate, but not for gradual, extinction of slavery.

One man who was in the political schemes of that day says that in Washington there were only three prominent politicians who were not seriously discontented with and opposed to Lincoln. The three named were Conkling, Sumner, and Wilson. Though there was undoubtedly a larger number who remained loyal to their chief, yet the discontent was general. The President himself felt this. Nicolay and Hay have published a note which impressively tells the sorrowful story.

Executive Mansion,
Washington,
August 28, 1864.
This morning, as for some days past, it seems exceedingly probable that this administration will not be re-elected. Then it will be my duty to so cooperate with the President-elect as to save the Union between the election and the inauguration, as he will have secured his election on such ground that he cannot possibly save it afterward.

A. LINCOLN

Early in the year this discontent had broken out in a disagreeable and dangerous form. The malcontents were casting about to find a candidate who would defeat Lincoln. They first tried General Rosecrans, and from him they got an answer of no uncertain sound. 'My place,' he declared, 'is here. The country gave me my education, and so has a right to my military services.'

Their next attempt was Grant, with whom they fared no better. Then they tried Vice-President Hamlin who was certainly dissatisfied with the slowness with which Lincoln moved in the direction of abolition. But Hamlin would not be a candidate against his chief.

Then the Secretary of the Treasury, Chase, entered the race as a rival of Lincoln. When this became known, the President was urged by his friends to dismiss from the cabinet this secretary who was so far out of sympathy with the administration he was serving. He refused to do this so long as Chase did his official duties well, and when Chase offered to resign he told him there was no need of it. But the citizens of Ohio, of which state Chase had in 1860 been the 'favorite son', did not take the same view of the matter. Both legislature and mass meetings demanded his resignation so emphatically that he could not refuse. He did resign and was for a short time in private life. In December, 1864, Lincoln, in the full knowledge of the fact that during the summer Chase had done his utmost to injure him, nominated him as Chief Justice, and from him received his oath of office at his second inaugural.

The search for a rival for Lincoln was more successful when Fremont was solicited. He was nominated by a convention of extreme abolitionists that met in the city of Cleveland. But it soon became apparent that his following was insignificant, and he withdrew his name.

The regular Republican convention was held in Baltimore, June 8, 1864. Lincoln's name was presented, as in 1860, by the state of Illinois. On the first ballot he received every vote except those from the state of Missouri. When this was done, the Missouri delegates changed their votes and he was nominated unanimously.

In reply to congratulations, he said, 'I do not allow myself to suppose that either the convention or the League have concluded to decide that I am either the greatest or best man in America, but rather that they have concluded that it is not best to swap horses while crossing the river, and have further concluded that I am not so poor a horse that they might not make a botch of it trying to swap.'

That homely figure of 'swapping horses while crossing the river' caught the attention of the country. It is doubtful if ever a campaign speech, or any series of campaign speeches, was so effective in winning and holding votes as that one phrase.

But, as has already been said, the prospects during the summer – for there was a period of five months from the nomination to the election – were anything but cheering. At this crisis there developed a means of vigorous support which had not previously been estimated at its full value. In every loyal state there was a 'war governor'. Upon these men the burdens of the war had rested so heavily that they understood, as they would not otherwise have understood, the superlative weight of cares that pressed on the President, and they saw more clearly than they otherwise could have seen, the danger in swapping horses while crossing the river. These war governors rallied with unanimity and with great earnestness to the support of the President. Other willing helpers were used. The plain people, as well as the leading patriots, rallied to the support of the President.

The Democrats nominated McClellan on the general theory that the war was a failure. As election day approached, the increased vigor with which the war was prosecuted made it look less like a failure, even though success was not in sight. The result of the election was what in later days would be called a landslide. There were two hundred and thirty-three electors. Of this number two hundred and twelve were for Lincoln. The loyal North was back of him. He might now confidently gird himself for finishing the work.

Such was his kindliness of spirit that he was not unduly elated by success, and never, either in trial or achievement, did he become vindictive or revengeful. After the election he was serenaded, and in acknowledgment he made a little speech. Among other things he said, 'Now that the election is over, may not all, having a common interest, reunite in a common effort to save our common country? For my own part, I have striven, and will strive, to place no obstacle in the way. So long as I have been here *I have not willingly planted a thorn in any man's bosom.*'

CHAPTER THIRTY–SEVEN
Close of the War

As the year 1864 wore towards its close, military events manifestly approached a climax. In 1861 the two armies were comparatively green. For obvious reasons the advantage was on the side of the South. The South had so long been in substantial control at Washington that they had the majority of the generals, they had nearly all the arms and ammunition, and, since they had planned the coming conflict, their militia were in the main in better condition. But matters were different after three years. The armies on both sides were now composed of veterans, the generals had been tried and their value was known. Not least of all, Washington, while by no means free from spies, was not so completely overrun with them as at the first. At the beginning the departments were simply full of spies, and every movement of the government was promptly reported to the authorities at Richmond. Three and a half years had sufficed to weed out most of these.

In that period a splendid navy had been constructed. The Mississippi River was open from Minnesota to the Gulf of Mexico. Every southern port was more or less successfully blockaded, and the power of the government in this was every month growing stronger.

Strange as it may seem, the available population of the North had increased. The figures which Lincoln gave prove this. The loyal states of the North gave in 1860 a sum total of 3,870,222 votes. The same states in 1864 gave a total of 3,982,011. That gave an excess of voters to the number of 111,789. To this should be added the number of all the soldiers in the field from Massachusetts, Rhode Island, New Jersey, Delaware, Indiana, Illinois, and California, who by the laws of those states could not vote away from their homes, and which number could not have been less than 90,000. Then there were two new states, Kansas and Nevada, that had cast 33,762 votes. This leaves an increase for the North of 234,551 votes. It is plain that the North was not becoming exhausted of men.

Nor had the manufactures of the North decreased. The manufacture of arms and all the munitions of war was continually improving, and other industrial interests were flourishing. There was indeed much poverty and great suffering. The financial problem was one of the most serious of all, but in all these the South was suffering more than the North. On the southern side matters were growing desperate. The factor of time now counted against them, for, except in military discipline, they were not improving with the passing years. There was little hope of foreign intervention, there was not much hope of a counter uprising in the North. It is now generally accepted as a certainty that, if the Confederate government had published the truth concerning the progress of the war, especially of such battles as Chattanooga, the southern people would have recognized the hopelessness of their cause and the wickedness of additional slaughter, and the war would have terminated sooner.

In the eighth volume of the History by Nicolay and Hay there is a succession of chapters of which the headings alone tell the glad story of progress. These headings are: 'Arkansas Free', 'Louisiana Free', 'Tennessee Free', 'Maryland Free', and 'Missouri Free'.

In August Admiral Farragut had captured Mobile. General Grant with his veterans was face to face with General Lee and his veterans in Virginia. General Sherman with his splendid army had in the early fall struck through the territory of the Southern Confederacy and on Christmas day had captured Savannah. The following letter from the President again shows his friendliness towards his generals.

Executive Mansion,
Washington,
December 26, 1864
MY DEAR GENERAL SHERMAN:
Many, many thanks for your Christmas gift, the capture of Savannah.

When you were about leaving Atlanta for the Atlantic, I was anxious, if not fearful; but feeling that you were the better judge, and remembering that 'nothing risked, nothing gained', I did not interfere. Now, the undertaking being a success, the honor is all yours; for I believe none of us went further than to acquiesce.

And taking the work of General Thomas into the count, as it should be taken, it is indeed a great success. Not only does it afford the obvious and immediate military advantages; but in showing to the world that your army could be divided, putting the stronger part to an important new service, and yet leaving enough to vanquish the old opposing force of the whole – Hood's army – it brings those who sat in darkness to see a great light. But what next?

I suppose it will be safe if I leave General Grant and yourself to decide.

Please make my grateful acknowledgment to your whole army – officers and men.

Yours very truly,

A. LINCOLN

The principal thing now to be done was the destruction of the Confederate army or armies in Virginia. That and that only could end the war. The sooner it should be done the better. Grant's spirit cannot in a hundred pages be better expressed than in his own epigram – 'I propose to fight it out on this line if it takes all summer.' It did take all summer and all winter too, for the

Confederates as well as the Federals had grown to be good fighters, and they were no cowards. They, too, were now acting on the defensive and were able to take advantage of swamp, hill, and river. This was an important factor. Grant had indeed captured two armies and destroyed one, but this was different.

It needed not an experienced eye or a military training to see that this could only be done at a costly sacrifice of life. But let it be remembered that the three years of no progress had also been at a costly sacrifice of life. The deadly malaria of Virginia swamps was quite as dangerous as a bullet or bayonet. Thousands upon thousands of soldiers were taken to hospital cursing in their wrath: 'If I could only have been shot on the field of battle, there would have been some glory in it. But to die of drinking the swamp water – this is awful!' The sacrifice of life under Grant was appalling, but it was not greater than the other sort of sacrifice had been. What is more, it accomplished its purpose. Inch by inch he fought his way through many bloody months to the evacuation of Richmond and the surrender of Lee's army at Appomattox, April 9, 1865. Then the war was over.

The sympathies of the President were not limited to his own friends or his own army. The author is permitted to narrate the following incident – doubtless there were many others like it – which is given by an eye-witness, the Reverend Lysander Dickerman, D.D., of New York City.

It was at Hatcher's Run on the last Sunday before the close of the war. A detachment of Confederate prisoners, possibly two thousand in all, had just been brought in. They were in rags, starved, sick, and altogether as wretched a sight as one would be willing to see in a lifetime. A train of cars was standing on the siding. The President came out of a car and stood on the platform. As he gazed at the pitiable sufferers, he said not a word, but his breast heaved with emotion, his frame quivered. The tears streamed down his cheeks and he raised his arm ('I don't suppose,' commented the Doctor, 'he had a handkerchief') and with his sleeve wiped away the tears. Then he silently turned, re-entered the car which but for him was empty, sat down on the further side, buried his face in his hands, and wept. That is the picture of the man Lincoln. Little did the Southerners suspect, as they in turn cursed and maligned that great and tender man, what a noble friend they really had in him.

As the end came in sight an awkward question arose, What shall we do with Jeff Davis – if we catch him? This reminded the President of a little story. 'I told Grant,' he said, 'the story of an Irishman who had taken Father Matthew's pledge. Soon thereafter, becoming very thirsty, he slipped into a saloon and applied for a lemonade, and whilst it was being mixed he whispered to the bartender, 'Av ye could drap a bit o' brandy in it, all unbeknown to myself, I'd make no fuss about it.' My notion was that if Grant could let Jeff Davis escape all unbeknown to himself, he was to let him go. I didn't want him.' Subsequent events proved the sterling wisdom of this suggestion, for the country had no use for Jeff Davis when he was caught.

Late in March, 1865, the President decided to take a short vacation, said to be the first he had had since entering the White House in 1861. With a few friends he went to City Point on the James River, where Grant had his headquarters. General Sherman came up for a conference. The two generals were confident that the end of the war was near, but they were also certain that there must be at least one more great battle. 'Avoid this if possible,' said the President. 'No more bloodshed, no more bloodshed.'

On the second day of April both Richmond and Petersburg were evacuated. The President was determined to see Richmond and started under the care of Admiral Porter. The river was tortuous and all knew that the channel was full of obstructions so that they had the sensation of being in suspense as to the danger of torpedoes and other devices. Admiral Farragut who was in Richmond came down the river on the same day, April 4th, to meet the presidential party. An accident happened to his boat and it swung across the channel and there stuck fast, completely obstructing the channel, and rendering progress in either direction impossible. The members of the presidential party were impatient and decided to proceed as best they could. They were transferred to the Admiral's barge and towed up the river to their destination.

The grandeur of that triumphal entry into Richmond was entirely moral, not in the least spectacular. There were no triumphal arches, no martial music, no applauding multitudes, no vast cohorts with flying banners and glittering arms. Only a few American citizens, in plain clothes, on foot, escorted by ten marines. The central figure was that of a man remarkably tall, homely, ill-dressed, but with a countenance radiating joy and good-will. It was only thirty-six hours since Jefferson Davis had fled, having set fire to the city, and the fire was still burning. There was no magnificent civic welcome to the modest party, but there was a spectacle more significant. It was the large number of negroes, crowding, kneeling, praying, shouting 'Bress de Lawd!' Their emancipator, their Moses, their Messiah, had come in person. To them it was the beginning of the millennium. A few poor whites added their welcome, such as it was, and that was all. But all knew that 'Babylon had fallen', and they realized the import of that fact.

Johnston did not surrender to Sherman until April 26th, but Lee had surrendered on the 9th, and it was conceded that it was a matter of but a few days when the rest also would surrender. On Good Friday, April 14th – a day glorious in its beginning, tragic at its close – the newspapers throughout the North published an order of the Secretary of War stopping the draft and the purchase of arms and munitions of war. The government had decreed that at twelve o'clock noon of that day the stars and stripes should be raised above Fort Sumter. The chaplain was the Reverend Matthias Harris who had officiated at the raising of the flag over that fort in 1860. The reading of the psalter was conducted by the Reverend Dr Storrs of Brooklyn. The orator of the occasion was the eloquent Henry Ward Beecher. And the flag was raised by Major (now General) Anderson, whose staunch loyalty and heroic defense has linked his name inseparably with Sumter.

The war was over and Lincoln at once turned his attention to the duties of reconstruction.

CHAPTER THIRTY-EIGHT
Assassination

Ward H. Lamon asserts that there was no day, from the morning Lincoln left Springfield to the night of his assassination, when his life was not in serious peril. If we make generous allowance for the fears which had their root in Lamon's devoted love for his chief, and for that natural desire to magnify his office – for his special charge was to guard the President from bodily harm – which would incline him to estimate trifles seriously, we are still compelled to believe that the life was in frequent, if not continual, danger. There are, and always have been, men whose ambition is in the direction of a startling crime. There were not less than three known attempts on the life of Lincoln between Springfield and Washington. There may have been others that are not known. If anyone was in a position to know of real and probable plots against the President's life, it was Lamon. It was he, too, who showed the greatest concern upon the subject, though he was personally a man of unlimited courage.

An event occurred early in 1862, which we here transcribe, not merely because of its intrinsic interest, but especially because it hints of dangers not known to the public. Lincoln was at this time residing at the Soldiers' Home and was accustomed to riding alone to and from this place. His friends could not prevail on him to accept an escort, though they were in daily fear of kidnapping or murder. Lamon narrates the occurrence (substantially in the President's words) as follows.

One day he rode up to the White House steps, where the Colonel met him, and with his face full of fun, he said, 'I have something to tell you.' The two entered the office, where the President locked the door and proceeded: 'You know I have always told you I thought you an *idiot* that ought to be put in a straitjacket for your apprehensions of my personal danger from assassination. You also know that the way we skulked into this city in the first place has been a source of shame and regret to me, for it did look so cowardly!'

'Yes, go on.'

'Well, I don't now propose to make you my father-confessor and acknowledge a change of heart, yet I am free to admit that just now I don't know what to think: I am staggered. Understand me, I do not want to oppose my pride of opinion against light and reason, but I am in such a state of "betweenity" in my conclusions, that I can't say that the judgment of *this court* is prepared to proclaim a decision upon the facts presented.'

After a pause he continued: 'Last night about eleven o'clock, I went to the Soldiers' Home alone, riding *Old Abe*, as you call him; and when I arrived at the foot of the hill on the road leading to the entrance to the Home grounds, I was jogging along at a slow gait, immersed in deep thought, when suddenly I was aroused – I may say the arousement lifted me out of my saddle as well as out of my wits – by the report of a rifle, and seemingly the gunner was not fifty yards from where my contemplations ended and my accelerated transit began. My erratic namesake, with little warning, gave proof of decided dissatisfaction at the racket, and with one reckless bound he unceremoniously separated me from my eight-dollar plug hat, with which I parted company without any assent, express or implied, upon my part. At a breakneck speed we soon arrived in a haven of safety. Meanwhile I was left in doubt whether death was more desirable from being thrown from a runaway Federal horse, or as the tragic result of a rifle-ball fired by a disloyal bushwhacker in the middle of the night.'

'I tell you there is no time on record equal to that made by the two Old Abes on that occasion. The historic ride of John Gilpin, and Henry Wilson's memorable display of bareback equestrianship on the stray army mule from the scenes of the battle of Bull Run, a year ago, are nothing in comparison to mine, either in point of time made or in ludicrous pageantry.'

'No good can result at this time from giving [this occurrence] publicity. It does seem to me that I am in more danger from the augmentation of an imaginary peril than from a judicious silence, be the danger ever so great; and, moreover, I do not want it understood that I share your apprehensions. I never have.'

When one takes into account the number of Lincoln's bitter enemies, and the desperate character of some of them, the wonder is that he was not shot sooner. There were multitudes of ruffians in Washington City and elsewhere, who had murder in their hearts and plenty of deadly weapons within reach. Yet Lincoln lived on for four years, and was reluctant to accept even a nominal body-guard. The striking parallel between him and William the Silent will at once occur to the reader. He, like Lincoln, would take no precaution. He exposed himself freely, and there were plots almost innumerable against his life before he was slain. Such persons seem to have invisible defenders.

Lincoln was not a fatalist, but he did believe that he would live to complete his specific work and that he would not live beyond that. Perhaps he was wise in this. Had he surrounded himself with pomp and defense after the manner of Fremont he could not have done his work at all, for his special calling required that he should keep near to the people, and not isolate himself. Moreover, it is a question whether an elaborate show of defense would not have invited a correspondingly elaborate ingenuity in attack. His very trustfulness must have disarmed some. The wonder is not that he was slain at last, but that under the circumstances he was not slain earlier.

Much has been written, and perhaps justly, of Lincoln's presentiments. It is not exceptional, it is common in all rural communities to multiply and magnify signs. The commonest occurrences are invested with an occult meaning. Seeing the new moon over the right shoulder or over the left shoulder, the howling of a dog at night, the chance assemblage of thirteen persons, the spilling of salt – these and a thousand other things are taken to be signs of something. The habit of attending to these things probably originates in mere amusements. It takes the place, or furnishes the material, of small talk. But years of attention to these things, especially in the susceptible period of childhood and youth, are almost certain to have a lasting effect. A person gets into the habit of noting them, of looking for them, and the influence becomes ingrained in his very nature so that it is next to impossible to shake it off. This condition is a feature of all rural communities, not only in the West, but in New England: in fact, in Europe, Asia, Africa, and Australia.

Lincoln shared the impressibility of the community in which he grew up; no more, no less. Like all the rest, indeed, like all of mankind, he counted the hits, not the misses. Being unusually outspoken, he often told of impressions which another would not have mentioned. The very telling of them magnified their importance. He had been having premonitions all his life, and it would be strange if he did not have some just before his death. He did, and these are the ones that are remembered.

In spite of all, he was in excellent spirits on Good Friday, April 14, 1865. The burdens and sorrows of bloodshed had made an old man of him. But the war was at an end, the stars and stripes were floating over Sumter, the Union was saved, and slavery was doomed. There came back into his eyes the light that had long been absent. Those who were about him said the elasticity of his movements and joyousness of his manner were marked. 'His mood all day was singularly happy and tender.'

The events of the day were simple. It was the day of the regular meeting of the cabinet. Grant, who had arrived in Washington that morning, attended this meeting. It was the President's idea that the leaders of the Confederacy should be allowed to escape – much as he had already jocularly advised Grant to let Jeff Davis escape 'all unbeknown to himself'. He spoke plainly on the subject. 'No one need expect me to take any part in hanging or killing these men, even the worst of them. Enough lives have been sacrificed.' After the discussion of various matters, when the cabinet adjourned until the following Tuesday, the last words he ever uttered to them were that 'they must now begin to act in the interests of peace.'

In the afternoon he went for a drive with Mrs Lincoln. The conversation embraced plans of living – in Chicago? or California? – after the expiration of his term of office. This fact shows that his presentiments did not make so real an impression on him as many people have believed.

Three days before this his devoted servant Colonel Lamon – we might almost call him his faithful watch-dog, so loving, loyal, and watchful was he – had gone on an errand for him to Richmond. Lamon, who was loath to start, tried to secure from him a promise in advance of divulging what it was to be. Lincoln, after much urging, said he thought he would venture to make the promise. It was that he would promise not to go out after night in Lamon's absence, and *particularly to the theater* (italics Lamon's). The President first joked about it, but being persistently entreated said at last: 'Well, I promise to do the best I can towards it.'

But for the evening of the day under consideration, Mrs Lincoln had got up a theater party – her husband was always fond of the diversion of the theater. The party was to include General and Mrs Grant. But the general's plans required him to go that evening to Philadelphia, and so Major Rathbone and Miss Harris were substituted. This party occupied the upper proscenium box on the right of the stage.

About ten o'clock, J. Wilkes Booth, a young actor twenty-six years of age, and very handsome, glided along the corridor towards that box. Being himself an actor and well known by the employees of the theater, he was suffered to proceed without hindrance. Passing through the corridor door he fastened it shut by means of a bar that fitted into a niche previously prepared, and making an effectual barricade. A hole had been bored through the door leading into the box so that he could survey the inmates without attracting their attention. With revolver in one hand and dagger in the other he noiselessly entered the box and stood directly behind the President who was enjoying the humor of the comedy.

The awful tragedy in the box makes everything else seem pale and unreal. Here were five human beings in a narrow space – the greatest man of his time, in the glory of the most stupendous success in our history, the idolized chief of a nation already mighty, with illimitable vistas of grandeur to come; his beloved wife, proud and happy; a pair of betrothed lovers, with all the promise of felicity that youth, social position, and wealth could give them; and this young actor, handsome as Endymion upon Latmos, the pet of his little world. The glitter of fame, happiness, and ease was upon the entire group, but in an instant everything was to be changed with the blinding swiftness of enchantment. Quick death was to come on the central figure of that company – the central figure, we believe, of the great and good men of the century. Over all the rest the blackest fates hovered menacingly – fates from which a mother might pray that kindly death would save her children in their infancy. One was to wander with the stain of murder on his soul, with the curses of a world upon his name, with a price set upon his head, in frightful physical pain, till he died a dog's death in a burning barn; the stricken wife was to pass the rest of her days in melancholy and madness; of those two young lovers, one was to slay the other, and then end his life a raving maniac.

(Nicolay and Hay, X. 295)

The revolver was thrust near to the back of the head of the unsuspecting victim – that kind man who had 'never willingly planted a thorn in any man's bosom', who could not bear to witness suffering even in an animal. The report of the pistol was somewhat muffled and was unnoticed by the majority of the audience. The ball penetrated the President's brain, and without word or sound his head dropped upon his breast. Major Rathbone took in the situation and sprang at the murderer who slashed him savagely with the dagger, tore himself free, and leaped over the balustrade upon the stage. It was not a high leap for an athletic young man, but his spur caught in a flag with which the box was draped, so that he did not strike quite squarely on his feet. The result was that he broke his leg or ankle. But gathering himself up, he flourished his dagger, declaiming the motto of Virginia, *Sic semper tyrannis* ['Thus ever to tyrants'], and before the audience could realize what was done, he disappeared. He ran out of the rear of the theater where a fleet horse was in waiting. He mounted and rode for his life. For eleven days he was in hiding, with the curse of Cain upon him, suffering all the while excruciating agonies from his broken leg, which could be but imperfectly cared for. He was finally corralled in a barn, the barn was set on fire, and while thus at bay he was shot down.

Aid came at once to the President, but the surgeons saw at a glance that the wound was mortal. They carried him out into the open air. When they reached the street the question arose, Where shall we take him? On the opposite side of the street was an unpretentious hotel. A man, standing on the front steps, saw the commotion and asked what it meant. On being told, he said, 'Take him to my room.' It was thus that the greatest man of the age died in a small room of a common hotel. But this was not unfitting; he was of the plain people, he always loved them, and among them he closed his earthly record. He lingered unconscious through the night, and at twenty minutes after seven o'clock, on the morning of April 15th, he died.

The band of assassins of which Booth was the head, planned to murder also other officials. Grant escaped, having suddenly left the city. The only other person who was actually attacked was Seward. Though the assassin was a giant in stature and in strength, though he fought like a madman, and though Seward was at the time in bed with his right arm and jaw fractured, he having been thrown from a horse, yet strangely enough he was not killed. The assassin inflicted many and terrible wounds, especially upon Frederick Seward, his son, who did not regain consciousness for weeks; but no one in that house was killed.

Surely never did the telegraph bear heavier news than when it flashed the message, 'Lincoln has been assassinated.' More than

one ex-Confederate stoutly declared that 'when Lincoln was murdered the South lost its best friend.' And thousands of others
replied, that was the truth! At the dedication of his monument in
1874 General Grant gave utterance again to this thought: 'In his
death the nation lost its greatest hero; in his death the South lost its
most just friend.'

CHAPTER THIRTY-NINE
A Nation's Sorrow

The outburst of sorrow and indignation over the foul murder of
the President was so great as to lead people to assume that Lincoln
was at all times and universally a favorite. Those who know better
have sometimes thought it discreet to preserve silence. But the
greatness of his work cannot be appreciated at its full value unless
one bears in mind that he had not the full measure of sympathy
and a reasonable help from those on whom he had a right to
depend. During the four years that he was in Washington he was
indeed surrounded by a band of devoted followers. But these
people were few in numbers. Those who sympathized with
Fremont, or McClellan, or Greeley, plus those who were against
Lincoln on general principles, constituted a large majority of the
people who ought to have sustained him. All of these factions, or
coteries, however much they differed among themselves, agreed
in hampering Lincoln. For one person Lincoln was too radical, for
another too conservative, but both joined hands to annoy him.

Much of this annoyance was thoughtless. The critics were conscientious, they sincerely believed that their plans were the best.
They failed to grasp the fact that the end desired might possibly be
better reached by other methods than their own. But on the other
hand much of this annoyance was malicious.

When the shock of the murder came, there was a great revulsion
of feeling. The thoughtless were made thoughtful, the malicious
were brought to their senses. Neither class had realized into what
diabolical hands they were playing by their opposition to the
administration. It was the greatness of the sorrow of the people –

the plain people whom he had always loved and who always loved him – that sobered the contentions. Even this was not fully accomplished at once. There is documentary evidence to show that the extreme radicals, represented by such men as George W. Julian, of Indiana, considered that the death of Lincoln removed an obstruction to the proper governing of the country. Julian's words (in part) are as follows.

> I spent most of the afternoon [April 15, 1864, the day of Lincoln's death] in a political caucus held for the purpose of considering the necessity for a new Cabinet and a line of policy less conciliating than that of Mr Lincoln; and while everybody was shocked at his murder, the feeling was nearly universal that the accession of Johnson to the presidency would prove a godsend to the country. . . . On the following day, in pursuance of a previous engagement, the Committee on the Conduct of the War met the President at his quarters at the Treasury Department. He received us with decided cordiality, and Mr Wade said to him: 'Johnson, we have faith in you. There will be no trouble now in running the government.' . . . While we were rejoiced that the leading conservatives of the country were not in Washington, we felt that the presence and influence of the committee, of which Johnson had been a member, would aid the Administration in getting on the right track. . . . The general feeling was . . . that he would act on the advice of General Butler by inaugurating a policy of his own, instead of administering on the political estate of his predecessor.
>
> (Julian, *Political Recollections*, p. 255, ff.)

The names of the patriots who attended this caucus on the day of Lincoln's death, are not given. It is not necessary to know them. It is not probable that there were many exhibitions of this spirit after the death of the President. This one, which is here recorded in the words of the confession of one of the chief actors, is an exception. But *before* the death of Lincoln, this spirit of fault-finding, obstruction, hostility, was not uncommon and was painfully aggressive. *After* his death there was a revulsion of feeling. Many who had failed to give the cheer, sympathy, and encouragement which they might have given in life, shed bitter and unavailing tears over his death.

On the other, the Confederate, side, it is significant that during the ten days the murderer was in hiding, no southern sympathizer whom he met wished to arrest him or have him arrested, although a large reward had been offered for his apprehension. As to the head of the Confederacy, Jeff Davis, there is no reasonable doubt that he approved the act and motive of Booth, whether he had given him a definite commission or not. Davis tried to defend himself by saying that he had greater objection to Johnson than to Lincoln. But since the conspiracy included the murder of both Lincoln and Johnson, as well as others, this defense is very lame. It was certainly more than a coincidence that Booth – a poor man who had plenty of ready money – and Jacob Thompson, the Confederate agent in Canada, had dealings with the same bank in Montreal. Davis himself said, 'For an enemy so relentless, in the war for our subjugation, I could not be expected to mourn.'

To put it in the mildest form, neither Jeff Davis in the South, nor the extreme radicals in the North, were sorry that Lincoln was out of the way. Extremes had met in the feeling of relief that the late President was now out of the way. This brings to mind a statement in an ancient book which records that 'Herod and Pilate became friends with each other that very day; for before they were at enmity between themselves.'

On Friday evening there had been general rejoicing throughout the loyal North. On Saturday morning there rose to heaven a great cry of distress – such a cry as has hardly been paralleled since the destruction of the first-born in Egypt. For the telegraph – invented since Lincoln had come into manhood – had carried the heavy news to every city and commercial center in the North. The shock plunged the whole community, in the twinkling of an eye, from the heights of exultation into the abyss of grief.

There was no business transacted that day. The whole nation was given up to grief. Offices, stores, exchanges were deserted. Men gathered in knots and conversed in low tones. By twelve o'clock noon there was scarcely a public building, store, or residence in any northern city that was not draped in mourning. The poor also procured bits of black crepe, or some substitute for it, and tied them to their door-knobs. The plain people were orphaned. 'Father Abraham' was dead.

Here and there some southern sympathizer ventured to express exultation – a very rash thing to do. Forbearance had ceased to be a virtue, and in nearly every such case the crowd organized a lynching bee in the fraction of a minute, and the offender was thankful to escape alive.

Though this wave of sorrow swept over the land from ocean to ocean, it was necessarily more manifest in Washington than elsewhere. There the crime had been committed. There the President's figure was a familiar sight and his voice was a familiar sound. There the tragedy was nearer at hand and more vivid. In the middle of the morning a squad of soldiers bore the lifeless body to the White House. It lay there in state until the day of the funeral, Wednesday. It is safe to say that on the intervening Sunday there was hardly a pulpit in the North, from which, by sermon and prayer, were not expressed the love of the chief. On Wednesday, the day of the funeral in Washington, all the churches in the land were invited to join in solemnizing the occasion.

The funeral service was held in the East room of the White House, conducted by the President's pastor Dr Gurley, and his eloquent friend, Bishop Simpson of the Methodist Episcopal church. Mrs Lincoln, prostrated by the shock, was unable to be present, and little Tad would not come. Only Robert, a recent graduate of Harvard and at the time a member of Grant's staff, was there to represent the family.

After the service, which was brief and simple, the body was borne with suitable pomp and magnificence, the procession fittingly headed by negro troops, to the Capitol, where it was placed in the rotunda until the evening of the next day. There, as at the White House, innumerable crowds passed to look upon that grave, sad, kindly face. The negroes came in great numbers, sobbing out their grief over the death of their Emancipator. The soldiers, too, who remembered so well his oft repeated 'God bless you, boys!' were not ashamed of their grief. There were also neighbors, friends, and the general public.

It was arranged that the cortège should return to Springfield over as nearly as possible the same route as that taken by the President in 1861 – Baltimore, Harrisburg, Philadelphia, New York, Albany, Cleveland, Columbus, Indianapolis, and Chicago. In the party there were three of those who had escorted him to Washington – David Davis, W. H. Lamon, and General Hunter.

At eight o'clock on Friday, April 21st, the funeral train left Washington. It is hardly too much to say that it was a funeral procession two thousand miles in length. All along the route people turned out, not daunted by darkness and rain – for it rained much of the time – and stood with streaming eyes to watch the train go by. At the larger cities named, the procession paused and the body lay for some hours in state while the people came in crowds so great that it seemed as if the whole community had turned out. At Columbus and Indianapolis those in charge said that it seemed as if the entire population of the state came to do him honor. The present writer has never witnessed another sight so imposing.

Naturally the ceremonies were most elaborate in New York City. But at Chicago the grief was most unrestrained and touching. He was there among his neighbors and friends. It was the state of Illinois that had given him to the nation and the world. They had the claim of fellow-citizenship, he was one of them. As a citizen of the state of which Chicago was the leading city, he had passed all his public life. The neighboring states sent thousands of citizens, for he was a western man like themselves, and for the forty-eight hours that he lay in state a continuous stream of all sorts and conditions of men passed by sorrowing.

In all these cities not a few mottoes were displayed. Most of these were from his own writings, such as, 'With malice toward none, with charity for all'; and, 'We here highly resolve that these dead shall not have died in vain.' Two others are firmly fixed in the mind of the writer which are here given as a sample of all. The first is from the Bible: 'He being dead yet speaketh.' The second is from Shakespeare.

> His life was gentle, and the elements
> So mix'd in him, that Nature might stand up
> And say to all the world, This was a man!

His final resting-place was Springfield. Here, and in all the neighboring country, he was known to everyone. He had always a kind word for everyone, and now all this came back in memory. His goodness had not been forgotten. Those whom he had be-friended had delighted to tell of it. They therefore came to do honor not merely to the great statesman, but to the beloved friend, the warm-hearted neighbor. Many could remember his grave face as he stood on the platform of the car that rainy morning in February, 1861, and said, 'I now leave, not knowing when or whether ever I shall return.' Between the two days, what a large and noble life had been lived.

The city had made elaborate preparations for the final services. The funeral in Springfield was on May 4th. The order of service included a dirge, a prayer, the reading of his second inaugural address, and an oration. The latter was by Bishop Simpson and was worthy of the noble and eloquent orator. It was a beautiful day, the rain which had been falling during the long journey was over, and May sunshine filled earth and sky. Near the close of the day the body of the President, together with that of his little son Willie, which also had been brought from Washington, was laid in a vault in Oak Ridge cemetery.

A movement was at once set on foot to erect a suitable monument. For this purpose a few large sums of money were subscribed, but most of it came in small sums from the plain people. The negro troops contributed $8,000. The sum of $180,000 in all was raised and a noble structure was erected. It was dedicated in 1874. The orator of the day was his old-time friend, Governor, afterwards General, Oglesby. Warm words of appreciation were added by Generals Grant and Sherman. The former, who served under him as general and for two terms succeeded him in office, among other things said, 'To know him personally was to love and respect him for his great qualities of heart and head, and for his patience and patriotism.'

Lincoln was never a resident of Chicago, but he was always a favorite in that city, even though it was the home of his great rival, Judge Douglas. It was there he was nominated in 1860, and the city always felt as if it had a personal claim on him. It has done itself honor by the construction of Lincoln Park. The chief ornament is a bronze statue of heroic size, by the sculptor St Gaudens. The statue represents Lincoln in the attitude of speaking, and the legend, which is lettered at the base, is the sublime paragraph that concludes the second inaugural. The beauty of the park – lawn, flowers, shrubbery, trees – and the majesty of the statue, constitute a noble memorial of the man whose name they perpetuate.

CHAPTER FORTY

The Measure of a Man

'God's plan
And measure of a stalwart man.' – *Lowell.*

Lincoln's physical characteristics have been sufficiently described –
his unmanageable height and his giant strength. His mental traits
have been treated in Chapter 35. We now consider his moral
qualities, that is to say his character.

Conspicuous was his honesty. The soubriquet 'Honest Abe Lincoln', which his neighbors fastened on him in his youth, was never
lost, shaken off, or outgrown. This was something more than the
exactness of commercial honesty which forbade him to touch a
penny of the funds that remained over from the extinct post-office
of New Salem, though the government was for years negligent in
the matter of settling up. In youth he always insisted on fairness in
sports so that he came to be the standing umpire of the neighborhood. It came out also in his practise of the law, when he would
not lend his influence to further scoundrel schemes, nor would he
consent to take an unfair advantage of an opponent. But the glory of
his honesty appeared in his administration. It is a wonderful fact that
there has never been any suspicion, even among his enemies, that
he used the high powers of his office for gain, or for the furtherance
of his political ambition. When contracts, to the amount of many
millions of dollars, were being constantly given out for a period of
four years, there was never a thought that a dishonest dollar would
find its way, either directly or indirectly, into the hands of the
President, or with his consent into the hands of his friends. When
he was a candidate for re-election he was fully aware that some
officials of high station were using their prerogatives for the purpose
of injuring him. It was in his power to dismiss these in disgrace –
and they deserved it. This he refused to do. So long as they did well
their official duties, he overlooked their injustice to him. No
President has surpassed him in the cleanness of his record, and only
Washington has equaled him.

His tenderness of heart overrode almost everything. In childhood he would not permit boys to put live coals on the back of a

turtle. In youth he stayed out all night with a drunkard to prevent his freezing to death, a fate which his folly had invited. In young manhood with the utmost gentleness he restored to their nest some birdlings that had been beaten out by the storm. When a lawyer on the circuit, be dismounted from his horse and rescued a pig that was stuck in the mud. This spoiled a suit of clothes, because he had to lift the pig in his arms. His explanation was that he could not bear to think of that animal in suffering, and so he did it simply for his own peace of mind.

But when he became President, his tenderness of heart was as beautiful as the glow of the sunset. To him the boys in blue were as sons. On him as on no one else the burden of the nation's troubles rested. It may with reverence be said that he 'bore our sorrows, he carried our grief'. Not only was this true in general, but in specific cases his actions showed it. When the soldiers were under sentence from court-martial – many of them mere boys – the sentence came to Lincoln for approval. If he could find any excuse whatever for pardon he would grant it. His tendency to pardon, his leaning towards the side of mercy, became proverbial and greatly annoyed some of the generals who feared military discipline would be destroyed. But he would not turn a deaf ear to the plea of mercy, and he could not see in it any permanent danger to the republic. One or two examples will stand fairly for a large number. When a boy was sentenced to death for desertion, he said: 'Must I shoot a simple-minded soldier boy who deserts, and not touch a hair of the wily agitator who induces him to desert? I think that in such a case, to silence the agitator and save the boy, is not only constitutional, but withal a great mercy.'

Early in the war he pardoned a boy who was sentenced to be shot for sleeping at his post as sentinel. By way of explanation the President said: 'I could not think of going into eternity with the blood of that poor young man on my skirts. It is not to be wondered at that a boy, raised on a farm, probably in the habit of going to bed at dark, should, when required to watch, fall asleep; and I cannot consent to shoot him for such an act.' The sequel is romantic. The dead body of this boy was found among the slain on the field of the battle of Fredericksburg. Next his heart was a photograph of the President on which he had written 'God bless President Abraham Lincoln!'

On the 21st day of November, 1864, he wrote to Mrs Bixby, of Boston, Mass., the following letter which needs no comment or explanation.

DEAR MADAM: I have been shown, in the files of the War Department, a statement of the Adjutant-General of Massachusetts, that you are the mother of five sons who have died gloriously on the field of battle. I feel how weak and fruitless must be any words of mine which should attempt to beguile you from the grief of a loss so overwhelming. But I cannot refrain from tendering to you the consolation that may be found in the thanks of the Republic they died to save. I pray that our Heavenly Father may assuage the anguish of your bereavement, and leave you only the cherished memory of the loved and lost, and the solemn pride that must be yours to have laid so costly a sacrifice upon the altar of freedom.

Yours, very sincerely and respectfully,

ABRAHAM LINCOLN

A different side of his character is shown in the following incident. A slave-trader had been condemned, in Newburyport, Mass., to a fine of one thousand dollars and imprisonment for five years. He served out his term of imprisonment, but he could not pay his fine, because he had no money and no way of getting any. Consequently he was still held for the fine which he was unable to pay. Some people of influence interested themselves in the case, and a congressman from eastern Massachusetts, who stood very near to the President, laid the facts before him with the request for a pardon. He was indeed much moved by the appeal, but he gave his decision in substantially the following words: 'My friend, this appeal is very touching to my feelings, and no one knows my weakness better than you. I am, if possible to be, too easily moved by appeals for mercy; and I must say that if this man had been guilty of the foulest murder that the arm of man could perpetrate, I might forgive him on such an appeal. But the man who could go to Africa, and rob her of her children, and then sell them into interminable bondage, with no other motive than that which is furnished by dollars and cents, is so much worse than the most depraved murderer that he can never receive pardon at my hand. No, sir; he may stay in jail forever before he shall have liberty by any act of mine.'

It was his magnanimity that constructed his cabinet. Hardly another man in the world would have failed to dismiss summarily both Seward and Chase. But, thanks to his magnanimous forbearance, Seward became not only useful to the country, but devotedly loyal to his chief. After Chase's voluntary retirement Lincoln appointed him Chief Justice. To his credit be it said that he adorned the judiciary, but he never did appreciate the man who saved him from oblivion, not to say disgrace. Up to the year 1862, his only personal knowledge of Stanton was such as to rouse only memories of indignation, but when he believed that Stanton would make a good Secretary of War he did not hesitate to appoint him. It is safe to say that this appointment gave Stanton the greatest surprise of his life.

He was always ready to set aside his preference, or to do the expedient thing when no moral principle was involved. When such a principle was involved he was ready to stand alone against the world. He was no coward. In early youth he championed the cause of temperance in a community where the use of liquors was almost universal. In the Illinois legislature and in Congress he expressed his repugnance to the whole institution of slavery, though this expression could do him no possible good, while it might do him harm. When he was a lawyer, he was almost the only lawyer of ability who did not dread the odium sure to attach to those who befriended negroes.

When in the White House, he stood out almost alone against the clamors of his constituents and directed the release of Mason and Slidell.

Personally he was a clean man. The masculine vices were abhorrent to him. He was not profane. He was not vulgar. He was as far removed from suspicion as Caesar could have demanded of his wife. He was not given to drink. When a young man he could not be tricked into swallowing whisky. At the close of the war, a barrel of whisky was sent him from some cellar in Richmond, as a souvenir of the fall of the city, but he declined to receive it. Wine was served at the table of the White House in deference to foreign guests who did not know, and could not be taught, how to dine without it. As a matter of courtesy he went through the form of touching the glass to his lips, but he never drank. How widely his life was separated from many of his associates! The atmosphere of the White House has been sweeter and purer ever since he occupied it, and this is largely due to the influence of his incorruptible purity.

In the matter of religion, he did not wear his heart on his sleeve, and some of his friends have refused to believe that he was religious. It is true that he was not a church member, but there were special reasons for this. The church with which he was naturally affiliated was the Presbyterian. The most eloquent preacher of that denomination was the Reverend Dr Palmer of New Orleans, who was an aggressive champion of slavery as a divine institution. His teachings were feebly echoed in thousands of other pulpits. Now Lincoln abhorred slavery. He incorporated human freedom into his religion. The one point on which he insisted all his life was that 'slavery is wrong!' It may therefore be seen that the church did not give him a cordial invitation. If this needs any proof, that proof is found in the fact that the pastors in Springfield voted almost unanimously against him. Even Peter Cartwright had denounced him as an atheist.

The marvel is that this did not embitter him against the church. But all his life long he kept up such bonds of sympathy with the church as were possible. He bore with the faults of the church and of ministers with that patience which made his whole character so remarkably genuine. He was a constant attendant at the services, he was favorable to all the legitimate work of the church, and he was exceptionally kind to ministers, though they were often a sore trial to him.

In childhood he would not rest until a clergyman had traveled many miles through the forests to preach a memorial discourse over the grave of his mother. When his father was ill he wrote a letter of religious consolation intended for him: 'Tell him to remember to call upon and confide in our great and good and merciful Maker, who will not turn away from him in any extremity. He notes the fall of a sparrow, and numbers the hairs of our heads, and He will not forget the dying man who puts his trust in Him.'

Hugh McCulloch, in a personal letter to the author, January 28, 1889, wrote: 'He was, as far as I could judge, a pure man, and "in spirit and temper" a Christian.' His pastor, Dr Gurley, regarded him as a Christian. Other clergymen who were acquainted with him did so.

J. G. Holland has preserved the following incident.

Colonel Loomis, who was commandant of Fort Columbus, Governor's Island, in New York Harbor, reached the age at which by law he should be put on the retired list. He was a very religious man, and his influence was so marked that the chaplain and some others, determined to appeal to the President to have him continued at the post. The Reverend Dr Duryea of Brooklyn was sent to Washington to prefer the request. 'What does the clergyman know of military matters?' inquired the President. 'Nothing,' was the reply. 'It is desired to retain Colonel Loomis solely for the sake of his Christian influence. He sustains religious exercises at the fort, leads a prayer-meeting, and teaches a Bible class in the Sunday School.' 'That is the highest possible recommendation,' replied the President. He approved the request, and the Christian officer was retained there until imperative military duty called him elsewhere.

The religious strain that runs through his papers and addresses cannot be overlooked. But there are two that deserve special mention. The first is the 'Sunday Order', which is as follows.

The importance for man and beast of the prescribed weekly rest, the sacred rights of Christian soldiers and sailors, a becoming deference to the best sentiment of a Christian people, and a due regard for the Divine will, demand that Sunday labor in the army and navy be reduced to the measure of strict necessity. The discipline and character of the national forces should not suffer, nor the cause they defend be imperiled, by the profanation of the day or the name of the Most High.

The other is his thanksgiving proclamation. He it was who nationalized this festival which had previously been local and irregular. His successors in office have done well to follow his example in the matter. Every November, when the entire population turns from daily toil to an hour of thanksgiving, they should not forget that they are thereby acting on his recommendation, and in doing this they are strengthening the best possible monument to the grand, good man whom the Most High mercifully gave to this country in the time of her direst need.

He was a *man*; take him for all in all
I shall not look upon his like again.

CHAPTER FORTY-ONE

Testimonies

We have now followed the career of Lincoln throughout. It is fitting that this book should conclude with a record of what some observant men have said about him. Accordingly this, the last, chapter is willingly given up to these testimonies. Of course such a list could easily be extended indefinitely, but the quotations here given are deemed sufficient for their purpose.

H. W. Beecher

Who shall recount our martyr's sufferings for this people? Since the November of 1860 his horizon has been black with storms. By day and by night, he trod a way of danger and darkness. On his shoulders rested a government dearer to him than his own life. At its integrity millions of men were striking home. Upon this government foreign eyes lowered. It stood like a lone island in a sea full of storms; and every tide and wave seemed eager to devour it. Upon thousands of hearts great sorrows and anxieties have rested, but not on one such, and in such measure, as upon that simple, truthful, noble soul, our faithful and sainted Lincoln. Never rising to the enthusiasm of more impassioned natures in hours of hope, and never sinking with the mercurial in hours of defeat to the depths of despondency, he held on with immovable patience and fortitude, putting caution against hope, that it might not be premature, and hope against caution, that it might not yield to dread and danger. He wrestled ceaselessly through four black and dreadful purgatorial years, wherein God was cleansing the sin of his people as by fire. ... .

Then the wail of a nation proclaimed that he had gone from among us. Not thine the sorrow, but ours, sainted soul! Thou hast indeed entered the promised land, while we are yet on the march. To us remains the rocking of the deep, the storm upon the land, days of duty and nights of watching; but thou art sphered high above all darkness and fear, beyond all sorrow and weariness. Rest, O weary heart! Rejoice exceedingly, thou that hast enough suffered! Thou hast beheld Him who invisibly led thee in this great wilderness. Thou standest among the elect. Around thee are the royal men that have ennobled human life in every age. Kingly art thou, with glory on thy brow as a diadem. And joy is upon thee for evermore. Over all this land, over all this little cloud of years, that now from thine infinite horizon moves back as a speck, thou art lifted up as high as the star is above the clouds that hide us, but never reach it. In the goodly company of Mount Zion thou shalt find that rest which thou hast sorrowing sought in vain; and thy name, an everlasting name in heaven, shall flourish in fragrance and beauty as long as men shall last upon the earth, or hearts remain, to revere truth, fidelity, and goodness.

. . . Four years ago, O Illinois, we took from your midst an untried man, and from among the people. We return him to you a mighty conqueror. Not thine any more but the Nation's; not ours, but the world's. Give him place, O ye prairies! In the midst of this great continent his dust shall rest, a sacred treasure to myriads who shall pilgrim to that shrine to kindle anew their zeal and patriotism. Ye winds that move over the mighty places of the West, chant his requiem! Ye people, behold a martyr whose blood, as so many articulate words, pleads for for fidelity, for law, for liberty!

Noah Brooks
He became the type, flower, and representative of all that is worthily American; in him the commonest of human traits were blended with an all-embracing charity and the highest human wisdom; with single devotion to the right he lived unselfishly, void of selfish personal ambition, and, dying tragically, left a name to be remembered with love and honor as one of the best and greatest of mankind.

W. C. Bryant

> Oh, slow to smite and swift to spare,
> Gentle and merciful and just!
> Who, in the fear of God, didst bear
> The sword of power, a nation's trust!
>
> In sorrow by thy bier we stand,
> Amid the awe that hushes all,
> And speak the anguish of a land
> That shook with horror at thy fall.

Thy task is done; the bond are free:
We bear thee to an honored grave,
Whose proudest monument shall be
The broken fetters of the slave.

Pure was thy life; its bloody close
Hath placed thee with the sons of light,
Among the noble host of those
Who perished in the cause of Right.

J. H. Choate

A rare and striking illustration of the sound mind in the sound body. He rose to every occasion. He led public opinion. He knew the heart and conscience of the people. Not only was there this steady growth of intellect, but the infinite delicacy of his nature and capacity for refinement developed also, as exhibited in the purity and perfection of his language and style of speech.

R. W. Emerson

He had a face and manner which disarmed suspicion, which inspired confidence, which confirmed good will. He was a man without vices. He had a strong sense of duty. . . . He had what the farmers call a long head. . . . He was a great worker; he had a prodigious faculty of performance; worked easily. . . . He had a vast good nature which made him accessible to all. . . . Fair-minded . . . affable . . . this wise man.

What an occasion was the whirlwind of the war! Here was the place for no holiday magistrate, no fair-weather sailor; the new pilot was hurled to the helm in a tornado. In four years – four years of battle-days – his endurance, his fertility of resources, his magnanimity, were sorely tried and never found wanting. There, by his courage, his justice, his even temper, his fertile counsel, his humanity, he stood a heroic figure in the center of a heroic epoch. He is the true history of the American people in his time. Step by step he walked before them; slow with their slowness, quickening his march by theirs, the true representative of this continent; an entirely public man; father of his country, the pulse of twenty millions throbbing in his heart, the thought of their minds articulated by his tongue.

J. G. Holland

Conscience, and not expediency, not temporary advantage, not popular applause, not the love of power, was the ruling and guiding motive of his life. He was patient with his enemies, and equally patient with equally unreasonable friends. No hasty act of his administration can be traced to his impatience. He had a tender, brotherly regard for every human being; and the thought of oppression was torment to him. . . . A statesman without a statesman's craftiness, a politician without a politician's mean-nesses, a great man without a great man's vices, a philanthropist without a philanthropist's impracticable dreams, a Christian with-out pretensions, a ruler without the pride of place and power, an ambitious man without selfishness, and a successful man without vanity.

O. W. Holmes

> Our hearts lie buried in the dust
>> With him so true and tender,
> The patriot's stay, the people's trust,
>> The shield of the offender.

J. R. Lowell

On the day of his death, this simple Western attorney, who, according to one party was a vulgar joker, and whom the *doctrin-aires* among his own supporters accused of wanting every element of statesmanship, was the most absolute ruler in Christendom, and this solely by the hold his good-humored sagacity had laid on the hearts and understandings of his countrymen. Nor was this all, for it appeared that he had drawn the great majority not only of his fellow-citizens, but of mankind also, to his side. So strong and so persuasive is honest manliness without a single quality of romance or unreal sentiment to help it! A civilian during times of the most captivating military achievement, awkward, with no skill in the lower technicalities of manners, he left behind a fame beyond that of any conqueror, the memory of a grace higher than that of out-ward person, and of a gentlemanliness deeper than mere breeding. Never before that startled April morning did such multitudes of men shed tears for the death of one whom they had never seen, as if with him a friendly presence had been taken away from their lives, leaving them colder and darker. Never was funeral panegyric so eloquent as the silent look of sympathy which strangers exchanged when they met on that day. Their common manhood had lost a kinsman.

> Wise, steadfast in the strength of God, and true.
>   How beautiful to see
> Once more a shepherd of mankind indeed,
> Who loved his charge, but never loved to lead;
> One whose meek flock the people joyed to be,
>   Not lured by any Cheat of birth,
>   But by his clear-grained human worth,
> And brave old wisdom of sincerity!

*   *   *

> Great Captains, with their guns and drums,
> Disturb our judgment for the hour,
>   But at last silence comes;
> These all are gone, and, standing like a tower,
> Our children shall behold his fame,
>   The kindly-earnest, brave, foreseeing man,
> Sagacious, patient, dreading praise, not blame,
> New birth of our new soil, the first American.

Clara Morris
God's anointed – the great, the blameless Lincoln. . . . The homely, tender-hearted 'Father Abraham' – rare combination of courage, justice, and humanity.

H. J. Raymond
But there was a native grace, the out-growth of kindness of heart, which never failed to shine through all his words and acts. His heart was as tender as a woman's – as accessible to grief and gladness as a child's – yet strong as Hercules to bear the anxieties and responsibilities of the awful burden that rested on it. Little incidents of the war – instances of patient suffering in devotion to duty – tales of distress from the lips of women, never failed to touch the innermost chords of his nature, and to awaken that sweet sympathy which carries with it, to those who suffer, all the comfort the human heart can crave. Those who have heard

him, as many have, relate such touching episodes of the war, cannot recall without emotion the quivering lip, the face gnarled and writhed to stifle the rising sob, and the patient, loving eyes swimming in tears, which mirrored the tender pity of his gentle and loving nature. He seemed a stranger to the harsher and stormier passions of man. Easily grieved, he seemed incapable of hate. . . . It is first among the marvels of a marvelous time, that to such a character, so womanly in all its traits, should have been committed, absolutely and with almost despotic power, the guidance of a great nation through a bloody and terrible civil war. . . .

Carl Schurz

As the state of society in which Abraham Lincoln grew up passes away, the world will read with increasing wonder of the man who, not only of the humblest origin, but remaining the simplest and most unpretending of citizens, was raised to a position of power unprecedented in our history; who was the gentlest and most peace-loving of mortals, unable to see any creature suffer without a pang in his own breast, and suddenly found himself called to conduct the greatest and bloodiest of our wars; who wielded the power of government when stern resolution and relentless force were the order of the day, and then won and ruled the popular mind and heart by the tender sympathies of his nature; who was a cautious conservative by temperament and mental habit, and led the most sudden and sweeping social revolution of our time; who, preserving his homely speech and rustic manner, even in the most conspicuous position of that period, drew upon himself the scoffs of polite society, and then thrilled the soul of mankind with utterances of wonderful beauty and grandeur; who, in his heart the best friend of the defeated South, was murdered because a crazy fanatic took him for its most cruel enemy; who, while in power, was beyond measure lampooned and maligned by sectional passion and an excited party spirit, and around whose bier friend and foe gathered to praise him – which they have since never ceased to do – as one of the greatest of Americans and the best of men.

Henry Watterson

He went on and on, and never backward, until his time was come, when his genius, fully developed, rose to the great exigencies intrusted to his hands.

Where did he get his style? Ask Shakespeare and Burns where they got their style. Where did he get his grasp upon affairs and his knowledge of men? Ask the Lord God, who created miracles in Luther and Bonaparte! . . . Where did Shakespeare get his genius? Where did Mozart get his music? Whose hand smote the lyre of the Scottish plowman, and stayed the life of the German priest? God, God, and God alone; and as surely as these were raised up by God, inspired by God, was Abraham Lincoln; and a thousand years hence, no drama, no tragedy, no epic poem, will be filled with greater wonder, or be followed by mankind with deeper feeling, than that which tells the story of his life and death.

THE END

SPEECHES AND LETTERS OF
ABRAHAM LINCOLN
1832-1865

Lincoln's First Public Speech. From an Address to the People of
Sangamon County. March 9, 1832

Upon the subject of education, not presuming to dictate any plan or system respecting it, I can only say that I view it as the most important subject which we, as a people, can be engaged in. That every man may receive at least a moderate education, and thereby be enabled to read the histories of his own and other countries, by which he may duly appreciate the value of our free institutions, appears to be an object of vital importance, even on this account alone, to say nothing of the advantages and satisfaction to be derived from all being able to read the Scriptures and other works, both of a religious and moral nature, for themselves.

For my part, I desire to see the time when education – and by its means morality, sobriety, enterprise, and industry – shall become much more general than at present; and should be gratified to have it in my power to contribute something to the advancement of any measure which might have a tendency to accelerate that happy period.

With regard to existing laws, some alterations are thought to be necessary. Many respectable men have suggested that our estray laws – the law respecting the issuing of executions, the road law, and some others – are deficient in their present form, and require alterations. But considering the great probability that the framers of those laws were wiser than myself, I should prefer not meddling with them, unless they were first attacked by others, in which case I should feel it both a privilege and a duty to take that stand which, in my view, might tend to the advancement of justice.

But, fellow-citizens, I shall conclude. Considering the great degree of modesty which should always attend youth, it is probable I have already been more presuming than becomes me. However, upon the subjects of which I have treated, I have spoken as I have thought. I may be wrong in regard to any or all of them; but, holding it a sound maxim that it is better only to be sometimes right than at all times wrong, so soon as I discover my opinions to be erroneous I shall be ready to renounce them.

Every man is said to have his peculiar ambition. Whether it be true or not, I can say, for one, that I have no other so great as that of being truly esteemed of my fellow-men by rendering myself worthy of their esteem. How far I shall succeed in gratifying this ambition is yet to be developed. I am young and unknown to many of you; I was born and have ever remained in the most humble walks of life. I have no wealthy or popular relations or friends to recommend me. My case is thrown exclusively upon the independent voters of the county, and if elected, they will have conferred a favour upon me for which I shall be unremitting in my labours to compensate. But if the good people in their wisdom shall see fit to keep me in the background, I have been too familiar with disappointments to be very much chagrined.

Your friend and fellow-citizen,

A. LINCOLN

Letter to Colonel Robert Allen. June 21, 1836

Dear Colonel, I am told that during my absence last week you passed through this place, and stated publicly that you were in possession of a fact or facts which, if known to the public, would entirely destroy the prospects of N. W. Edwards and myself at the ensuing election; but that, through favour to us, you should forbear to divulge them. No one has needed favours more than I, and, generally, few have been less unwilling to accept them; but in this case favour to me would be injustice to the public, and therefore I must beg your pardon for declining it. That I once had the confidence of the people of Sangamon, is sufficiently evident; and if I have since done anything, either by design or misadventure, which if known would subject me to a forfeiture of that confidence, he that knows of that thing, and conceals it, is a traitor to his country's interest.

I find myself wholly unable to form any conjecture of what fact or facts, real or supposed, you spoke; but my opinion of your veracity will not permit me for a moment to doubt that you at least believed what you said. I am flattered with the personal regard you manifested for me; but I do hope that, on more mature reflection, you will view the public interest as a paramount consideration, and therefore determine to let the worst come. I here assure you that the candid statement of facts on your part, however low it may sink me, shall never break the tie of personal friendship between us. I wish an answer to this, and you are at liberty to publish both, if you choose.

Lincoln's Opinion on Universal Suffrage. From a Letter published in the Sangamon Journal. June 13, 1836

I go for all sharing the privileges of the government who assist in bearing its burdens: consequently I go for admitting all whites to the right of suffrage who pay taxes or bear arms.

From an Address before the Young Men's Lyceum of Springfield, Illinois. January 27, 1837

As a subject for the remarks of the evening 'The perpetuation of our political institutions' is selected. In the great journal of things happening under the sun, we, the American people, find our account running under the date of the nineteenth century of the Christian era. We find ourselves in the peaceful possession of the fairest portion of the earth, as regards extent of territory, fertility of soil, and salubrity of climate. We find ourselves under the government of a system of political institutions conducing more essentially to the ends of civil and religious liberty, than any of which the history of former times tells us. We, when remounting the stage of existence, found ourselves the legal inheritors of these fundamental blessings. We toiled not in the acquirement or the establishment of them; they are a legacy bequeathed to us by a once hardy, brave, and patriotic, but now lamented and departed race of ancestors.

Theirs was the task (and nobly they performed it) to possess themselves, and through themselves us, of this goodly land, and to rear upon its hills and valleys a political edifice of liberty and equal rights; 'tis ours only to transmit these – the former unprofaned by the foot of the invader; the latter undecayed by lapse of time. This, our duty to ourselves and to our posterity, and love for our species in general, imperatively require us to perform.

How, then, shall we perform it? At what point shall we expect the approach of danger? By what means shall we fortify against it? Shall we expect some transatlantic military giant to step across the ocean and crush us at a blow? Never. All the armies of Europe, Asia and Africa combined, with all the treasure of the earth (our own excepted) in their military chest, with a Bonaparte for a commander, could not, by force, take a drink from the Ohio, or make a track on the Blue Ridge, in a trial of a thousand years.

At what point, then, is the approach of danger to be expected? I answer, if it ever reaches us, it must spring up among us. It cannot come from abroad. If destruction be our lot, we must ourselves be its author and finisher. As a nation of freemen, we must live through all time, or die by suicide.

There is even now something of ill omen among us. I mean the increasing disregard for law which pervades the country; the growing disposition to substitute wild and furious passions in lieu of the sober judgment of courts; and the worse than savage mobs for the executive ministers of justice. This disposition is awfully fearful in any community; and that it now exists in ours, though grating to our feelings to admit, it would be a violation of truth and an insult to our intelligence to deny.

*   *   *

I know the American people are *much* attached to their government. I know they would suffer *much* for its sake. I know they would endure evils long and patiently before they would ever think of exchanging it for another. Yet, notwithstanding all this, if the laws be continually despised and disregarded, if their rights to be secure in their persons and property are held by no better tenure than the caprice of a mob, the alienation of their affection for the government is the natural consequence, and to that sooner or later it must come.

Here, then, is one point at which danger may be expected. The question recurs, how shall we fortify against it? The answer is simple. Let every American, every lover of liberty, every well-wisher to his posterity, swear by the blood of the Revolution never to violate in the least particular the laws of the country, and never to tolerate their violation by others. As the patriots of seventy-six did to the support of the Declaration of Independence, so to the support of the Constitution and the laws let every American pledge his life, his property, and his sacred honour; let every man remember that to violate the law is to trample on the blood of his father, and to tear the charter of his own and his children's liberty. Let reverence for the laws be breathed by every American mother to the lisping babe that prattles on her lap. Let it be taught in schools, in seminaries, and in colleges. Let it be written in primers, spelling-books, and in almanacs. Let it be preached from the pulpit, proclaimed in legislative halls, and enforced in courts of justice. And, in short, let it become the political religion of the nation.

When I so pressingly urge a strict observance of all the laws, let me not be understood as saying that there are no bad laws, or that grievances may not arise for the redress of which no legal provisions have been made. I mean to say no such thing. But I do mean to say that although bad laws, if they exist, should be repealed as soon as possible, still, while they continue in force, for the sake of example they should be religiously observed. So also in unprovided cases. If such arise, let proper legal provisions be made for them with the least possible delay, but till then let them, if not too intolerable, be borne with.

There is no grievance that is a fit object of redress by mob law. In any case that may arise, as, for instance, the promulgation of abolitionism, one of two positions is necessarily true – that is, the thing is right within itself, and therefore deserves the protection of all law and all good citizens, or it is wrong, and therefore proper to be prohibited by legal enactments; and in neither case is the interposition of mob law either necessary, justifiable, or excusable. . . .

They [histories of the Revolution] were pillars of the temple of liberty; and now that they have crumbled away, that temple must fall unless we, their descendants, supply their places with other pillars, hewn from the solid quarry of sober reason. Passion has helped us, but can do so no more. It will in future be our enemy. Reason – cold, calculating, unimpassioned reason – must furnish all the materials for our future support and defence. Let those materials be moulded into general intelligence, sound morality, and, in particular, a reverence for the Constitution and laws; and that we improved to the last, that we remained free to the last, that we revered his name to the last, that during his long sleep we permitted no hostile foot to pass over or desecrate his resting-place, shall be that which to learn the last trump shall awaken our Washington.

Upon these let the proud fabric of freedom rest, as the rock of its basis; and as truly as has been said of the only greater institution, 'the gates of hell shall not prevail against it.'

Many great and good men, sufficiently qualified for any task they should undertake, may ever be found, whose ambition would aspire to nothing beyond a seat in Congress, a gubernatorial or a presidential chair. But such belong not to the family of the lion or the brood of the eagle. What? Think you these places would satisfy an Alexander, a Cæsar, or a Napoleon? Never! Towering genius disdains a beaten path. It seeks regions hitherto unexplored. It sees no distinction in adding story to story upon the monuments of fame erected to the memory of others. It denies that it is glory enough to serve under any chief. It scorns to tread in the footsteps of any predecessor, however illustrious. It thirsts and burns for distinction; and, if possible, it will have it, whether at the expense of emancipating slaves, or enslaving free men. Is it unreasonable, then, to expect that some men, possessed of the loftiest genius, coupled with ambition sufficient to push it to its utmost stretch, will at some time spring up among us? And when such a one does, it will require the people to be united with each other, attached to the government and laws, and generally intelligent, to successfully frustrate his design.

Distinction will be his paramount object, and although he would as willingly, perhaps more so, acquire it by doing good as harm, yet that opportunity being passed, and nothing left to be done in the way of building up, he would sit down boldly to the task of pulling down. Here, then, is a probable case, highly dangerous, and such a one as could not well have existed heretofore.

* * *

All honour to our Revolutionary ancestors, to whom we are indebted for these institutions. They will not be forgotten. In history we hope they will be read of, and recounted, so long as the Bible shall be read. But even granting that they will, their influence cannot be what it heretofore has been. Even then, they cannot be so universally known, nor so vividly felt, as they were by the generation just gone to rest. At the close of that struggle, nearly every adult male had been a participator in some of its scenes. The consequence was, that of those scenes, in the form of a husband, a father, a son, or a brother, a living history was to be found in every family – a history bearing the indubitable testimonies to its own authenticity in the limbs mangled, in the scars of wounds received in the midst of the very scenes related; a history, too, that could be read and understood alike by all, the wise and the ignorant, the learned and the unlearned. But those histories are gone. They can be read no more for ever. They were a fortress of strength; but what the invading foemen could never do, the silent artillery of time has done – the levelling of its walls. They are gone. They were a forest of giant oaks; but the resistless hurricane has swept over them, and left only here and there a lonely trunk, despoiled of its verdure, shorn of its foliage, unshading and unshaded, to murmur in a few more gentle breezes, and to combat with its mutilated limbs a few more ruder storms, and then to sink and be no more.

HUMOROUS ACCOUNT OF HIS EXPERIENCES WITH A LADY HE WAS REQUESTED TO MARRY

A Letter to Mrs O. H. Browning. Springfield, Illinois. April 1, 1838
Dear Madam, Without apologising for being egotistical, I shall make the history of so much of my life as has elapsed since I saw you the subject of this letter. And, by the way, I now discover that in order to give a full and intelligible account of the things I have done and suffered since I saw you, I shall necessarily have to relate some that happened before.

It was, then, in the autumn of 1836 that a married lady of my acquaintance, and who was a great friend of mine, being about to pay a visit to her father and other relatives residing in Kentucky, proposed to me that on her return she would bring a sister of hers with her on condition that I would engage to become her brother-in-law with all convenient dispatch. I, of course, accepted the proposal, for you know I could not have done otherwise had I really been averse to it; but privately, between you and me, I was most confoundedly well pleased with the project. I had seen the said sister some three years before, thought her intelligent and agreeable, and saw no good objection to plodding life through hand-in-hand with her. Time passed on, the lady took her journey, and in due time returned, sister in company, sure enough. This astonished me a little, for it appeared to me that her coming so readily showed that she was a trifle too willing, but on reflection it occurred to me that she might have been prevailed on by her married sister to come, without anything concerning me having been mentioned to her, and so I concluded that if no other objection presented itself, I would consent to waive this. All this occurred to me on hearing of her arrival in the neighbourhood – for, be it remembered, I had not yet seen her, except about three years previous, as above mentioned. In a few days we had an interview, and, although I had seen her before, she did not look as my imagination had pictured her. I knew she was over-size, but she now appeared a fair match for Falstaff. I knew she was called an 'old maid', and I felt no doubt of the truth of at least half of the appellation, but now, when I beheld her, I could not for my life avoid thinking of my mother; and this, not from withered features – for her skin was too full of fat to permit of its contracting into wrinkles – but from her want of teeth, weather-beaten appearance in general, and from a kind of notion that ran in my head that nothing could have commenced at the size of infancy and reached her present bulk in less than thirty-five or forty years; and, in short, I was not at all pleased with her. But what could I do? I had told her sister that I would take her for better or for worse, and I made a point of honour and conscience in all things to stick to my word, especially if others had been induced to act on it, which in this case I had no doubt they had, for I was now fairly convinced that no other man on earth would have her, and hence the conclusion that they were bent on holding me to my bargain. 'Well,' thought I, 'I have said it, and, be the consequences what they may, it shall not be my fault if I fail to do it.' At once I determined to consider her my wife, and this done, all my powers of discovery were put to work in search of perfections in her which might be fairly set off against her defects. I tried to imagine her handsome, which, but for her unfortunate corpulency, was actually true. Exclusive of this, no woman that I have ever seen has a finer face. I also tried to convince myself that the mind was much more to be valued than the person, and in this she was not inferior, as I could discover, to any with whom I had been acquainted.

Shortly after this, without attempting to come to any positive understanding with her, I set out for Vandalia, when and where you first saw me. During my stay there I had letters from her which did not change my opinion of either her intellect or intention, but, on the contrary, confirmed it in both.

All this while, although I was fixed 'firm as the surge-repelling rock' in my resolution, I found I was continually repenting the rashness which had led me to make it. Through life I have been in no bondage, either real or imaginary, from the thraldom of which I so much desired to be free. After my return home I saw nothing to change my opinion of her in any particular. She was the same, and so was I. I now spent my time in planning how I might get along in life after my contemplated change of circumstances should have taken place, and how I might procrastinate the evil day for a time, which I really dreaded as much, perhaps more, than an Irishman does the halter.

After all my sufferings upon this deeply interesting subject, here I am, wholly, unexpectedly, completely out of the 'scrape', and I now want to know if you can guess how I got out of it – out, clear, in every sense of the term – no violation of word, honour, or conscience. I don't believe you can guess, and so I might as well tell you at once. As the lawyer says, it was done in the manner following, to wit: After I had delayed the matter as long as I thought I could in honour do (which, by the way, had brought me round into the last fall), I concluded I might as well bring it to a consummation without further delay, and so I mustered my resolution and made the proposal to her direct; but, shocking to relate, she answered, No. At first I supposed she did it through an affectation of modesty, which I thought but ill became her under the peculiar circumstances of the case, but on my renewal of the charge I found she repelled it with greater firmness than before. I tried it again and again, but with the same success, or rather with the same want of success.

I finally was forced to give it up, at which I very unexpectedly found myself mortified almost beyond endurance. I was mortified, it seemed to me, in a hundred different ways. My vanity was deeply wounded by the reflection that I had so long been too stupid to discover her intentions, and at the same time never doubting that I understood them perfectly; and also that she, whom I had taught myself to believe nobody else would have, had actually rejected me with all my fancied greatness. And, to cap the whole, I then for the first time began to suspect that I was really a little in love with her. But let it all go! I'll try and outlive it. Others have been made fools of by the girls, but this can never in truth be said of me. I most emphatically, in this instance, made a fool of myself. I have now come to the conclusion never again to think of marrying, and for this reason – I can never be satisfied with anyone who would be blockhead enough to have me.

When you receive this, write me a long yarn about something to amuse me. Give my respects to Mr Browning.

From a Debate between Lincoln, E. D. Baker, and others against Douglas, Lamborn, and others. Springfield. December 1839

* * *

. . . Mr Lamborn insists that the difference between the Van Buren party and the Whigs is, that although the former sometimes err in practice, they are always correct in principle, whereas the latter are wrong in principle; and the better to impress this proposition, he uses a figurative expression in these words: 'The Democrats are vulnerable in the heel, but they are sound in the heart and in the head.' The first branch of the figure – that is, that the Democrats are vulnerable in the heel – I admit is not merely figuratively but literally true. Who that looks but for a moment at their Swartwouts, their Prices, their Harringtons, and their hundreds of others, scampering away with the public money to Texas, to Europe, and to every spot of the earth where a villain may hope to find refuge from justice, can at all doubt that they are most distressingly affected in their heels with a species of running fever? It seems that this malady of their heels operates on the sound-headed and honest-hearted creatures very much like the cork leg in the song did on its owner, which, when he had once got started on it, the more he tried to stop it, the more it would run away. At the hazard of wearing this point threadbare, I will relate an anecdote which seems to be too strikingly in point to be omitted. A witty Irish soldier who was always boasting of his bravery when no danger was near, but who invariably retreated without orders at the first charge of the engagement, being asked by his captain why he did so, replied, 'Captain, I have as brave a heart as Julius Caesar ever had; but somehow or other, whenever danger approaches, my cowardly legs will run away with it.' So it is with Mr Lamborn's party. They take the public money into their hands for the most laudable purpose that wise heads and honest hearts can dictate, but before they can possibly get it out again, their rascally vulnerable heels will run away with them. . . .

Letter to W. G. Anderson. Lawrenceville, Illinois. October 31, 1840

Dear Sir, Your note of yesterday is received. In the difficulty between us of which you speak, you say you think I was the aggressor. I do not think I was. You say my 'words imported insult'. I meant them as a fair set-off to your own statements, and not otherwise; and in that light alone I now wish you to understand them. You ask for my present 'feelings on the subject'. I entertain no unkind feelings to you, and none of any sort upon the subject, except a sincere regret that I permitted myself to get into such an altercation.

Extract from a Letter to John T. Stuart. Springfield, Illinois.
January 23, 1841

For not giving you a general summary of news, you must pardon me; it is not in my power to do so. I am now the most miserable man living. If what I feel were equally distributed to the whole human family, there would not be one cheerful face on earth. Whether I shall ever be better, I cannot tell; I awfully forebode I shall not. To remain as I am is impossible; I must die or be better, it appears to me. The matter you speak of on my account you may attend to as you say, unless you shall hear of my condition forbidding it. I say this because I fear I shall be unable to attend to any business here, and a change of scene might help me. If I could be myself, I would rather remain at home with Judge Logan. I can write no more.

From an Address before the Washingtonian Temperance Society.
Springfield, Illinois. February 22, 1842

Although the temperance cause has been in progress for nearly twenty years, it is apparent to all that it is just now being crowned with a degree of success hitherto unparalleled.

The list of its friends is daily swelled by the additions of fifties, of hundreds, and of thousands. The cause itself seems suddenly transformed from a cold abstract theory to a living, breathing, active and powerful chieftain, going forth conquering and to conquer. The citadels of his great adversary are daily being stormed and dismantled; his temples and his altars, where the rites of his idolatrous worship have long been performed, and where human sacrifices have long been wont to be made, are daily desecrated and deserted. The trump of the conqueror's fame is sounding from hill to hill, from sea to sea, and from land to land, and calling millions to his standard at a blast.

*   *   *

'But,' say some, 'we are no drunkards, and we shall not acknowledge ourselves such by joining a reform drunkard's society, whatever our influence might be.' Surely no Christian will adhere to this objection.

If they believe, as they profess, that Omnipotence condescended to take on himself the form of sinful man, and, as such, to die an ignominious death for their sakes, surely they will not refuse submission to the infinitely lesser condescension for the temporal and perhaps eternal salvation of a large, erring, and unfortunate class of their fellow-creatures; nor is the condescension very great. In my judgment, such of us as have never fallen victims have been spared more from the absence of appetite, than from any mental or moral superiority over those who have. Indeed I believe, if we take habitual drunkards as a class, their heads and their hearts will bear an advantageous comparison with those of any other class. There seems ever to have been a proneness in the brilliant and warm-blooded to fall into this vice. The demon of intemperance ever seems to have delighted in sucking the blood of genius and generosity. What one of us but can call to mind some relative more promising in youth than all his fellows, who has fallen a sacrifice to his rapacity? He ever seems to have gone forth like the Egyptian angel of death, commissioned to slay, if not the first, the fairest born of every family. Shall he now be arrested in his desolating career? In that arrest all can give aid that will; and who shall be excused that can and will not? Far around as human breath has ever blown, he keeps our fathers, our brothers, our sons, and our friends prostrate in the chains of moral death. . . .

When the conduct of men is designed to be influenced, persuasion, kind, unassuming persuasion, should ever be adopted. It is an old and a true maxim 'that a drop of honey catches more flies than a gallon of gall.' So with men. If you would win a man to your cause, first convince him that you are his sincere friend. Therein is a drop of honey that catches his heart, which, say what you will, is the great high-road to his reason, and which, when once gained, you will find but little trouble in convincing his judgment of the justice of your cause, if indeed that cause really be a just one. On the contrary, assume to dictate to his judgment, or to command his action, or to mark him as one to be shunned and despised, and he will retreat within himself, close all the avenues to his head and his heart; and though your cause be naked truth itself, transformed to the heaviest lance, harder than steel, and sharper than steel can be made, and though you throw it with more than herculean force and precision, you shall be no more able to pierce him than to penetrate the hard shell of a tortoise with a rye straw. Such is man, and so must he be understood by those who would lead him, even to his own best interests. . . .

Another error, as it seems to me, into which the old reformers fell, was the position that all habitual drunkards were utterly incorrigible, and therefore must be turned adrift and damned without remedy in order that the grace of temperance might abound, to the temperate then, and to all mankind some hundreds of years thereafter. There is in this something so repugnant to humanity, so uncharitable, so cold-blooded and feelingless, that it never did, nor never can enlist the enthusiasm of a popular cause. We could not love the man who taught it – we could not hear him with patience. The heart could not throw open its portals to it, the generous man could not adopt it – it could not mix with his blood. It looked so fiendishly selfish, so like throwing fathers and brothers overboard to lighten the boat for our security, that the noble-minded shrank from the manifest meanness of the thing. And besides this, the benefits of a reformation to be effected by such a system were too remote in point of time to warmly engage many in its behalf. Few can be induced to labour exclusively for posterity; and none will do it enthusiastically. Posterity has done nothing for us; and theorize on it as we may, practically we shall do very little for it, unless we are made to think we are at the same time doing something for ourselves.

What an ignorance of human nature does it exhibit, to ask or expect a whole community to rise up and labour for the temporal happiness of others, after themselves shall be consigned to the dust, a majority of which community take no pains whatever to secure their own eternal welfare at no more distant day! Great distance in either time or space has wonderful power to lull and render quiescent the human mind. Pleasures to be enjoyed, or pains to be endured, after we shall be dead and gone, are but little regarded even in our own cases, and much less in the cases of others. Still, in addition to this there is something so ludicrous in promises of good or threats of evil a great way off as to render the whole subject with which they are connected easily turned into ridicule. 'Better lay down that spade you are stealing, Paddy; if you don't you'll pay for it at the day of judgment.' 'Be the powers, if ye'll credit me so long I'll take another jist.'

From the Circular of the Whig Committee. An Address to the People of Illinois. March 4, 1843

. . . The system of loans is but temporary in its nature, and must soon explode. It is a system not only ruinous while it lasts, but one that must soon fail and leave us destitute.

As an individual who undertakes to live by borrowing soon finds his original means devoured by interest, and next, no one left to borrow from, so must it be with a government.

We repeat, then, that a tariff sufficient for revenue, or a direct tax, must soon be resorted to; and, indeed, we believe this alternative is now denied by no one. But which system shall be adopted? Some of our opponents in theory admit the propriety of a tariff sufficient for revenue, but even they will not in practice vote for such a tariff; while others boldly advocate direct taxation. Inasmuch, therefore, as some of them boldly advocate direct taxation, and all the rest – or so nearly all as to make exceptions needless – refuse to adopt the tariff, we think it is doing them no injustice to class them all as advocates of direct taxation. Indeed, we believe they are only delaying an open avowal of the system till they can assure themselves that the people will tolerate it. Let us, then, briefly compare the two systems. The tariff is the cheaper system, because the duties, being collected in large parcels, at a few commercial points, will require comparatively few officers in their collection; while by the direct tax system the land must be literally covered with assessors and collectors, going forth like swarms of Egyptian locusts, devouring every blade of grass and other green thing. And, again, by the tariff system the whole revenue is paid by the consumers of foreign goods, and those chiefly the luxuries and not the necessaries of life. By this system, the man who contents himself to live upon the products of his own country pays nothing at all. And surely that country is extensive enough, and its products abundant and varied enough, to answer all the real wants of its people. In short, by this system the burden of revenue falls almost entirely on the wealthy and luxurious few, while the substantial and labouring many, who live at home and upon home products, go entirely free. By the direct tax system, none can escape. However strictly the citizen may exclude from his premises all foreign luxuries, fine cloths, fine silks, rich wines, golden chains, and diamond rings – still, for the possession of his house, his barn, and his homespun he is to be perpetually haunted and harassed by the tax-gatherer. With these views, we leave it to be determined whether we or our opponents are more truly democratic on the subject.

From a Letter to Martin M. Morris. Springfield, Illinois.
March 26, 1843

It is truly gratifying to me to learn that while the people of Sangamon have cast me off, my old friends of Menard, who have known me longest and best, stick to me. It would astonish, if not amuse, the older citizens to learn that I (a stranger, friendless, uneducated, penniless boy, working on a flatboat at ten dollars per month) have been put down here as the candidate of pride, wealth, and aristocratic family distinction. Yet so, chiefly, it was. There was, too, the strangest combination of church influence against me. Baker is a Campbellite; and therefore, as I suppose, with few exceptions, got all that church. My wife has some relations in the Presbyterian churches, and some with the Episcopal churches; and therefore, wherever it would tell, I was set down as either the one or the other, while it was everywhere contended that no Christian ought to go for me, because I belonged to no church, was suspected of being a deist, and had talked about fighting a duel. With all these things, Baker, of course, had nothing to do. Nor do I complain of them. As to his own church going for him, I think that was right enough, and as to the influences I have spoken of in the other, though they were very strong, it would be grossly untrue and unjust to charge that they acted upon them in a body, or were very near so. I only mean that those influences levied a tax of a considerable per cent. upon my strength throughout the religious controversy. But enough of this.

From a Letter to Joshua F. Speed. Springfield. October 22, 1846

We have another boy, born the 10th of March. He is very much such a child as Bob was at his age, rather of a longer order. Bob is 'short and low', and I expect always will be. He talks very plainly – almost as plainly as anybody. He is quite smart enough. I sometimes fear that he is one of the little rare-ripe sort that are smarter at about five than ever after. He has a great deal of that sort of mischief that is the offspring of such animal spirits. Since I began this letter, a messenger came to tell me Bob was lost; but by the time I reached the house his mother had found him and had him whipped, and by now, very likely, he is run away again.

From a Letter to William H. Herndon. Washington. January 8, 1848

Dear William, Your letter of December 27th was received a day or two ago. I am much obliged to you for the trouble you have taken, and promise to take in my little business there. As to speech-making, by way of getting the hang of the House, I made a little speech two or three days ago on a post-office question of no general interest. I find speaking here and elsewhere about the same thing. I was about as badly scared, and no worse, as I am when I speak in court. I expect to make one within a week or two, in which I hope to succeed well enough to wish you to see it.

It is very pleasant to learn from you that there are some who desire that I should be re-elected. I most heartily thank them for their partiality; and I can say, as Mr Clay said of the annexation of Texas, that 'personally I would not object' to a re-election, although I thought at the time, and still think, it would be quite as well for me to return to the law at the end of a single term. I made the declaration that I would not be a candidate again, more from a wish to deal fairly with others, to keep peace among our friends, and to keep the district from going to the enemy, than for any cause personal to myself; so that, if it should so happen that nobody else wishes to be elected, I could refuse the people the right of sending me again. But to enter myself as a competitor of others, or to authorize anyone so to enter me, is what my word and honour forbid.

From a Letter to William H. Herndon. Washington. June 22, 1848

As to the young men. You must not wait to be brought forward by the older men. For instance, do you suppose that I should ever have got into notice if I had waited to be hunted up and pushed forward by older men? You young men get together and form a 'Rough and Ready Club', and have regular meetings and speeches. Take in everybody you can get. Harrison Grimsley, L. A. Enos, Lee Kimball and C. W. Matheny will do to begin the thing; but as you go along gather up all the shrewd, wild boys about town, whether just of age or a little under age – Chris. Logan, Reddick Ridgley, Lewis Zwizler, and hundreds such. Let every one play the part he can play best – some speak, some sing, and all 'holler'. Your meetings will be of evenings; the older men, and the women, will go to hear you; so that it will not only contribute to the election of 'Old Zach', but will be an interesting pastime, and improving to the intellectual faculties of all engaged. Don't fail to do this.

From a Letter to William H. Herndon. Washington. July 10, 1848

The way for a young man to rise is to improve himself every way he can, never suspecting that anybody wishes to hinder him. Allow me to assure you that suspicion and jealousy never did help any man in any situation. There may sometimes be ungenerous attempts to keep a young man down; and they will succeed, too, if he allows his mind to be diverted from its true channel to brood over the attempted injury. Cast about, and see if this feeling has not injured every person you have ever known to fall into it.

Letter to John D. Johnston. January 2, 1851

Dear Johnston, Your request for eighty dollars I do not think it best to comply with now. At the various times when I have helped you a little you have said to me, 'We can get along very well now'; but in a very short time I find you in the same difficulty again. Now, this can only happen by some defect in your conduct. What that defect is, I think I know. You are not lazy, and still you are an idler. I doubt whether, since I saw you, you have done a good whole day's work in any one day. You do not very much dislike to work, and still you do not work much, merely because it does not seem to you that you could get much for it. This habit of uselessly wasting time is the whole difficulty; it is vastly important to you, and still more so to your children, that you should break the habit. It is more important to them, because they have longer to live, and can keep out of an idle habit before they are in it, easier than they can get out after they are in.

You are now in need of some money; and what I propose is, that you shall go to work, 'tooth and nail', for somebody who will give you money for it. Let father and your boys take charge of your things at home, prepare for a crop, and make the crop, and you go to work for the best money wages, or in discharge of any debt you owe, that you can get; and, to secure you a fair reward for your labour, I now promise you, that for every dollar you will, between this and the first of May, get for your own labour, either in money or as your own indebtedness, I will then give you one other dollar. By this, if you hire yourself at ten dollars a month, from me you will get ten more, making twenty dollars a month for your work. In this I do not mean you shall go off to St Louis, or the lead mines, or the gold mines in California, but I mean for you to go at it for the best wages you can get close to home in Coles County. Now, if you will do this, you will be soon out of debt, and, what is better, you will have a habit that will keep you from getting in debt again. But, if I should now clear you out of debt, next year you would be just as deep in as ever. You say you would almost give your place in heaven for seventy or eighty dollars. Then you value your place in heaven very cheap, for I am sure you can, with the offer I make, get the seventy or eighty dollars for four or five months' work. You say if I will furnish you the money you will deed me the land, and, if you don't pay the money back, you will deliver possession. Nonsense! If you can't now live with the land, how will you then live without it? You have always been kind to me, and I do not mean to be unkind to you. On the contrary, if you will but follow my advice, you will find it worth more than eighty times eighty dollars to you.

Letter to John D. Johnston. Shelbyville. November 4, 1851

Dear Brother, When I came into Charleston day before yesterday, I learned that you are anxious to sell the land where you live and move to Missouri. I have been thinking of this ever since, and cannot but think such a notion is utterly foolish. What can you do in Missouri better than here? Is the land any richer? Can you there, any more than here, raise corn and wheat and oats without work? Will anybody there, any more than here, do your work for you? If you intend to go to work, there is no better place than right where you are; if you do not intend to go to work, you cannot get along anywhere. Squirming and crawling about from place to place can do no good. You have raised no crop this year; and what you really want is to sell the land, get the money, and spend it. Part with the land you have, and, my life upon it, you will never after own a spot big enough to bury you in. Half you will get for the land you will spend in moving to Missouri, and the other half you will eat, drink, and wear out, and no foot of land will be bought. Now, I feel it my duty to have no hand in such a piece of foolery. I feel that it is so even on your own account, and particularly on mother's account. The eastern forty acres I intend to keep for mother while she lives; if you will not cultivate it, it will rent for enough to support her – at least, it will rent for something. Her dower in the other two forties she can let you have, and no thanks to me. Now, do not misunderstand this letter; I do not write it in any unkindness. I write it in order, if possible, to get you to face the truth, which truth is, you are destitute because you have idled away all your time. Your thousand pretences for not getting along better are all nonsense; they deceive nobody but yourself. Go to work is the only cure for your case.

A word to mother. Chapman tells me he wants you to go and live with him. If I were you I would try it awhile. If you get tired of it (as I think you will not), you can return to your own home. Chapman feels very kindly to you, and I have no doubt he will make your situation very pleasant.

Note for Law Lecture. Written about July 1, 1852

I am not an accomplished lawyer. I find quite as much material for a lecture in those points wherein I have failed, as in those wherein I have been moderately successful. The leading rule for a lawyer, as for the man of every other calling, is diligence. Leave nothing for tomorrow which can be done today. Never let your correspondence fall behind. Whatever piece of business you have in hand, before stopping, do all the labour pertaining to it which can then be done. When you bring a common law-suit, if you have the facts for doing so, write the declaration at once. If a law point be involved, examine the books, and note the authority you rely on upon the declaration itself, where you are sure to find it when wanted. The same of defences and pleas. In business not likely to be litigated – ordinary collection cases, foreclosures, partitions, and the like – make all examinations of titles, and note them and even draft orders and decrees in advance. The course has a triple advantage; it avoids omissions and neglect, saves your labour when once done, performs the labour out of court when you have leisure, rather than in court when you have not.

Extemporaneous speaking should be practised and cultivated. It is the lawyer's avenue to the public. However able and faithful he may be in other respects, people are slow to bring him business if he cannot make a speech. And yet there is not a more fatal error to young lawyers than relying too much on speech-making. If anyone, upon his rare powers of speaking, shall claim an exemption from the drudgery of the law, his case is a failure in advance.

Discourage litigation. Persuade your neighbours to compromise whenever you can. Point out to them how the nominal winner is often a real loser – in fees, expenses, and waste of time. As a peace-maker the lawyer has a superior opportunity of being a good man. There will still be business enough.

Never stir up litigation. A worse man can scarcely be found than one who does this. Who can be more nearly a fiend than he who habitually overhauls the register of deeds in search of defects in titles, whereon to stir up strife, and put money in his pocket? A moral tone ought to be infused into the profession which should drive such men out of it.

The matter of fees is important, far beyond the mere question of bread and butter involved. Properly attended to, fuller justice is done to both lawyer and client. An exorbitant fee should never be claimed. As a general rule, never take your whole fee in advance, nor any more than a small retainer. When fully paid beforehand, you are more than a common mortal if you can feel the same interest in the case as if something was still in prospect for you, as well as for your client. And when you lack interest in the case the job will very likely lack skill and diligence in the performance. Settle the amount of fee and take a note in advance. Then you will feel that you are working for something, and you are sure to do your work faithfully and well. Never sell a fee-note – at least not before the consideration service is performed. It leads to negligence and dishonesty – negligence by losing interest in the case, and dishonesty in refusing to refund when you have allowed the consideration to fail.

There is a vague popular belief that lawyers are necessarily dishonest. I say vague, because when we consider to what extent confidence and honours are reposed in and conferred upon lawyers by the people, it appears improbable that their impression of dishonesty is very distinct and vivid. Yet the impression is common, almost universal. Let no young man choosing the law for a calling for a moment yield to the popular belief. Resolve to be honest at all events; and if in your own judgment you cannot be an honest lawyer, resolve to be honest without being a lawyer. Choose some other occupation, rather than one in the choosing of which you do, in advance, consent to be a knave.

A Fragment. Written about July 1, 1854

Equality in society alike beats inequality, whether the latter be of the British aristocratic sort or of the domestic slavery sort.

We know Southern men declare that their slaves are better off than hired labourers amongst us. How little they know whereof they speak! There is no permanent class of hired labourers amongst us. Twenty-five years ago I was a hired labourer. The hired labourer of yesterday labours on his own account today, and will hire others to labour for him tomorrow.

Advancement – improvement in condition – is the order of things in a society of equals. As labour is the common burden of our race, so the effort of some to shift their share of the burden on to the shoulders of others is the great durable curse of the race. Originally a curse for transgression upon the whole race, when, as by slavery, it is concentrated on a part only, it becomes the double-refined curse of God upon his creatures.

Free labour has the inspiration of hope; pure slavery has no hope. The power of hope upon human exertion and happiness is wonderful. The slave-master himself has a conception of it, and hence the system of tasks among slaves. The slave whom you cannot drive with the lash to break seventy-five pounds of hemp in a day, if you will task him to break a hundred, and promise him pay for all he does over, he will break you a hundred and fifty. You have substituted hope for the rod.

And yet perhaps it does not occur to you that, to the extent of your gain in the case, you have given up the slave system and adopted the free system of labour.

A Fragment on Slavery. July 1854

If A can prove, however conclusively, that he may of right enslave B, why may not B snatch the same argument and prove equally that he may enslave A? You say A is white and B is black. It is colour, then; the lighter having the right to enslave the darker? Take care. By this rule you are to be slave to the first man you meet with a fairer skin than your own.

You do not mean colour exactly? You mean the whites are intellectually the superiors of the blacks, and therefore have the right to enslave them? Take care again. By this rule you are to be slave to the first man you meet with an intellect superior to your own.

But, say you, it is a question of interest, and if you make it your interest you have the right to enslave another. Very well. And if he can make it his interest he has the right to enslave you.

Lincoln's Reply to Senator Douglas at Peoria, Illinois. The Origin of the Wilmot Proviso. October 16, 1854

. . . Our war with Mexico broke out in 1846. When Congress was about adjourning that session, President Polk asked them to place two millions of dollars under his control, to be used by him in the recess, if found practicable and expedient, in negotiating a treaty of peace with Mexico, and acquiring some part of her territory. A bill was duly gotten up for the purpose, and was progressing swimmingly in the House of Representatives, when a Democratic member from Pennsylvania by the name of David Wilmot moved as an amendment, 'Provided, that in any territory thus acquired there shall never be slavery.' *This is the origin of the far-famed Wilmot Proviso*. It created a great flutter; but it stuck like wax, was voted into the bill, and the bill passed with it through the House. The Senate, however, adjourned without final action on it, and so both the appropriation and the proviso were lost for the time.

. . . This declared indifference, but, as I must think, real, covert zeal, for the spread of slavery, I cannot but hate. I hate it because of the monstrous injustice of slavery itself. I hate it because it deprives our republican example of its just influence in the world, enables the enemies of free institutions with plausibility to taunt us as hypocrites, causes the real friends of freedom to doubt our sincerity, and especially because it forces so many good men amongst ourselves into an open war with the very fundamental principles of civil liberty, criticizing the Declaration of Independence, and insisting that there is no right principle of action but self-interest.

Before proceeding let me say that I think I have no prejudice against the Southern people. They are just what we would be in their situation. If slavery did not now exist among them, they would not introduce it. If it did now exist among us, we should not instantly give it up. This I believe of the masses North and South. Doubtless there are individuals on both sides who would not hold slaves under any circumstances, and others who would gladly introduce slavery anew if it were out of existence. We know that some Southern men do free their slaves, go North and become tip-top Abolitionists, while some Northern ones go South and become most cruel slave-masters.

When Southern people tell us they are no more responsible for the origin of slavery than we are, I acknowledge the fact. When it is said that the institution exists, and that it is very difficult to get rid of it in any satisfactory way, I can understand and appreciate the saying. I surely will not blame them for not doing what I should not know how to do myself. If all earthly power were given me, I should not know what to do as to the existing institution. My first impulse would be to free all the slaves, and send them to Liberia, to their own native land. But a moment's reflection would convince me that whatever of high hope (as I think there is) there may be in this in the long run, its sudden execution is impossible. If they were all landed there in a day, they would all perish in the next ten days; and there are not surplus shipping and surplus money enough to carry them there in many times ten days. What then? Free them all, and keep them among us as underlings? Is it quite certain that this betters their condition? I think I would not hold one in slavery at any rate, yet the point is not clear enough for me to denounce people upon. What next? Free them, and make them politically and socially our equals? My own feelings will not admit of this, and if mine would, we well know that those of the great mass of whites will not. Whether this feeling accords with justice and sound judgment is not the sole question, if indeed it is any part of it. A universal feeling, whether well or ill founded, cannot be safely disregarded. We cannot then make them equals. It does seem to me that systems of gradual emancipation might be adopted, but for their tardiness in this I will not undertake to judge our brethren of the South.

Equal justice to the South, it is said, requires us to consent to the extension of slavery to new countries. That is to say, that inasmuch as you do not object to my taking my hog to Nebraska, therefore I must not object to your taking your slave. Now, I admit that this is perfectly logical, if there is no difference between hogs and slaves. But while you thus require me to deny the humanity of the negro, I wish to ask whether you of the South, yourselves, have ever been willing to do as much? It is kindly provided that of all those who come into the world, only a small percentage are natural tyrants. That percentage is no larger in the slave States than in the free. The great majority, South as well as North, have human sympathies, of which they can no more divest themselves than they can of their sensibility to physical pain. These sympathies in the bosoms of the Southern people manifest in many ways their sense of the wrong of slavery, and their consciousness that, after all, there is humanity in the negro. If they deny this let me address them a few plain questions.

In 1820 you joined the North almost unanimously in declaring the African slave-trade piracy, and in annexing to it the punishment of death. Why did you do this? If you did not feel that it was wrong, why did you join in providing that men should be hung for it? The practice was no more than bringing wild negroes from Africa to such as would buy them. But you never thought of hanging men for catching and selling wild horses, wild buffaloes, or wild bears.

Again, you have among you a sneaking individual of the class of native tyrants known as the *slave-dealer*. He watches your necessities, and crawls up to buy your slave at a speculating price. If you cannot help it, you sell to him; but if you can help it, you drive him from your door. You despise him utterly; you do not recognize him as a friend, or even as an honest man. Your children must not play with his; they may rollick freely with the little negroes, but not with the slave-dealer's children. If you are obliged to deal with him, you try to get through the job without so much as touching him. It is common with you to join hands with the men you meet; but with the slave-dealer you avoid the ceremony – instinctively shrinking from the snaky contact. If he grows rich and retires from business, you still remember him, and still keep up the ban of non-intercourse upon him and his family. Now, why is this? You do not so treat the man who deals in cotton, corn, or tobacco.

And yet again. There are in the United States and Territories, including the District of Columbia, over four hundred and thirty thousand free blacks. At five hundred dollars per head, they are worth over two hundred millions of dollars. How comes this vast amount of property to be running about without owners? We do not see free horses or free cattle running at large. How is this? All these free blacks are the descendants of slaves, or have been slaves themselves; and they would be slaves now but for something that has operated on their white owners, inducing them at vast pecuniary sacrifice to liberate them. What is that something? Is there any mistaking it? In all these cases it is your sense of justice and human sympathy continually telling you that the poor negro has some natural right to himself – that those who deny it and make mere merchandise of him deserve kickings, contempt, and death.

And now why will you ask us to deny the humanity of the slave, and estimate him as only the equal of the hog? Why ask us to do what you will not do yourselves? Why ask us to do for nothing what two hundred millions of dollars could not induce you to do?

But one great argument in support of the repeal of the Missouri Compromise is still to come. That argument is 'the sacred right of self-government'. . . . Some poet has said –

Fools rush in where angels fear to tread.

At the hazard of being thought one of the fools of this quotation, I meet that argument – I rush in – I take that bull by the horns. . . . My faith in the proposition that each man should do precisely as he pleases with all which is exclusively his own, lies at the foundation of the sense of justice there is in me. I extend the principle to communities of men as well as to individuals. I so extend it because it is politically wise as well as naturally just – politically wise in saving us from broils about matters which do not concern us. Here, or at Washington, I would not trouble myself with the oyster laws of Virginia, or the cranberry laws of Indiana. The doctrine of self-government is right – absolutely and internally right; but it has no just application as here attempted. Or perhaps I should rather say that whether it has any application here depends upon whether a negro is not or is a man. If he is not a man, in that case he who is a man may, as a matter of self-government, do just what he pleases with him. But if the negro is a man, is it not to that extent a total destruction of self-government to say that he, too, shall not govern himself? When the white man governs himself, that is self-government; but when he governs himself and also governs another man, that is more than self-government – that is despotism. If the negro is a man, then my ancient faith teaches me that 'all men are created equal', and that there can be no moral right in connection with one man's making a slave of another.

Judge Douglas frequently, with bitter irony and sarcasm, paraphrases our argument by saying: 'The white people of Nebraska are good enough to govern themselves, but they are not good enough to govern a few miserable negroes!'

Well, I doubt not that the people of Nebraska are and will continue to be as good as the average of people elsewhere. I do not say the contrary. What I do say is that no man is good enough to govern another man without that other's consent. I say this is the leading principle – the sheet-anchor of American republicanism.

. . . Slavery is founded in the selfishness of man's nature – opposition to it in his love of justice. These principles are in eternal antagonism, and when brought into collision so fiercely as slavery extension brings them, shocks and throes and convulsions must ceaselessly follow. Repeal the Missouri Compromise; repeal all compromises; repeal the Declaration of Independence; repeal all past history – you still cannot repeal human nature. It still will be the abundance of man's heart that slavery extension is wrong, and out of the abundance of his heart his mouth will continue to speak. . . .

The Missouri Compromise ought to be restored. Slavery may or may not be established in Nebraska. But whether it be or not, we shall have repudiated – discarded from the councils of the nation – the spirit of compromise; for who, after this, will ever trust in a national compromise? The spirit of mutual concession – that spirit which first gave us the Constitution, and has thrice saved the Union – we shall have strangled and cast from us for ever. And what shall we have in lieu of it? The South flushed with triumph and tempted to excess; the North betrayed, as they believed, brooding on wrong and burning for revenge. One side will provoke, the other resent. The one will taunt, the other defy; one aggresses, the other retaliates. Already a few in the North defy all constitutional restraints, resist the execution of the Fugitive Slave Law, and even menace the institution of slavery in the States where it exists. Already a few in the South claim the constitutional right to take and hold slaves in the free States, demand the revival of the slave-trade, and demand a treaty with Great Britain by which fugitive slaves may be reclaimed from Canada. As yet they are but few on either side. It is a grave question for lovers of the Union, whether the final destruction of the Missouri Compromise, and with it the spirit of all compromise, will or will not embolden and embitter each of these, and fatally increase the number of both.

. . . Some men, mostly Whigs, who condemn the repeal of the Missouri Compromise, nevertheless hesitate to go for its restoration, lest they be thrown in company with the Abolitionists. Will they allow me, as an old Whig, to tell them good-humouredly that I think this is very silly? Stand with anybody that stands right. Stand with him while he is right, and part with him when he goes wrong. Stand with the Abolitionist in restoring the Missouri Compromise, and stand against him when he attempts to repeal the Fugitive Slave Law. In the latter case you stand with the Southern disunionist. What of that? You are still right. In both cases you are right In both cases you expose the dangerous extremes. In both you stand on the middle ground and hold the ship level and steady. In both you are national, and nothing less than national. This is the good old Whig ground. To desert such ground because of any company is to be less than a Whig, less than a man, less than an American.

I particularly object to the new position which the avowed principle of this Nebraska law gives to slavery in the body politic. I object to it because it assumes that there can be moral right in the enslaving of one man by another. I object to it as a dangerous dalliance for free people – a sad evidence that, feeling over-prosperity, we forget right; that liberty as a principle we have ceased to revere. I object to it because the Fathers of the Republic eschewed and rejected it. The argument of 'necessity' was the only argument they ever admitted in favour of slavery, and so far, and so far only as it carried them, did they ever go. They found the institution existing among us, which they could not help, and they cast the blame on the British king for having permitted its introduction. Thus we see the plain, unmistakable spirit of their age towards slavery was hostility to the principle, and toleration only by necessity.

But now it is to be transformed into a *sacred right*. . . . Henceforth it is to be the chief jewel of the nation – the very figure-head of the ship of State. Little by little, but steadily as man's march to the grave, we have been giving up the old for the new faith. Near eighty years ago we began by declaring that all men are created equal; but now from that beginning we have run down to the other declaration, that for some men to enslave others is a sacred right of self-government. These principles cannot stand together. They are as opposite as God and Mammon; and whoever holds to the one must despise the other. . . .

Our Republican robe is soiled and trailed in the dust. Let us purify it. Let us turn and wash it white in the spirit if not the blood of the Revolution. Let us turn slavery from its claims of moral right, back upon its existing legal rights and its arguments of necessity. Let us return it to the position our fathers gave it, and there let it rest in peace. Let us re-adopt the Declaration of Independence, and with it the practices and policy which harmonize with it. Let North and South, let all Americans, let all lovers of liberty everywhere, join in the great and good work. If we do this, we shall not only have saved the Union, but we shall have so saved it as to make and to keep it for ever worthy of the saving.

From Letter to the Hon. Geo. Robertson, Lexington, Kentucky. Springfield, Illinois. August 15, 1855

My dear Sir, . . . You are not a friend of slavery in the abstract. In that speech you spoke of 'the peaceful extinction of slavery' and used other expressions indicating your belief that the thing was, at some time, to have an end. Since then we have had thirty-six years of experience; and this experience has demonstrated, I think, that there is no peaceful extinction of slavery in prospect for us. The signal failure of Henry Clay and other good and great men, in 1849, to effect anything in favour of gradual emancipation in Kentucky, together with a thousand other signs, extinguishes that hope utterly. On the question of liberty, as a principle, we are not what we have been. When we were the political slaves of King George, and wanted to be free, we called the maxim that 'all men are created equal' a self-evident truth; but now when we have grown fat, and have lost all dread of being slaves ourselves, we have become so greedy to be *masters* that we call the same maxim 'a self-evident lie'. The Fourth of July has not quite dwindled away; it is still a great day for burning fire-crackers!

That spirit which desired the peaceful extinction of slavery has itself become extinct with the *occasion* and the *men* of the Revolution. Under the impulse of that occasion, nearly half the States adopted systems of emancipation at once; and it is a significant fact that not a single State has done the like since. So far as peaceful, voluntary emancipation is concerned, the condition of the negro slave in America, scarcely less terrible to the contemplation of the free mind, is now as fixed and hopeless of change for the better as that of the lost souls of the finally impenitent. The Autocrat of all the Russias will resign his crown and proclaim his subjects free republicans, sooner than will our American masters voluntarily give up their slaves.

Our political problem now is, 'Can we as a nation continue together *permanently* − *for ever* − half slave, and half free?' The problem is too mighty for me. May God in his mercy superintend the solution.

> Your much obliged friend, and humble servant,
>
> A. LINCOLN

Extracts from Letter to Joshua F. Speed. August 24, 1855

You suggest that in political action now, you and I would differ. I suppose we would; not quite so much, however, as you may think. You know I dislike slavery, and you fully admit the abstract wrong of it. So far there is no cause of difference. But you say that sooner than yield your legal right to the slave, especially at the bidding of those who are not themselves interested, you would see the Union dissolved. I am not aware that anyone is bidding you yield that right; very certainly I am not. I leave that matter entirely to yourself. I also acknowledge your rights and my obligations under the Constitution in regard to your slaves. I confess I hate to see the poor creatures hunted down and caught and carried back to their stripes and unrequited toil; but I bite my lips and keep quiet. In 1841, you and I had together a tedious low-water trip on a steamboat, from Louisville to St Louis. You may remember, as I well do, that from Louisville to the mouth of the Ohio, there were on board ten or a dozen slaves shackled together with irons. That sight was a continued torment to me, and I see something like it every time I touch the Ohio or any other slave border. It is not fair for you to assume that I have no interest in a thing which has, and continually exercises, the power of making me miserable. You ought rather to appreciate how·much the great body of the Northern people do crucify their feelings in order to maintain their loyalty to the Constitution and the Union. I do oppose the extension of slavery, because my judgment and feeling so prompt me, and I am under no obligations to the contrary. If for this you and I must differ, differ we must. You say if you were President, you would send an army and hang the leaders of the Missouri outrages upon the Kansas elections; still, if Kansas fairly votes herself a slave State she must be admitted, or the Union must be dissolved. But how if she votes herself a slave State unfairly; that is, by the very means for which you say you would hang men? Must she still be admitted, or the Union dissolved? That will be the phase of the question when it first becomes a practical one. In your assumption that there may be a fair decision of the slavery question in Kansas, I plainly see that you and I would differ about the Nebraska law. I look upon that enactment, not as a law, but as a violence from the beginning. It was conceived in violence, is maintained in violence, and is being executed in violence. I say it was conceived in violence, because the destruction of the Missouri Compromise, under the circumstances, was nothing less than violence. It was passed in violence, because it could not have passed at all but for the votes of many members in violence of the known will of their constituents. It is maintained in violence, because the elections since clearly demand its repeal, and the demand is openly disregarded.

You say men ought to be hung for the way they are executing the law; I say that the way it is being executed is quite as good as any of its antecedents. It is being executed in the precise way which was intended from the first, else why does no Nebraska man express astonishment or condemnation? Poor Reeder is the only public man who has been silly enough to believe that anything like fairness was ever intended, and he has been bravely undeceived.

That Kansas will form a slave constitution, and with it ask to be admitted into the Union, I take to be already a settled question, and so settled by the very means you so pointedly condemn. By every principle of law ever held by any court North or South, every negro taken to Kansas *is* free; yet in utter disregard of this –

in the spirit of violence merely – that beautiful Legislature gravely passes a law to hang any man who shall venture to inform a negro of his legal rights. This is the subject and real object of the law. If, like Haman, they should hang upon the gallows of their own building, I shall not be among the mourners for their fate. In my humble sphere, I shall advocate the restoration of the Missouri Compromise so long as Kansas remains a Territory; and when, by all these foul means, it seeks to come into the Union as a slave State, I shall oppose it. I am very loath in any case to withhold my assent to the enjoyment of property acquired or located in good faith; but I do not admit that good faith in taking a negro to Kansas to be held in slavery is a probability with any man. Any man who has sense enough to be the controller of his own property has too much sense to misunderstand the outrageous character of the whole Nebraska business. But I digress. In my opposition to the admission of Kansas, I shall have some company, but we may be beaten. If we are, I shall not, on that account, attempt to dissolve the Union. I think it probable, however, we shall be beaten. Standing as a unit among yourselves, you can, directly and indirectly, bribe enough of our men to carry the day, as you could on the open proposition to establish a monarchy. Get hold of some man in the North whose position and ability are such that he can make the support of your measure, whatever it may be, a Democratic-party necessity, and the thing is done. Apropos of this, let me tell you an anecdote. Douglas introduced the Nebraska Bill in January. In February afterward, there was a called session of the Illinois Legislature. Of the one hundred members composing the two branches of that body, about seventy were Democrats. These latter held a caucus, in which the Nebraska Bill was talked of, if not formally discussed. It was thereby discovered that just three, and no more, were in favour of the measure. In a day or two Douglas's orders came on to have resolutions passed approving the bill; and they were passed by large majorities! The truth of this is vouched for by a bolting Democratic member. The masses too, Democratic as well as Whig, were even nearer unanimous against it; but as soon as the party necessity of supporting it became apparent, the way the Democrats began to see the wisdom and justice of it was perfectly astonishing.

You say that if Kansas fairly votes herself a free State, as a Christian you will rejoice at it. All decent slaveholders talk that way, and I do not doubt their candour; but they never vote that way. Although in a private letter or conversation you will express your preference that Kansas should be free, you would vote for no man for Congress who would say the same thing publicly. No such man could be elected from any district in a slave State. You think Stringfellow and company ought to be hung. . . . The slave-breeders and slave-traders are a small, odious, and detested class among you; and yet in politics they dictate the course of all of you, and are as completely your masters as you are the master of your own negroes. You inquire where I now stand. That is a disputed point. I think I am a Whig; but others say there are no Whigs, and that I am an Abolitionist. When I was at Washington, I voted for the Wilmot Proviso as good as forty times; and I never heard of anyone attempting to unwhig me for that. I now do no more than oppose the extension of slavery. I am not a Know-nothing; that is certain. How could I be? How can anyone who abhors the oppression of negroes be in favour of degrading classes of white people? Our progress in degeneracy appears to me to be pretty rapid. As a nation, we began by declaring that *all men are created equal*. We now practically read it, *all men are created equal except negroes*. When the Know-nothings get control, it will read, *all men are created equal except negroes* and foreigners and Catholics. When it comes to this, I shall prefer emigrating to some country where they make no pretence of loving liberty – to Russia, for instance, where despotism can be taken pure, and without the base alloy of hypocrisy. . . . My kindest regards to Mrs Speed. On the leading subject of this letter I have more of her sympathy than I have of yours; and yet let me say I am your friend for ever.

A. LINCOLN

Mr Lincoln's Speech. Bloomington. May 29, 1856

Mr Chairman and Gentlemen, I was over at [cries of 'Platform!' 'Take the platform!'] – I say, that while I was at Danville Court, some of our friends of anti-Nebraska got together in Springfield and elected me as one delegate to represent old Sangamon with them in this convention, and I am here certainly as a sympathizer in this movement and by virtue of that meeting and selection. But we can hardly be called delegates strictly, inasmuch as, properly speaking, we represent nobody but ourselves. I think it altogether fair to say that we have no anti-Nebraska party in Sangamon, although there is a good deal of anti-Nebraska feeling there; but I say for myself, and I think I may speak also for my colleagues, that we who are here fully approve of the platform and of all that has been done [A voice: 'Yes!']; and even if we are not regularly delegates, it will be right for me to answer your call to speak. I suppose we truly stand for the public sentiment of Sangamon on the great question of the repeal, although we do not yet represent many numbers who have taken a distinct position on the question.

We are in a trying time – it ranges above mere party – and this movement to call a halt and turn our steps backward needs all the help and good counsels it can get; for unless popular opinion makes itself very strongly felt, and a change is made in our present course, *blood will flow on account of Nebraska, and brother's hand will be raised against brother!* [The last sentence was uttered in such an earnest, impressive, if not, indeed, tragic, manner, as to make a cold chill creep over me. Others gave a similar experience.]

I have listened with great interest to the earnest appeal made to Illinois men by the gentleman from Lawrence [James S. Emery] who has just addressed us so eloquently and forcibly. I was deeply moved by his statement of the wrongs done to free-State men out there. I think it just to say that all true men North should sympathize with them, and ought to be willing to do any possible and needful thing to right their wrongs. But we must not promise what we ought not, lest we be called on to perform what we cannot; we must be calm and moderate, and consider the whole difficulty, and determine what is possible and just. We must not be led by excitement and passion to do that which our sober judgments would not approve in our cooler moments. We have higher aims; we will have more serious business than to dally with temporary measures.

We are here to stand firmly for a principle – to stand firmly for a right. We know that great political and moral wrongs are done, and outrages committed, and we denounce those wrongs and outrages, although we cannot, at present, do much more. But we desire to reach out beyond those personal outrages and establish a rule that will apply to all, and so prevent any future outrages.

We have seen today that every shade of popular opinion is represented here, with *Freedom* or rather *Free-Soil* as the basis. We have come together as in some sort representatives of popular opinion against the extension of slavery into territory now free in fact as well as by law, and the pledged word of the statesmen of the nation who are now no more. We come – we are here assembled together – to protest as well as we can against a great wrong, and to take measures, as well as we now can, to make that wrong right; to place the nation, as far as it may be possible now, as it was before the repeal of the Missouri Compromise; and the plain way to do this is to restore the Compromise, and to demand and determine that *Kansas shall be free!* [Immense applause.] While we affirm, and reaffirm, if necessary, our devotion to the principles of the Declaration of Independence, let our practical work here be limited to the above. We know that there is not a perfect agreement of sentiment here on the public questions which might be rightfully considered in this convention, and that the indignation which we all must feel cannot be helped; but all of us must give up something for the good of the cause. There is one desire which is uppermost in the mind, one wish common to us all – to which no dissent will be made; and I counsel you earnestly to bury all resentment, to sink all personal feeling, make all things work to a common purpose in which we are united and agreed about, and which all present will agree is absolutely necessary – which *must* be done by any rightful mode if there be such: *Slavery must be kept out of Kansas!* [Applause.] The test – the pinch – is right there. If we lose Kansas to freedom, an example will be set which will prove fatal to freedom in the end. We, therefore, in the language of the Bible, must 'lay the axe to the root of the tree'. Temporizing will not do longer; now is the time for decision – for firm, persistent, resolute action. [Applause.]

The Nebraska bill, or rather Nebraska law, is not one of wholesome legislation, but was and is an act of legislative usurpation, whose result, if not indeed intention, is to make slavery national; and unless headed off in some effective way, we are in a fair way to see this land of boasted freedom converted into a land of slavery in fact. [Sensation.] Just open your two eyes, and see if this be not so.

I need do no more than state, to command universal approval, that almost the entire North, as well as a large following in the border States, is radically opposed to the planting of slavery in free territory. Probably in a popular vote throughout the nation nine-tenths of the voters in the free States, and at least one-half in the border States, if they could express their sentiments freely, would vote NO on such an issue; and it is safe to say that two-thirds of the votes of the entire nation would be opposed to it. And yet, in spite of this overbalancing of sentiment in this free country, we are in a fair way to see Kansas present itself for admission as a slave State. Indeed, it is a felony, by the local law of Kansas, to deny that slavery exists there even now. By every principle of law, a negro in Kansas is free; yet the *bogus* legislature makes it an infamous crime to tell him that he is free!

The party lash and the fear of ridicule will overawe justice and liberty; for it is a singular fact, but none the less a fact, and well known by the most common experience, that men will do things under the terror of the party lash that they would not on any account or for any consideration do otherwise; while men who will march up to the mouth of a loaded cannon without shrinking, will run from the terrible name of 'Abolitionist', even when pronounced by a worthless creature whom they, with good reason, despise. For instance – to press this point a little – Judge Douglas introduced his anti-Nebraska bill in January; and we had an extra session of our legislature in the succeeding February, in which were seventy-five Democrats; and at a party caucus, fully attended, there were just three votes out of the whole seventy-five, for the measure. But in a few days orders came on from Washington, commanding them to approve the measure; the party lash was applied, and it was brought up again in caucus, and passed by a large majority. The masses were against it, but party necessity carried it; and it was passed through the lower house of Congress against the will of the people, for the same reason. Here is where the greatest danger lies – that, while we profess to be a government of law and reason, law will give way to violence on demand of this awful and crushing power. Like the great Juggernaut – I think that is the name – the great idol, it crushes everything that comes in its way, and makes a – or as I read once, in a black-letter law book, 'a slave is a human being who is legally not a *person*, but a *thing*.' And if the safeguards to liberty are broken down, as is now attempted, when they have made *things* of all the free negroes, how long, think you, before they will begin to make *things* of poor white men? [Applause.] Be not deceived. Revolutions do not go backward. The founder of the Democratic party declared that *all* men were created equal. His successor in the leadership has written the word 'white' before men, making it read 'all *white* men are created equal.' Pray, will or may not the Know-nothings, if they should get in power, add the word 'protestant', making it read '*all protestant white men*'?

Meanwhile the hapless negro is the fruitful subject of reprisals in other quarters. John Pettit, whom Tom Benton paid his respects to, you will recollect, calls the immortal Declaration 'a self-evident lie'; while at the birth-place of freedom – in the shadow of Bunker Hill and of the 'cradle of liberty', at the home of the Adamses and Warren and Otis – Choate, from our side of the house, dares to fritter away the birthday promise of liberty by proclaiming the Declaration to be 'a string of glittering generalities'; and the Southern Whigs, working hand in hand with pro-slavery Democrats, are making Choate's theories practical. Thomas Jefferson, a slaveholder, mindful of the moral element in slavery, solemnly declared that he 'trembled for his country when he remembered that God is just'; while Judge Douglas, with an insignificant wave of the hand, 'don't care whether slavery is voted up or voted down'. Now, if slavery is right, or even negative, he has a right to treat it in this trifling manner. But if it is a moral and political wrong, as all Christendom considers it to be, how can he answer to God for this attempt to spread and fortify it? [Applause.]

But no man, and Judge Douglas no more than any other, can maintain a negative, or merely neutral, position on this question; and, accordingly, he avows that the Union was made *by* white men and *for* white men and their descendants. As matter of fact, the first branch of the proposition is historically true; the government was made by white men, and they were and are the superior race. This I admit. But the cornerstone of the government, so to speak, was the declaration that '*all* men are created equal', and all entitled to 'life, liberty, and the pursuit of happiness'. [Applause.]

And not only so, but the framers of the Constitution were particular to keep out of that instrument the word 'slave', the reason being that slavery would ultimately come to an end, and they did not wish to have any reminder that in this free country human beings were ever prostituted to slavery. [Applause.] Nor is it any argument that we are superior and the negro inferior – that he has but one talent while we have ten. Let the negro possess the little he has in independence; if he has but one talent, he should be permitted to keep the little he has. [Applause.] But slavery will endure no test of reason or logic; and yet its advocates, like Douglas, use a sort of bastard logic, or noisy assumption, it might better be termed, like the above, in order to prepare the mind for the gradual, but none the less certain, encroachments of the Moloch of slavery upon the fair domain of freedom. But however much you may argue upon it, or smother it in soft phrases, slavery can only be maintained by force – by violence. The repeal of the Missouri Compromise was by violence. It was a violation of both law and the sacred obligations of honour, to overthrow and trample underfoot a solemn compromise, obtained by the fearful loss to freedom of one of the fairest of our Western domains. Congress violated the will and confidence of its constituents in voting for the bill; and while public sentiment, as shown by the elections of 1854, demanded the restoration of this compromise, Congress violated its trust by refusing, simply because it had the force of numbers to hold on to it. And murderous violence is being used now, in order to force slavery on to Kansas; for it cannot be done in any other way. [Sensation.]

The necessary result was to establish the rule of violence – force, instead of the rule of law and reason; to perpetuate and spread slavery, and, in time, to make it general. We see it at both ends of the line. In Washington, on the very spot where the outrage was started, the fearless Sumner is beaten to insensibility, and is now slowly dying; while senators who claim to be gentlemen and Christians stood by, countenancing the act, and even applauding it afterward in their places in the Senate. Even Douglas, our man, saw it all and was within helping distance, yet let the murderous blows fall unopposed. Then, at the other end of the line, at the very time Sumner was being murdered, Lawrence was being destroyed for the crime of Freedom. It was the most prominent stronghold of liberty in Kansas, and must give way to the all-dominating power of slavery. Only two days ago, Judge Trumbull found it necessary to propose a bill in the Senate to prevent a general civil war and to restore peace in Kansas.

We live in the midst of alarms; anxiety beclouds the future; we expect some new disaster with each newspaper we read. Are we in a healthful political state? Are not the tendencies plain? Do not the signs of the times point plainly the way in which we are going? [Sensation.]

In the early days of the Constitution slavery was recognized, by South and North alike, as an evil, and the division of sentiment about it was not controlled by geographical lines or considerations of climate, but by moral and philanthropic views. Petitions for the abolition of slavery were presented to the very first Congress by Virginia and Massachusetts alike. To show the harmony which prevailed, I will state that a fugitive slave law was passed in 1793, with no dissenting voice in the Senate, and but seven dissenting votes in the House. It was, however, a wise law, moderate, and, under the Constitution, a just one. Twenty-five years later, a more stringent law was proposed and defeated; and thirty-five years after that, the present law, drafted by Mason of Virginia, was passed by Northern votes. I am not, just now, complaining of this law, but I am trying to show how the current sets; for the proposed law of 1817 was far less offensive than the present one. In 1774 the Continental Congress pledged itself, without a dissenting vote, to wholly discontinue the slave trade, and to neither purchase nor import any slave: and less than three months before the passage of the Declaration of Independence, the same Congress which adopted that declaration unanimously resolved 'that *no slave be imported into any of the thirteen United Colonies.*' [Great applause.]

On the second day of July, 1776, the draft of a Declaration of Independence was reported to Congress by the committee, and in it the slave trade was characterized as 'an execrable commerce', as 'a piratical warfare', as the 'opprobrium of infidel powers', and as 'a cruel war against human nature'. [Applause.] All agreed on this except South Carolina and Georgia, and in order to preserve harmony, and from the necessity of the case, these expressions were omitted. Indeed, abolition societies existed as far south as Virginia; and it is a well-known fact that Washington, Jefferson, Madison, Lee, Henry, Mason, and Pendleton were qualified abolitionists, and much more radical on that subject than we of the

Whig and Democratic parties claim to be today. On March 1, 1784, Virginia ceded to the confederation all its lands lying northwest of the Ohio River. Jefferson, Chase of Maryland, and Howell of Rhode Island, as a committee on that and territory thereafter *to be ceded*, reported that no slavery should exist after the year 1800. Had this report been adopted, not only the Northwest, but Kentucky, Tennessee, Alabama, and Mississippi also would have been free; but it required the assent of nine States to ratify it. North Carolina was divided, and thus its vote was lost; and Delaware, Georgia, and New Jersey refused to vote. In point of fact, as it was, it was assented to by six States. Three years later, on a square vote to exclude slavery from the Northwest, only one vote, and that from New York, was against it. And yet, thirty-seven years later, five thousand citizens of Illinois out of a voting mass of less than twelve thousand, deliberately, after a long and heated contest, voted to introduce slavery in Illinois; and, today, a large party in the free State of Illinois are willing to vote to fasten the shackles of slavery on the fair domain of Kansas, notwithstanding it received the dowry of freedom long before its birth as a political community. I repeat, therefore, the question, Is it not plain in what direction we are tending? [Sensation.] In the colonial time, Mason, Pendleton, and Jefferson were as hostile to slavery in Virginia as Otis, Ames, and the Adamses were in Massachusetts; and Virginia made as earnest an effort to get rid of it as old Massachusetts did. But circumstances were against them and they failed; but not that the goodwill of its leading men was lacking. Yet within less than fifty years Virginia changed its tune, and made negro-breeding for the cotton and sugar States one of its leading industries. [Laughter and applause.]

In the Constitutional Convention, George Mason of Virginia made a more violent abolition speech than my friends Lovejoy or Codding would desire to make here today – a speech which could not be safely repeated anywhere on Southern soil in this enlightened year. But while there were some differences of opinion on this subject even then, discussion was allowed; but as you see by the Kansas slave code, which, as you know, is the Missouri slave code, merely ferried across the river, it is a felony to even express an opinion hostile to that foul blot in the land of Washington and the Declaration of Independence. [Sensation.]

In Kentucky – my State – in 1849, on a test vote, the mighty influence of Henry Clay and many other good men there could not get a symptom of expression in favour of gradual emancipation on a plain issue of marching toward the light of civilization with Ohio and Illinois; but the State of Boone and Hardin and Henry Clay, with a *nigger* under each arm, took the black trail toward the deadly swamps of barbarism. Is there – can there be – any doubt about this thing? And is there any doubt that we must all lay aside our prejudices and march, shoulder to shoulder, in the great army of Freedom? [Applause.]

Every Fourth of July our young orators all proclaim this to be 'the land of the *free* and the home of the brave!' Well, now, when you orators get that off next year, and, may be, this very year, how would you like some old grizzled farmer to get up in the grove and deny it? [Laughter.] How would you like that? But suppose Kansas comes in as a slave State, and all the 'border ruffians' have barbecues about it, and free-State men come trailing back to the dishonoured North, like whipped dogs with their tails between their legs, it is – ain't it? – evident that this is no more the 'land of the free'; and if we let it go so, we won't dare to say 'home of the brave' out loud. [Sensation and confusion.]

Can any man doubt that, even in spite of the people's will, slavery will triumph through violence, unless that will be made manifest and enforced? Even Governor Reeder claimed at the outset that the contest in Kansas was to be fair, but he got his eyes open at last; and I believe that, as a result of this moral and physical violence, Kansas will soon apply for admission as a slave State. And yet we can't mistake that the people don't want it so, and that it is a land which is free both by natural and political law. *No law is free law!* Such is the understanding of all Christendom. In the Somerset case, decided nearly a century ago, the great Lord Mansfield held that slavery was of such a nature that it must take its rise in *positive* (as distinguished from *natural*) law; and that in no country or age could it be traced back to any other source. Will someone please tell me where is the *positive* law that establishes slavery in Kansas? [A voice: 'The *bogus* laws.'] Aye, the *bogus* laws! And, on the same principle, a gang of Missouri horse-thieves could come into Illinois and declare horse-stealing to be legal [Laughter], and it would be just as legal as slavery is in Kansas. But by express statute, in the land of Washington and Jefferson, we may soon be brought face to face with the discreditable fact of showing to the world by our acts that we prefer slavery to freedom — darkness to light! [Sensation.]

It is, I believe, a principle in law that when one party to a contract violates it so grossly as to chiefly destroy the object for which it is made, the other party may rescind it. I will ask Browning if that ain't good law. [Voices: 'Yes!'] Well, now if that be right, I go for rescinding the whole, entire Missouri Compromise and thus turning Missouri into a free State; and I should like to know the difference — should like for anyone to point out the difference — between *our* making a free State of Missouri and *their* making a slave State of Kansas. [Great applause.] There ain't one bit of difference, except that our way would be a great mercy to humanity. But I have never said — and the Whig party has never said — and those who oppose the Nebraska bill do not as a body say, that they have any intention of interfering with slavery in the slave States. Our platform says just the contrary. We allow slavery to exist in the slave States — not because slavery is right or good, but from the necessities of our Union. We grant a fugitive slave law because it is so 'nominated in the bond'; because our fathers so stipulated — had to — and we are bound to carry out this agreement. But they did not agree to introduce slavery in regions where it did not previously exist. On the contrary, they said by their example and teachings that they did not deem it expedient — did not consider it right — to do so; and it is wise and right to do just as they did about it [Voices: 'Good!'], and that is what we propose — not to interfere with slavery where it exists (we have never tried to do it), and to give them a reasonable and efficient fugitive slave law. [A voice: 'No!'] I say YES! [Applause.] It was part of the bargain, and I'm for living up to it; but I go no further; I'm not bound to do more, and I won't agree any further. [Great applause.]

We, here in Illinois, should feel especially proud of the provision of the Missouri Compromise excluding slavery from what is now Kansas; for an Illinois man, Jesse B. Thomas, was its father. Henry Clay, who is credited with the authorship of the Compromise in general terms, did not even vote for that provision, but only advocated the ultimate admission by a second compromise; and, Thomas was, beyond all controversy, the real author of the 'slavery restriction' branch of the Compromise. To show the generosity of the Northern members toward the Southern side; on a test vote to exclude slavery from Missouri, ninety voted not to exclude, and eighty-seven to exclude, every vote from the slave States being ranged with the former and fourteen votes from the free States, of whom seven were from New England alone; while on a vote to exclude slavery from what is now Kansas, the vote was one hundred and thirty-four *for* to forty-two *against*. The scheme, as a whole, was, of course, a Southern triumph. It is idle to contend otherwise, as is now being done by the Nebraskaites; it was so shown by the votes and quite as emphatically by the expressions of representative men. Mr Lowndes of South Carolina was never known to commit a political mistake; his was the great judgment of that section; and he declared that this measure 'would restore tranquillity to the country – a result demanded by every consideration of discretion, of moderation, of wisdom, and of virtue.' When the measure came before President Monroe for his approval, he put to each member of his cabinet this question: 'Has Congress the constitutional power to prohibit slavery in a territory?' And John C. Calhoun and William H. Crawford from the South, equally with John Quincy Adams, Benjamin Rush, and Smith Thompson from the North, alike answered, '*Yes!*' without qualification or equivocation; and this measure, of so great consequence to the South, was passed; and Missouri was, by means of it, finally enabled to knock at the door of the Republic for an open passage to its brood of slaves. And, in spite of this, Freedom's share is about to be taken by violence – by the force of misrepresentative votes, not called for by the popular will. What name can I, in common decency, give to this wicked transaction? [Sensation.]

But even then the contest was not over; for when the Missouri constitution came before Congress for its approval, it forbade any free negro or mulatto from entering the State. In short, our Illinois 'black laws' were hidden away in their constitution [Laughter], and the controversy was thus revived. Then it was that Mr Clay's talents shone out conspicuously, and the controversy that shook the Union to its foundation was finally settled to the satisfaction of the conservative parties on both sides of the line, though not to the extremists on either, and Missouri was admitted by the small majority of six in the lower House. How great a majority, do you think, would have been given had Kansas also been secured for slavery? [A voice: 'A majority the other way.'] 'A majority the other way,' is answered. Do you think it would have been safe for a Northern man to have confronted his constituents after having voted to consign both Missouri and Kansas to hopeless slavery? And yet this man Douglas, who misrepresents his constituents, and who has exerted his highest talents in that direction, will be carried in triumph through the State, and hailed with honour while applauding that act. [Three groans for '*Dug*!'] And this shows whither we are tending. This thing of slavery is more powerful than its supporters – even than the high priests that minister at its altar. It debauches even our greatest men. It gathers strength, like a rolling snowball, by its own infamy. Monstrous crimes are committed in its name by persons collectively which they would not dare to commit as individuals. Its aggressions and encroachments almost surpass belief. In a despotism, one might not wonder to see slavery advance steadily and remorselessly into new dominions; but is it not wonderful, is it not even alarming, to see its steady advance in a land dedicated to the proposition that 'all men are created equal'? [Sensation.]

It yields nothing itself; it keeps all it has, and gets all it can besides. It really came dangerously near securing Illinois in 1824; it did get Missouri in 1821. The first proposition was to admit what is now Arkansas *and* Missouri as one slave State. But the territory was divided, and Arkansas came in, without serious question, as a slave State; and afterward Missouri, not as a sort of equality, *free*, but also as a slave State. Then we had Florida and Texas; and now Kansas is about to be forced into the dismal procession. [Sensation.] And so it is wherever you look. We have not forgotten – it is but six years since – how dangerously near California came to being a slave State. Texas is a slave State, and four other slave States may be carved from its vast domain. And yet, in the year 1829, slavery was abolished throughout that vast region by a royal decree of the then sovereign of Mexico. Will you please tell me by what *right* slavery exists in Texas today? By the same right as, and no higher or greater than, slavery is seeking dominion in Kansas: by political force – peaceful, if that will suffice; by the torch (as in Kansas) and the bludgeon (as in the Senate chamber), if required. And so history repeats itself; and even as slavery has kept its course by craft, intimidation, and violence in the past, so it will persist, in my judgment, until met and dominated by the will of a people bent on its restriction.

We have, this very afternoon, heard bitter denunciations of Brooks in Washington, and Titus, Stringfellow, Atchison, Jones, and Shannon in Kansas – the battle-ground of slavery. I certainly am not going to advocate or shield them; but they and their acts are but the necessary outcome of the Nebraska law. We should reserve our highest censure for the authors of the mischief, and not for the catspaws which they use. I believe it was Shakespeare who said, 'Where the offence lies, there let the axe fall'; and, in my opinion, this man Douglas and the Northern men in Congress who advocate 'Nebraska' are more guilty than a thousand Joneses and Stringfellows, with all their murderous practices, can be. [Applause.]

We have made a good beginning here today. As our Methodist friends would say, 'I feel it is good to be here.' While extremists may find some fault with the moderation of our platform, they should recollect that 'the battle is not always to the strong, nor the race to the swift.' In grave emergencies, moderation is generally safer than radicalism: and as this struggle is likely to be long and earnest, we must not, by our action, repel any who are in sympathy with us in the main, but rather win all that we can to our standard. We must not belittle nor overlook the facts of our condition – that we are new and comparatively weak, while our enemies are entrenched and relatively strong. They have the administration and the political power; and, right or wrong, at present they have the numbers. Our friends who urge an appeal to arms with so much force and eloquence, should recollect that the government is arrayed against us, and that the numbers are now arrayed against us as well; or, to state it nearer to the truth, they are not yet expressly and affirmatively for us; and we should repel friends rather than gain them by anything savouring of revolutionary methods. As it now stands, we must appeal to the sober sense and patriotism of the people. We will make converts day by day; we will grow strong by calmness and moderation; we will grow strong by the violence and injustice of our adversaries. And, unless truth be a mockery and justice a hollow lie, we will be in the majority after a while, and then the revolution which we will accomplish will be none the less radical from being the result of pacific measures. The battle of freedom is to be fought out on principle. Slavery is a violation of the eternal right. We have temporized with it from the necessities of our condition; but *as sure as God reigns and school children read*, THAT BLACK FOUL LIE CAN NEVER BE CONSECRATED INTO GOD'S HALLOWED TRUTH! [Immense applause lasting some time.] One of our greatest difficulties is, that men who *know* that slavery is a detestable crime and ruinous to the nation, are compelled, by our peculiar condition and other circumstances, to advocate it concretely, though damning it in the raw. Henry Clay was a brilliant example of this tendency; others of our purest statesmen are compelled to do so; and thus slavery secures actual support from those who detest it at heart. Yet Henry Clay perfected and forced through the Compromise which secured to slavery a great State as well as a political advantage. Not that he hated slavery less, but that he loved the whole Union more. As long as slavery profited by his great Compromise, the hosts of pro-slavery could not sufficiently cover him with praise; but now that this Compromise stands in their way –

> . . . they never mention him,
> His name is never heard:
> Their lips are now forbid to speak
> That once familiar word.

They have slaughtered one of his most cherished measures, and his ghost would arise to rebuke them. [Great applause.]

Now, let us harmonize, my friends, and appeal to the moderation and patriotism of the people: to the sober second thought; to the awakened public conscience. The repeal of the sacred Missouri Compromise has installed the weapons of violence: the bludgeon, the incendiary torch, the death-dealing rifle, the bristling cannon – the weapons of kingcraft, of the inquisition, of ignorance, of barbarism, of oppression. We see its fruits in the dying bed of the heroic Sumner; in the ruins of the 'Free State' hotel; in the smoking embers of the *Herald of Freedom*; in the free-State Governor of Kansas chained to a stake on freedom's soil like a horse-thief, for the crime of freedom. [Applause.] We see it in Christian statesmen, and Christian newspapers, and Christian pulpits, applauding *the cowardly act of a low bully*, WHO CRAWLED UPON HIS VICTIM

BEHIND HIS BACK AND DEALT THE DEADLY BLOW. [Sensation and applause.] We note our political demoralization in the catch-words that are coming into such common use; on the one hand, 'freedom-shriekers', and sometimes 'freedom-screechers' [Laughter]; and, on the other hand, 'border ruffians', and that fully deserved. And the significance of catch-words cannot pass unheeded, for they constitute a sign of the times. Everything in this world 'jibes' in with everything else, and all the fruits of this Nebraska bill are like the poisoned source from which they come. I will not say that we may not sooner or later be compelled to meet force by force; but the time has not yet come, and if we are true to ourselves, may never come. Do not mistake that the ballot is stronger than the bullet. Therefore let the legions of slavery use bullets; but let us wait patiently till November, and fire ballots at them in return; and by that peaceful policy, I believe we shall ultimately win. [Applause.]

It was by that policy that here in Illinois the early fathers fought the good fight and gained the victory. In 1824 the free men of our State, led by Governor Coles (who was a native of Maryland and President Madison's private secretary), determined that those beautiful groves should never re-echo the dirge of one who has no title to himself. By their resolute determination, the winds that sweep across our broad prairies shall never cool the parched brow, nor shall the unfettered streams that bring joy and gladness to our free soil water the tired feet, of a *slave*; but so long as those heavenly breezes and sparkling streams bless the land, or the groves and their fragrance or their memory remain, the humanity to which they minister SHALL BE FOR EVER FREE! [Great applause.] Palmer, Yates, Williams, Browning, and some more in this convention came from Kentucky to Illinois (instead of going to Missouri), not only to better their conditions, but also to get away from slavery. They have said so to me, and it is understood among us Kentuckians that we don't like it one bit. Now, can we, mindful of the blessings of liberty which the early men of Illinois left to us, refuse a like privilege to the free men who seek to plant Freedom's banner on our Western outposts? ['No! No!'] Should we not stand by our neighbours who seek to better their conditions in Kansas and Nebraska? ['Yes! Yes!'] Can we as Christian men, and strong and free ourselves, wield the sledge or hold the iron which is to manacle anew an already oppressed race? ['No! No!'] 'Woe unto them,' it is written, 'that decree unrighteous decrees and that write grievousness which they have prescribed.' Can we afford to sin any more deeply against human liberty? ['No! No!']

One great trouble in the matter is, that slavery is an insidious and crafty power, and gains equally by open violence of the brutal as well as by sly management of the peaceful. Even after the ordinance of 1787, the settlers in Indiana and Illinois (it was all one government then) tried to get Congress to allow slavery temporarily, and petitions to that end were sent from Kaskaskia, and General Harrison, the Governor, urged it from Vincennes the capital. If that had succeeded, good-bye to liberty here. But John Randolph of Virginia made a vigorous report against it; and although they persevered so well as to get three favourable reports for it, yet the United States Senate, with the aid of some slave States, finally *squelched* it for good. [Applause.] And that is why this hall is today a temple for free men instead of a negro livery stable. [Great applause and laughter.] Once let slavery get planted in a locality, by ever so weak or doubtful a title, and in ever so small numbers, and it is like the Canada thistle or Bermuda grass – you can't root it out. You yourself may detest slavery; but your neighbour has five or six slaves, and he is an excellent neighbour, or your son has married his daughter, and they beg you to help save their property, and you vote against your interest and principles to accommodate a neighbour, hoping that your vote will be on the losing side. And others do the same; and in those ways slavery gets a sure foothold. And when that is done the whole mighty Union – the force of the nation – is committed to its support. And that very process is working in Kansas today. And you must recollect that the slave property is worth a billion of dollars ($1,000,000,000); while free-State men must work for sentiment alone. Then there are 'blue lodges' – as they call them – everywhere doing their secret and deadly work.

It is a very strange thing, and not solvable by any moral law that I know of, that if a man loses his horse, the whole country will turn out to help hang the thief; but if a man but a shade or two darker than I am is himself stolen, the same crowd will hang one who aids in restoring him to liberty. Such are the inconsistencies of slavery, where a horse is more sacred than a man; and the essence of *squatter* or popular sovereignty – I don't care how you call it – is that if one man chooses to make a slave of another, no third man shall be allowed to object. And if you can do this in free Kansas, and it is allowed to stand, the next thing you will see is ship-loads of negroes from Africa at the wharf at Charleston; for one thing is as truly lawful as the other; and these are the bastard notions we have got to stamp out, else they will stamp us out. [Sensation and applause.]

Two years ago, at Springfield, Judge Douglas avowed that Illinois came into the Union as a slave State, and that slavery was weeded out by the operation of his great, patent, everlasting principle of 'popular sovereignty'. [Laughter.] Well, now, that argument must be answered, for it has a little grain of truth at the bottom. I do not mean that it is true in essence, as he would have us believe. It could not be essentially true if the ordinance of '87 was valid. But, in point of fact, there were some degraded beings called slaves in Kaskaskia and the other French settlements when our first State constitution was adopted; that is a fact, and I don't deny it. Slaves were brought here as early as 1720, and were kept here in spite of the ordinance of 1787 against it. But slavery did not thrive here. On the contrary, under the influence of the ordinance, the number *decreased* fifty-one from 1810 to 1820; while under the influence of *squatter* sovereignty, right across the river in Missouri, they *increased* seven thousand two hundred and eleven in the same time; and slavery finally faded out in Illinois, under the influence of the law of freedom, while it grew stronger and stronger in Missouri, under the law or practice of 'popular sovereignty'. In point of fact there were but one hundred and seventeen slaves in Illinois one year after its admission, or one to every four hundred and seventy of its population; or, to state it in another way, if Illinois was a slave State in 1820, so were New York and New Jersey much greater slave States from having had greater numbers, slavery having been established there in very early times. But there is this vital difference between all these States and the judge's Kansas experiment: that they sought to disestablish slavery which had been already established, while the judge seeks, so far as he can, to disestablish freedom, which had been established there by the Missouri Compromise. [Voices: 'Good!']

The Union is undergoing a fearful strain; but it is a stout old ship, and has weathered many a hard blow, and 'the stars in their courses', aye, an invisible power, greater than the puny efforts of men, will fight for us. But we ourselves must not decline the burden of responsibility, nor take counsel of unworthy passions. Whatever duty urges us to do or to omit, must be done or omitted; and the recklessness with which our adversaries break the laws, or counsel their violation, should afford no example for us. Therefore, let us revere the Declaration of Independence; let us continue to obey the Constitution and the laws; let us keep step to the music of the Union. Let us draw a cordon, so to speak, around the slave States, and the hateful institution, like a reptile poisoning itself, will perish by its own infamy. [Applause.]

But we cannot be free men if this is, by our national choice, to be a land of slavery. Those who deny freedom to others, deserve it not for themselves; and, under the rule of a just God, cannot long retain it. [Loud applause.]

Did you ever, my friends, seriously reflect upon the speed with which we are tending downward? Within the memory of men now present the leading statesmen of Virginia could make genuine, red-hot abolitionist speeches in old Virginia; and, as I have said, now even in 'free Kansas' it is a crime to declare that it is 'free Kansas'. The very sentiments that I and others have just uttered would entitle us, and each of us, to the ignominy and seclusion of a dungeon; and yet I suppose that, like Paul, we were 'free born'. But if this thing is allowed to continue, it will be but one step further to impress the same rule in Illinois. [Sensation.]

The conclusion of all is, that we must restore the Missouri Compromise. We must highly resolve that *Kansas must be free!* [Great applause.] We must reinstate the birthday promise of the Republic; we must reaffirm the Declaration of Independence; we must make good in essence as well as in form Madison's vowal that 'the word *slave* ought not to appear in the Constitution'; and we must even go further, and decree that only local law, and not that time-honoured instrument, shall shelter a slave-holder. We must make this a land of liberty in fact, as it is in name. But in seeking to attain these results – so indispensable if the liberty which is our pride and boast shall endure – we will be loyal to the Con-stitution and to the 'flag of our Union', and no matter what our grievance – even though Kansas shall come in as a slave State; and no matter what theirs – even if we shall restore the Compromise – WE WILL SAY TO THE SOUTHERN DISUNIONISTS, WE WON'T GO OUT OF THE UNION, AND YOU SHAN'T!!! [This was the climax; the audience rose to its feet *en masse*, applauded, stamped, waved handkerchiefs, threw hats in the air, and ran riot for several minutes. The arch-enchanter who wrought this transformation looked, meanwhile, like the personification of political justice.]

But let us, meanwhile, appeal to the sense and patriotism of the people, and not to their prejudices; let us spread the floods of enthusiasm here aroused all over these vast prairies, so suggestive of freedom. Let us commence by electing the gallant soldier Governor (Colonel) Bissell who stood for the honour of our State alike on the plains and amidst the chaparral of Mexico and on the floor of Congress, while he defied the Southern Hotspur; and that will have a greater moral effect than all the border ruffians can accomplish in all their raids on Kansas. There is both a power and a magic in popular opinion. To that let us now appeal; and while, in all probability, no resort to force will be needed, our moderation and forbearance will stand us in good stead when, if ever, WE MUST MAKE AN APPEAL TO BATTLE AND TO THE GOD OF HOSTS!! [Immense applause and a rush for the orator.]

This speech has been called Lincoln's 'Lost Speech', because all the reporters present were so carried away by his eloquence that they one and all forgot to take any notes. If it had not been for a young lawyer, a Mr H. C. Whitney, who kept his head sufficiently to take notes, we would have no record of it. Mr Whitney wrote out the speech for McClure's Magazine in 1896. It was submitted to several people who were present at the Bloomington Convention, and they said it was remarkably accurate considering that it was not taken down stenographically.

From his Speech on the Dred Scott Decision. Springfield, Illinois.
June 26, 1857

. . . And now as to the Dred Scott decision. That decision declares two propositions – first, that a negro cannot sue in the United States courts; and secondly, that Congress cannot prohibit slavery in the Territories. It was made by a divided court – dividing differently on the different points. Judge Douglas does not discuss the merits of the decision, and in that respect I shall follow his example, believing I could no more improve on McLean and Curtis than he could on Taney.

He denounces all who question the correctness of that decision, as offering violent resistance to it. But who resists it? Who has, in spite of the decision, declared Dred Scott free, and resisted the authority of his master over him?

Judicial decisions have two uses: first, to absolutely determine the case decided; and secondly, to indicate to the public how other similar cases will be decided when they arise. For the latter use, they are called 'precedents' and 'authorities'.

We believe as much as Judge Douglas (perhaps more) in obedience to and respect for the judicial department of government. We think its decisions on constitutional questions, when fully settled, should control not only the particular cases decided, but the general policy of the country, subject to be disturbed only by amendments of the Constitution, as provided in that instrument itself. More than this would be revolution. But we think the Dred Scott decision is erroneous. We know the court that made it has often overruled its own decisions, and we shall do what we can to have it overrule this. We offer no resistance to it.

Judicial decisions are of greater or less authority as precedents according to circumstances. That this should be so, accords both with common-sense and the customary understanding of the legal profession.

If this important decision had been made by the unanimous concurrence of the judges, and without any apparent partisan bias, and in accordance with legal public expectation, and with the steady practice of the departments throughout our history, and had been in no part based on assumed historical facts, which are not really true; or if wanting in some of these, it had been before the court more than once, and had there been affirmed and reaffirmed through a course of years – it then might be, perhaps would be factious, nay, even revolutionary, not to acquiesce in it as a precedent.

But when, as is true, we find it wanting in all these claims to the public confidence, it is not resistance, it is not factious, it is not even disrespectful to treat it as not having yet quite established a settled doctrine for the country.

I have said in substance, that the Dred Scott decision was in part based on assumed historical facts which were not really true, and I ought not to leave the subject without giving some reasons for saying this, I therefore give an instance or two, which I think fully sustain me. Chief Justice Taney, in delivering the opinion of the majority of the court, insists at great length that negroes were no part of the people who made, or for whom was made, the Declaration of Independence, or the Constitution of the United States.

On the contrary, Judge Curtis, in his dissenting opinion, shows that in five of the then thirteen States – to wit, New Hampshire, Massachusetts, New York, New Jersey, and North Carolina – free negroes were voters, and in proportion to their numbers had the same part in making the Constitution that the white people had. He shows this with so much particularity as to leave no doubt of its truth; and as a sort of conclusion on that point, holds the following language.

> The Constitution was ordained and established by the people of the United States, through the action, in each State, of those persons who were qualified by its laws to act thereon in behalf of themselves and all other citizens of the State. In some of the States, as we have seen, coloured persons were among those qualified by law to act on the subject. These coloured persons were not only included in the body of 'the people of the United States' by whom the Constitution was ordained and established; but in at least five of the States they had the power to act, and doubtless did act, by their suffrages, upon the question of its adoption.

Again, Chief Justice Taney says:

> It is difficult at this day to realize the state of public opinion, in relation to that unfortunate race, which prevailed in the civilized and enlightened portions of the world at the time of the Declaration of Independence, and when the Constitution of the United States was framed and adopted.

And again, after quoting from the Declaration, he says: 'The general words above quoted would seem to include the whole human family, and if they were used in a similar instrument at this day, would be so understood.'

In these the Chief Justice does not directly assert, but plainly assumes as a fact, that the public estimate of the black man is more favourable now than it was in the days of the Revolution. This assumption is a mistake. In some trifling particulars the condition of that race has been ameliorated; but as a whole, in this country, the change between then and now is decidedly the other way; and their ultimate destiny has never appeared so hopeless as in the last three or four years. In two of the five States – New Jersey and North Carolina – that then gave the free negro the right of voting, the right has since been taken away; and in a third – New York – it has been greatly abridged: while it has not been extended, so far as I know, to a single additional State, though the number of the States has more than doubled. In those days, as I understand, masters could, at their own pleasure, emancipate their slaves; but since then such legal restraints have been made upon emancipation as to amount almost to prohibition. In those days legislatures held the unquestioned power to abolish slavery in their respective States; but now it is becoming quite fashionable for State constitutions to withhold that power from the legislatures. In those days, by common consent, the spread of the black man's bondage to the new countries was prohibited; but now Congress decides that it will not continue the prohibition, and the Supreme Court decides that it could not if it would. In those days our Declaration of Independence was held sacred by all, and thought to include all; but now, to aid in making the bondage of the negro universal and eternal, it is assailed and sneered at, and construed, and hawked at, and torn, till, if its framers could rise from their graves, they could not at all recognize it. All the powers of earth seem rapidly combining against him. Mammon is after him; ambition follows, philosophy follows, and the theology of the day is fast joining in the cry. They have him in his prison-house; they have searched his person, and left no prying instrument with him. One after another they have closed the heavy iron doors upon him; and now they have him, as it were, bolted in with a lock of a hundred keys, which can never be unlocked without the concurrence of every key; the keys in the hands of a hundred different men, and they scattered to a hundred different and distant places; and they stand musing as to what invention, in all the dominions of mind and matter, can be produced to make the impossibility of escape more complete than it is. It is grossly incorrect to say or assume that the public estimate of the negro is more favourable now than it was at the origin of the government.

. . . There is a natural disgust in the minds of nearly all white people at the idea of an indiscriminate amalgamation of the white and black races; and Judge Douglas evidently is basing his chief hope upon the chances of his being able to appropriate the benefit of this disgust to himself. If he can, by much drumming and repeating, fasten the odium of that idea upon his adversaries, he thinks he can struggle through the storm. He therefore clings to this hope as a drowning man to the last plank. He makes an occasion for lugging it in from the opposition to the Dred Scott decision. He finds the Republicans insisting that the Declaration of Independence includes *all* men, black as well as white; and forthwith he boldly denies that it includes negroes at all, and proceeds to argue gravely that all who contend it does, do so only because they want to vote, and eat, and sleep, and marry with negroes! He will have it that they cannot be consistent else. Now I protest against the counterfeit logic which concludes that because I do not want a black woman for a slave, I must necessarily want her for a wife. I need not have her for either. I can just leave her alone. In some respects she certainly is not my equal; but in her natural right to eat the bread she earns with her own hands without asking leave of anyone else, she is my equal, and the equal of all others.

Chief Justice Taney, in his opinion in the Dred Scott case, admits that the language of the Declaration is broad enough to include the whole human family; but he and Judge Douglas argue that the authors of that instrument did not intend to include negroes, by the fact that they did not at once actually place them on an equality with the whites. Now this grave argument comes to just nothing at all, by the other fact that they did not at once, nor ever afterward, actually place all white people on an equality with one another. And this is the staple argument of both the Chief Justice and the senator, for doing this obvious violence to the plain, unmistakable language of the Declaration.

I think the authors of that notable instrument intended to include *all* men, but they did not intend to declare all men equal *in all respects*. They did not mean to say that all were equal in colour, size, intellect, moral developments, or social capacity. They defined with tolerable distinctness in what respects they did consider all men created equal – equal with 'certain inalienable rights, among which are life, liberty, and the pursuit of happiness'. This they said, and this they meant. They did not mean to assert the obvious untruth that all were then actually enjoying that equality, nor yet that they were about to confer it immediately upon them. In fact, they had no power to confer such a boon. They meant simply to declare the right, so that the enforcement of it might follow as fast as circumstances should permit.

They meant to set up a standard maxim for free society, which should be familiar to all and revered by all – constantly looked to, constantly laboured for, and, even though never perfectly attained, constantly approximated, and thereby constantly spreading and deepening its influence, and augmenting the happiness and value of life to all people of all colours everywhere. The assertion that 'all men are created equal', was of no practical use in effecting our separation from Great Britain; and it was placed in the Declaration, not for that, but for future use. Its authors meant it to be as, thank God, it is now proving itself, a stumbling-block to all those who in after times might seek to turn a free people back into the hateful paths of despotism. They knew the proneness of prosperity to breed tyrants, and they meant, when such should reappear in this fair land and commence their vocation, that they should find left for them at least one hard nut to crack.

I have now briefly expressed my view of the meaning and object of that part of the Declaration of Independence which declares that all men are created equal. Now let us hear Judge Douglas's view of the same subject, as I find it in the printed report of his late speech. Here it is:

No man can vindicate the character, motives and conduct of the signers of the Declaration of Independence except upon the hypothesis that they referred to the white race alone, and not to the African, when they declared all men to have been created equal; that they were speaking of British subjects on this continent being equal to British subjects born and residing in Great Britain; that they were entitled to the same inalienable rights, and among them were enumerated life, liberty, and the pursuit of happiness. The Declaration was adopted for the purpose of justifying the colonists in the eyes of the civilized world in withdrawing their allegiance from the British crown, and dissolving their connection with the mother-country.

My good friends, read that carefully over some leisure hour, and ponder well upon it; see what a mere wreck and mangled ruin Judge Douglas makes of our once glorious Declaration. He says 'they were speaking of British subjects on this continent being equal to British subjects born and residing in Great Britain!' Why, according to this, not only negroes but white people outside of Great Britain and America were not spoken of in that instrument. The English, Irish, and Scotch, along with white Americans, were included, to be sure; but the French, Germans, and other white people of the world are all gone to pot along with the Judge's inferior races!

I had thought that the Declaration promised something better than the condition of British subjects; but no, it only meant that we should be equal to them in their own oppressed and unequal condition. According to that, it gave no promise that, having kicked off the king and lords of Great Britain, we should not at once be saddled with a king and lords of our own.

I had thought the Declaration contemplated the progressive improvement in the condition of all men, everywhere; but no, it merely 'was adopted for the purpose of justifying the colonists in the eyes of the civilized world in withdrawing their allegiance from the British crown, and dissolving their connection with the mother-country.' Why, that object having been effected some eighty years ago, the Declaration is of no practical use now – mere rubbish – old wadding, left to rot on the battlefield after the victory is won.

I understand you are preparing to celebrate the 'Fourth', to-morrow week. What for? The doings of that day had no reference to the present; and quite half of you are not even descendants of those who were referred to at that day. But I suppose you will celebrate, and will even go so far as to read the Declaration. Suppose, after you read it once in the old-fashioned way, you read it once more with Judge Douglas's version. It will then run thus: 'We hold these truths to be self-evident, that all British subjects who were on this continent eighty-one years ago, were created equal to all British subjects born and then residing in Great Britain!'

. . . The very Dred Scott case affords a strong test as to which party most favours amalgamation, the Republicans or the dear Union-saving Democracy. Dred Scott, his wife and two daughters, were all involved in the suit. We desired the court to have held that they were citizens, so far at least as to entitle them to a hearing as to whether they were free or not; and then also, that they were in fact and in law really free. Could we have had our way, the chances of these black girls ever mixing their blood with that of white people would have been diminished at least to the extent that it could not have been without their consent. But Judge Douglas is delighted to have them decided to be slaves, and not human enough to have a hearing, even if they were free, and thus left subject to the forced concubinage of their masters, and liable to become the mothers of mulattoes in spite of themselves – the very state of the case that produces nine-tenths of all the mulattoes, all the mixing of the blood of the nation.

'A house divided against itself cannot stand.'
On Lincoln's Nomination to the United States Senate.
Springfield, Illinois. June 17, 1858

If we could first know where we are, and whither we are tending, we could better judge what to do, and how to do it. We are now far into the fifth year since a policy was initiated with the avowed object and confident promise of putting an end to slavery agitation. Under the operation of that policy, that agitation has not only not ceased, but has constantly augmented. In my opinion it will not cease until a crisis shall have been reached and passed. 'A house divided against itself cannot stand.' I believe this government cannot endure permanently, half slave and half free. I do not expect the Union to be dissolved – I do not expect the house to fall; but I do expect it will cease to be divided. It will become all one thing, or all the other. Either the opponents of slavery will arrest the further spread of it, and place it where the public mind shall rest in the belief that it is in the course of ultimate extinction; or its advocates will push it forward till it shall become alike lawful in all the States, old as well as new, North as well as South.

Have we no tendency to the latter condition? Let anyone who doubts, carefully contemplate that now almost complete legal combination – piece of machinery, so to speak – compounded of the Nebraska doctrine and the Dred Scott decision. Let him consider not only what work the machinery is adapted to do, and how well adapted; but also let him study the history of its construction, and trace, if he can, or rather fail, if he can, to trace the evidences of design and concert of action among its chief architects from the beginning.

The new year of 1854 found slavery excluded from more than half the States by State constitutions, and from most of the national territory by congressional prohibition. Four days later commenced the struggle which ended in repealing that congressional prohibition. This opened all the national territory to slavery, and was the first point gained.

But so far, Congress only had acted; and an indorsement by the people, real or apparent, was indispensable to save the point already gained and give chance for more.

This necessity had not been overlooked, but had been provided for, as well as might be, in the notable argument of *Squatter Sovereignty*, otherwise called *sacred right of self-government*, which latter phrase, though expressive of the only rightful basis of any government, was so perverted in this attempted use of it, as to amount to just this: That if any one man choose to enslave another, no third man shall be allowed to object. That argument was incorporated into the Nebraska bill itself, in the language which follows: 'It being the true intent and meaning of this act, not to legislate slavery into any Territory or State, nor to exclude it therefrom; but to leave the people thereof perfectly free to form and regulate their domestic institutions in their own way, subject only to the Constitution of the United States.' Then opened the roar of loose declamation in favour of *Squatter Sovereignty* and *sacred right of self-government*. 'But,' said opposition members, 'let us amend the bill so as to expressly declare that the people of the Territory may exclude slavery.' 'Not we,' said the friends of the measure, and down they voted the amendment.

While the Nebraska bill was passing through Congress, a *law case*, involving the question of a negro's freedom, by reason of his owner having voluntarily taken him first into a free State and then into a Territory covered by the congressional prohibition, and held him as a slave for a long time in each, was passing through the

United States Circuit Court for the District of Missouri; and both Nebraska bill and law-suit were brought to a decision, in the same month of May, 1854. The negro's name was 'Dred Scott', which name now designates the decision finally rendered in the case. Before the then next presidential election, the law case came to, and was argued, in the Supreme Court of the United States; but the decision of it was deferred until after the election. Still, before the election, Senator Trumbull, on the floor of the Senate, requested the leading advocate of the Nebraska bill to state *his opinion* whether the people of a Territory can constitutionally exclude slavery from their limits, and the latter answers: 'That is a question for the Supreme Court.'

The election came. Mr Buchanan was elected, and the indorsement, such as it was, secured. That was the second point gained. The indorsement, however, fell short of a clear popular majority by nearly four hundred thousand votes, and so, perhaps, was not overwhelmingly reliable and satisfactory. The outgoing President, in his last annual message, as impressively as possible echoed back upon the people the weight and authority of the indorsement. The Supreme Court met again; did not announce their decision, but ordered a reargument. The presidential inauguration came, and still no decision of the Court; but the incoming President in his inaugural address fervently exhorted the people to abide by the forthcoming decision, whatever it might be. Then, in a few days, came the decision.

The reputed author of the Nebraska bill finds an early occasion to make a speech at this capitol, indorsing the Dred Scott decision, and vehemently denouncing all opposition to it. The new President, too, seizes the early occasion of the Silliman letter to indorse and strongly construe that decision, and to express his astonishment that any different view had ever been entertained!

At length a squabble springs up between the President and the author of the Nebraska bill, on the mere question of *fact* whether the Lecompton constitution was, or was not, in any just sense, made by the people of Kansas; and in that quarrel, the latter declares that all he wants is a fair vote for the people, and that he cares not whether slavery be voted *down* or *voted up*. I do not understand his declaration that he cares not whether slavery be voted down or voted up, to be intended by him other than as an apt definition of the policy he would impress upon the public mind – the principle for which he declares he has suffered so much, and is ready to suffer to the end. And well may he cling to that principle. If he has any parental feeling, well may he cling to it. That principle is the only shred left of his original Nebraska doctrine. Under the Dred Scott decision, 'squatter sovereignty' squatted out of existence, tumbled down like temporary scaffolding; like the mould at the foundry, it served through one blast, and fell back into loose sand – helped to carry an election, and then was kicked to the winds. His late joint struggle with the Republicans against the Lecompton constitution, involves nothing of the original Nebraska doctrine. That struggle was made on a point – the right of the people to make their own constitution – upon which he and the Republicans have never differed.

The several points of the Dred Scott decision in connection with Senator Douglas's 'care not' policy, constitute the piece of machinery in its present state of advancement. This was the third point gained. The working points of that machinery are:

First. That no negro slave, imported as such from Africa, and no descendant of such slave, can ever be a citizen of any State, in the sense of that term as used in the Constitution of the United States. This point is made in order to deprive the negro, in every possible event, of the benefit of that provision of the United States Constitution which declares that 'citizens of each State shall be entitled to all privileges and immunities of citizens in the several States.'

Secondly. That 'subject to the Constitution of the United States', neither Congress nor a territorial legislature can exclude slavery from any United States Territory. This point is made in order that individual men may fill up the Territories with slaves, without danger of losing them as property, and thus enhance the chances of permanency to the institution through all the future.

Thirdly. That whether the holding a negro in actual slavery in a free State makes him free as against the holder, the United States Courts will not decide, but will leave to be decided by the courts of any slave State the negro may be forced into by the master. This point is made, not to be pressed immediately; but if acquiesced in for a while, and apparently indorsed by the people at an election, then to sustain the logical conclusion that what Dred Scott's master might lawfully do with Dred Scott in the free State of

Illinois, every other master may lawfully do, with any other one, or one thousand slaves in Illinois, or in any other free State.

Auxiliary to all this, and working hand-in-hand with it, the Nebraska doctrine, or what is left of it, is to educate and mould public opinion not to care whether slavery is voted down or voted up. This shows exactly where we now are, and partially, also, whither we are tending.

It will throw additional light on the latter, to go back, and run the mind over the string of historical facts already stated. Several things will now appear less dark and mysterious than they did when they were transpiring. The people were to be left 'perfectly free', 'subject only to the Constitution'. What the Constitution had to do with it, outsiders could not then see. Plainly enough now: it was an exactly fitted niche for the Dred Scott decision to afterwards come in, and declare the perfect freedom of the people to be just no freedom at all. Why was the amendment expressly declaring the right of the people voted down? Plainly enough now: the adoption of it would have spoiled the niche for the Dred Scott decision. Why was the Court decision held up? Why even a Senator's individual opinion withheld till after the presidential election? Plainly enough now: the speaking out then would have damaged the perfectly free argument upon which the election was to be carried. Why the outgoing President's felicitation on the indorsement? Why the delay of a reargument? Why the incoming President's advance exhortation in favour of the decision? These things look like the cautious patting and petting of a spirited horse, preparatory to mounting him, when it is dreaded that he may give the rider a fall. And why the hasty after-indorsement of the decision by the President and others?

We cannot absolutely know that all these adaptations are the result of preconcert. But when we see a lot of framed timbers, different portions of which we know have been gotten out at different times and places, and by different workmen – Stephen, Franklin, Roger, and James, for instance (Douglas, Pierce, Taney, Buchanan) – and when we see those timbers joined together, and see they exactly make the frame of a house or a mill, all the tenons and mortices exactly fitting, and all the lengths and proportions of the different pieces exactly adapted to their respective places, and not a piece too many or too few, not omitting even scaffolding –

or if a single piece be lacking, we see the place in the frame exactly fitted and prepared yet to bring such piece in – in such a case, we find it impossible not to believe that Stephen and Franklin and Roger and James all understood one another from the beginning, and all worked upon a common plan or draft, drawn up before the first blow was struck.

It should not be overlooked that by the Nebraska bill the people of a State as well as Territory were to be left 'perfectly free', 'subject only to the Constitution'. Why mention a State? They were legislating for Territories, and not for or about States. Certainly the people of a State are and ought to be subject to the Constitution of the United States; but why is mention of this lugged into this merely territorial law? Why are the people of a Territory and the people of a State therein lumped together, and their relation to the Constitution therein treated as being precisely the same? While the opinion of the Court by Chief Justice Taney, in the Dred Scott case, and the separate opinions of all the concurring judges, expressly declare that the Constitution of the United States neither permits Congress nor a territorial legislature to exclude slavery from any United States Territory, they all omit to declare whether or not the same Constitution permits a State or the people of a State to exclude it. *Possibly* this is a mere omission; but who can be quite sure if McLean or Curtis had sought to get into the opinion a declaration of unlimited power in the people of a State to exclude slavery from their limits – just as Chase and Mace sought to get such declaration in behalf of the people of a Territory, into the Nebraska Bill – I ask, who can be quite sure that it would not have been voted down in the one case as it had been in the other? The nearest approach to the point of declaring the power of a State over slavery is made by Judge Nelson. He approaches it more than once, using the precise idea, and almost the language too, of the Nebraska act. On one occasion his exact language is 'except in cases where the power is restrained by the Constitution of the United States, the law of the State is supreme over the subject of slavery within its jurisdiction.' In what cases the power of the State is so restrained by the United States Constitution is left an open question, precisely as the same question, as to the restraint on the power of the Territories, was left open in the Nebraska act. Put this and that together, and we have another nice little niche, which we may, ere long, see filled with another Supreme Court decision, declaring that the Constitution of the United States does not permit *a State* to exclude slavery from its limits. And this may especially be expected if the doctrine of 'care not whether slavery be voted down or voted up' shall gain upon the public mind sufficiently to give promise that such a decision can be maintained when made.

Such a decision is all that slavery now lacks of being alike lawful in all the States. Welcome or unwelcome, such decision is probably coming, and will soon be upon us, unless the power of the present political dynasty shall be met and overthrown. We shall lie down, pleasantly dreaming that the people of Missouri are on the verge of making their State free, and we shall awake to the reality instead, that the Supreme Court has made Illinois a slave State. To meet and overthrow the power of that dynasty is the work now before all those who would prevent that consummation. That is what we have to do. How can we best do it?

There are those who denounce us openly to their own friends, and yet whisper to us softly that Senator Douglas is the aptest instrument there is with which to effect that object. They wish us to *infer* all from the fact that he now has a little quarrel with the present head of that dynasty, and that he has regularly voted with us on a single point, upon which he and we have never differed. They remind us that he is a great man and that the largest of us are very small ones. Let this be granted. But 'a living dog is better than a dead lion.' Judge Douglas, if not a dead lion, for this work is at least a caged and toothless one. How can he oppose the advances of slavery? He don't care anything about it. His avowed mission is impressing the 'public heart' to *care nothing about it.* A leading Douglas Democratic newspaper thinks Douglas's superior talent will be needed to resist the revival of the African slave-trade. Does Douglas believe an effort to revive that trade is approaching? He has not said so. Does he really think so? But if it is, how can he resist it? For years he has laboured to prove it a sacred right of white men to take negro slaves into the new territories. Can he possibly show that it is a less sacred right to buy them where they can be bought cheapest? And unquestionably they can be bought cheaper in Africa than in Virginia. He has done all in his power to reduce the whole question of slavery to one of a mere right of property: and, as such, how can he oppose the foreign slave-trade? – how can he refuse that trade in that property shall be 'perfectly free', unless he does it as a protection to home production? And as the home producers will probably not ask the protection, he will be wholly without a ground of opposition.

Senator Douglas holds, we know, that a man may rightfully be wiser today than he was yesterday – that he may rightfully change when he finds himself wrong. But can we, for that reason, run ahead, and infer that he will make any particular change, of which he himself has given no intimation? Can we safely base our action upon any such vague inference?

Now, as ever, I wish not to misrepresent Judge Douglas's position, question his motives, or do aught that can be personally offensive to him. Whenever, if ever, he and we can come together on principle, so that our cause may have assistance from his great ability, I hope to have interposed no adventitious obstacle. But, clearly, he is not now with us – he does not pretend to be – he does not promise ever to be.

Our cause, then, must be intrusted to, and conducted by, its own undoubted friends – those whose hands are free, whose hearts are in the work, who do care for the result. Two years ago the Republicans of the nation mustered over thirteen hundred thousand strong. We did this under the single impulse of resistance to a common danger, with every external circumstance against us. Of strange, discordant, and even hostile elements, we gathered from the four winds, and formed and fought the battle through, under the constant hot fire of a disciplined, proud, and pampered enemy. Did we brave all then to falter now? – now, when that same enemy is wavering, dissevered, and belligerent? The result is not doubtful. We shall not fail. If we stand firm, we shall not fail. Wise counsels may accelerate or mistakes delay it; but sooner or later the victory is sure to come.

Lincoln's Reply to Judge Douglas at Chicago on Popular Sovereignty, the Nebraska Bill, etc. July 10, 1858

. . . Popular sovereignty! everlasting popular sovereignty! Let us for a moment inquire into this vast matter of popular sovereignty. What is popular sovereignty? We recollect that at an early period in the history of this struggle, there was another name for the same thing – *squatter sovereignty*. It was not exactly popular sovereignty, but squatter sovereignty. What do these terms mean? What do those terms mean when used now? And vast credit is taken by our friend, the Judge, in regard to his support of it, when he declares the last years of his life have been, and all the future years of his life shall be, devoted to this matter of popular sovereignty. What is it? Why, it is the sovereignty of the people! What was squatter sovereignty? I suppose, if it had any signification at all, it was the right of the people to govern themselves, to be sovereign in their own affairs, while they were squatted down in a country not their own – while they had squatted on a territory that did not belong to them, in the sense that a State belongs to the people who inhabit it – when it belonged to the nation; such right to govern them-selves was called 'squatter sovereignty'.

Now, I wish you to mark, What has become of that squatter sovereignty? What has become of it? Can you get anybody to tell you now that the people of a Territory have any authority to govern themselves, in regard to this mooted question of slavery, before they form a State constitution? No such thing at all, although there is a general running fire, and although there has been a hurrah made in every speech on that side, assuming that policy had given to the people of a Territory the right to govern themselves upon this question; yet the point is dodged. Today it has been decided – no more than a year ago it was decided by the Supreme Court of the United States, and is insisted upon today – that the people of a Territory have no right to exclude slavery from a Territory; that if any one man chooses to take slaves into a Territory, all the rest of the people have no right to keep them out. This being so, and this decision being made, one of the points that the Judge approved, and one in the approval of which he says he means to keep me down – *put* me down I should not say, for I have never been up! He says he is in favour of it, and sticks to it, and expects to win his battle on that decision, which says that there is no such thing as squatter sovereignty, but that any one man may take slaves into a Territory, and all the other men in the Territory may be opposed to it, and yet by reason of the Constitution they cannot prohibit it. When that is so, how much is left of this vast matter of squatter sovereignty, I should like to know?

When we get back, we get to the point of the right of the people to make a constitution. Kansas was settled, for example, in 1854. It was a Territory yet, without having formed a constitution; in a very regular way, for three years. All this time negro slavery could be taken in by any few individuals, and by that decision of the Supreme Court, which the Judge approves, all the rest of the people cannot keep it out; but when they come to make a constitution they may say they will not have slavery. But it is there; they are obliged to tolerate it in some way, and all experience shows it will be so – for they will not take the negro slaves and absolutely deprive the owners of them. All experience shows this to be so. All that space of time that runs from the beginning of the settlement of the Territory until there is a sufficiency of people to make a State constitution – all that portion of time popular sovereignty is given up. The seal is absolutely put down upon it by the court decision, and Judge Douglas puts his own upon the top of that; yet he is appealing to the people to give him vast credit for his devotion to popular sovereignty.

Again, when we get to the question of the right of the people to form a State constitution as they please, to form it with slavery or without slavery – if that is anything new I confess I don't know it. Has there ever been a time when anybody said that any other than the people of a Territory itself should form a constitution? What is now in it that Judge Douglas should have fought several years of his life, and pledge himself to fight all the remaining years of his life for? Can Judge Douglas find anybody on earth that said that anybody else should form a constitution for a people? . . . It is enough for my purpose to ask, whenever a Republican said anything against it? They never said anything against it, but they have constantly spoken for it; and whosoever will undertake to examine the platform and the speeches of responsible men of the party, and of irresponsible men, too, if you please, will be unable to find one word from anybody in the Republican ranks opposed to that popular sovereignty which Judge Douglas thinks he has invented. I suppose that Judge Douglas will claim in a little while that he is the inventor of the idea that the people should govern themselves; that nobody ever thought of such a thing until he brought it forward. We do not remember that in that old Declaration of Independence it is said that 'We hold these truths to be self-evident, that all men are created equal; that they are endowed by their Creator with certain inalienable rights; that among these are life, liberty, and the pursuit of happiness; that to secure these rights, governments are instituted among men, deriving their just powers from the consent of the governed.' There is the origin of popular sovereignty. Who, then, shall come in at this day and claim that he invented it? The Lecompton constitution connects itself with this question, for it is in this matter of the Lecompton constitution that our friend Judge Douglas claims such vast credit. I agree that in opposing the Lecompton constitution, so far as I can perceive, he was right. I do not deny that at all; and, gentlemen, you will readily see why I could not deny it, even if I wanted to. But I do not wish to, for all the Republicans in the nation opposed it, and they would have opposed it just as much without Judge Douglas's aid as with it. They had all taken ground against it long before he did. Why, the reason that he urges against that constitution I urged against him a year before. I have the printed speech in my hand. The argument that he makes why that constitution should not be adopted, that the people were not fairly represented nor allowed to vote, I pointed out in a speech a year ago, which I hold in my hand now, that no fair chance was to be given to the people.

. . . A little more now as to this matter of popular sovereignty and the Lecompton constitution. The Lecompton constitution, as the Judge tells us, was defeated. The defeat of it was a good thing, or it was not. He thinks the defeat of it was a good thing, and so do I; and we agree in that. Who defeated it? [A voice: 'Judge Douglas.'] Yes, he furnished himself; and if you suppose he controlled the other Democrats that went with him, he furnished three votes, while the Republicans furnished twenty.

That is what he did to defeat it. In the House of Representatives he and his friends furnished some twenty votes, and the Republicans furnished ninety odd. Now, who was it that did the work? [A voice: 'Douglas.'] Why, yes, Douglas did it? To be sure he did!

Let us, however, put that proposition another way. The Republicans could not have done it without Judge Douglas. Could he have done it without them? Which could have come the nearest to doing it without the other? Ground was taken against it by the Republicans long before Douglas did it. The proposition of opposition to that measure is about five to one. [A voice: 'Why don't they come out on it?'] You don't know what you are talking about, my friend; I am quite willing to answer any gentleman in the crowd who asks an intelligent question.

Now, who in all this country has ever found any of our friends of Judge Douglas's way of thinking, and who have acted upon this main question, that have ever thought of uttering a word in behalf of Judge Trumbull? I defy you to show a printed resolution passed in a Democratic meeting. I take it upon myself to defy any man to show a printed resolution, large or small, of a Democratic meeting in favour of Judge Trumbull, or any of the five to one Republicans who beat that bill. Everything must be for the Democrats! They did everything, and the five to the one that really did the thing, they snub over, and they do not seem to remember that they have an existence upon the face of the earth.

Gentlemen, I fear that I shall become tedious. I leave this branch of the subject to take hold of another. I take up that part of Judge Douglas's speech in which he respectfully attended to me.

Judge Douglas made two points upon my recent speech at Springfield. He says they are to be the issues of this campaign. The first one of these points he bases upon the language in a speech which I delivered at Springfield, which I believe I can quote correctly from memory. I said that 'we are now far into the fifth year since a policy was instituted for the avowed object and with the confident promise of putting an end to slavery agitation; under the operation of that policy, that agitation has not only not ceased, but has constantly augmented. I believe it will not cease until a crisis shall have been reached and passed. "A house divided against itself cannot stand." I believe this government cannot endure permanently half slave and half free. I do not expect the Union to be dissolved,' – I am quoting from my speech – 'I do not expect the house to fall, but I do expect it will cease to be divided. It will become all one thing or all the other. Either the opponents of slavery will arrest the further spread of it, and place it where the public mind shall rest in the belief that it is in the course of ultimate extinction, or its advocates will push it forward until it shall become alike lawful in all the States, old as well as new; North as well as South.'

That is the paragraph! In this paragraph which I have quoted in your hearing, and to which I ask the attention of all, Judge

Douglas thinks he discovers great political heresy. I want your attention particularly to what he has inferred from it. He says I am in favour of making all the States of this Union uniform in all their internal regulations; that in all their domestic concerns I am in favour of making them entirely uniform. He draws this inference from the language I have quoted to you. He says that I am in favour of making war by the North upon the South for the extinction of slavery; that I am also in favour of inviting (as he expresses it) the South to a war upon the North for the purpose of nationalizing slavery. Now, it is singular enough, if you will carefully read that passage over, that I did not say that I was in favour of anything in it. I only said what I expected would take place. I made a prediction only – it may have been a foolish one, perhaps. I did not even say that I desired that slavery should be put in course of ultimate extinction. I do say so now, however; so there need be no longer any difficulty about that. It may be written down in the great speech.

Gentlemen, Judge Douglas informed you that this speech of mine was probably carefully prepared. I admit that it was. I am not master of language; I have not a fine education; I am not capable of entering into a disquisition upon dialectics, as I believe you call it; but I do not believe the language I employed bears any such construction as Judge Douglas puts upon it. But I don't care about a quibble in regard to words. I know what I meant, and I will not leave this crowd in doubt, if I can explain it to them, what I really meant in the use of that paragraph.

I am not, in the first place, unaware that this government has endured eighty-two years, half slave and half free. I know that. I am tolerably well acquainted with the history of the country, and I know that it has endured eighty-two years, half slave and half free. I believe – and that is what I meant to allude to there – I believe it has endured, because, during all that time, until the introduction of the Nebraska bill, the public mind did rest all the time in the belief that slavery was in course of ultimate extinction. That was what gave us the rest that we had through that period of eighty-two years; at least, so I believe. I have always hated slavery, I think, as much as any Abolitionist – I have been an old-line Whig – I have always hated it, but I have always been quiet about it until this new era of the introduction of the

Nebraska bill began. I always believed that everybody was against it, and that it was in course of ultimate extinction. . . . They had reason so to believe.

The adoption of the Constitution and its attendant history led the people to believe so, and that such was the belief of the framers of the Constitution itself. Why did those old men, about the time of the adoption of the Constitution, decree that slavery should not go into the new Territory where it had not already gone? Why declare that within twenty years the African slave-trade, by which slaves are supplied, might be cut off by Congress? Why were all these acts? I might enumerate more of these acts; but enough. What were they but a clear indication that the framers of the Constitution intended and expected the ultimate extinction of that institution? And now when I say – as I said in my speech that Judge Douglas has quoted from – when I say that I think the opponents of slavery will resist the further spread of it, and place it where the public mind shall rest in the belief that it is in the course of ultimate extinction, I only mean to say that they will place it where the founders of this government originally placed it.

I have said a hundred times, and I have now no inclination to take it back, that I believe there is no right, and ought to be no inclination in the people of the free States, to enter into the slave States and interfere with the question of slavery at all. I have said that always; Judge Douglas has heard me say it. And when it is said that I am in favour of interfering with slavery where it exists, I know it is unwarranted by anything I have ever intended, and, as I believe, by anything I have ever said. If by any means I have ever used language which could fairly be so construed (as, however, I believe I never have), I now correct it.

So much, then, for the inference that Judge Douglas draws, that I am in favour of setting the sections at war with one another. I know that I never meant any such thing, and I believe that no fair mind can infer any such thing from anything I have said.

Now, in relation to his inference that I am in favour of a general consolidation of all the local institutions of the various States. . . . I have said very many times in Judge Douglas's hearing that no man believed more than I in the principle of self-government; that it lies at the bottom of all my ideas of just government from beginning to end. I have denied that his use of that term applies properly. But for the thing itself I deny that any man has ever gone ahead of me in his devotion to the principle, whatever he may have done in efficiency in advocating it. I think that I have said it in your hearing, that I believe each individual is naturally entitled to do as he pleases with himself and the fruit of his labour, so far as it in no wise interferes with any other man's rights; that each community, as a State, has a right to do exactly as it pleases with all the concerns within that State that interfere with the right of no other State; and that the general government upon principle has no right to interfere with anything other than that general class of things that does concern the whole. I have said that at all times; I have said as illustrations that I do not believe in the right of Illinois to interfere with the cranberry laws of Indiana, the oyster laws of Virginia, or the liquor laws of Maine.

How is it, then, that Judge Douglas infers, because I hope to see slavery put where the public mind shall rest in the belief that it is in the course of ultimate extinction, that I am in favour of Illinois going over and interfering with the cranberry laws of Indiana? What can authorize him to draw any such inference? I suppose there might be one thing that at least enabled him to draw such an inference, that would not be true with me or many others; that is, because he looks upon all this matter of slavery as an exceedingly little thing – this matter of keeping one-sixth of the population of the whole nation in a state of oppression and tyranny unequalled in the world. He looks upon it as being an exceedingly little thing, only equal to the question of the cranberry laws of Indiana; as something having no moral question in it; as something on a par with the question of whether a man shall pasture his land with cattle or plant it with tobacco; so little and so small a thing that he concludes, if I could desire that anything should be done to bring about the ultimate extinction of that little thing, I must be in favour of bringing about an amalgamation of all the other little things in the Union. Now, it so happens – and there, I presume, is the foundation of this mistake – that the Judge thinks thus; and it so happens that there is a vast portion of the American people that do not look upon that matter as being this very little thing. They look upon it as a vast moral evil; they can prove it as such by the writings of those who gave us the blessings of liberty which we enjoy, and that they so looked upon it, and not as an evil merely confining itself to the States where it is situated; and while we agree that by the Constitution we assented to, in the States where it exists we have no right to interfere with it, because it is in the Constitution, we are both by duty and inclination to stick by that Constitution in all its letter and spirit from beginning to end.

So much, then, as to my disposition, my wish, to have all the State legislatures blotted out and to have one consolidated government and a uniformity of domestic regulations in all the States; by which I suppose it is meant, if we raise corn here we must make sugar-cane grow here too, and we must make those things which grow North grow in the South. All this I suppose he understands I am in favour of doing. Now, so much for all this nonsense – for I must call it so. The Judge can have no issue with me on a question of establishing uniformity in the domestic regulations of the States.

A little now on the other point – the Dred Scott decision. Another of the issues, he says, that is to be made with me is upon his devotion to the Dred Scott decision and my opposition to it.

I have expressed heretofore, and I now repeat, my opposition to the Dred Scott decision; but I should be allowed to state the nature of that opposition, and I ask your indulgence while I do so. What is fairly implied by the term Judge Douglas has used, 'resistance to the decision'? I do not resist it. If I wanted to take Dred Scott from his master I would be interfering with property, and that terrible difficulty that Judge Douglas speaks of, of interfering with property, would arise. But I am doing no such thing as that; all that I am doing is refusing to obey it as a political rule. If I were in Congress, and a vote should come up on a question whether slavery should be prohibited in a new Territory, in spite of the Dred Scott decision, I would vote that it should.

That is what I would do. Judge Douglas said last night that before the decision he might advance his opinion, and it might be contrary to the decision when it was made; but after it was made he would abide by it until it was reversed. Just so! We let this property abide by the decision, but we will try to reverse that decision. We will try to put it where Judge Douglas would not object, for he says he will obey it until it is reversed. Somebody has to reverse that decision, since it is made; and we mean to reverse it, and we mean to do it peaceably.

What are the uses of decisions of courts? They have two uses. First, they decide upon the question before the court. They decide in this case that Dred Scott is a slave. Nobody resists that. Not only that, but they say to everybody else that persons standing just as Dred Scott stands are as he is. That is, they say that when a question comes up upon another person it will be so decided again, unless the court decides another way, unless the court overrules its decision. Well, we mean to do what we can to have the court decide the other way. That is one thing we mean to try to do.

The sacredness that Judge Douglas throws around this decision is a degree of sacredness that has never been before thrown around any other decision. I have never heard of such a thing. Why, decisions apparently contrary to that decision, or that good lawyers thought were contrary to that decision, have been made by that very court before. It is the first of its kind; it is an astonisher in legal history; it is a new wonder of the world; it is based upon falsehood in the main as to the facts – allegations of facts upon which it stands are not facts at all in many instances – and no decision made on any question – the first instance of a decision made under so many unfavourable circumstances – thus placed, has ever been held by the profession as law, and it has always needed confirmation before the lawyers regarded it as settled law; but Judge Douglas will have it that all hands must take this extraordinary decision made under these extraordinary circumstances and give their vote in Congress in accordance with it, yield to it, and obey it in every possible sense. Circumstances alter cases. Do not gentlemen here remember the case of that same Supreme Court some twenty-five or thirty years ago, deciding that a national bank was con-stitutional? I ask if somebody does not remember that a national bank was declared to be constitutional? Such is the truth, whether it be remembered or not. The bank charter ran out, and a re-charter was granted by Congress. That re-charter was laid before General Jackson. It was urged upon him, when he denied the constitutionality of the bank, that the Supreme Court had decided that it was constitutional; and General Jackson then said that the Supreme Court had no right to lay down a rule to govern a coordinate branch of the government, the members of which had sworn to support the Constitution – that each member had sworn to support the Constitution as he understood it. I will venture here to say that I have heard Judge Douglas say that he approved of General Jackson for that act. What has now become of all his tirade against 'resistance to the Supreme Court'?

My fellow-citizens, getting back a little – for I pass from these points – when Judge Douglas makes his threat of annihilation upon the 'alliance', he is cautious to say that that warfare of his is to fall upon the leaders of the Republican party. Almost every word he utters and every distinction he makes has its significance. He means for the Republicans who do not count themselves as leaders to be his friends; he makes no fuss over them, it is the leaders that he is making war upon. He wants it understood that the mass of the Republican party are really his friends. It is only the leaders that are doing something, that are intolerant, and require extermination at his hands. As this is clearly and unquestionably the light in which he presents that matter, I want to ask your attention, addressing myself to Republicans here, that I may ask you some questions as to where you, as the Republican party, would be placed if you sustained Judge Douglas in his present position by a re-election? I do not claim, gentlemen, to be unselfish; I do not pretend that I would not like to go to the United States Senate – I make no such hypocritical pretence; but I do say to you, that in this mighty issue it is nothing to you, nothing to the mass of the people of the nation, whether or not Judge Douglas or myself shall ever be heard of after this night. It may be a trifle to either of us; but in connection with this mighty question, upon which hang the destinies of the nation, perhaps, it is absolutely nothing. But where will you be placed if you reindorse Judge Douglas? Don't you know how apt he is, how exceedingly anxious he is, at all times to seize upon anything and everything to persuade you that something he has done you did yourselves? Why, he tried to persuade you last night that our Illinois Legislature instructed him to introduce the Nebraska bill. There was nobody in that Legislature ever thought of it; but still he fights furiously for the proposition; and that he did it because there was a standing instruction to our senators to be always introducing Nebraska bills. He tells you he is for the Cincinnati platform; he tells you he is for the Dred Scott decision; he tells you – not in his speech last night, but substantially in a former speech – that he cares not if slavery is voted up or down; he tells you the struggle on Lecompton is past – it may come up again or not, and if it does, he stands where he stood when, in spite of him and his opposition, you built up the Republican party. If you indorse him, you tell him you do not care whether slavery be voted up or down, and he will close, or try to close, your mouths with his declaration, repeated by the day, the week, the month, and the year. I think, in the position in which Judge Douglas stood in opposing the Lecompton constitution, he was right; he does not know that it will return, but if it does we may know where to find him; and if it does not, we may know where to look for him, and that is on the Cincinnati platform. Now, I could ask the Republican party, after all the hard names Judge Douglas has called them by, . . . all his declarations of Black Republicanism – (by the way, we are improving, the black has got rubbed off), but with all that, if he be indorsed by Republican votes, where do you stand? Plainly, you stand ready saddled, bridled, and harnessed, and waiting to be driven over to the slavery-extension camp of the nation – just ready to be driven over, tied together in a lot – to be driven over, every man with a rope around his neck, that halter being held by Judge Douglas. That is the question. If Republican men have been in earnest in what they have done, I think they had better not do it; but I think the Republican party is made up of those who, as far as they can peaceably, will oppose the extension of slavery, and who will hope for its ultimate extinction. If they believe it is wrong in grasping up the new lands of the continent, and keeping them from the settlement of free white labourers, who want the land to bring up their families upon; if they are in earnest – although they may make a mistake, they will grow restless, and the time will come when they will come back again and reorganize, if not by the same name, at least upon the same principles as their party now has. It is better, then, to save the work while it is begun. You have done the labour; maintain it, keep it. If men choose to serve you, go with them; but as you have made up your organization upon principle, stand by it; for, as surely as God reigns over you, and has inspired your minds and given you a sense of propriety and continues to give you hope, so surely will you still cling to these ideas, and you will at last come back again after your wanderings, merely to do your work over again.

We were often – more than once, at least – in the course of Judge Douglas's speech last night, reminded that this government was made for white men – that he believed it was made for white men. Well, that is putting it into a shape in which no one wants to deny it; but the Judge then goes into his passion for drawing inferences that are not warranted. I protest, now and for ever, against that counterfeit logic which presumes that, because I do not want a negro woman for a slave, I do necessarily want her for a wife. My understanding is, that I need not have her for either; but, as God made us separate, we can leave one another alone, and do one another much good thereby. There are white men enough to marry all the white women, and enough black men to marry all the black women; and in God's name let them be so married. The Judge regales us with the terrible enormities that take place by the mixture of races; that the inferior race bears the superior down. Why, Judge, if we do not let them get together in the Territories, they won't mix there. I should say at least that that was a self-evident truth.

Now, it happens that we meet together once every year, some-where about the 4th of July, for some reason or other. These 4th of July gatherings, I suppose, have their uses. If you will indulge me, I will state what I suppose to be some of them.

We are now a mighty nation: we are thirty, or about thirty, millions of people, and we own and inhabit about one-fifteenth part of the dry land of the whole earth. We run our memory back over the pages of history for about eighty-two years, and we discover that we were then a very small people in point of numbers, vastly inferior to what we are now, with a vastly less extent of country, with vastly less of everything we deem desirable among men. We look upon the change as exceedingly advant-ageous to us and to our posterity, and we fix upon something that happened away back, as in some way or other being connected with this rise of prosperity. We find a race of men living in that day whom we claim as our fathers and grandfathers; they were iron men; they fought for the principle that they were contending for, and we understand that by what they then did, it has followed that the degree of prosperity which we now enjoy has come to us. We hold this annual celebration to remind ourselves of all the good done in this process of time – of how it was done, and who did it, and how we are historically connected with it; and we go from these meetings in better humour with ourselves – we feel more attached the one to the other, and more firmly bound to the country we inhabit. In every way we are better men, in the age and race and country in which we live, for these celebrations. But after we have done all this, we have not yet reached the whole. There is something else connected with it. We have, besides these men – descended by blood from our ancestors – among us, perhaps half our people who are not descendants at all of these men; they are men who have come from Europe – German, Irish, French, and Scandinavian – men that have come from Europe themselves, or whose ancestors have come hither and settled here, finding themselves our equal in all things. If they look back through this history, to trace their connection with those days by blood, they find they have none: they cannot carry themselves back into that glorious epoch and make themselves feel that they are part of us; but when they look through that old Declaration of Independence, they find that those old men say that 'we hold these truths to be self-evident, that all men are created equal', and then they feel that that moral sentiment taught in that day evidences their relation to those men, that it is the father of all moral principle in them, and that they have a right to claim it as though they were blood of the blood, and flesh of the flesh, of the men who wrote that Declaration; and so they are. That is the electric cord in that Declaration that links the hearts of patriotic and liberty-loving men together; that will link those patriotic hearts as long as the love of freedom exists in the minds of men throughout the world.

Now, sirs, for the purpose of squaring things with this idea of 'don't care if slavery is voted up or voted down'; for sustaining the Dred Scott decision; for holding that the Declaration of Independence did not mean anything at all – we have Judge Douglas giving his exposition of what the Declaration of Independence means, and we have him saying that the people of America are equal to the people of England. According to his construction, you Germans are not connected with it. Now, I ask you in all soberness, if all these things, if indulged in, if ratified, if confirmed and indorsed, if taught to our children and repeated to them, do not tend to rub out the sentiment of liberty in the country, and to transform this

government into a government of some other form? Those arguments that are made, that the inferior race are to be treated with as
much allowance as they are capable of enjoying; that as much is to
be done for them as their condition will allow – what are these
arguments? They are the arguments that kings have made for
enslaving the people in all ages of the world. You will find that all
the arguments in favour of kingcraft were of this class; they always
bestrode the necks of the people – not that they wanted to do it,
but because the people were better off for being ridden. That is
their argument; and this argument of the Judge is the same old
serpent, that says, 'You work, and I eat; you toil, and I will enjoy
the fruits of it.' Turn in whatever way you will – whether it come
from the mouth of a king, an excuse for enslaving the people of his
country, or from the mouth of men of one race as a reason for
enslaving the men of another race – it is all the same old serpent;
and I hold, if that course of argumentation that is made for the
purpose of convincing the public mind that we should not care
about this, should be granted, it does not stop with the negro. I
should like to know – taking this old Declaration of Independence, which declares that all men are equal, upon principle, and
making exceptions to it – where will it stop? If one man says it
does not mean a negro, why not another say it does not mean
some other man? If that Declaration is not the truth, let us get the
statute-book in which we find it, and tear it out! Who is so bold as
to do it? If it is not true, let us tear it out. [Cries of 'No! No!'] Let
us stick to it, then; let us stand firmly by it, then.

It may be argued that there are certain conditions that make
necessities and impose them upon us, and to the extent that a
necessity is imposed upon a man, he must submit to it. I think that
was the condition in which we found ourselves when we established this government. We had slaves among us; we could not get
our Constitution unless we permitted them to remain in slavery;
we could not secure the good we did secure, if we grasped for
more; but, having by necessity submitted to that much, it does not
destroy the principle that is the charter of our liberties. Let that
charter stand as our standard.

My friend has said to me that I am a poor hand to quote
Scripture. I will try it again, however. It is said in one of the
admonitions of our Lord, 'Be ye [therefore] perfect even as your

Father which is in heaven is perfect.' The Saviour, I suppose, did not expect that any human creature could be perfect as the Father in heaven; but He said: 'As your Father in heaven is perfect, be ye also perfect.' He set that up as a standard, and he who did most toward reaching that standard attained the highest degree of moral perfection. So I say in relation to the principle that all men are created equal, let it be as nearly reached as we can. If we cannot give freedom to every creature, let us do nothing that will impose slavery upon any other creature. Let us, then, turn this government back into the channel in which the framers of the Constitution originally placed it. Let us stand firmly by each other. If we do not do so, we are tending in the contrary direction, that our friend Judge Douglas proposes – not intentionally – working in the traces that tend to make this one universal slave nation. He is one that runs in that direction, and as such I resist him.

My friends, I have detained you about as long as I desired to do, and I have only to say, let us discard all this quibbling about this man and the other man, this race and that race and the other race being inferior, and therefore they must be placed in an inferior position. Let us discard all these things, and unite as one people throughout this land, until we shall once more stand up declaring that all men are created equal.

My friends, I could not, without launching off upon some new topic, which would detain you too long, continue tonight. I thank you for this most extensive audience that you have furnished me tonight. I leave you, hoping that the lamp of liberty will burn in your bosoms until there shall no longer be a doubt that all men are created free and equal.

From a Speech at Springfield, Illinois. July 17, 1858

. . . There is still another disadvantage under which we labour, and to which I will ask your attention. It arises out of the relative positions of the two persons who stand before the State as candidates for the Senate. Senator Douglas is of worldwide renown. All the anxious politicians of his party, or who have been of his party for years past, have been looking upon him as certainly, at no distant day, to be the President of the United States. They have seen, in his round, jolly, fruitful face, post-offices, land-offices, marshalships, and cabinet appointments, chargéships and foreign missions, bursting and sprouting out in wonderful exuberance, ready to be laid hold of by their greedy hands. And as they have been gazing upon this attractive picture so long, they cannot, in the little distraction that has taken place in the party, bring themselves to give up the charming hope. But with greedier anxiety they rush about him, sustain him, and give him marches, triumphal entries, and receptions, beyond what, even in the days of his highest prosperity, they could have brought about in his favour. On the contrary, nobody has ever expected me to be President. In my poor, lean, lank face, nobody has ever seen that any cabbages were sprouting out. These are disadvantages, all taken together, that the Republicans labour under. We have to fight this battle upon principle, and upon principle alone. I am in a certain sense made the standard-bearer in behalf of the Republicans. I was made so merely because there had to be someone so placed − I being in no wise preferable to any other one of the twenty-five, perhaps a hundred, we have in the Republican ranks. Then I say, I wish it to be distinctly understood and borne in mind, that we have to fight this battle without many − perhaps without any − of the external aids which are brought to bear against us. So I hope those with whom I am surrounded have principle enough to nerve themselves for the task, and leave nothing undone that can fairly be done to bring about the right result. As appears by two speeches I have heard him deliver since his arrival in Illinois, he gave special attention to the speech of mine delivered on the sixteenth of June. He says that he carefully read that speech. He told us that at Chicago a week ago last night, and he repeated it at Bloomington last night. . . . He says it was evidently prepared with great care. I freely admit it was prepared with care. . . . But I was very careful not to put anything in that speech as a matter of fact, or make any inferences which did not appear to me to be true and fully warrantable. If I had made any mistake I was willing to be corrected; if I had drawn any inference in regard to Judge Douglas or anyone else, which was not warranted, I was fully prepared to modify it as soon as discovered. I planted myself upon the truth and the truth only, so far as I knew it, or could be brought to know it.

Having made that speech with the most kindly feelings toward Judge Douglas, as manifested therein, I was gratified when I found that he had carefully examined it, and had detected no error of fact, nor any inference against him, nor any misrepresentations, of which he thought fit to complain. . . . He seizes upon the doctrines he supposes to be included in that speech, and declares that upon them will turn the issues of the campaign. He then quotes, or attempts to quote, from my speech. I will not say that he wilfully misquotes, but he does fail to quote accurately. His attempt at quoting is from a passage which I believe I can quote accurately from memory. I shall make the quotation now, with some comments upon it, as I have already said, in order that the Judge shall be left entirely without excuse for misrepresenting me. I do so now, as I hope, for the last time. I do this in great caution, in order that if he repeats his misrepresentation, it shall be plain to all that he does so wilfully. If, after all, he still persists, I shall be compelled to reconstruct the course I have marked out for myself, and draw upon such humble resources as I have for a new course, better suited to the real exigencies of the case. I set out in this campaign with the intention of conducting it strictly as a gentleman, in substance at least, if not in the outside polish. The latter I shall never be, but that which constitutes the inside of a gentleman I hope I understand, and am not less inclined to practise than others. It was my purpose and expectation that this canvass would be conducted upon principle, and with fairness on both sides, and it shall not be my fault if this purpose and expectation shall be given up.

He charges, in substance, that I invite a war of sections; that I propose all local institutions of the different States shall become consolidated and uniform. What is there in the language of that speech which expresses such purpose or bears such construction? I have again and again said that I would not enter into any one of the States to disturb the institution of slavery. Judge Douglas said at Bloomington that I used language most able and ingenious for concealing what I really meant; and that while I had protested against entering into the slave States, I nevertheless did mean to go on the banks of the Ohio and throw missiles into Kentucky, to disturb them in their domestic institutions.

. . . I have said that I do not understand the Declaration to mean that all men were created equal in all respects. The negroes are not our equals in colour; but I suppose it does mean to declare that all men are equal in some respects; they are equal in their right to 'life, liberty, and the pursuit of happiness'. Certainly the negro is not our equal in colour, perhaps not in many other respects. Still, in the right to put into his mouth the bread that his own hands have earned, he is the equal of every other man, white or black. In pointing out that more has been given you, you cannot be justified in taking away the little which has been given him. All I ask for the negro is, that if you do not like him, let him alone. If God gave him but little, that little let him enjoy.

. . . One more point on this Springfield speech, which Judge Douglas says he has read so carefully. I expressed my belief in the existence of a conspiracy to perpetuate and nationalize slavery. I did not profess to know it, nor do I now. I showed the part Judge Douglas had played in the string of facts, constituting to my mind the proof of that conspiracy. I showed the parts played by others.

I charged that the people had been deceived into carrying the last presidential election, by the impression that the people of the Territories might exclude slavery if they chose, when it was known in advance by the conspirators that the court was to decide that neither Congress nor the people could so exclude slavery. These charges are more distinctly made than anything else in the speech.

Judge Douglas has carefully read and re-read that speech. He has not, so far as I know, contradicted those charges. In the two speeches which I heard he certainly did not. On his own tacit admission I renew that charge. I charge him with having been a party to that conspiracy and to that deception, for the sole purpose of nationalizing slavery.

From Lincoln's Reply to Douglas in the First Joint Debate at Ottawa, Illinois. August 21, 1858

When a man bears himself somewhat misrepresented, it provokes him – at least, I find it so with myself; but when misrepresentation becomes very gross and palpable, it is more apt to amuse him. . . . [After stating the charge of an arrangement between himself and Judge Trumbull.]

Now, all I have to say upon that subject is, that I think no man – not even Judge Douglas – can prove it, because it is not true. I have no doubt he is 'conscientious' in saying it. As to those resolutions that he took such a length of time to read, as being the platform of the Republican party in 1854, I say I never had anything to do with them, and I think Trumbull never had. Judge Douglas cannot show that either of us ever had anything to do with them. . . .

Now, about this story that Judge Douglas tells of Trumbull bargaining to sell out the old Democratic party, and Lincoln agreeing to sell out the old Whig party, I have the means of knowing about that; Judge Douglas cannot have; and I know there is no substance to it whatever. . . .

A man cannot prove a negative, but he has a right to claim that when a man makes an affirmative charge, he must offer some proof to show the truth of what he says. I certainly cannot introduce testimony to show the negative about things, but I have a right to claim that if a man says he knows a thing, then he must show how he knows it. I always have a right to claim this; and it is not satisfactory to me that he may be 'conscientious' on the subject.

. . . Anything that argues me into his idea of perfect social and political equality with the negro is but a specious and fantastic arrangement of words, by which a man can prove a horse-chestnut to be a chestnut horse. I will say here, while upon this subject, that I have no purpose, either directly or indirectly, to interfere with the institution of slavery in the States where it exists. I believe I have no lawful right to do so, and I have no inclination to do so. I have no purpose to introduce political and social equality between the white and the black races. There is a physical difference between the two, which, in my judgment, will probably for ever forbid their living together upon the footing of perfect equality; and inasmuch as it becomes a necessity that there must be a difference, I, as well as Judge Douglas, am in favour of the race to which I belong having the superior position. I have never said anything to the contrary; but I hold, that, notwithstanding all this, there is no reason in the world why the negro is not entitled to all the natural rights enumerated in the Declaration of Independence – the right to life, liberty, and the pursuit of happiness. I hold that he is as much entitled to these as the white man. I agree with Judge Douglas, he is not my equal in many respects, certainly not in colour, perhaps not in moral or intellectual endowment. But in the right to eat the bread, without the leave of anybody, which his own hand earns, he is my equal, and the equal of Judge Douglas, and the equal of any living man.

. . . As I have not used up so much of my time as I had supposed, I will dwell a little longer upon one or two of these minor topics upon which the Judge has spoken. He has read from my speech at Springfield, in which I say that 'a house divided against itself cannot stand.' Does the Judge say it can stand? I don't know whether he does or not. The Judge does not seem to be attending to me just now, but I would like to know if it is his opinion that a house divided against itself can stand? If he does, then there is a question of veracity, not between him and me, but between the Judge and an authority of a somewhat higher character.

Now, my friends, I ask your attention to this matter for the purpose of saying something seriously, I know that the Judge may readily enough agree with me that the maxim which was put forth by the Saviour is true, but he may allege that I misapply it; and the Judge has a right to urge that in my application I do misapply it, and then I have a right to show that I do not misapply it. When he undertakes to say that because I think this nation, so far as the question of slavery is concerned, will all become one thing or all the other, I am in favour of bringing about a dead uniformity in the various States, in all their institutions, he argues erroneously. The great variety of local institutions in the States, springing from differences in the soil, differences in the face of the country, and in the climate, are bonds of union. They do not make 'a house divided against itself', but they make a house united. If they produce in one section of the country what is called for by the wants of another section, and this other section can supply the wants of the first, they are not matters of discord, but bonds of union, true bonds of union. But can this question of slavery be considered as among these varieties in the institutions of the country? I leave it for you to say, whether in the history of our government, this institution of slavery has not always failed to be a bond of union, and, on the contrary, been an apple of discord and an element of division in the house. I ask you to consider whether so long as the moral constitution of men's minds shall continue to be the same, after this generation and assemblage shall sink into the grave, and another race shall arise with the same moral and intellectual development we have – whether, if that institution is standing in the same irritating position in which it now is, it will not continue an element of division?

If so, then I have a right to say that, in regard to this question, the Union is a house divided against itself; and when the Judge reminds me that I have often said to him that the institution of slavery has existed for eighty years in some States, and yet it does not exist in some others, I agree to the fact, and I account for it by looking at the position in which our fathers originally placed it – restricting it from the new Territories where it had not gone, and legislating to cut off its source by the abrogation of the slave-trade, thus putting the seal of legislation against its spread. The public mind did rest in the belief that it was in the course of ultimate extinction. But lately, I think – and in this I charge nothing on the Judge's motives – lately, I think that he and those acting with him have placed that institution on a new basis, which looks to the perpetuity and nationalization of slavery. And while it is placed on this new basis, I say, and I have said, that I believe we shall not have peace upon the question, until the opponents of slavery arrest the further spread of it, and place it where the public mind shall rest in the belief that it is in the course of ultimate extinction; or, on the other hand, that its advocates will push it forward until it shall become alike lawful in all the States, old as well as new, North as well as South. Now, I believe if we could arrest the spread, and place it where Washington and Jefferson and Madison placed it, it would be in the course of ultimate extinction, and the public mind would, as for eighty years past, believe that it was in the course of ultimate extinction. The crisis would be past, and the institution might be let alone for a hundred years – if it should live so long – in the States where it exists, yet it would be going out of existence in the way best for both the black and the white races. [A voice: 'Then do you repudiate popular sovereignty?'] Well, then, let us talk about popular sovereignty. What is popular sovereignty? Is it the right of the people to have slavery or not to have it, as they see fit, in the Territories? I will state – and I have an able man to watch me – my understanding is that popular sovereignty, as now applied to the question of slavery, does allow the people of a Territory to have slavery if they want to, but does not allow them not to have it if they do not want it. I do not mean that if this vast concourse of people were in a Territory of the United States, any one of them would be obliged to have a slave if he did not want one; but I do say that, as I understand the Dred Scott decision, if any one man wants slaves, all the rest have no way of keeping that one man from holding them.

When I made my speech at Springfield, of which the Judge complains, and from which he quotes, I really was not thinking of the things which he ascribes to me at all. I had no thought in the world that I was doing anything to bring about a war between the free and slave States. I had no thought in the world that I was doing anything to bring about a political and social equality of the black and white races. It never occurred to me that I was doing anything or favouring anything to reduce to a dead uniformity all the local institutions of the various States. But I must say, in all fairness to him, if he thinks I am doing something which leads to these bad results, it is none the better that I did not mean it. It is just as fatal to the country, if I have any influence in producing it, whether I intend it or not. But can it be true that placing this institution upon the original basis – the basis upon which our fathers placed it – can have any tendency to set the Northern and the Southern States at war with one another, or that it can have any tendency to make the people of Vermont raise sugar-cane, because they raise it in Louisiana, or that it can compel the people of Illinois to cut pine logs on the Grand Prairie, where they will not grow, because they cut pine logs in Maine, where they do grow? The Judge says this is a new principle started in regard to this question. Does the Judge claim that he is working on the plan of the founders of the government? I think he says in some of his speeches – indeed, I have one here now – that he saw evidence of a policy to allow slavery to be south of a certain line, while north of it it should be excluded, and he saw an indisposition on the part of the country to stand upon that policy, and, therefore, he set about studying the subject upon original principles, and upon original principles he got up the Nebraska bill! I am fighting it upon these 'original principles' – fighting it in the Jeffersonian, Washingtonian, Madisonian fashion. . . .

If I have brought forward anything not a fact, if he (Judge Douglas) will point it out, it will not even ruffle me to take it back. But if he will not point out anything erroneous in the evidence, is it not rather for him to show by a comparison of the evidence that I have reasoned falsely, than to call the 'kind, amiable, intelligent gentleman' a liar?

I want to ask your attention to a portion of the Nebraska bill which Judge Douglas has quoted: 'It being the true intent and meaning of this act, not to legislate slavery into any Territory or State, nor to exclude it therefrom, but to leave the people thereof perfectly free to form and regulate their domestic institutions in their own way, subject only to the Constitution of the United States.' Thereupon Judge Douglas and others began to argue in favour of 'popular sovereignty' – the right of the people to have slaves if they wanted them, and to exclude slavery if they did not want them. 'But,' said, in substance, a senator from Ohio (Mr Chase, I believe), 'we more than suspect that you do not mean to allow the people to exclude slavery if they wish to; and if you do mean it, accept an amendment which I propose, expressly authorizing the people to exclude slavery.' I believe I have the amendment here before me, which was offered, and under which the people of the Territory, through their proper representatives, might, if they saw fit, prohibit the existence of slavery therein.

And now I state it as a fact, to be taken back if there is any mistake about it, that Judge Douglas and those acting with him voted that amendment down. I now think that those who voted it down had a real reason for doing so. They know what that reason was. It looks to us, since we have seen the Dred Scott decision pronounced, holding that 'under the Constitution' the people cannot exclude slavery – I say it looks to outsiders, poor, simple, 'amiable, intelligent gentlemen', as though the niche was left as a place to put that Dred Scott decision in, a niche that would have been spoiled by adopting the amendment. And now I say again, if this was not the reason, it will avail the Judge much more to calmly and good-humouredly point out to these people what that other reason was for voting the amendment down, than swelling himself up to vociferate that he may be provoked to call somebody a liar.

Again, there is in that same quotation from the Nebraska bill this clause: 'it being the true intent and meaning of this bill not to legislate slavery into any Territory or State'. I have always been puzzled to know what business the word 'State' had in that connection. Judge Douglas knows – he put it there. He knows what he put it there for. We outsiders cannot say what he put it there for. The law they were passing was not about States, and was not making provision for States. What was it placed there for? After seeing the Dred Scott decision, which holds that the people cannot exclude slavery from a Territory, if another Dred Scott decision shall come, holding that they cannot exclude it from a State, we shall discover that when the word was originally put there, it was in view of something that was to come in due time; we shall see that it was the other half of something. I now say again, if there was any different reason for putting it there, Judge Douglas, in a good-humoured way, without calling anybody a liar, can tell what the reason was. . . .

Now, my friends, . . . I ask the attention of the people here assembled, and elsewhere, to the course that Judge Douglas is pursuing every day as bearing upon this question of making slavery national. Not going back to the records, but taking the speeches he makes, the speeches he made yesterday and the day before, and makes constantly, all over the country, I ask your attention to them. In the first place, what is necessary to make the institution national? Not war: there is no danger that the people of Kentucky will shoulder their muskets and . . . march into Illinois to force the blacks upon us. There is no danger of our going over there, and making war upon them. Then what is necessary for the nationalization of slavery? It is simply the next Dred Scott decision. It is merely for the Supreme Court to decide that no State under the Constitution can exclude it, just as they have already decided that under the Constitution neither Congress nor the territorial legislature can do it. When that is decided and acquiesced in, the whole thing is done. This being true and this being the way, as I think, that slavery is to be made national, let us consider what Judge Douglas is doing every day to that end. In the first place, let us see what influence he is exerting on public sentiment. In this and like communities, public sentiment is everything. With public sentiment nothing can fail; without it nothing can succeed. Consequently he who moulds public sentiment goes deeper than he who enacts statutes or pronounces decisions. He makes statutes and decisions possible or impossible to be executed. This must be borne in mind, as also the additional fact that Judge Douglas is a man of vast influence, so great that it is enough for many men to profess to believe anything when they once find out that Judge Douglas professes to believe it. Consider also the attitude he occupies at the head of a large party – a party which he claims has a majority of all the voters in the country.

This man sticks to a decision which forbids the people of a Territory to exclude slavery, and he does so not because he says it is right in itself – he does not give any opinion on that – but because it has been decided by the Court, and, being decided by the Court, he is, and you are, bound to take it in your political action as law – not that he judges at all of its merits, but because a decision of the Court is to him a 'Thus saith the Lord'. He places it on that ground alone, and you will bear in mind that thus committing himself unreservedly to this decision, commits himself just as firmly to the next one as to this. He did not commit himself on account of the merit or demerit of the decision, but it is a 'Thus saith the Lord'. The next decision as much as this will be a 'Thus saith the Lord'. There is nothing that can divert or turn him away from this decision. It is nothing that I point out to him that his great prototype, General Jackson, did not believe in the binding force of decisions. It is nothing to him that Jefferson did not so believe. I have said that I have often heard him approve of Jackson's course in disregarding the decision of the Supreme Court pronouncing a national bank constitutional. He says I did not hear him say so. He denies the accuracy of my recollection. I say he ought to know better than I, but I will make no question about this thing, though it still seems to me that I heard him say it twenty times. I will tell him, though, that he now claims to stand on the Cincinnati platform, which affirms that Congress cannot charter a national bank in the teeth of that old standing decision that Congress can charter a bank. And I remind him of another piece of Illinois history on the question of respect for judicial decisions, and it is a piece of Illinois history belonging to a time when a large party to which Judge Douglas belonged, were displeased with a decision of the Supreme Court of Illinois, because they had decided that a Governor could not remove a secretary of State, and I know that Judge Douglas will not deny that he was then in favour of overslaughing that decision, by the mode of adding five new Judges, so as to vote down the four old ones. Not only so, but it ended in the Judge's sitting down on the very bench as one of the five new judges to break down the four old ones. It was in this way precisely that he got his title of Judge. Now, when the Judge tells me that men appointed conditionally to sit as members of a Court will have to be catechized beforehand upon some subject, I say, 'You know, Judge; you have tried it!' When he says a Court of this kind will lose the confidence of all men, will be prostituted and disgraced by such a proceeding, I say, 'You know best, Judge; you have been through the mill.'

But I cannot shake Judge Douglas's teeth loose from the Dred Scott decision. Like some obstinate animal (I mean no disrespect) that will hang on when he has once got his teeth fixed – you may cut off a leg, or you may tear away an arm, still he will not relax his hold. And so I may point out to the Judge, and say that he is bespattered all over, from the beginning of his political life to the present time, with attacks upon judicial decisions – I may cut off limb after limb of his public record, and strive to wrench from him a single dictum of the Court, yet I cannot divert him from it. He hangs to the last to the Dred Scott decision. . . . Henry Clay, my beau ideal of a statesman, . . . once said of a class of men who would repress all tendencies to liberty and ultimate emancipation, that they must, if they would do this, go back to the era of our independence, and muzzle the cannon that thunders its annual joyous return; that they must blow out the moral lights around us; they must penetrate the human soul, and eradicate there the love of liberty; and then, and not till then, could they perpetuate slavery in this country! To my thinking, Judge Douglas is, by his example and vast influence, doing that very thing in this community when he says that the negro has nothing in the Declaration of Independence. Henry Clay plainly understood the contrary. Judge Douglas is going back to the era of our Revolution, and, to the extent of his ability, muzzling the cannon which thunders its annual joyous return. When he invites any people, willing to have slavery, to establish it, he is blowing out the moral lights around us. When he says 'cares not whether slavery is voted down or voted up' – that it is a sacred right of self-government – he is, in my judgment, penetrating the human soul and eradicating the light of reason and the love of liberty in this American people. And now I will only say, that when, by all these means and appliances, Judge Douglas shall succeed in bringing public sentiment to an exact accordance with his own views; when these vast assemblages shall echo back all these sentiments; when they shall come to repeat his views and avow his principles, and to say all that he says on these mighty questions – then it needs only the formality of a second Dred Scott decision, which he indorses in advance, to make slavery alike lawful in all the States, old as well as new, North as well as South.

Lincoln's Reply to Judge Douglas in the Second Joint Debate. Freeport, Illinois. August 27, 1858

. . . The plain truth is this. At the introduction of the Nebraska policy, we believed there was a new era being introduced in the history of the Republic, which tended to the spread and perpetuation of slavery. But in our opposition to that measure we did not agree with one another in everything. The people in the north end of the State were for stronger measures of opposition than we of the southern and central portions of the State, but we were all opposed to the Nebraska doctrine. We had that one feeling and one sentiment in common. You at the north end met in your conventions, and passed your resolutions. We in the middle of the State and further south did not hold such conventions and pass the same resolutions, although we had in general a common view and a common sentiment. So that these meetings which the Judge has alluded to, and the resolutions he has read from, were local, and did not spread over the whole State. We at last met together in 1856, from all parts of the State, and we agreed upon a common platform. You who held more extreme notions, either yielded those notions, or if not wholly yielding them, agreed to yield them practically, for the sake of embodying the opposition to the measures which the opposite party were pushing forward at that time. We met you then, and if there was anything yielded, it was for practical purposes. We agreed then upon a platform for the party throughout the entire State of Illinois, and now we are all bound as a party to that platform. And I say here to you, if anyone expects of me in the case of my election, that I will do anything not signified by our Republican platform and my answers here today, I tell you very frankly, that person will be deceived. I do not ask for the vote of anyone who supposes that I have secret purposes or pledges that I dare not speak out. . . . If I should never be elected to any office, I trust I may go down with no stain of falsehood upon my reputation, notwithstanding the hard opinions Judge Douglas chooses to entertain of me.

From Lincoln's Reply at Jonesboro'. September 15, 1858

Ladies and Gentlemen, There is very much in the principles that Judge Douglas has here enunciated that I most cordially approve, and over which I shall have no controversy with him. In so far as he insisted that all the States have the right to do exactly as they please about all their domestic relations, including that of slavery, I agree entirely with him. He places me wrong in spite of all I tell him, though I repeat it again and again, insisting that I have made no difference with him upon this subject. I have made a great many speeches, some of which have been printed, and it will be utterly impossible for him to find anything that I have ever put in print contrary to what I now say on the subject. I hold myself under constitutional obligations to allow the people in all the States, without interference, direct or indirect, to do exactly as they please, and I deny that I have any inclination to interfere with them, even if there were no such constitutional obligation. I can only say again that I am placed improperly – altogether improperly, in spite of all that I can say – when it is insisted that I entertain any other view or purpose in regard to that matter.

While I am upon this subject, I will make some answers briefly to certain propositions that Judge Douglas has put. He says, 'Why can't this Union endure permanently half slave and half free?' I have said that I supposed it could not, and I will try, before this new audience, to give briefly some of the reasons for entertaining that opinion. Another form of his question is, 'Why can't we let it stand as our fathers placed it?' That is the exact difficulty between us. I say that Judge Douglas and his friends have changed it from the position in which our fathers originally placed it.

I say in the way our fathers originally left the slavery question, the institution was in the course of ultimate extinction. I say when this government was first established, it was the policy of its founders to prohibit the spread of slavery into the new Territories of the United States where it had not existed. But Judge Douglas and his friends have broken up that policy, and placed it upon a new basis, by which it is to become national and perpetual. All I have asked or desired anywhere is that it should be placed back again upon the basis that the fathers of our government originally placed it upon. I have no doubt that it would become extinct for all time to come, if we had but readopted the policy of the fathers by restricting it to the limits it has already covered – restricting it from the new Territories.

I do not wish to dwell on this branch of the subject at great length at this time, but allow me to repeat one thing that I have stated before. Brooks, the man who assaulted Senator Sumner on the floor of the Senate, and who was complimented with dinners and silver pitchers and gold-headed canes, and a good many other things for that feat, in one of his speeches declared that when this government was originally established, nobody expected that the institution of slavery would last until this day. That was but the opinion of one man, but it is such an opinion as we can never get from Judge Douglas or anybody in favour of slavery in the North at all. You can sometimes get it from a Southern man. He said at the same time that the framers of our government did not have the knowledge that experience has taught us – that experience and the invention of the cotton gin have taught us that the perpetuation of slavery is a necessity. He insisted therefore upon its being changed from the basis upon which the fathers of the government left it to the basis of perpetuation and nationalization.

I insist that this is the difference between Judge Douglas and myself – that Judge Douglas is helping the change along. I insist upon this government being placed where our fathers originally placed it. . . . When he asks me why we cannot get along with it [slavery] in the attitude where our fathers placed it, he had better clear up the evidences that he has himself changed it from that basis; that he has himself been chiefly instrumental in changing the policy of the fathers. Any one who will read his speech of the twenty-second of March last, will see that he there makes an open confession, showing that he set about fixing the institution upon an altogether different set of principles. . . .

Now, fellow-citizens, in regard to this matter about a contract between myself and Judge Trumbull, and myself and all that long portion of Judge Douglas's speech on this subject. I wish simply to say, what I have said to him before, that he cannot know whether it is true or not, and I do know that there is not a word of truth in it. And I have told him so before. I don't want any harsh language indulged in, but I do not know how to deal with this persistent insisting on a story that I know to be utterly without truth. It used to be the fashion amongst men that when a charge was made, some sort of proof was brought forward to establish it, and if no proof was found to exist, it was dropped. I don't know how to meet this kind of an argument. I don't want to have a fight with Judge Douglas, and I have no way of making an argument up into the consistency of a corn-cob and stopping his mouth with it. All I can do is good-humouredly to say, that from the beginning to the end of all that story about a bargain between Judge Trumbull and myself, there is not a word of truth in it. . . .

When that compromise [of 1850] was made, it did not repeal the old Missouri Compromise. It left a region of United States territory half as large as the present territory of the United States, north of the line of 36° 30', in which slavery was prohibited by act of Congress. This compromise did not repeal that one. It did not affect nor propose to repeal it. But at last it became Judge Douglas's duty, as he thought (and I find no fault with him), as chairman of the Committee on Territories, to bring in a bill for the organization of a territorial government – first of one, then of two Territories north of that line. When he did so, it ended in his inserting a provision substantially repealing the Missouri Compromise. That was because the Compromise of 1850 had not repealed it. And now I ask why he could not have left that compromise alone? We were quiet from the agitation of the slavery question. We were making no fuss about it. All had acquiesced in the compromise measures of 1850. We never had been seriously disturbed by any Abolition agitation before that period. . . . I close this part of the discussion on my part by asking him the question again, Why, when we had peace under the Missouri Compromise, could you not have let it alone?

* * *

He tries to persuade us that there must be a variety in the different institutions of the States of the Union; that that variety necessarily proceeds from the variety of soil, climate, of the face of the country, and the difference of the natural features of the States. I agree to all that. Have these very matters ever produced any difficulty amongst us? Not at all. Have we ever had any quarrel over the fact that they have laws in Louisiana designed to regulate the commerce that springs from the production of sugar, or because we have a different class relative to the production of flour in this State? Have they produced any differences? Not at all. They are the very cements of this Union. They don't make the house a house divided against itself. They are the props that hold up the house and sustain the Union.

But has it been so with this element of slavery? Have we not always had quarrels and difficulties over it? And when will we cease to have quarrels over it? Like causes produce like effects. It is worth while to observe that we have generally had comparative peace upon the slavery question, and that there has been no cause for alarm until it was excited by the effort to spread it into new territory. Whenever it has been limited to its present bounds, and there has been no effort to spread it, there has been peace. All the trouble and convulsion has proceeded from efforts to spread it over more territory. It was thus at the date of the Missouri Compromise. It was so again with the annexation of Texas; so with the territory acquired by the Mexican War; and it is so now. Whenever there has been an effort to spread it, there has been agitation and resistance. Now, I appeal to this audience (very few of whom are my political friends), as rational men, whether we have reason to expect that the agitation in regard to this subject will cease while the causes that tend to reproduce agitation are actively at work? Will not the same cause that produced agitation in 1820, when the Missouri Compromise was formed — that which produced the agitation upon the annexation of Texas, and at other times — work out the same results always? Do you think that the nature of man will be changed; that the same causes that produced agitation at one time will not have the same effect at another?

This has been the result so far as my observation of the slavery question and my reading in history extend. What right have we then to hope that the trouble will cease, that the agitation will come to an end, until it shall either be placed back where it originally stood, and where the fathers originally placed it, or, on the other hand, until it shall entirely master all opposition? This is the view I entertain, and this is the reason why I entertained it, as Judge Douglas has read from my Springfield speech.

. . . At Freeport I answered several interrogatories that had been propounded to me by Judge Douglas at the Ottawa meeting. . . . At the same time I propounded four interrogatories to him, claiming it as a right that he should answer as many for me as I did for him, and I would reserve myself for a future instalment when I got them ready. The Judge, in answering me upon that occasion, put in what I suppose he intends as answers to all four of my interrogatories. The first one of these I have before me, and it is in these words:

> Question 1. If the people of Kansas shall by means entirely unobjectionable in all other respects, adopt a State constitution and ask admission into the Union under it, before they have the requisite number of inhabitants according to the English bill – some 93,000 – will you vote to admit them?

As I read the Judge's answer in the newspaper, and as I remember it as pronounced at the time, he does not give any answer which is equivalent to yes or no – I will or I won't. He answers at very considerable length, rather quarrelling with me for asking the question, and insisting that Judge Trumbull had done something that I ought to say something about; and finally, getting out such statements as induce me to infer that he means to be understood, he will, in that supposed case, vote for the admission of Kansas. I only bring this forward now, for the purpose of saying that, if he chooses to put a different construction upon his answer, he may do it. But if he does not, I shall from this time forward assume that he will vote for the admission of Kansas in disregard of the English bill. He has the right to remove any misunderstanding I may have. I only mention it now, that I may hereafter assume this to have been the true construction of his answer, if he does not now choose to correct me.

The second interrogatory I propounded to him was this:

> Question 2. Can the people of a United States Territory in any lawful way, against the wish of any citizen of the United States, exclude slavery from its limits prior to the formation of a State constitution?

To this Judge Douglas answered that they can lawfully exclude slavery from the Territory prior to the formation of a constitution.

He goes on to tell us how it can be done. As I understand him, he holds that it can be done by the territorial legislature refusing to make any enactments for the protection of slavery in the Territory, and especially by adopting unfriendly legislation to it. For the sake of clearness, I state it again: that they can exclude slavery from the Territory – first, by withholding what he assumes to be an indispensable assistance to it in the way of legislation; and second, by unfriendly legislation. If I rightly understand him, I wish to ask your attention for a while to his position.

In the first place, the Supreme Court of the United States has decided that any congressional prohibition of slavery in the Territories is unconstitutional: they have reached this proposition as a conclusion from their former proposition that the Constitution of the United States expressly recognizes property in slaves; and from that other constitutional provision that no person shall be deprived of property without due process of law. Hence they reach the conclusion that as the Constitution of the United States expressly recognizes property in slaves, and prohibits any person from being deprived of property without due process of law, to pass an act of Congress by which a man who owned a slave on one side of a line would be deprived of him if he took him on the other side, is depriving him of that property without due process of law. That I understand to be the decision of the Supreme Court. I understand also that Judge Douglas adheres most firmly to that decision; and the difficulty is, how is it possible for any power to exclude slavery from the Territory unless in violation of that decision? That is the difficulty.

In the Senate of the United States, in 1856, Judge Trumbull in a speech, substantially if not directly, put the same interrogatory to Judge Douglas, as to whether the people of a Territory had the lawful power to exclude slavery prior to the formation of a constitution? Judge Douglas then answered at considerable length, and his answer will be found in the *Congressional Globe*, under date of June 9, 1856. The Judge said that whether the people could exclude slavery prior to the formation of a constitution or not, was a question to be decided by the Supreme Court. He put that proposition, as will be seen by the *Congressional Globe*, in a variety of forms, all running to the same thing in substance – that it was a question for the Supreme Court. I maintain that when he says, after the Supreme Court has decided the question, that the people may yet exclude slavery by any means whatever, he does virtually say that it is not a question for the Supreme Court. He shifts his ground. I appeal to you whether he did not say it was a question for the Supreme Court? Has not the Supreme Court decided that question? When he now says that the people may exclude slavery, does he not make it a question for the people? Does he not virtually shift his ground and say that it is not a question for the court, but for the people? This is a very simple proposition – a very plain and naked one. It seems to me that there is no difficulty in deciding it. In a variety of ways he said that it was a question for the Supreme Court. He did not stop then to tell us that, whatever the Supreme Court decides, the people can by withholding necessary 'police regulations' keep slavery out. He did not make any such answer. I submit to you now, whether the new state of the case has not induced the Judge to sheer away from his original ground? Would not this be the impression of every fair-minded man?

I hold that the proposition that slavery cannot enter a new country without police regulations is historically false. It is not true at all. I hold that the history of this country shows that the institution of slavery was originally planted upon this continent without these 'police regulations' which the Judge now thinks necessary for the actual establishment of it. Not only so, but is there not another fact – how came this Dred Scott decision to be made? It was made upon the case of a negro being taken and actually held in slavery in Minnesota Territory, claiming his freedom because the act of Congress prohibited his being so held there. Will the Judge pretend that Dred Scott was not held there without police regulations? There is at least one matter of record as to his having been held in slavery in the Territory, not only with-out police regulations, but in the teeth of congressional legislation supposed to be valid at the time. This shows that there is vigour enough in slavery to plant itself in a new country, even against unfriendly legislation. It takes not only law, but the enforcement of law to keep it out. That is the history of this country upon the subject.

I wish to ask one other question. It being understood that the Constitution of the United States guarantees property in slaves in the Territories, if there is any infringement of the right of that property, would not the United States courts, organized for the government of the Territory, apply such remedy as might be necessary in that case? It is a maxim held by the courts that there is no wrong without its remedy; and the courts have a remedy for whatever is acknowledged and treated as a wrong.

Again: I will ask you, my friends, if you were elected members of the legislature, what would be the first thing you would have to do before entering upon your duties? Swear to support the Constitution of the United States. Suppose you believe as Judge Douglas does, that the Constitution of the United States guarantees to your neighbour the right to hold slaves in that Territory – that they are his property – how can you clear your oaths unless you give him such legislation as is necessary to enable him to enjoy that property? What do you understand by supporting the Constitution of a State or of the United States? Is it not to give such constitutional helps to the rights established by that Constitution as may be practically needed? Can you, if you swear to support the Constitution and believe that the Constitution establishes a right, clear your oath without giving it support? Do you support the Constitution if, knowing or believing there is a right established under it which needs specific legislation, you withhold that legislation? Do you not violate and disregard your oath? I can conceive of nothing plainer in the world. There can be nothing in the words 'support the Constitution', if you may run counter to it by refusing support to any right established under the Constitution. And what I say here will hold with still more force against the Judge's doctrine of 'unfriendly legislation'. How could you, having sworn to support the Constitution, and believing that it guaranteed the right to hold slaves in the Territories, assist in legislation intended to defeat that right? That would be violating your own view of the Constitution. Not only so, but if you were to do so, how long would it take the courts to hold your votes unconstitutional and void? Not a moment.

Lastly, I would ask, is not Congress itself under obligation to give legislative support to any right that is established under the United States Constitution? I repeat the question, is not Congress itself bound to give legislative support to any right that is established in the United States Constitution? A member of Congress swears to support the Constitution of the United States, and if he sees a right established by that Constitution which needs specific legislative protection, can he clear his oath without giving that protection? Let me ask you why many of us, who are opposed to slavery upon principle, give our acquiescence to a fugitive-slave law? Why do we hold ourselves under obligations to pass such a law, and abide by it when passed? Because the Constitution makes provision that the owners of slaves shall have the right to reclaim them. It gives the right to reclaim slaves; and that right is, as Judge Douglas says, a barren right, unless there is legislation that will enforce it.

The mere declaration, 'No person held to service or labour in one State, under the laws thereof, escaping into another, shall, in consequence of any law or regulation therein, be discharged from such service or labour, but shall be delivered up on claim of the party to whom such service or labour may be due,' is powerless without specific legislation to enforce it. Now, on what ground would a member of Congress who is opposed to slavery in the abstract, vote for a fugitive law, as I would deem it my duty to do? Because there is a constitutional right which needs legislation to enforce it. And, although it is distasteful to me, I have sworn to support the Constitution; and, having so sworn, I cannot conceive that I do support it if I withhold from that right any necessary legislation to make it practical. And if that is true in regard to a fugitive-slave law, is the right to have fugitive slaves reclaimed any better fixed in the Constitution than the right to hold slaves in the Territories? For this decision is a just exposition of the Constitution, as Judge Douglas thinks. Is the one right any better than the other? If I wished to refuse to give legislative support to slave property in the Territories, if a member of Congress, I could not do it, holding the view that the Constitution establishes that right. If I did it at all, it would be because I deny that this decision properly construes the Constitution. But if I acknowledge with Judge Douglas that this decision properly construes the Constitution, I cannot conceive that I would be less than a perjured man if I should refuse in Congress to give such protection to that property as in its nature it needed. . . .

From Lincoln's Reply to Judge Douglas at Charleston, Illinois.
September 18, 1858

Judge Douglas has said to you that he has not been able to get from me an answer to the question whether I am in favour of negro citizenship. So far as I know, the Judge never asked me the question before. He shall have no occasion ever to ask it again, for I tell him very frankly that I am not in favour of negro citizenship. . . . Now my opinion is, that the different States have the power to make a negro a citizen under the Constitution of the United States, if they choose. The Dred Scott decision decides that they have not that power. If the State of Illinois had that power, I should be opposed to the exercise of it. That is all I have to say about it.

Judge Douglas has told me that he heard my speeches north and my speeches south, . . . and there was a very different cast of sentiment in the speeches made at the different points. I will not charge upon Judge Douglas that he wilfully misrepresents me, but I call upon every fair-minded man to take these speeches and read them, and I dare him to point out any difference between my speeches north and south. While I am here, perhaps I ought to say a word, if I have the time, in regard to the latter portion of the Judge's speech, which was a sort of declamation in reference to my having said that I entertained the belief that this government would not endure, half slave and half free. I have said so, and I did not say it without what seemed to me good reasons. It perhaps would require more time than I have now to set forth those reasons in detail; but let me ask you a few questions. Have we ever had any peace on this slavery question? When are we to have peace upon it if it is kept in the position it now occupies? How are we ever to have peace upon it? That is an important question. To be sure, if we will all stop and allow Judge Douglas and his friends to march on in their present career until they plant the institution all over the nation, here and wherever else our flag waves, and we acquiesce in it, there will be peace. But let me ask Judge Douglas how he is going to get the people to do that? They have been wrangling over this question for forty years. This was the cause of the agitation resulting in the Missouri Compromise; this produced the troubles at the annexation of Texas, in the acquisition of the territory acquired in the Mexican War. Again, this was the trouble quieted by the Compromise of 1850, when it was settled 'for ever', as both the great political parties declared in their national conventions. That 'for ever' turned out to be just four years, when Judge Douglas himself reopened it.

When is it likely to come to an end? He introduced the Nebraska bill in 1854, to put another end to the slavery agitation. He promised that it would finish it all up immediately, and he has never made a speech since, until he got into a quarrel with the President about the Lecompton constitution, in which he has not declared that we are just at the end of the slavery agitation. But in one speech, I think last winter, he did say that he didn't quite see when the end of the slavery agitation would come. Now he tells us again that it is all over, and the people of Kansas have voted down the Lecompton constitution. How is it over? That was only one of the attempts to put an end to the slavery agitation – one of these 'final settlements'. Is Kansas in the Union? Has she formed a constitution that she is likely to come in under? Is not the slavery agitation still an open question in that Territory? . . . If Kansas should sink today, and leave a great vacant space in the earth's surface, this vexed question would still be among us. I say, then, there is no way of putting an end to the slavery agitation amongst us, but to put it back upon the basis where our fathers placed it; no way but to keep it out of our new Territories – to restrict it for ever to the old States where it now exists. Then the public mind will rest in the belief that it is in the course of ultimate extinction. That is one way of putting an end to the slavery agitation.

The other way is for us to surrender, and let Judge Douglas and his friends have their way, and plant slavery over all the States – cease speaking of it as in any way a wrong – regard slavery as one of the common matters of property, and speak of our negroes as we do of our horse and cattle.

From Lincoln's Reply to Judge Douglas at Galesburg, Illinois. October 7, 1858

. . . The Judge has alluded to the Declaration of Independence, and insisted that negroes are not included in that Declaration; and that it is a slander on the framers of that instrument to suppose that negroes were meant therein; and he asks you, Is it possible to believe that Mr Jefferson, who penned that immortal paper, could have supposed himself applying the language of that instrument to the negro race, and yet held a portion of that race in slavery? Would he not at once have freed them? I only have to remark upon this part of his speech (and that too, very briefly, for I shall not detain myself or you upon that point for any great length of time), that I believe the entire records of the world, from the date of the Declaration of Independence up to within three years ago, may be searched in vain for one single affirmation from one single man, that the negro was not included in the Declaration of Independence; I think I may defy Judge Douglas to show that he ever said so, that Washington ever said so, that any President ever said so, that any member of Congress ever said so, or that any living man upon the whole earth ever said so, until the necessities of the present policy of the Democratic party in regard to slavery had to invent that affirmation. And I will remind Judge Douglas and this audience, that while Mr Jefferson was the owner of slaves, as undoubtedly he was, in speaking on this very subject, he used the strong language that 'he trembled for his country when he remembered that God was just;' and I will offer the highest premium in my power to Judge Douglas if he will show that he, in all his life, ever uttered a sentiment at all akin to that of Jefferson.

. . . I want to call to the Judge's attention an attack he made upon me in the first one of these debates. . . . In order to fix extreme Abolitionism upon me, Judge Douglas read a set of resolutions which he declared had been passed by a Republican State Convention, in October 1854, held at Springfield, Illinois, and he declared that I had taken a part in that convention. It turned out that although a few men calling themselves an anti-Nebraska State Convention had sat at Springfield about that time, yet neither did I take any part in it, nor did it pass the resolutions or any such resolutions as Judge Douglas read. So apparent had it become that the resolutions that he read had not been passed at Springfield at all, nor by any State Convention in which I had taken part, that seven days later at Freeport . . . Judge Douglas declared that he had been misled . . . and promised . . . that when he went to Springfield he would investigate the matter. . . . I have waited as I think a sufficient time for the report of that investigation.

. . . A fraud, an absolute forgery, was committed, and the per-petration of it was traced to the three – Lanphier, Harris, and Douglas. . . . Whether it can be narrowed in any way, so as to exonerate any one of them, is what Judge Douglas's report would probably show. The main object of that forgery at that time was to beat Yates and elect Harris to Congress, and that object was known to be exceedingly dear to Judge Douglas at that time.

. . . The fraud having been apparently successful upon that occasion, both Harris and Douglas have more than once since then been attempting to put it to new uses. As the fisherman's wife, whose drowned husband was brought home with his body full of eels, said, when she was asked what was to be done with him, 'Take out the eels and set him again', so Harris and Douglas have shown a disposition to take the eels out of that stale fraud by which they gained Harris's election, and set the fraud again, more than once. . . . And now that it has been discovered publicly to be a fraud, we find that Judge Douglas manifests no surprise at all. . . . But meanwhile the three are agreed that each is a most honourable man.

Notes for Speeches. October 1858

Suppose it is true that the negro is inferior to the white in the gifts of nature; is it not the exact reverse of justice that the white should for that reason take from the negro any part of the little which he has had given him? 'Give to him that is needy' is the Christian rule of charity; but 'Take from him that is needy' is the rule of slavery.

The sum of pro-slavery theology seems to be this: 'Slavery is not universally right, nor yet universally wrong; it is better for some people to be slaves; and, in such cases, it is the will of God that they be such.'

Certainly there is no contending against the will of God; but still there is some difficulty in ascertaining and applying it to particular cases. For instance, we will suppose the Rev. Dr Ross has a slave named Sambo, and the question is, 'Is it the will of God that Sambo shall remain a slave, or be set free?' The Almighty gives no audible answer to the question, and his revelation, the Bible, gives none – or at most none but such as admits of a squabble as to its meaning; no one thinks of asking Sambo's opinion on it. So at last it comes to this, that Dr Ross is to decide the question; and while he considers it, he sits in the shade, with gloves on his hands, and subsists on the bread that Sambo is earning in the burning sun. If he decides that God wills Sambo to continue a slave, he thereby retains his own comfortable position; but if he decides that God wills Sambo to be free, he thereby has to walk out of the shade, throw off his gloves, and delve for his own bread. Will Dr Ross be actuated by the perfect impartiality which has ever been considered most favourable to correct decisions?

We have in this nation the element of domestic slavery. It is a matter of absolute certainty that it is a disturbing element. It is the opinion of all the great men who have expressed an opinion upon it, that it is a dangerous element. We keep up a controversy in regard to it. That controversy necessarily springs from difference of opinion, and if we can learn exactly – can reduce to the lowest elements – what that difference of opinion is, we perhaps shall be better prepared for discussing the different systems of policy that we would propose in regard to that disturbing element.

I suggest that the difference of opinion, reduced to its lowest terms, is no other than the difference between the men who think slavery a wrong and those who do not think it wrong. The Republican party think it wrong – we think it is a moral, a social, and a political wrong. We think it is a wrong not confining itself merely to the persons or the States where it exists, but that it is a wrong which in its tendency, to say the least, affects the existence of the whole nation. Because we think it wrong, we propose a course of policy that shall deal with it as a wrong.

We deal with it as with any other wrong, in so far as we can prevent its growing any larger, and so deal with it that in the run of time there may be some promise of an end to it. We have a due regard to the actual presence of it amongst us, and the difficulties of getting rid of it in any satisfactory way, and all the constitutional obligations thrown about it. I suppose that in reference both to its actual existence in the nation, and to our constitutional obligations, we have no right at all to disturb it in the States where it exists, and we profess that we have no more inclination to disturb it than we have the right to do it. We go further than that: we don't propose to disturb it where, in one instance, we think the Constitution would permit us. We think the Constitution would permit us to disturb it in the District of Columbia. Still we do not propose to do that, unless it should be in terms which I don't suppose the nation is very likely soon to agree to – the terms of making the emancipation gradual and compensating the unwilling owners. Where we suppose we have the constitutional right, we restrain ourselves in reference to the actual existence of the institution and the difficulties thrown about it. We also oppose it as an evil so far as it seeks to spread itself. We insist on the policy that shall restrict it to its present limits. We don't suppose that in doing this we violate anything due to the actual presence of the institution, or anything due to the constitutional guaranties thrown around it.

We oppose the Dred Scott decision in a certain way, upon which I ought perhaps to address you in a few words. We do not propose that when Dred Scott has been decided to be a slave by the court, we, as a mob, will decide him to be free. We do not propose that, when any other one, or one thousand, shall be decided by that court to be slaves, we will in any violent way disturb the rights of property thus settled; but we nevertheless do oppose that decision as a political rule, which shall be binding on the voter to vote for nobody who thinks it wrong, which shall be binding on the members of Congress or the President to favour no measure that does not actually concur with the principles of that decision. We do not propose to be bound by it as a political rule in that way, because we think it lays the foundation not merely of enlarging and spreading out what we consider an evil, but it lays the foundation for spreading that evil into the States themselves. We propose so resisting it as to have it reversed if we can, and a new judicial rule established upon this subject.

I will add this, that if there be any man who does not believe that slavery is wrong in the three aspects which I have mentioned, or in any one of them, that man is misplaced and ought to leave us. While, on the other hand, if there be any man in the Republican party who is impatient over the necessity springing from its actual presence, and is impatient of the constitutional guaranties thrown around it, and would act in disregard of these, he too is misplaced, standing with us. He will find his place somewhere else; for we have a due regard, so far as we are capable of understanding them, for all these things. This, gentlemen, as well as I can give it, is a plain statement of our principles in all their enormity.

I will say now that there is a sentiment in the country contrary to me – a sentiment which holds that slavery is not wrong, and therefore goes for the policy that does not propose dealing with it as a wrong. That policy is the Democratic policy, and that sentiment is the Democratic sentiment. If there be a doubt in the mind of any one of this vast audience that this is really the central idea of the Democratic party, in relation to this subject, I ask him to bear with me while I state a few things tending, as I think, to prove that proposition.

In the first place, the leading man – I think I may do my friend Judge Douglas the honour of calling him such – advocating the present Democratic policy, never himself says it is wrong. He has the high distinction, so far as I know, of never having said slavery is either right or wrong. Almost everybody else says one or the other, but the Judge never does. If there be a man in the Democratic party who thinks it is wrong, and yet clings to that party, I suggest to him in the first place that his leader don't talk as he does, for he never says that it is wrong.

In the second place, I suggest to him that if he will examine the policy proposed to be carried forward, he will find that he carefully excludes the idea that there is anything wrong in it. If you will examine the arguments that are made on it, you will find that every one carefully excludes the idea that there is anything wrong in slavery.

Perhaps that Democrat who says he is as much opposed to slavery as I am will tell me that I am wrong about this. I wish him to examine his own course in regard to this matter a moment, and then see if his opinion will not be changed a little. You say it is wrong; but don't you constantly object to anybody else saying so? Do you not constantly argue that this is not the right place to oppose it? You say it must not be opposed in the free States, because slavery is not there; it must not be opposed in the slave States, because it is there; it must not be opposed in politics, because that will make a fuss; it must not be opposed in the pulpit, because it is not religion. Then where is the place to oppose it? There is no suitable place to oppose it. There is no plan in the country to oppose this evil overspreading the continent, which you say yourself is coming. Frank Blair and Gratz Brown tried to get up a system of gradual emancipation in Missouri, had an election in August, and got beat; and you, Mr Democrat, threw up your hat and hallooed, 'Hurrah for Democracy!'

So I say again, that in regard to the arguments that are made, when Judge Douglas says he 'don't care whether slavery is voted up or voted down', whether he means that as an individual expression of sentiment, or only as a sort of statement of his views on national policy, it is alike true to say that he can thus argue logically if he don't see anything wrong in it; but he cannot say so logically if he admits that slavery is wrong. He cannot say that he would as soon see a wrong voted up as voted down. When Judge Douglas says that whoever or whatever community wants slaves, they have a right to have them, he is perfectly logical if there is nothing wrong in the institution; but if you admit that it is wrong, he cannot logically say that anybody has a right to do wrong. When he says that slave property and horse and hog property are alike to be allowed to go into the Territories, upon the principles of equality, he is reasoning truly if there is no difference between them as property; but if the one is property, held rightfully, and the other is wrong, then there is no equality between the right and wrong; so that, turn it in any way you can, in all the arguments sustaining the Democratic policy, and in that policy itself, there is a careful, studied exclusion of the idea that there is anything wrong in slavery.

Let us understand this. I am not, just here, trying to prove that we are right and they are wrong. I have been stating where we and they stand, and trying to show what is the real difference between us; and I now say that whenever we can get the question distinctly stated – can get all these men who believe that slavery is in some of these respects wrong, to stand and act with us in treating it as a wrong – then, and not till then, I think, will we in some way come to an end of this slavery agitation.

Mr Lincoln's Reply to Judge Douglas in the Seventh and Last Debate. Alton, Illinois. October 15, 1858

. . . But is it true that all the difficulty and agitation we have in regard to this institution of slavery springs from office-seeking – from the mere ambition of politicians? Is that the truth? How many times have we had danger from this question? Go back to the day of the Missouri Compromise. Go back to the nullification question, at the bottom of which lay this same slavery question. Go back to the time of the annexation of Texas. Go back to the troubles that led to the Compromise of 1850. You will find that every time, with the single exception of the nullification question, they sprung from an endeavour to spread this institution. There never was a party in the history of this country, and there probably never will be, of sufficient strength to disturb the general peace of the country. Parties themselves may be divided and quarrel on minor questions, yet it extends not beyond the parties themselves. But does not this question make a disturbance outside of political circles? Does it not enter into the churches and rend them asunder? What divided the great Methodist Church into two parts, North and South? What has raised this constant disturbance in every Presbyterian General Assembly that meets? What disturbed the Unitarian Church in this very city two years ago? What has jarred and shaken the great American Tract Society recently – not yet splitting it, but sure to divide it in the end? Is it not this same mighty, deep-seated power, that somehow operates on the minds of men, exciting and stirring them up in every avenue of society, in politics, in religion, in literature, in morals, in all the manifold relations of life? Is this the work of politicians? Is that irresistible power which for fifty years has shaken the government and agitated the people, to be stilled and subdued by pretending that it is an exceedingly simple thing, and we ought not to talk about it? If you will get everybody else to stop talking about it, I assure you that I will quit before they have half done so. But where is the philosophy or statesmanship which assumes that you can quiet that disturbing element in our society, which has disturbed us for more than half a century, which has been the only serious danger that has threatened our institutions? I say where is the philosophy or the statesmanship, based on the assumption that we are to quit talking about it, and that the public mind is all at once to cease being agitated by it? Yet this is the policy here in the North that Douglas is advocating – that we are to care nothing about it! I ask you if it is not a false philosophy? Is it not a false statesmanship that undertakes to build up a system of policy upon the basis of caring nothing about the very thing that everybody does care the most about – a thing which all experience has shown we care a very great deal about?

. . . The Judge alludes very often in the course of his remarks to the exclusive right which the States have to decide the whole thing for themselves. I agree with him very readily. . . . Our controversy with him is in regard to the new Territories. We agree that when States come in as States they have the right and power to do as they please. . . . We profess constantly that we have no more inclination than belief in the power of the government to disturb it; yet we are driven constantly to defend ourselves from the assumption that we are warring upon the rights of the States. What I insist upon is, that the new Territories shall be kept free from it while in the territorial condition . . .

. . . These are false issues, upon which Judge Douglas has tried to force the controversy. . . .

The real issue in this controversy – the one pressing upon every mind – is the sentiment on the part of one class that looks upon the institution of slavery as a wrong, and of another class that does not look upon it as a wrong. The sentiment that contemplates the institution of slavery in this country as a wrong is the sentiment of the Republican party. It is the sentiment around which all their actions, all their arguments, circle; from which all their propositions radiate. They look upon it as being a moral, social, and political wrong; and while they contemplate it as such, they nevertheless have due regard for its actual existence among us, and the difficulties of getting rid of it in any satisfactory way, and to all the constitutional obligations thrown about it. Yet, having a due regard for these, they desire a policy in regard to it that looks to its not creating any more danger. They insist that it, as far as may be, be treated as a wrong; and one of the methods of treating it as a wrong is to make provision that it shall grow no larger. They also desire a policy that looks to a peaceful end of slavery some time, as being a wrong. These are the views they entertain in regard to it, as I understand them; and all their sentiments, all their arguments and propositions are brought within this range. I have said, and I here repeat it, that if there be a man amongst us who does not think that the institution of slavery is wrong in any one of the aspects of which I have spoken, he is misplaced, and ought not to be with us. And if there be a man amongst us who is so impatient of it as a wrong as to disregard its actual presence among us, and the difficulty of getting rid of it suddenly in a satisfactory way, and to disregard the constitutional obligations thrown about it, that man is misplaced if he is on our platform. We disclaim sympathy with him in practical action. He is not placed properly with us.

On this subject of treating it as a wrong and limiting its spread, let me say a word. Has anything ever threatened the existence of this Union save and except this very institution of slavery? What is it that we hold most dear amongst us? Our own liberty and prosperity. What has ever threatened our liberty and prosperity save and except this institution of slavery? If this is true, how do you propose to improve the condition of things by enlarging slavery – by spreading it out and making it bigger? You may have a wen or a cancer upon your person, and not be able to cut it out lest you bleed to death; but surely it is no way to cure it, to engraft it and spread it over your whole body. That is no proper way of treating what you regard as a wrong. You see this peaceful way of dealing with it as a wrong – restricting the spread of it, and not allowing it to go into new countries where it has not already existed. That is the peaceful way – the old-fashioned way – the way in which the fathers themselves set us the example.

On the other hand, I have said there is a sentiment which treats it as not being wrong. That is the Democratic sentiment of this day. I do not mean to say that every man who stands within that range positively asserts that it is right. That class will include all who positively assert that it is right, and all who, like Judge Douglas, treat it as indifferent, and do not say it is either right or wrong. These two classes of men fall within the general class of those who do not look upon it as a wrong. And if there be among you anybody who supposes that he, as a Democrat, can consider himself 'as much opposed to slavery as anybody', I would like to reason with him. You never treat it *as* a wrong. What other thing that you consider a wrong do you deal with as you deal with that? Perhaps you say it is wrong, but your leader never does, and you quarrel with anybody who says it is wrong. Although you pretend to say so yourself, you can find no fit place to deal with it as a wrong. You must not say anything about it in the free States, because it is not here. You must not say anything about it in the slave States, because it is there. You must not say anything about it in the pulpit, because that is religion, and has nothing to do with it. You must not say anything about it in politics, because that will disturb the security of 'my place'. There is no place to talk about it as being a wrong, although you say yourself it is a wrong. But, finally, you will screw yourself up to the belief that if the people of the slave States should adopt a system of gradual emancipation on the slavery question, you would be in favour of it. You would be in favour of it! You say that is getting it in the right place, and you would be glad to see it succeed. But you are deceiving yourself. You all know that Frank Blair and Gratz Brown, down there in St Louis, undertook to introduce that system in Missouri. They fought as valiantly as they could for the system of gradual emancip-ation, which you pretend you would be glad to see succeed. Now I will bring you to the test. After a hard fight they were beaten; and when the news came over here, you threw up your hats and hurrahed for Democracy! More than that; take all the argument made in favour of the system you have proposed, and it carefully excludes the idea that there is anything wrong in the institution of slavery. The arguments to sustain that policy carefully exclude it. Even here today, you heard Judge Douglas quarrel with me, because I uttered a wish that it might sometime come to an end. Although Henry Clay could say he wished every slave in the United States was in the country of his ancestors, I am denounced by those who pretend to respect Henry Clay, for uttering a wish that it might sometime, in some peaceful way, come to an end.

The Democratic policy in regard to that institution will not tolerate the merest breath, the slightest hint, of the least degree of wrong about it. Try it by some of Judge Douglas's arguments. He says he 'don't care whether it is voted up or voted down in the Territories'. I do not care myself in dealing with that expression whether it is intended to be expressive of his individual sentiments on the subject or only of the national policy he desires to have established.

But no man can logically say it who does see a wrong in it, because no man can logically say he don't care whether a wrong is voted up or voted down. . . . Any man can say that who does not see anything wrong in slavery. . . . But if it is a wrong, he cannot say that people have a right to do wrong. He says that, upon the score of equality, slaves should be allowed to go into a new Territory like other property. This is strictly logical if there is no difference between it and other property. . . . But if you insist that one is wrong and the other right, there is no use to institute a comparison between right and wrong. . . . The Democratic policy everywhere carefully excludes the idea that there is anything wrong in it.

That is the real issue. That is the issue that will continue in this country when these poor tongues of Judge Douglas and myself shall be silent. It is the eternal struggle between these two principles – right and wrong – throughout the world. They are the two principles that have stood face to face from the beginning of time, and will ever continue to struggle.

The one is the common right of humanity, and the other the divine right of kings. It is the same principle in whatever shape it develops itself. It is the same spirit that says, 'You toil and work and earn bread, and I'll eat it.' No matter in what shape it comes, whether from the mouth of a king, who seeks to bestride the people of his own nation and live by the fruit of their labour, or from one race of men as an apology for enslaving another race – it is the same tyrannical principle. . . . Whenever the issue can be distinctly made, and all extraneous matter thrown out, so that men can fairly see the real difference between the parties, this controversy will soon be settled, and it will be done peaceably, too. There will be no war, no violence. It will be placed again where the wisest and best men of the world placed it.

From a Speech at Columbus, Ohio, on the Slave Trade, Popular Sovereignty, etc. September 16, 1859

. . . The Republican party, as I understand its principles and policy, believes that there is great danger of the institution of slavery being spread out and extended, until it is ultimately made alike lawful in all the States of this Union; so believing, to prevent that incidental and ultimate consummation is the original and chief purpose of the Republican organization.

I say 'chief purpose' of the Republican organization; for it is certainly true that if the national House shall fall into the hands of the Republicans, they will have to attend to all the matters of national house-keeping as well as this. The chief and real purpose of the Republican party is eminently conservative. It proposes nothing save and except to restore this Government to its original tone in regard to this element of slavery, and there to maintain it, looking for no further change in reference to it than that which the original framers of the Government themselves expected and looked forward to.

The chief danger to this purpose of the Republican party is not just now the revival of the African slave-trade, or the passage of a Congressional slave-code . . . but the most imminent danger that now threatens that purpose is that insidious Douglas popular sovereignty. This is the miner and sapper. While it does not propose to revive the African slave-trade, nor to pass a slave-code, nor to make a second Dred Scott decision, it is preparing us for the onslaught and charge of these ultimate enemies when they shall be ready to come on, and the word of command for them to advance shall be given. I say this *Douglas* popular sovereignty – for there is a broad distinction, as I now understand it, between that article and a genuine popular sovereignty.

I believe there is a genuine popular sovereignty. I think a definition of genuine popular sovereignty in the abstract would be about this: that each man shall do precisely as he pleases with himself, and with all those things which exclusively concern him. Applied to governments, this principle would be, that a general government shall do all those things which pertain to it; and all the local governments shall do precisely as they please in respect to those matters which exclusively concern them. I understand that this government of the United States under which we live, is based upon this principle; and I am misunderstood if it is supposed that I have any war to make upon that principle.

Now, what is Judge Douglas's popular sovereignty? It is, as a principle, no other than that if one man chooses to make a slave of another man, neither that other man nor anybody else has a right to object. Applied in government, as he seeks to apply it, it is this: If, in a new Territory into which a few people are beginning to enter for the purpose of making their homes, they choose to either exclude slavery from their limits or to establish it there, however one or the other may affect the persons to be enslaved, or the infinitely greater number of persons who are afterward to inhabit that Territory, or the other members of the families of communities of which they are but an incipient member, or the general head of the family of States as parent of all – however their action may affect one or the other of these, there is no power or right to interfere. That is Douglas popular sovereignty applied.

. . . I cannot but express my gratitude that this true view of this element of discord among us, as I believe it is, is attracting more and more attention. I do not believe that Governor Seward uttered that sentiment because I had done so before, but because he reflected upon this subject, and saw the truth of it. Nor do I believe, because Governor Seward or I uttered it, that Mr Hickman of Pennsylvania, in different language, since that time, has declared his belief in the utter antagonism which exists between the principles of liberty and slavery. You see we are multiplying. Now, while I am speaking of Hickman, let me say, I know but little about him. I have never seen him, and know scarcely anything about the man; but I will say this much about him: of all the anti-Lecompton Democracy that have been brought to my notice, he alone has the true, genuine ring of the metal.

. . . Judge Douglas . . . proceeds to assume, without proving it, that slavery is one of those little, unimportant, trivial matters which are of just about as much consequence as the question would be to me, whether my neighbour should raise horned cattle or plant tobacco; that there is no moral question about it, but that it is altogether a matter of dollars and cents; that when a new Territory is opened for settlement, the first man who goes into it may plant there a thing which, like the Canada thistle or some other of those pests of the soil, cannot be dug out by the millions of men who will come thereafter; that it is one of those little things that is so trivial in its nature that it has no effect upon anybody save the few men who first plant upon the soil; that it is not a thing which in any way affects the family of communities composing these States, nor any way endangers the general government. Judge Douglas ignores altogether the very well-known fact that we have never had a serious menace to our political existence except it sprang from this thing, which he chooses to regard as only upon a par with onions and potatoes.

. . . Did you ever, five years ago, hear of anybody in the world saying that the negro had no share in the Declaration of National Independence; that it did not mean negroes at all; and when 'all men' were spoken of, negroes were not included?

. . . Then I suppose that all now express the belief that the Declaration of Independence never did mean negroes. I call upon one of them to say that he said it five years ago. If you think that now, and did not think it then, the next thing that strikes me is to remark that there has been a *change* wrought in you, and a very significant change it is, being no less than changing the negro, in your estimation, from the rank of a man to that of a brute. . . .

Is not this change wrought in your minds a very important change? Public opinion in this country is everything. In a nation like ours this popular sovereignty and squatter sovereignty have already wrought a change in the public mind to the extent I have stated. . . .

. . . Now, if you are opposed to slavery honestly, I ask you to note that fact (the popular-sovereignty of Judge Douglas), and the like of which is to follow, to be plastered on, layer after layer, until very soon you are prepared to deal with the negro everywhere as with the brute. If public sentiment has not been debauched already to this point, a new turn of the screw in that direction is all that is wanting; and this is constantly being done by the teachers of this insidious popular sovereignty. You need but one or two turns further, until your minds, now ripening under these teachings, will be ready for all these things, and you will receive and support or submit to the slave-trade, revived with all its horrors – a slave-code enforced in our Territories – and a new Dred Scott decision to bring slavery up into the very heart of the free North.

. . . I ask attention to the fact that in a pre-eminent degree these popular sovereigns are at this work: blowing out the moral lights around us; teaching that the negro is no longer a man, but a brute; that the Declaration has nothing to do with him; that he ranks with the crocodile and the reptile; that man with body and soul is a matter of dollars and cents. I suggest to this portion of the Ohio Republicans, or Democrats, if there be any present, the serious consideration of this fact, that there is now going on among you a steady process of debauching public opinion on this subject. With this, my friends, I bid you adieu.

From a Speech at Cincinnati, Ohio, on the Intentions of
'Black Republicans', the Relation of Labour and Capital, etc.
September 17, 1859

. . . I say, then, in the first place to the Kentuckians that I am what they call, as I understand it, a 'Black Republican'. I think slavery is wrong, morally and politically. I desire that it should be no further spread in these United States, and I should not object if it should gradually terminate in the whole Union. While I say this for myself, I say to you, Kentuckians, that I understand you differ radically with me upon this proposition; that you believe slavery is a good thing; that slavery is right; that it ought to be extended and perpetuated in this Union. Now, there being this broad difference between us, I do not pretend, in addressing myself to you, Kentuckians, to attempt proselyting you. That would be a vain effort. I do not enter upon it. I only propose to try to show you that you ought to nominate for the next presidency, at Charleston, my distinguished friend, Judge Douglas. In all that, there is no real difference between you and him; I understand he is as sincerely for you, and more wisely for you than you are for yourselves. I will try to demonstrate that proposition.

In Kentucky perhaps – in many of the slave States certainly – you are trying to establish the rightfulness of slavery by reference to the Bible. You are trying to show that slavery existed in the Bible times by Divine ordinance. Now, Douglas is wiser than you, for your own benefit, upon that subject. Douglas knows that whenever you establish that slavery was right by the Bible, it will occur that that slavery was the slavery of the white man – of men without reference to colour – and he knows very well that you may entertain that idea in Kentucky as much as you please, but you will never win any Northern support upon it. He makes a wiser argument for you. He makes the argument that the slavery of the black man – the slavery of the man who has a skin of a different colour from your own – is right. He thereby brings to your support Northern voters, who could not for a moment be brought by your own argument of the Bible right of slavery.

. . . At Memphis he [Judge Douglas] declared that in all contests between the negro and the white man, he was for the white man, but that in all questions between the negro and the crocodile, he was for the negro. He did not make that declaration accidentally . . . he made it a great many times.

The first inference seems to be that if you do not enslave the negro, you are wronging the white man in some way or other; and that whoever is opposed to the negro being enslaved is in some way or other against the white man. Is not that a falsehood? If there was a necessary conflict between the white man and the negro, I should be for the white man as much as Judge Douglas; but I say there is no such necessary conflict. I say there is room enough for us all to be free, and that it not only does not wrong the white man that the negro should be free, but it positively wrongs the mass of the white men that the negro should be enslaved – that the mass of white men are really injured by the effects of slave labour in the vicinity of the fields of their own labour. . . .

There is one other thing that I will say to you in this relation. It is but my opinion; I give it to you without a fee. It is my opinion that it is for you to take him or be defeated; and that if you do take him you may be beaten. You will surely be beaten if you do not take him. We, the Republicans and others forming the opposition of the country, intend 'to stand by our guns', to be patient and firm; and in the long run to beat you, whether you take him or not. We know that before we fairly beat you, we have to beat you both together. We know that 'you are all of a feather', and that we have to beat you all together, and we expect to do it. We don't intend to be very impatient about it. We mean to be as deliberate and calm about it as it is possible to be, but as firm and resolved as it is possible for men to be. When we do as we say, beat you, you perhaps want to know what we will do with you.

I will tell you, so far as I am authorized to speak for the opposition, what we mean to do with you. We mean to treat you, as near as we possibly can, as Washington, Jefferson, and Madison treated you. We mean to leave you alone, and in no way to interfere with your institution; to abide by all and every compromise of the Constitution, and, in a word, coming back to the original proposition, to treat you, so far as degenerate men (if we have degenerated) may, according to the example of those noble fathers – Washington, Jefferson, and Madison. We mean to remember that you are as good as we; that there is no difference between us other than the difference of circumstances. We mean to recognize and bear in mind always, that you have as good hearts in your bosoms as other people, or as we claim to have, and to treat you accordingly. We mean to marry your girls when we have a chance – the white ones, I mean, and I have the honour to inform you that I once did have a chance in that way.

I have told you what we mean to do. I want to know, now, when that thing takes place, what do you mean to do? I often hear it intimated that you mean to divide the Union whenever a Republican, or anything like it, is elected President of the United States. [A voice: 'That is so.'] 'That is so,' one of them says; I wonder if he is a Kentuckian? [A voice: 'He is a Douglas man.'] Well, then, I want to know what you are going to do with your half of it. Are you going to split the Ohio down through, and push your half off a piece? Or are you going to keep it right alongside of us outrageous fellows? Or are you going to build up a wall some way between your country and ours, by which that movable property of yours can't come over here any more, to the danger of your losing it? Do you think you can better yourselves on that subject by leaving us here under no obligation whatever to return those specimens of your movable property that come hither?

You have divided the Union because we would not do right with you, as you think, upon that subject; when we cease to be under obligation to do anything for you, how much better off do you think you will be? Will you make war upon us and kill us all? Why, gentlemen, I think you are as gallant and as brave men as live; that you can fight as bravely in a good cause, man for man, as any other people living; that you have shown yourselves capable of this upon various occasions; but man for man, you are not better than we are, and there are not so many of you as there are of us. You will never make much of a hand at whipping us. If we were fewer in numbers than you, I think that you could whip us; if we were equal it would likely be a drawn battle; but being inferior in numbers, you will make nothing by attempting to master us. . . .

Labour is the great source from which nearly all, if not all, human comforts and necessities are drawn. There is a difference in opinion about the elements of labour in society. Some men assume that there is a necessary connection between capital and labour, and that connection draws within it the whole of the labour of the community. They assume that nobody works unless capital excites them to work. They begin next to consider what is the best way. They say there are but two ways – one is to hire men and to allure them to labour by their consent; the other is to buy the men, and drive them to it, and that is slavery. Having assumed that, they proceed to discuss the question of whether the labourers themselves are better off in the condition of slaves or of hired labourers, and they usually decide that they are better off in the condition of slaves.

In the first place, I say the whole thing is a mistake. That there is a certain relation between capital and labour, I admit. That it does exist, and rightfully exist, I think is true. That men who are industrious and sober and honest in the pursuit of their own interests should after a while accumulate capital, and after that should be allowed to enjoy it in peace, and also if they should choose, when they have accumulated it, to use it to save themselves from actual labour, and hire other people to labour for them – is right. In doing so, they do not wrong the man they employ, for they find men who have not their own land to work upon, or shops to work in, and who are benefited by working for others – hired labourers, receiving their capital for it. Thus a few men that own capital hire a few others, and these establish the relation of capital and labour rightfully – a relation of which I make no complaint. But I insist that that relation, after all, does not embrace more than one-eighth of the labour of the country.

There are a plenty of men in the slave States that are altogether good enough for me, to be either President or Vice-President, provided they will profess their sympathy with our purpose, and will place themselves on such ground that our men upon principle can vote for them. There are scores of them – good men in their character for intelligence, for talent and integrity. If such an one will place himself upon the right ground, I am for his occupying one place upon the next Republican or opposition ticket. I will go heartily for him. But unless he does so place himself, I think it is perfect nonsense to attempt to bring about a union upon any other basis; that if a union be made, the elements will so scatter that there can be no success for such a ticket. The good old maxims of the Bible are applicable, and truly applicable, to human affairs; and in this, as in other things, we may say that he who is not for us is against us; he who gathereth not with us, scattereth. I should be glad to have some of the many good and able and noble men of the South place themselves where we can confer upon them the high honour of an election upon one or the other end of our ticket. It would do my soul good to do that thing. It would enable us to teach them that inasmuch as we select one of their own number to carry out our principles, we are free from the charge that we mean more than we say. . . .

From a Letter to J. W. Fell. December 20, 1859

I was born February 12, 1809, in Hardin County, Kentucky. My parents were both born in Virginia, of undistinguished families – second families, perhaps I should say. My mother, who died in my tenth year, was of a family of the name of Hanks, some of whom now reside in Adams, and others in Macon County, Illinois. My paternal grandfather, Abraham Lincoln, emigrated from Rocking-ham County, Virginia, to Kentucky about 1781 or 1782, where a year or two later he was killed by the Indians, not in battle, but by stealth, when he was labouring to open a farm in the forest. His ancestors, who were Quakers, went to Virginia from Berks County, Pennsylvania. An effort to identify them with the New England family of the same name ended in nothing more definite than a similarity of Christian names in both families, such as Enoch, Levi, Mordecai, Solomon, Abraham, and the like.

My father, at the death of his father, was but six years of age, and he grew up literally without education. He removed from Kentucky to what is now Spencer County, Indiana, in my eighth year. We reached our new home about the time the State came into the Union. It was a wild region, with many bears and other wild animals still in the woods. There I grew up. There were some schools, so called, but no qualification was ever required of a teacher beyond 'readin', writin', and cipherin'' to the rule of three. If a straggler supposed to understand Latin happened to sojourn in the neighbourhood, he was looked upon as a wizard. There was absolutely nothing to excite ambition for education. Of course, when I came of age I did not know much. Still, somehow, I could read, write, and cipher to the rule of three, but that was all. I have not been to school since. The little advance I now have upon this store of education I have picked up from time to time under the pressure of necessity.

I was raised to farm work, which I continued till I was twenty-two. At twenty-one I came to Illinois, Macon County. Then I got to New Salem, at that time in Sangamon, now in Menard County, where I remained a year as a sort of clerk in a store.

Then came the Black Hawk War; and I was elected a captain of volunteers, a success which gave me more pleasure than any I have had since. I went the campaign, was elated, ran for the legislature the same year (1832), and was beaten – the only time I ever have been beaten by the people. The next and three succeeding biennial elections I was elected to the legislature. I was not a candidate afterward. During this legislative period I had studied law, and removed to Springfield to practise it. In 1846 I was once elected to the lower House of Congress. Was not a candidate for re-election. From 1849 to 1854, both inclusive, practised law more assiduously than ever before. Always a Whig in politics; and generally on the Whig electoral tickets, making active canvasses. I was losing interest in politics when the repeal of the Missouri Compromise aroused me again. What I have done since then is pretty well known.

If any personal description of me is thought desirable, it may be said I am, in height, six feet four inches, nearly; lean in flesh, weighing on an average one hundred and eighty pounds; dark complexion, with coarse black hair and gray eyes. No other marks or brands recollected.

From an Address delivered at Cooper Institute, New York.
February 27, 1860

. . . Now, and hear, let me guard a little against being misunderstood. I do not mean to say we are bound to follow implicitly in whatever our fathers did. To do so, would be to discard all the lights of current experience – to reject all progress, all improvement. What I do say is, that if we would supplant the opinions and policy of our fathers in any case, we should do so on evidence so conclusive, and argument so clear, that even their great authority, fairly considered and weighed, cannot stand; and most surely not in a case whereof we ourselves declare they understood the question better than we.

If any man at this day sincerely believes that the proper division of local from Federal authority, or any part of the Constitution, forbids the Federal Government to control as to slavery in the Federal Territories, he is right to say so, and to enforce his position by all truthful evidence and fair argument he can. But he has no right to mislead others who have less access to history, and less leisure to study it, into the false belief that 'our fathers who framed the government under which we live' were of the same opinion – thus substituting falsehood and deception for truthful evidence and fair argument. If any man at this day sincerely believes 'our fathers who framed the government under which we live' used and applied principles, in other cases, which ought to have led them to understand that a proper division of local from Federal authority, or some part of the Constitution, forbids the Federal Government to control as to slavery in the Federal Territories, he is right to say so. But he should, at the same time, have the responsibility of declaring that, in his opinion, he understands their principles better than they did themselves; and especially should he not shirk the responsibility by asserting that they understood the question just as well and even better than we do now.

But enough! Let all who believe that 'our fathers who framed the government under which we live understood this question just as well, and even better than we do now,' speak as they spoke, and act as they acted upon it. This is all Republicans ask, all Republicans desire, in relation to slavery. As those fathers marked it, so let it again be marked, as an evil not to be extended, but to be tolerated and protected only because of and so far as its actual presence among us makes that toleration and protection a necessity. Let all the guaranties those fathers gave it be not grudgingly, but fully and fairly maintained. For this Republicans contend, and with this, so far as I know or believe, they will be content.

And now, if they would listen – as I suppose they will not – I would address a few words to the Southern people.

I would say to them: You consider yourselves a reasonable and a just people; and I consider that in the general qualities of reason and justice you are not inferior to any other people. Still, when you speak of us Republicans, you do so only to denounce us as reptiles, or, at the best, as no better than outlaws. You will grant a hearing to pirates or murderers, but nothing like it to 'Black Republicans.' In all your contentions with one another, each of you deems an unconditional condemnation of 'Black

Republicanism' as the first thing to be attended to. Indeed, such condemnation of us seems to be an indispensable prerequisite – license, so to speak – among you to be admitted or permitted to speak at all. Now, can you or not be prevailed upon to pause and to consider whether this is quite just to us, or even to yourselves? Bring forward your charges and specifications, and then be patient long enough to hear us deny or justify.

You say we are sectional. We deny it. That makes an issue; and the burden of proof is upon you. You produce your proof; and what is it? Why, that our party has no existence in your section – gets no votes in your section. The fact is substantially true; but does it prove the issue? If it does, then, in case we should, without change of principle, begin to get votes in your section, we should thereby cease to be sectional. You cannot escape this conclusion; and yet, are you willing to abide by it? If you are, you will probably soon find that we have ceased to be sectional, for we shall get votes in your section this very year. You will then begin to discover, as the truth plainly is, that your proof does not touch the issue. The fact that we get no votes in your section is a fact of your making, and not of ours.

And if there be fault in that fact, that fault is primarily yours, and remains so until you show that we repel you by some wrong principle or practice. If we do repel you by any wrong principle or practice, the fault is ours; but this brings you to where you ought to have started – to a discussion of the right or wrong of our principle. If our principle, put in practice, would wrong your section for the benefit of ours, or for any other object, then our principle, and we with it, are sectional, and are justly opposed and denounced as such. Meet us, then, on the question of whether our principle, put in practice, would wrong your section; and so meet us as if it were possible that something may be said on our side. Do you accept the challenge? No! Then you really believe that the principle which 'our fathers who framed the government under which we live' thought so clearly right as to adopt it, and indorse it again and again, upon their official oaths, is in fact so clearly wrong as to demand your condemnation without a moment's consideration.

Some of you delight to flaunt in our faces the warning against sectional parties given by Washington in his Farewell Address. Less than eight years before Washington gave that warning he had, as President of the United States, approved and signed an act of Congress enforcing the prohibition of slavery in the Northwestern Territory, which act embodied the policy of the government upon that subject up to and at the very moment he penned that warning; and about one year after he penned it, he wrote Lafayette that he considered that prohibition a wise measure, expressing in the same connection his hope that we should at some time have a confederacy of free States.

Bearing this in mind, and seeing that sectionalism has since arisen upon this same subject, is that warning a weapon in your hands against us, or in our hands against you? Could Washington himself speak, would he cast the blame of that sectionalism upon us, who sustain his policy, or upon you, who repudiate it? We respect that warning of Washington, and we commend it to you, together with his example pointing to the right application of it.

But you say you are conservative – eminently conservative – while we are revolutionary, destructive, or something of the sort.

What is conservatism? Is it not adherence to the old and tried, against the new and untried? We stick to, contend for, the identical old policy on the point in controversy which was adopted by 'our fathers who framed the government under which we live'; while you with one accord reject, and scout, and spit upon that old policy, and insist upon substituting something new.

True, you disagree among yourselves as to what that substitute shall be. You are divided on new propositions and plans, but you are unanimous in rejecting and denouncing the old policy of the fathers. Some of you are for reviving the foreign slave-trade; some for a Congressional slave-code for the Territories; some for Congress forbidding the Territories to prohibit slavery within their limits; some for maintaining slavery in the Territories through the judiciary; some for the 'gur-reat pur-rinciple' that 'if one man would enslave another, no third man should object', fantastically called 'popular sovereignty'; but never a man among you is in favour of Federal prohibition of slavery in Federal Territories, according to the practice of 'our fathers who framed the government under which we live.' Not one of all your various plans can show a precedent or an advocate in the century within which our government originated.

Consider, then, whether your claim for conservatism for yourselves, and your charge of destructiveness against us, are based on the most clear and stable foundations.

Again, you say we have made the slavery question more prominent than it formerly was. We deny it. We admit that it is more prominent, but we deny that we made it so. It was not we, but you, who discarded the old policy of the fathers. We resisted, and still resist, your innovation; and thence comes the greater prominence of the question. Would you have that question reduced to its former proportions? Go back to that old policy. What has been will be again, under the same conditions. If you would have the peace of the old times, readopt the precepts and policy of the old times.

You charge that we stir up insurrections among your slaves. We deny it; and what is your proof? Harper's Ferry! John Brown! John Brown was no Republican; and you have failed to implicate a single Republican in his Harper's Ferry enterprise. If any member of our party is guilty in that matter, you know it, or you do not know it. If you do know it, you are inexcusable for not designating the man and proving the fact. If you do not know it, you are inexcusable for asserting it, and especially for persisting in the assertion after you have tried and failed to make the proof. You need not be told that persisting in a charge which one does not know to be true is simply malicious slander.

Some of you admit that no Republican designedly aided or encouraged the Harper's Ferry affair, but still insist that our doctrines and declarations necessarily lead to such results. We do not believe it. We know we hold no doctrine, and make no declaration, which were not held to and made by 'our fathers who framed the government under which we live'. You never dealt fairly by us in relation to this affair. When it occurred, some important State elections were near at hand, and you were in evident glee with the belief that, by charging the blame upon us, you could get an advantage of us in those elections. The elections came, and your expectations were not quite fulfilled. Every Republican man knew that, as to himself at least, your charge was a slander, and he was not much inclined by it to cast his vote in your favour. Republican doctrines and declarations are accompanied with a continual protest against any interference whatever with your slaves, or with you about your slaves. Surely this does not encourage them to revolt. True, we do, in common with 'our fathers who framed the government under which we live', declare our belief that slavery is wrong; but the slaves do not hear us declare even this. For anything we say or do, the slaves would scarcely know there is a Republican party. I believe they would not, in fact, generally know it but for your misrepresentations of us in their hearing. In your political contests among yourselves, each faction charges the other with sympathy with Black Republicanism; and then, to give point to the charge, defines Black Republicanism to simply be insurrection, blood, and thunder among the slaves.

Slave insurrections are no more common now than they were before the Republican party was organized. What induced the Southampton insurrection, twenty-eight years ago, in which at least three times as many lives were lost as at Harper's Ferry? You can scarcely stretch your very elastic fancy to the conclusion that Southampton was 'got up by Black Republicanism'. In the present state of things in the United States, I do not think a general, or even a very extensive, slave insurrection is possible. The indispensable concert of action cannot be attained. The slaves have no means of rapid communication; nor can incendiary freemen, black or white, supply it. The explosive materials are everywhere in parcels; but there neither are, nor can be supplied, the indispensable connecting trains.

Much is said by Southern people about the affection of slaves for their masters and mistresses; and a part of it, at least, is true. A plot for an uprising could scarcely be devised and communicated to twenty individuals before some one of them, to save the life of a favourite master or mistress, would divulge it. This is the rule; and the slave revolution in Haiti was not an exception to it, but a case occurring under peculiar circumstances. The Gunpowder Plot of British history, though not connected with slaves, was more in point. In that case, only about twenty were admitted to the secret; and yet one of them, in his anxiety to save a friend, betrayed the plot to that friend, and, by consequence, averted the calamity. Occasional poisonings from the kitchen, and open or stealthy assassinations in the field, and local revolts extending to a score or so, will continue to occur as the natural results of slavery; but no general insurrection of slaves, as I think, can happen in this country for a long time. Whoever much fears, or much hopes, for such an event, will be alike disappointed.

In the language of Mr Jefferson, uttered many years ago, 'It is still in our power to direct the process of emancipation and deportation peaceably, and in such slow degrees as that the evil will wear off insensibly, and their places be, *pari passu*, filled up by free white labourers. If, on the contrary, it is left to force itself on, human nature must shudder at the prospect held up.'

Mr Jefferson did not mean to say, nor do I, that the power of emancipation is in the Federal Government. He spoke of Virginia; and, as to the power of emancipation, I speak of the slaveholding States only. The Federal Government, however, as we insist, has the power of restraining the extension of the institution – the power to insure that a slave insurrection shall never occur on any American soil which is now free from slavery.

John Brown's effort was peculiar. It was not a slave insurrection. It was an attempt by white men to get up a revolt among slaves, in which the slaves refused to participate. In fact, it was so absurd that the slaves, with all their ignorance, saw plainly enough it could not succeed. That affair, in its philosophy, corresponds with the many attempts, related in history, at the assassination of kings and emperors. An enthusiast broods over the oppression of a people till he fancies himself commissioned by Heaven to liberate them. He ventures the attempt, which ends in little else than his own execution. Orsini's attempt on Louis Napoleon, and John Brown's attempt at Harper's Ferry, were, in their philosophy, precisely the same. The eagerness to cast blame on Old England in the one case, and on New England in the other, does not disprove the sameness of the two things.

And how much would it avail you if you could, by the use of John Brown, Helper's book, and the like, break up the Republican organization? Human action can be modified to some extent, but human nature cannot be changed. There is a judgment and a feeling against slavery in this nation, which cast at least a million and a half of votes. You cannot destroy that judgment and feeling – that sentiment – by breaking up the political organization which rallies around it. You can scarcely scatter and disperse an army which has been formed into order in the face of your heaviest fire; but if you could, how much would you gain by forcing the sentiment which created it out of the peaceful channel of the ballot-box into some other channel? What would that other channel probably be? Would the number of John Browns be lessened or enlarged by the operation?

But you will break up the Union rather than submit to a denial of your constitutional rights.

That has a somewhat reckless sound; but it would be palliated, if not fully justified, were we proposing, by the mere force of numbers, to deprive you of some right plainly written down in the Constitution. But we are proposing no such thing.

When you make these declarations you have a specific and well-understood allusion to an assumed constitutional right of yours to take slaves into the Federal Territories, and to hold them there as property. But no such right is specifically written in the Constitution. That instrument is literally silent about any such right. We, on the contrary, deny that such a right has any existence in the Constitution, even by implication.

Your purpose, then, plainly stated, is that you will destroy the government, unless you be allowed to construe and force the Constitution as you please, on all points in dispute between you and us. You will rule or ruin in all events.

This, plainly stated, is your language. Perhaps you will say the Supreme Court has decided the disputed constitutional question in your favour. Not quite so. But waiving the lawyer's distinction between dictum and decision, the court has decided the question for you in a sort of way. The court has substantially said, it is your constitutional right to take slaves into the Federal Territories, and to hold them there as property. When I say the decision was made in a sort of way, I mean it was made in a divided court, by a bare majority of the judges, and they not quite agreeing with one another in the reasons for making it; that it is so made as that its avowed supporters disagree with one another about its meaning, and that it was mainly based upon a mistaken statement of fact – the statement in the opinion that 'the right of property in a slave is distinctly and expressly affirmed in the Constitution'.

An inspection of the Constitution will show that the right of property in a slave is not 'distinctly and expressly affirmed' in it. Bear in mind, the judges do not pledge their judicial opinion that such right is impliedly affirmed in the Constitution; but they pledge their veracity that it is 'distinctly and expressly' affirmed there – 'distinctly', that is, not mingled with anything else; 'expressly', that is, in words meaning just that, without the aid of any inference, and susceptible of no other meaning.

If they had only pledged their judicial opinion that such right is affirmed in the instrument by implication, it would be open to others to show that neither the word 'slave' nor 'slavery' is to be found in the Constitution, nor the word 'property', even, in any connection with language alluding to the things slave or slavery; and that wherever in that instrument the slave is alluded to, he is called a 'person'; and wherever his master's legal right in relation to him is alluded to, it is spoken of as 'service or labour which may be due' – as a debt payable in service or labour. Also it would be open to show, by contemporaneous history, that this mode of alluding to slaves and slavery, instead of speaking of them, was employed on purpose to exclude from the Constitution the idea that there could be property in man.

To show all this is easy and certain.

When this obvious mistake of the judges shall be brought to their notice, is it not reasonable to expect that they will withdraw the mistaken statement, and reconsider the conclusion based upon it?

And then it is to be remembered that 'our fathers who framed the government under which we live' – the men who made the Constitution – decided this same constitutional question in our favour long ago; decided it without division among themselves when making the decision; without division among themselves about the meaning of it after it was made, and, so far as any evidence is left, without basing it upon any mistaken statement of facts.

Under all these circumstances, do you really feel yourselves justified to break up this government unless such a court decision as yours is shall be at once submitted to as a conclusive and final rule of political action? But you will not abide the election of a Republican President! In that supposed event, you say, you will destroy the Union; and then, you say, the great crime of having destroyed it will be upon us! That is cool. A highwayman holds a pistol to my ear, and mutters through his teeth, 'Stand and deliver, or I shall kill you, and then you will be a murderer!'

To be sure, what the robber demanded of me – my money – was my own; and I had a clear right to keep it; but it was no more my own than my vote is my own; and the threat of death to me, to extort my money, and the threat of destruction to the Union, to extort my vote, can scarcely be distinguished in principle.

*   *   *

Wrong as we think slavery is, we can yet afford to let it alone where it is, because that much is due to the necessity arising from its actual presence in the nation; but can we, while our votes will prevent it, allow it to spread into the national Territories, and to overrun us here in these free States? If our sense of duty forbids this, then let us stand by our duty fearlessly and effectively. Let us be diverted by none of those sophistical contrivances wherewith we are so industriously plied and belaboured – contrivances such as groping for some middle ground between the right and the wrong, vain as the search for a man who should be neither a living man nor a dead man; such as a policy of 'don't care', on a question about which all true men do care; such as Union appeals beseeching true Union men to yield to disunionists, reversing the Divine rule, and calling not the sinners, but the righteous to repentance; such as invocations to Washington, imploring men to unsay what Washington said, and undo what Washington did.

Neither let us be slandered from our duty by false accusations against us, nor frightened from it by menaces of destruction to the government, nor of dungeons to ourselves. Let us have faith that right makes might, and in that faith let us to the end dare to do our duty as we understand it.

A Letter to the Hon. Geo. Ashmun accepting his Nomination for the Presidency. May 23, 1860

I accept the nomination tendered me by the Convention over which you presided, and of which I am formally apprized in the letter of yourself and others, acting as a committee of the Convention for that purpose.

The declaration of principles and sentiments which accompanies your letter, meets my approval; and it shall be my care not to violate or disregard it in any part.

Imploring the assistance of Divine Providence, and with due regard to the views and feelings of all who were represented in the Convention; to the rights of all the States and Territories and people of the nation; to the inviolability of the Constitution; and the perpetual union, harmony, and prosperity of all – I am most happy to co-operate for the practical success of the principles declared by the Convention.

Your obliged friend and fellow-citizen,

A. LINCOLN

Letter to Miss Grace Bedell. Springfield, Illinois.
October 19, 1860

My dear little Miss, Your very agreeable letter of the 15th is received. I regret the necessity of saying I have no daughter. I have three sons – one seventeen, one nine, and one seven years of age. They, with their mother, constitute my whole family. As to the whiskers, having never worn any, do you not think people would call it a piece of silly affectation if I were to begin it now?

Lincoln's Farewell Address at Springfield, Illinois.
February 11, 1861

My Friends, No one not in my situation can appreciate my feeling of sadness at this parting. To this place, and the kindness of these people, I owe everything. Here I have lived a quarter of a century, and have passed from a young to an old man. Here my children have been born, and one is buried. I now leave, not knowing when or whether ever I may return, with a task before me greater than that which rested upon Washington. Without the assistance of that Divine Being who ever attended him I cannot succeed. With that assistance I cannot fail. Trusting in Him, who can go with me and remain with you, and be everywhere for good, let us confidently hope that all will yet be well. To His care commending you, as I hope in your prayers you will commend me, I bid you an affectionate farewell.

From an Address to the Legislature at Indianapolis, Indiana.
February 12, 1861

Fellow-citizens of the State of Indiana, I am here to thank you much for this magnificent welcome, and still more for the generous support given by your State to that political cause which I think is the true and just cause of the whole country and the whole world.

Solomon says 'there is a time to keep silence', and when men wrangle by the mouth with no certainty that they mean the same thing while using the same word, it perhaps were as well if they would keep silence.

The words 'coercion' and 'invasion' are much used in these days, and often with some temper and hot blood. Let us make sure, if we can, that we do not misunderstand the meaning of those who use them. Let us get exact definitions of these words, not from dictionaries, but from the men themselves, who certainly deprecate the things they would represent by the use of words. What then is *coercion*? What is *invasion*? Would the marching of an army into South Carolina, without the consent of her people and with hostile intent towards them, be invasion? I certainly think it would; and it would be coercion also, if the South Carolinians were forced to submit. But if the United States should merely retake and hold its own forts and other property, and collect the duties on foreign importations, or even withhold the mails from places where they were habitually violated, would any or all these things be invasion or coercion? Do our professed lovers of the Union, but who spitefully resolve that they will resist coercion and invasion, understand that such things as these, on the part of the United States, would be coercion or invasion of a State? If so, their idea of means to preserve the object of their affection would seem exceedingly thin and airy. If sick, the little pills of the homoeopathist would be much too large for them to swallow. In their view, the Union as a family relation would seem to be no regular marriage, but a sort of free-love arrangement to be maintained only on *passional attraction*.

By the way, in what consists the special sacredness of a State? I speak not of the position assigned to a State in the Union by the Constitution; for that, by the bond, we all recognize. That position, however, a State cannot carry out of the Union with it. I speak of that assumed primary right of a State to rule all which is *less* than itself, and ruin all which is larger than itself. If a State and a county in a given case should be equal in extent of territory, and equal in number of inhabitants, in what, as a matter of principle, is the State better than the county? Would an exchange of *names* be an exchange of *rights* upon principle? On what rightful principle may a State, being not more than one-fiftieth part of the nation in soil and population, break up the nation, and then coerce a proportionally larger subdivision of itself in the most arbitrary way? What mysterious right to play tyrant is conferred on a district of country, with its people, by merely calling it a State?

Fellow-citizens, I am not asserting anything: I am merely asking questions for you to consider. And now allow me to bid you farewell.

From his Address to the Legislature at Columbus, Ohio.
February 13, 1861

It is true, as has been said by the president of the Senate, that a very great responsibility rests upon me in the position to which the votes of the American people have called me. I am deeply sensible of that weighty responsibility. I cannot but know, what you all know, that without a name, perhaps without a reason why I should have a name, there has fallen upon me a task such as did not rest even upon the Father of his Country; and so feeling, I cannot but turn and look for that support without which it will be impossible for me to perform that great task. I turn then, and look to the great American people, and to that God who has never forsaken them. Allusion has been made to the interest felt in relation to the policy of the new Administration. In this I have received from some a degree of credit for having kept silence, and from others, some deprecation. I still think I was right.

In the varying and repeatedly shifting scenes of the present, and without a precedent which could enable me to judge by the past, it has seemed fitting that before speaking upon the difficulties of the country, I should have gained a view of the whole field, being at liberty to modify and change the course of policy as future events may make a change necessary.

I have not maintained silence from any want of real anxiety. It is a good thing that there is no more than anxiety, for there is nothing going wrong. It is a consoling circumstance that when we look out, there is nothing that really hurts anybody. We entertain different views upon political questions, but nobody is suffering anything. This is a most consoling circumstance, and from it we may conclude that all we want is time, patience, and a reliance on that God who has never forsaken this people.

From his Remarks at Pittsburgh, Pennsylvania. February 15, 1861

. . . The condition of the country is an extraordinary one, and fills the mind of every patriot with anxiety. It is my intention to give this subject all the consideration I possibly can, before specially deciding in regard to it, so that when I do speak, it may be as nearly right as possible. When I do speak, I hope I may say nothing in opposition to the spirit of the Constitution, contrary to the integrity of the Union, or which will prove inimical to the liberties of the people or to the peace of the whole country. And furthermore, when the time arrives for me to speak on this great subject, I hope I may say nothing to disappoint the people generally throughout the country, especially if the expectation has been based upon anything which I have heretofore said.

. . . If the great American people only keep their temper on both sides of the line, the troubles will come to an end, and the question which now distracts the country will be settled, just as surely as all other difficulties of a like character which have originated in this government have been adjusted. Let the people on both sides keep their self-possession, and just as other clouds have cleared away in due time, so will this great nation continue to prosper as heretofore.

. . . It is often said that the tariff is the specialty of Pennsylvania. Assuming that direct taxation is not to be adopted, the tariff question must be as durable as the government itself. It is a question of national house-keeping. It is to the government what replenishing the meal-tub is to the family. Ever-varying circumstances will require frequent modifications as to the amount needed and the sources of supply. So far there is little difference of opinion among the people. It is only whether, and how far, duties on imports shall be adjusted to favour home productions. In the home market that controversy begins. One party insists that too much protection oppresses one class for the advantage of another; while the other party argues that, with all its incidents, in the long run all classes are benefited. In the Chicago platform there is a plank upon this subject, which should be a general law to the incoming Administration. We should do neither more nor less than we gave the people reason to believe we would when they gave us their votes. That plank is as I now read:

> That while providing revenue for the support of the general government by duties upon imports, sound policy requires such an adjustment of these imposts as will encourage the development of the industrial interest of the whole country; and we commend that policy of national exchanges which secures to working-men liberal wages, to agriculture remunerating prices, to mechanics and manufacturers adequate reward for their skill, labour, and enterprise, and to the nation commercial prosperity and independence.

. . . My political education strongly inclines me against a very free use of any of the means by the Executive to control the legislation of the country. As a rule, I think it better that Congress should originate as well as perfect its measures without external bias. I therefore would rather recommend to every gentleman who knows he is to be a member of the next Congress, to take an enlarged view, and post himself thoroughly, so as to contribute his part to such an adjustment of the tariff as shall provide a sufficient revenue, and in its other bearings, so far as possible, be just and equal to all sections of the country and classes of the people.

Address at Utica, New York. February 18, 1861

Ladies and Gentlemen, I have no speech to make to you, and no time to speak in. I appear before you that I may see you, and that you may see me; and I am willing to admit, that, so far as the ladies are concerned, I have the best of the bargain, though I wish it to be understood that I do not make the same acknowledgment concerning the men.

From his Speech at Trenton to the Senate of New Jersey.
February 21, 1861

. . . I cannot but remember the place that New Jersey holds in our early history. In the early Revolutionary struggle few of the States among the old thirteen had more of the battlefields of the country within their limits than old New Jersey. May I be pardoned if, upon this occasion, I mention that away back in my childhood, the earliest days of my being able to read, I got hold of a small book, such a one as few of the younger members have ever seen – *Weems's Life of Washington.* I remember all the accounts there given of the battlefields and struggles for the liberties of the country, and none fixed themselves upon my imagination so deeply as the struggle here at Trenton, New Jersey. The crossing of the river, the contest with the Hessians, the great hardships endured at that time – all fixed themselves upon my memory more than any single Revolutionary event; and you all know, for you have all been boys, how those early impressions last longer than any others. I recollect thinking then, boy even though I was, that there must have been something more than common that these men struggled for. I am exceedingly anxious that that thing – that something even more than national independence; that something that held out a great promise to all the people of the world for all time to come – I am exceedingly anxious that this Union, the Constitution, and the liberties of the people shall be perpetuated in accordance with the original idea for which the struggle was made, and I shall be most happy indeed if I shall be an humble instrument in the hands of the Almighty, and of this, His most chosen people, for perpetuating the object of that great struggle.

Address in Independence Hall, Philadelphia. February 22, 1861

I am filled with deep emotion at finding myself standing in this place, where were collected together the wisdom, the patriotism, the devotion to principle, from which sprang the institutions under which we live.

You have kindly suggested to me that in my hands is the task of restoring peace to our distracted country. I can say in return, sir, that all the political sentiments I entertain have been drawn, so far as I have been able to draw them, from the sentiments which originated in and were given to the world from this hall. I have never had a feeling, politically, that did not spring from the sentiments embodied in the Declaration of Independence.

I have often pondered over the dangers which were incurred by the men who assembled here and framed and adopted that Declaration. I have pondered over the toils that were endured by the officers and soldiers of the army who achieved that independence. I have often inquired of myself what great principle or idea it was that kept this Confederacy so long together. It was not the mere matter of separation of the colonies from the motherland, but that sentiment in the Declaration of Independence which gave liberty not alone to the people of this country, but hope to all the world, for all future time. It was that which gave promise that in due time the weights would be lifted from the shoulders of all men, and that all should have an equal chance. This is the sentiment embodied in the Declaration of Independence.

Now, my friends, can this country be saved on that basis? If it can, I will consider myself one of the happiest men in the world if I can help to save it. If it cannot be saved upon that principle, it will be truly awful. But if this country cannot be saved without giving up that principle, I was about to say I would rather be assassinated on this spot than surrender it.

Now, in my view of the present aspect of affairs, there is no need of bloodshed and war. There is no necessity for it. I am not in favour of such a course; and I may say in advance that there will be no bloodshed unless it is forced upon the government. The government will not use force unless force is used against it.

My friends, this is wholly an unprepared speech. I did not expect to be called on to say a word when I came here. I supposed I was merely to do something toward raising a flag. I may, therefore, have said something indiscreet. But I have said nothing but what I am willing to live by, and, if it be the pleasure of Almighty God, to die by.

Reply to the Mayor of Washington, D.C. February 27, 1861
Mr Mayor, I thank you, and through you the municipal authorities of this city who accompany you, for this welcome. And as it is the first time in my life, since the present phase of politics has presented itself in this country, that I have said anything publicly

within a region of country where the institution of slavery exists, I will take this occasion to say that I think very much of the ill-feeling that has existed and still exists between the people in the section from which I came and the people here, is dependent upon a misunderstanding of one another. I therefore avail myself of this opportunity to assure you, Mr Mayor, and all the gentlemen present, that I have not now, and never have had, any other than as kindly feelings towards you as to the people of my own section. I have not now and never have had any disposition to treat you in any respect otherwise than as my own neighbours. I have not now any purpose to withhold from you any of the benefits of the Constitution under any circumstances, that I would not feel myself constrained to withhold from my own neighbours; and I hope, in a word, that when we become better acquainted – and I say it with great confidence – we shall like each other the more. I thank you for the kindness of this reception.

First Inaugural Address. March 4, 1861

Fellow-citizens of the United States, In compliance with a custom as old as the government itself, I appear before you to address you briefly, and to take in your presence the oath prescribed by the Constitution of the United States to be taken by the President 'before he enters on the execution of his office'.

I do not consider it necessary at present for me to discuss those matters of administration about which there is no special anxiety or excitement.

Apprehension seems to exist among the people of the Southern States that by the accession of a Republican administration their property and their peace and personal security are to be endangered. There has never been any reasonable cause for such apprehension. Indeed, the most ample evidence to the contrary has all the while existed and been open to their inspection. It is found in nearly all the published speeches of him who now addresses you. I do but quote from one of those speeches when I declare that 'I have no purpose, directly or indirectly, to interfere with the institution of slavery in the States where it exists. I believe I have no lawful right to do so, and I have no inclination to do so.' Those who nominated and elected me did so with full knowledge that I had made this and many similar declarations, and had never recanted them. And, more than this, they placed in the platform for my acceptance, and as a law to themselves and to me, the clear and emphatic resolution which I now read –

> *Resolved*, That the maintenance inviolate of the rights of the States, and especially the right of each State to order and control its own domestic institutions according to its own judgment exclusively, is essential to that balance of power on which the perfection and endurance of our political fabric depend, and we denounce the lawless invasion by armed force of the soil of any State or Territory, no matter under what pretext, as among the gravest of crimes.

I now reiterate these sentiments; and, in doing so, I only press upon the public attention the most conclusive evidence of which the case is susceptible, that the property, peace, and security of no section are to be in any wise endangered by the now incoming administration. I add, too, that all the protection which, consistently with the Constitution and the laws, can be given, will be cheerfully given to all the States when lawfully demanded, for whatever cause – as cheerfully to one section as to another.

There is much controversy about the delivering up of fugitives from service or labour. The clause I now read is as plainly written in the Constitution as any other of its provisions –

> No person held to service or labour in one State, under the laws thereof, escaping into another, shall in consequence of any law or regulation therein be discharged from such service or labour, but shall be delivered up on claim of the party to whom such service or labour may be due.

It is scarcely questioned that this provision was intended by those who made it for the reclaiming of what we call fugitive slaves; and the intention of the lawgiver is the law. All members of Congress swear their support to the whole Constitution – to this provision as much as to any other. To the proposition, then, that slaves whose cases come within the terms of this clause 'shall be delivered up', their oaths are unanimous. Now, if they would make the effort in good temper, could they not with nearly equal unanimity frame and pass a law by means of which to keep good that unanimous oath?

There is some difference of opinion whether this clause should be enforced by national or by State authority; but surely that difference is not a very material one. If the slave is to be surrendered, it can be of but little consequence to him or to others by which authority it is done. And should anyone in any case be content that his oath shall go unkept on a merely unsubstantial controversy as to how it shall be kept?

Again, in any law upon this subject, ought not all the safeguards of liberty known in civilized and humane jurisprudence to be introduced, so that a free man be not, in any case, surrendered as a slave? And might it not be well at the same time to provide by law for the enforcement of that clause in the Constitution which guarantees that 'the citizen of each State shall be entitled to all privileges and immunities of citizens in the several States'?

I take the official oath today with no mental reservations, and with no purpose to construe the Constitution or laws by any hypercritical rules. And while I do not choose now to specify particular acts of Congress as proper to be enforced, I do suggest that it will be much safer for all, both in official and private stations, to conform to and abide by all those acts which stand unrepealed, than to violate any of them, trusting to find impunity in having them held to be unconstitutional.

It is seventy-two years since the first inauguration of a President under our National Constitution. During that period fifteen different and greatly distinguished citizens have, in succession, administered the executive branch of the government. They have conducted it through many perils, and generally with great success. Yet, with all this scope of precedent, I now enter upon the same task for the brief constitutional term of four years under great and peculiar difficulty. A disruption of the Federal Union, heretofore only menaced, is now formidably attempted.

I hold that, in contemplation of universal law and of the Constitution, the Union of these States is perpetual. Perpetuity is implied, if not expressed, in the fundamental law of all national governments. It is safe to assert that no government proper ever had a provision in its organic law for its own termination.

Continue to execute all the express provisions of our National Constitution, and the Union will endure for ever – it being impossible to destroy it except by some action not provided for in the instrument itself.

Again, if the United States be not a government proper, but an association of States in the nature of contract merely, can it, as a contract, be peaceably unmade by less than all the parties who made it? One party to a contract may violate it – break it, so to speak; but does it not require all to lawfully rescind it?

Descending from these general principles, we find the proposition that in legal contemplation the Union is perpetual confirmed by the history of the Union itself. The Union is much older than the Constitution. It was formed, in fact, by the Articles of Association in 1774. It was matured and continued by the Declaration of Independence in 1776. It was further matured, and the faith of all the then thirteen States expressly plighted and engaged that it should be perpetual, by the Articles of Confederation in 1778. And, finally, in 1787 one of the declared objects for ordaining and establishing the Constitution was 'to form a more perfect Union'.

But if the destruction of the Union by one or by a part only of the States be lawfully possible, the Union is less perfect than before the Constitution, having lost the vital element of perpetuity.

It follows from these views that no State upon its own mere motion can lawfully get out of the Union; that resolves and ordinances to that effect are legally void; and that acts of violence, within any State or States, against the authority of the United States, are insurrectionary or revolutionary, according to circumstances.

I therefore consider that, in view of the Constitution and the laws, the Union is unbroken; and to the extent of my ability I shall take care, as the Constitution itself expressly enjoins upon me, that the laws of the Union be faithfully executed in all the States. Doing this I deem to be only a simple duty on my part; and I shall perform it so far as practicable, unless my rightful masters, the American people, shall withhold the requisite means, or in some authoritative manner direct the contrary. I trust this will not be regarded as a menace, but only as the declared purpose of the Union that it will constitutionally defend and maintain itself.

In doing this there needs to be no bloodshed or violence; and there shall be none, unless it be forced upon the national authority.

The power confided to me will be used to hold, occupy, and possess the property and places belonging to the government, and to collect the duties and imposts; but beyond what may be necessary for these objects, there will be no invasion, no using of force against or among the people anywhere. Where hostility to the United States, in any interior locality, shall be so great and universal as to prevent competent resident citizens from holding the Federal offices, there will be no attempt to force obnoxious strangers among the people for that object. While the strict legal right may exist in the government to enforce the exercise of these offices, the attempt to do so would be so irritating, and so nearly impracticable withal, that I deem it better to forego for the time the uses of such offices.

The mails, unless repelled, will continue to be furnished in all parts of the Union. So far as possible, the people everywhere shall have that sense of perfect security which is most favourable to calm thought and reflection. The course here indicated will be followed unless current events and experience shall show a modification or change to be proper, and in every case and exigency my best discretion will be exercised according to circumstances actually existing, and with a view and a hope of a peaceful solution of the national troubles and the restoration of fraternal sympathies and affections.

That there are persons in one section or another who seek to destroy the Union at all events, and are glad of any pretext to do it, I will neither affirm nor deny; but if there be such, I need address no word to them. To those, however, who really love the Union may I not speak?

Before entering upon so grave a matter as the destruction of our national fabric, with all its benefits, its memories, and its hopes, would it not be wise to ascertain precisely why we do it? Will you hazard so desperate a step while there is any possibility that any portion of the ills you fly from have no real existence? Will you, while the certain ills you fly to are greater than all the real ones you fly from – will you risk the commission of so fearful a mistake?

All profess to be content in the Union if all constitutional rights can be maintained. Is it true, then, that any right, plainly written in the Constitution, has been denied? I think not. Happily the human mind is so constituted that no party can reach to the audacity of doing this. Think, if you can, of a single instance in which a plainly written provision of the Constitution has ever been denied. If by the mere force of numbers a majority should deprive a minority of any clearly written constitutional right, it might, in a moral point of view, justify revolution – certainly would if such a right were a vital one. But such is not our case. All the vital rights of minorities and of individuals are so plainly assured to them by affirmations and negations, guaranties and prohibitions, in the Constitution, that controversies never arise concerning them. But no organic law can ever be framed with a provision specifically applicable to every question which may occur in practical administration. No foresight can anticipate, nor any document of reasonable length contain, express provisions for all possible questions. Shall fugitives from labour be surrendered by national or by State authority? The Constitution does not expressly say. *May* Congress prohibit slavery in the Territories? The Constitution does not expressly say. *Must* Congress protect slavery in the Territories? The Constitution does not expressly say.

From questions of this class spring all our constitutional controversies, and we divide upon them into majorities and minorities. If the minority will not acquiesce, the majority must, or the government must cease. There is no other alternative; for continuing the government is acquiescence on one side or the other.

If a minority in such case will secede rather than acquiesce, they make a precedent which in turn will divide and ruin them; for a minority of their own will secede from them whenever a majority refuses to be controlled by such minority. For instance, why may not any portion of a new confederacy a year or two hence arbitrarily secede again, precisely as portions of the present Union now claim to secede from it? All who cherish disunion sentiments are now being educated to the exact temper of doing this.

Is there such perfect identity of interests among the States to compose a new Union, as to produce harmony only, and prevent renewed secession?

Plainly, the central idea of secession is the essence of anarchy. A majority held in restraint by constitutional checks and limitations, and always changing easily with deliberate changes of popular opinions and sentiments, is the only true sovereign of a free people. Whoever rejects it does, of necessity, fly to anarchy or to despotism. Unanimity is impossible; the rule of a minority, as a permanent arrangement, is wholly inadmissible; so that, rejecting the majority principle, anarchy or despotism in some form is all that is left.

I do not forget the position, assumed by some, that constitutional questions are to be decided by the Supreme Court; nor do I deny that such decisions must be binding, in any case, upon the parties to a suit, as to the object of that suit, while they are also entitled to very high respect and consideration in all parallel cases by all other departments of the government. And while it is obviously possible that such decision may be erroneous in any given case, still the evil effect following it, being limited to that particular case, with the chance that it may be overruled and never become a precedent for other cases, can better be borne than could the evils of a different practice. At the same time, the candid citizen must confess that if the policy of the government, upon vital questions affecting the whole people, is to be irrevocably fixed by decisions of the Supreme Court, the instant they are made, in ordinary litigation between parties in personal actions, the people will have ceased to be their own rulers, having to that extent practically resigned their government into the hands of that eminent tribunal. Nor is there in this view any assault upon the court or the judges. It is a duty from which they may not shrink to decide cases properly brought before them, and it is no fault of theirs if others seek to turn their decisions to political purposes.

One section of our country believes slavery is right, and ought to be extended, while the other believes it is wrong, and ought not to be extended. This is the only substantial dispute. The fugitive-slave clause of the Constitution, and the law for the suppression of the foreign slave-trade, are each as well enforced, perhaps, as any law can ever be in a community where the moral sense of the people imperfectly supports the law itself. The great body of the people abide by the dry legal obligation in both cases, and a few break over in each. This, I think, cannot be perfectly cured; and it would be worse in both cases after the separation of the sections than before. The foreign slave-trade, now imperfectly suppressed, would be ultimately revived, without restriction, in one section, while fugitive slaves, now only partially surrendered, would not be surrendered at all by the other.

Physically speaking, we cannot separate. We cannot remove our respective sections from each other, nor build an impassable wall between them. A husband and wife may be divorced, and go out of the presence and beyond the reach of each other; but the different parts of our country cannot do this. They cannot but remain face to face, and intercourse, either amicable or hostile, must continue between them. Is it possible, then, to make that intercourse more advantageous or more satisfactory after separation than before? Can aliens make treaties easier than friends can make laws? Can treaties be more faithfully enforced between aliens than laws can among friends? Suppose you go to war, you cannot fight always; and when, after much loss on both sides, and no gain on either, you cease fighting, the identical old questions as to terms of intercourse are again upon you.

This country, with its institutions, belongs to the people who inhabit it. Whenever they shall grow weary of the existing government, they can exercise their constitutional right of amending it, or their revolutionary right to dismember or overthrow it. I cannot be ignorant of the fact that many worthy and patriotic citizens are desirous of having the National Constitution amended. While I make no recommendation of amendments, I fully recognize the rightful authority of the people over the whole subject, to be exercised in either of the modes prescribed in the instrument itself; and I should, under existing circumstances, favour rather than oppose a fair opportunity being afforded the people to act upon it. I will venture to add that to me the convention mode seems preferable, in that it allows amendments to originate with the people themselves, instead of only permitting them to take or reject propositions originated by others not especially chosen for the purpose, and which might not be precisely such as they would wish to either accept or refuse. I understand a proposed amendment to the Constitution – which amendment, however, I have not seen – has passed Congress, to the effect that the Federal Government shall never interfere with the domestic institutions of the States, including that of persons held to service. To avoid misconstruction of what I have said, I depart from my purpose not to speak of particular amendments so far as to say that, holding such a provision to now be implied constitutional law, I have no objection to its being made express and irrevocable.

The chief magistrate derives all his authority from the people, and they have conferred none upon him to fix terms for the separation of the States. The people themselves can do this also if they choose; but the Executive, as such, has nothing to do with it. His duty is to administer the present government, as it came to his hands, and to transmit it, unimpaired by him, to his successor.

Why should there not be a patient confidence in the ultimate justice of the people? Is there any better or equal hope in the world? In our present differences, is either party without faith of being in the right? If the Almighty Ruler of Nations, with his eternal truth and justice, be on your side of the North, or on yours of the South, that truth and that justice will surely prevail by the judgment of this great tribunal of the American people.

By the frame of the government under which we live, this same people have wisely given their public servants but little power for mischief; and have, with equal wisdom, provided for the return of that little to their own hands at very short intervals. While the people retain their virtue and vigilance, no administration, by any extreme of wickedness or folly, can very seriously injure the government in the short space of four years.

My countrymen, one and all, think calmly and well upon this whole subject. Nothing valuable can be lost by taking time. If there be an object to hurry any of you in hot haste to a step which you would never take deliberately, that object will be frustrated by taking time; but no good object can be frustrated by it. Such of you as are now dissatisfied still have the old Constitution unimpaired, and, on the sensitive point, the laws of your own framing under it; while the new administration will have no immediate power, if it would, to change either. If it were admitted that you who are dissatisfied hold the right side in the dispute, there still is no single good reason for precipitate action. Intelligence, patriotism, Christianity, and a firm reliance on Him who has never yet forsaken this favoured land, are still competent to adjust in the best way all our present difficulty.

In your hands, my dissatisfied fellow-countrymen, and not in mine, is the momentous issue of civil war. The government will not assail you. You can have no conflict without being yourselves the aggressors. You have no oath registered in heaven to destroy the government, while I shall have the most solemn one to 'preserve, protect, and defend it'.

I am loath to close. We are not enemies, but friends. We must not be enemies. Though passion may have strained, it must not break our bonds of affection. The mystic chords of memory, stretching from every battlefield and patriot grave to every living heart and hearthstone all over this broad land, will yet swell the chorus of the Union when again touched, as surely they will be, by the better angels of our nature.

From his First Message to Congress, at the Special Session.
July 4, 1861

. . . It is thus seen that the assault upon and reduction of Fort Sumter was in no sense a matter of self-defence on the part of the assailants. They well knew that the garrison in the fort could by no possibility commit aggression upon them. They knew – they were expressly notified – that the giving of bread to the few brave and hungry men of the garrison was all which would on that occasion be attempted, unless themselves, by resisting so much, should provoke more. They knew that this government desired to keep the garrison in the fort, not to assail them, but merely to maintain visible possession, and thus to preserve the Union from actual and immediate dissolution – trusting, as hereinbefore stated, to time, discussion, and the ballot-box, for final adjustment; and they assailed and reduced the fort for precisely the reverse object – to drive out the visible authority of the Federal Union, and thus force it to immediate dissolution. . . .

That this was their object the Executive well understood; and having said to them in the inaugural address, 'You can have no conflict without being yourselves the aggressors', he took pains not only to keep this declaration good, but also to keep the case so free from the power of ingenious sophistry that the world should not be able to misunderstand it. . . .

By the affair at Fort Sumter, with its surrounding circumstances, that point was reached. Then and thereby the assailants of the government began the conflict of arms, without a gun in sight, or in expectancy to return their fire, save only the few in the fort sent to that harbour years before for their own protection, and still ready to give that protection in whatever was lawful. In this act, discarding all else, they have forced upon the country the distinct issue, 'immediate dissolution or blood'.

And this issue embraces more than the fate of these United States. It presents to the whole family of man the question whether a constitutional republic or democracy – a government of the people by the same people – can or cannot maintain its territorial integrity against its own domestic foes. It presents the question whether discontented individuals, too few in numbers to control administration according to organic law in any case, can always, upon the pretences made in this case or any other pretences, or arbitrarily without any pretence, break up their government, and thus practically put an end to free government upon the earth. It forces us to ask: 'Is there, in all republics, this inherent and fatal weakness?' 'Must a government, of necessity, be too strong for the liberties of its own people, or too weak to maintain its own existence?'

So viewing the issue, no choice was left but to call out the war power of the government, and so to resist force employed for its destruction by force for its preservation.

The call was made, and the response of the country was most gratifying, surpassing in unanimity and spirit the most sanguine expectation.

. . . The people of Virginia have thus allowed this giant insurrection to make its nest within her borders – and this government has no choice left but to deal with it where it finds it. And it has the less regret, as the loyal citizens have in due form claimed its protection. Those loyal citizens this government is bound to recognize and protect, as being Virginia.

In the border States, so called – in fact, the Middle States – there are those who favour a policy which they call 'armed neutrality'; that is, an arming of those States to prevent the Union forces passing one way, or the disunion the other, over their soil. This would be disunion completed. Figuratively speaking, it would be the building of an impassable wall along the line of separation – and yet not quite an impassable one, for under the guise of neutrality, it would tie the hands of Union men, and freely pass supplies from among them to the insurrectionists, which it could not do as an open enemy. At a stroke, it would take all the trouble off the hands of secession, except only what proceeds from the external blockade. It would do for the disunionists that which of all things they most desire – feed them well and give them disunion without a struggle of their own. It recognizes no fidelity to the Constitution, no obligation to maintain the Union; and while very many who have favoured it are doubtless loyal citizens, it is, nevertheless, very injurious in effect.

. . . The forbearance of this government had been so extraordinary and so long continued, as to lead some foreign nations to shape their action as if they supposed the early destruction of our National Union was probable. While this, on discovery, gave the Executive some concern, he is now happy to say that the sovereignty and rights of the United States are now everywhere practically respected by foreign powers, and a general sympathy with the country is manifested throughout the world.

. . . It is now recommended that you give the legal means for making this contest a short and decisive one; that you place at the control of the government for the work, at least four hundred thousand men, and $400,000,000. That number of men is about one-tenth of those of proper ages within the regions where, apparently, all are willing to engage; and the sum is less than a twenty-third part of the money value owned by the men who seem ready to devote the whole.

. . . A right result at this time, will be worth more to the world than ten times the men and ten times the money. The evidences reaching us from the country leave no doubt that the material for the work is abundant, and that it needs only the hand of legislation to give it legal sanction, and the hand of the Executive to give it practical shape and efficiency. One of the greatest perplexities of the government is to avoid receiving troops faster than it can provide for them. In a word, the people will save their government, if the government itself will do its part only indifferently well.

It might seem at first thought to be of little difference whether the present movement at the South be called *secession* or *rebellion*. The movers, however, well understand the difference. At the beginning they knew they could never raise their treason to any respectable magnitude by any name which implies violation of law. They knew their people possessed as much of moral sense, as much of devotion to law and order, and as much pride in and reverence for the history and government of their common country as any other civilized and patriotic people. They knew they could make no advancement directly in the teeth of these strong and noble sentiments. Accordingly, they commenced by an insidious debauching of the public mind. They invented an ingenious sophism which, if conceded, was followed by perfectly logical steps, through all the incidents, to the complete destruction of the Union. The sophism itself is that any State of the Union may consistently with the national Constitution, and therefore lawfully and peacefully, withdraw from the Union without the consent of the Union or of any other State. The little disguise that the supposed right is to be exercised only for just cause, themselves to be the sole judges of its justice, is too thin to merit any notice.

With rebellion thus *sugar-coated* they have been drugging the public mind of their section for more than thirty years, and until at length they have brought many good men to a willingness to take up arms against the government the day after some assemblage of men have enacted the farcical pretence of taking their State out of the Union, who could have been brought to no such thing the day before.

This sophism derives much, perhaps the whole of its currency from the assumption that there is some omnipotent and sacred supremacy pertaining to a State – to each State of our Federal Union. Our States have neither more nor less power than that reserved to them in the Union by the Constitution, no one of them ever having been a State out of the Union. The original ones passed into the Union even before they cast off their British colonial dependence, and the new ones each came into the Union directly from a condition of dependence, excepting Texas. And even Texas in its temporary independence was never designated a State. The new ones only took the designation of States on coming into the Union, while that name was first adopted for the old ones in and by the Declaration of Independence. Therein the 'United Colonies' were declared to be 'free and independent States'; but even then the object plainly was, not to declare their independence of one another or of the Union, but directly the contrary, as their mutual pledges and their mutual action before, at the time, and afterward abundantly show. The express plighting of faith by each and all of the original thirteen in the Articles of Confederation two years later, that the Union shall be perpetual, is most conclusive. Having never been States, either in substance or name, outside of the Union, whence this magical omnipotence of 'State-Rights', asserting a claim of power to lawfully destroy the Union itself? Much is said about the 'sovereignty' of the States; but the word is not in the National Constitution, nor, as is believed, in any of the State constitutions. What is *sovereignty* in the political sense of the term? Would it be far wrong to define it 'a political community without a political superior'? Tested by this, no one of our States, except Texas, ever was a sovereignty. And even Texas gave up the character on coming into the Union, by which act she acknowledged the Constitution of the United States, and the laws and treaties of the United States made in pursuance of the Constitution, to be for her the supreme law of the land. The States have their status in the Union, and they have no other legal status. If they break from this, they can only do so against law and by revolution. The Union, and not themselves separately, procured their independence and their liberty. By conquest or purchase, the Union gave each of them whatever of independence or liberty it has. The Union is older than any of the States, and, in fact, it created them as States. Originally some dependent colonies made the Union, and in turn the Union threw off their old dependence for them, and made them States, such as they are. Not one of them ever had a State constitution independent of the Union. Of course it is not forgotten that all the new States framed their constitutions before they entered the Union – nevertheless, dependent upon and preparatory to coming into the Union.

Unquestionably the States have the powers and the rights reserved to them in and by the National Constitution; but among these, surely, are not included all conceivable powers, however mischievous or destructive; but, at most, such only as were known in the world at the time, as governmental powers; and, certainly, a power to destroy the government itself had never been known as a governmental – as a merely administrative power. This relative matter of National power and States rights, as a principle, is no other than the principle of generality and locality. Whatever concerns the whole world should be confided to the whole – to the General Government; while whatever concerns only the State should be left exclusively to the State. This is all there is of original principle about it. . . . What is now combated, is the position that secession is consistent with the Constitution – is lawful and peaceful. It is not contended that there is any express law for it; and nothing should ever be implied as law which leads to unjust or absurd consequences.

The nation purchased with money the countries out of which several of these States were formed; is it just that they shall go off without leave and without refunding? The nation paid very large sums (in the aggregate, I believe, nearly a hundred millions) to relieve Florida of the aboriginal tribes; is it just that she shall now be off without consent, or without making any return? The nation is now in debt for money applied to the benefit of these so-called seceding States in common with the rest; is it just that the creditors shall go unpaid, or the remaining States pay the whole? . . . Again, if one State may secede, so may another; and when all shall have seceded, none is left to pay the debts. Is this quite just to the creditors? Did we notify them of this sage view of ours when we borrowed their money? If we now recognize this doctrine by allowing the seceders to go in peace, it is difficult to see what we can do if others choose to go, or to extort terms upon which they will promise to remain.

The seceders insist that our Constitution admits of secession. They have assumed to make a national constitution of their own, in which, of necessity, they have either discarded or retained the right of secession, as they insist it exists in ours. If they have discarded it, they thereby admit that, on principle, it ought not to be in ours. If they have retained it, by their own construction of ours, they show that to be consistent they must secede from one another whenever they shall find it the easiest way of settling their debts, or effecting any other or selfish or unjust object. The principle itself is one of disintegration, and upon which no government can stand.

If all the States save one should assert the power to drive that one out of the Union, it is presumed the whole class of seceder politicians would at once deny the power, and denounce the act as the greatest outrage upon State rights. But suppose that precisely the same act, instead of being called 'driving the one out', should be called 'the seceding of the others from that one', it would be exactly what the seceders claim to do; unless, indeed, they make the point that the one, because it is a minority, may rightfully do what the others, because they are a majority, may not rightfully do. . . .

It may be affirmed without extravagance that the free institutions we enjoy have developed the powers and improved the condition of our whole people, beyond any example in the world. Of this we now have a striking and an impressive illustration. So large an army as the government has now on foot was never before known, without a soldier in it but who has taken his place there of his own free choice. But more than this, there are many single regiments, whose members, one and another, possess full practical knowledge of all the arts, sciences, and professions, and whatever else, whether useful or elegant, is known in the world; and there is scarcely one from which there could not be selected a President, a cabinet, a congress, and perhaps a court, abundantly competent to administer the government itself. Nor do I say that this is not true also in the army of our late friends, now adversaries in this contest; but if it is, so much the better reason why the government which has conferred such benefits on both them and us should not be broken up. Whoever in any section proposes to abandon such a government, would do well to consider in deference to what principle it is that he does it; what better he is likely to get in its stead; whether the substitute will give, or be intended to give, so much of good to the people? There are some foreshadowings on this subject. Our adversaries have adopted some declarations of independence in which, unlike the good old one penned by Jefferson, they omit the words, 'all men are created equal'. Why? They have adopted a temporary national constitution, in the preamble of which, unlike our good old one signed by Washington, they omit 'We, the people', and substitute 'We, the deputies of the sovereign and independent States'. Why? Why this deliberate pressing out of view the rights of men and the authority of the people?

This is essentially a people's contest. On the side of the Union it is a struggle for maintaining in the world that form and substance of government whose leading object is to elevate the condition of men – to lift artificial weights from all shoulders, to clear the paths of laudable pursuit for all, to afford all an unfettered start and a fair chance in the race of life. Yielding to partial and temporary departures from necessity, this is the leading object of the government for the existence of which we contend.

I am most happy to believe that the plain people understand and appreciate this. It is worthy of note that while in this, the government's hour of trial, large numbers of those in the army and navy who have been favoured with the offices have resigned and proved false to the hand which had pampered them, not one common soldier or common sailor is known to have deserted his flag.

Our popular government has often been called an experiment. Two points in it our people have already settled – the successful establishing and the successful administering of it. One still remains – its successful maintenance against a formidable internal attempt to overthrow it. It is now for them to demonstrate to the world that those who can fairly carry an election can also suppress a rebellion; that ballots are the rightful and peaceful successors of bullets; and that when ballots have fairly and constitutionally decided, there can be no successful appeal back to bullets; that there can be no successful appeal, except to ballots themselves, at succeeding elections. Such will be a great lesson of peace; teaching men that what they cannot take by an election, neither can they take by a war; teaching all the folly of being the beginners of a war.

From his Message to Congress at its Regular Session.
December 3, 1861

Fellow-citizens of the Senate and House of Representatives, In the midst of unprecedented political troubles, we have cause of great gratitude to God for unusual good health and abundant harvests.

You will not be surprised to learn that in the peculiar exigencies of the times, our intercourse with foreign nations has been attended with profound solicitude, chiefly turning upon our own domestic affairs.

A disloyal portion of the American people have, during the whole year, been engaged in an attempt to divide and destroy the Union. A nation which endures factious domestic division is exposed to disrespect abroad; and one party, if not both, is sure, sooner or later, to invoke foreign intervention. Nations thus tempted to interfere are not always able to resist the counsels of seeming expediency and ungenerous ambition, although measures adopted under such influences seldom fail to be injurious and unfortunate to those adopting them.

The disloyal citizens of the United States who have offered the ruin of our country in return for the aid and comfort which they have invoked abroad, have received less patronage and encouragement than they probably expected. If it were just to suppose, as the insurgents have seemed to assume, that foreign nations in this case, discarding all moral, social, and treaty obligations, would act solely and selfishly for the most speedy restoration of commerce, including especially the acquisition of cotton, those nations appear as yet not to have seen their way to their object more directly or clearly through the destruction than through the preservation of the Union. If we could dare to believe that foreign nations are actuated by no higher principle than this, I am quite sure a sound argument could be made to show them that they can reach their aim more readily and easily by aiding to crush this rebellion than by giving encouragement to it.

The principal lever relied on by the insurgents for exciting foreign nations to hostility against us, as already intimated, is the embarrassment of commerce. Those nations, however, not improbably saw from the first that it was the Union which made as well our foreign as our domestic commerce. They can scarcely have failed to perceive that the effort for disunion produces the existing difficulty; and that one strong nation promises a more durable peace and a more extensive, valuable, and reliable commerce than can the same nation broken into hostile fragments.

*   *   *

It continues to develop that the insurrection is largely, if not exclusively, a war upon the first principle of popular government – the rights of the people. Conclusive evidence of this is found in the most grave and maturely considered public documents, as well as in the general tone of the insurgents. In those documents we find the abridgment of the existing right of suffrage, and the denial to the people of all right to participate in the selection of public officers, except the legislative, boldly advocated, with laboured arguments to prove that large control of the people in government is the source of all political evil. Monarchy itself is sometimes hinted at, as a possible refuge from the power of the people.

In my present position, I could scarcely be justified were I to omit raising a warning voice against this approach of returning despotism.

It is not needed nor fitting here that a general argument should be made in favour of popular institutions; but there is one point, with its connections, not so hackneyed as most others, to which I ask a brief attention. It is the effort to place capital on an equal footing with, if not above, labour, in the structure of government. It is assumed that labour is available only in connection with capital; that nobody labours, unless somebody else, owning capital, somehow, by the use of it, induces him to labour. This assumed, it is next considered whether it is best that capital shall hire labourers, and thus induce them to work by their own consent, or buy them and drive them to it without their consent. Having proceeded thus far, it is naturally concluded that all labourers are either hired labourers, or what we call slaves. And further, it is assumed that whoever is once a hired labourer is fixed in that condition for life.

Now, there is no such relation between capital and labour as assumed, nor is there any such thing as a free man being fixed for life in the condition of a hired labourer. Both these assumptions are false, and all inferences from them are groundless.

Labour is prior to and independent of capital. Capital is only the fruit of labour, and could never have existed if labour had not first existed. Labour is the superior of capital, and deserves much the higher consideration. Capital has its rights, which are as worthy of protection as any other rights. Nor is it denied that there is, and probably always will be, a relation between labour and capital, producing mutual benefits. The error is in assuming that the whole labour of the community exists within that relation. A few men own capital, and that few avoid labour themselves, and with their capital hire or buy another few to labour for them. A large majority belong to neither class – neither work for others, nor have others working for them. In most of the Southern States, a majority of the whole people, of all colours, are neither slaves nor masters; while in the Northern, a majority are neither hirers nor hired. Men with their families – wives, sons, and daughters – work for themselves, on their farms, in their houses, and in their shops, taking the whole product to themselves, and asking no favours of capital on the one hand, nor of hired labourers or slaves on the other. It is not forgotten that a considerable number of persons mingle their own labour with capital – that is, they labour with their own hands, and also buy or hire others to labour for them; but this is only a mixed and not a distinct class. No principle stated is disturbed by the existence of this mixed class.

Again, as has already been said, there is not of necessity any such thing as the free, hired labourer being fixed to that condition for life. Many independent men, everywhere in these States, a few years back in their lives were hired labourers. The prudent, penniless beginner in the world labours for wages a while, saves a surplus with which to buy tools or land for himself, then labours on his own account another while, and at length hires another new beginner to help him. This is the just and generous and prosperous system which opens the way to all, gives hope to all, and consequent energy and progress and improvement of condition to all. No men living are more worthy to be trusted than those who toil up from poverty, none less inclined to take or touch aught which they have not honestly earned. Let them beware of surrendering a political power which they already possess, and which, if surrendered, will surely be used to close the door of advancement against such as they, and to fix new disabilities and burdens upon them, till all of liberty shall be lost.

Letter to General G. B. McClellan. Washington. February 3, 1862

My dear Sir, You and I have distinct and different plans for a movement of the Army of the Potomac – yours to be down the Chesapeake, up the Rappahannock to Urbana and across land to the terminus of the railroad on the York River; mine to move directly to a point on the railroad southwest of Manassas.

If you will give me satisfactory answers to the following questions, I shall gladly yield my plan to yours.

First. Does not your plan involve a greatly larger expenditure of time and money than mine?

Second. Wherein is a victory more certain by your plan than mine?

Third. Wherein is a victory more valuable by your plan than mine?

Fourth. In fact, would it not be less valuable in this, that it would break no great line of the enemy's communications, while mine would?

Fifth. In case of disaster, would not a retreat be more difficult by your plan than mine?

I have just assisted the Secretary of War in framing part of a despatch to you, relating to army corps, which despatch of course will have reached you long before this will.

I wish to say a few words to you privately on this subject. I ordered the army corps organization, not only on the unanimous opinion of the twelve generals whom you had selected and assigned as generals of division, but also on the unanimous opinion of every *military man* I could get an opinion from (and every modern military book), yourself only excepted. Of course I did not on my own judgment pretend to understand the subject. I now think it indispensable for you to know how your struggle against it is received in quarters which we cannot entirely disregard. It is looked upon as merely an effort to pamper one or two pets and to persecute and degrade their supposed rivals. I have had no word from Sumner, Heintzelman, or Keyes. The commanders of these corps are of course the three highest officers with you, but I am constantly told that you have no consultation or communication with them – that you consult and communicate with nobody but General Fitz John Porter, and perhaps General Franklin. I do not say these complaints are true or just, but at all events it is proper you should know of their existence. Do the commanders of corps disobey your orders in anything?

. . . Are you strong enough – are you strong enough, even with my help – to set your foot upon the necks of Sumner, Heintzelman, and Keyes, all at once? This is a practical and a very serious question for you.

Lincoln's Proclamation revoking General Hunter's Order setting the Slaves free. May 19, 1862

. . . General Hunter nor any other commander or person has been authorized by the Government of the United States to make proclamation declaring the slaves of any State free, and that the supposed proclamation now in question, whether genuine or false, is altogether void so far as respects such declaration. . . . On the sixth day of March last, by a special Message, I recommended to Congress the adoption of a joint resolution, to be substantially as follows – *Resolved, That the United States ought to co-operate with any State which may adopt a gradual abolishment of slavery, giving to such State earnest expression to compensate for its inconveniences, public and private, produced by such change of system.*

The resolution in the language above quoted was adopted by large majorities in both branches of Congress, and now stands an authentic, definite, and solemn proposal of the nation to the States and people most immediately interested in the subject-matter. To the people of those States I now earnestly appeal. I do not argue – I beseech you to make arguments for yourselves. You cannot, if you would, be blind to the signs of the times. I beg of you a calm and enlarged consideration of them, ranging, if it may be, far above personal and partisan politics. The proposal makes common cause for a common object, casting no reproaches upon any. It acts not the Pharisee. The change it contemplates would come gently as the dews of heaven, not rending or wrecking anything. Will you not embrace it? So much good has not been done by one effort in all past time as in the providence of God it is now your high privilege to do. May the vast future not have to lament that you have neglected it.

Appeal to the Border States in behalf of Compensated Emancipation. July 12, 1862

After the adjournment of Congress, now near, I shall have no opportunity of seeing you for several months. Believing that you of the border States hold more power for good than any other equal number of members, I feel it a duty which I cannot justifiably waive, to make this appeal to you.

I do not speak of emancipation at once, but of a decision at once to emancipate gradually. Room in South America for colonization can be obtained cheaply and in abundance, and when numbers shall be large enough to be company and encouragement for one another, the freed people will not be so reluctant to go.

I am pressed with a difficulty not yet mentioned – one which threatens division among those who, united, are none too strong. General Hunter is an honest man. He was, and I hope still is, my friend. I valued him none the less for his agreeing with me in the general wish that all men everywhere could be free. He proclaimed all men free within certain States, and I repudiated the proclamation. He expected more good and less harm from the measure than I could believe would follow. Yet in repudiating it, I gave dissatisfaction if not offence to many whose support the country cannot afford to lose. And this is not the end of it. The pressure in this direction is still upon me, and is increasing. By conceding what I now ask, you can relieve me, and, much more, can relieve the country, in this important point.

Upon these considerations I have again begged your attention to the message of March last. Before leaving the Capitol, consider and discuss it among yourselves. You are patriots and statesmen, and as such, I pray you, consider this proposition, and at the least commend it to the consideration of your States and people. As you would perpetuate popular government for the best people in the world, I beseech you that you do in no wise omit this. Our common country is in great peril, demanding the loftiest views and boldest action to bring it speedy relief. Once relieved, its form of government is saved to the world, its beloved history and cherished memories are vindicated, and its happy future fully assured and rendered inconceivably grand.

I intend no reproach or complaint when I assure you that, in my opinion, if you all had voted for the resolution in the gradual-emancipation message of last March, the war would now be substantially ended. And the plan therein proposed is yet one of the most potent and swift means of ending it. Let the States which are in rebellion see, definitely and certainly, that in no event will the States you represent ever join their proposed confederacy, and they cannot much longer maintain the contest. But you cannot divest them of their hope to ultimately have you with them, so long as you show a determination to perpetuate the institution within your own States. Beat them at elections, as you have overwhelmingly done, and, nothing daunted, they still claim you as their own. You and I know what the lever of their power is. Break that lever before their faces, and they can shake you no more for ever.

Most of you have treated me with kindness and consideration, and I trust you will not now think I improperly touch what is exclusively your own, when, for the sake of the whole country, I ask, Can you, for your States, do better than to take the course I urge? Discarding punctilio and maxims adapted to more manageable times, and looking only to the unprecedentedly stern facts of our case, can you do better in any possible event? You prefer that the constitutional relation of the States to the nation shall be practically restored without disturbance of the institution; and if this were done, my whole duty in this respect, under the Constitution and my oath of office, would be performed. But it is not done, and we are trying to accomplish it by war. The incidents of the war cannot be avoided. If the war continues long, as it must if the object be not sooner attained, the institution in your States will be extinguished by mere friction and abrasion – by the mere incidents of the war. It will be gone, and you will have nothing valuable in lieu of it. Much of its value is gone already. How much better for you and for your people to take the step which at once shortens the war and secures substantial compensation for that which is sure to be wholly lost in any other event! How much better to thus save the money which else we sink for ever in the war! How much better to do it while we can, lest the war ere long render us pecuniarily unable to do it! How much better for you as seller, and the nation as buyer, to sell out and buy out that without which the war could never have been, than to sink both the thing to be sold and the price of it in cutting one another's throats!

From a Letter to Cuthbert Bullitt. July 28, 1862

Now, I think the true remedy is very different from that suggested by Mr Durant. It does not lie in rounding the rough angles of the war, but in removing the necessity for the war. The people of Louisiana who wish protection to person and property, have but to reach forth their hands and take it. Let them in good faith reinaugurate the national authority, and set up a State government conforming thereto under the Constitution. They know how to do it, and can have the protection of the army while doing it. The army will be withdrawn as soon as such government can dispense with its presence, and the people of the State can then, upon the old constitutional terms, govern themselves to their own liking. This is very simple and easy.

If they will not do this, if they prefer to hazard all for the sake of destroying the government, it is for them to consider whether it is probable that I will surrender the government to save them from losing all. If they decline what I suggest, you will scarcely need to ask what I will do.

What would you do in my position? Would you drop the war where it is, or would you prosecute it in future with elder-stalk squirts charged with rose-water? Would you deal lighter blows rather than heavier ones? Would you give up the contest, leaving any available means untried?

I am in no boastful mood. I shall not do more than I can; but I shall do all I can to save the government, which is my sworn duty as well as my personal inclination. I shall do nothing in malice. What I deal with is too vast for malicious dealing.

Letter to August Belmont. July 31, 1862

Dear Sir, You send to Mr W— an extract from a letter written at New Orleans the 9th instant, which is shown to me. You do not give the writer's name; but plainly he is a man of ability, and probably of some note. He says: 'The time has arrived when Mr Lincoln must take a decisive course. Trying to please everybody, he will satisfy nobody. A vacillating policy in matters of importance is the very worst. Now is the time, if ever, for honest men who love their country to rally to its support. Why will not the North say officially that it wishes for the restoration of the Union as it was?'

And so, it seems, this is the point on which the writer thinks I have no policy. Why will he not read and understand what I have said?

The substance of the very declaration he desires is in the inaugural, in each of the two regular messages to Congress, and in many, if not all, the minor documents issued by the Executive since the Inauguration.

Broken eggs cannot be mended; but Louisiana has nothing to do now but to take her place in the Union as it was, barring the already broken eggs. The sooner she does so, the smaller will be the amount of that which will be past mending. This government cannot much longer play a game in which it stakes all, and its enemies stake nothing. Those enemies must understand that they cannot experiment for ten years trying to destroy the government, and if they fail still come back into the Union unhurt. If they expect in any contingency to ever have the Union as it was, I join with the writer in saying, 'Now is the time.'

How much better it would have been for the writer to have gone at this, under the protection of the army at New Orleans, than to have sat down in a closet writing complaining letters northward.

His Letter to Horace Greeley. August 22, 1862

I have just read yours of the 19th instant, addressed to myself through the *New York Tribune*.

If there be in it any statements or assumptions of fact which I may know to be erroneous, I do not now and here controvert them.

If there be in it any inferences which I may believe to be falsely drawn, I do not now and here argue against them.

If there be perceptible in it an impatient and dictatorial tone, I waive it, in deference to an old friend whose heart I have always supposed to be right.

As to the policy I 'seem to be pursuing', as you say, I have not meant to leave anyone in doubt. I would save the Union. I would save it in the shortest way under the Constitution.

The sooner the national authority can be restored, the nearer the Union will be – the Union as it was.

If there be those who would not save the Union unless they could at the same time save slavery, I do not agree with them.

If there be those who would not save the Union unless they could at the same time destroy slavery, I do not agree with them.

My paramount object in this struggle is to save the Union, and not either to save or to destroy slavery.

If I could save the Union without freeing any slave, I would do it; if I could save it by freeing all the slaves, I would do it; and if I could save it by freeing some and leaving others alone, I would also do that.

What I do about slavery and the coloured race, I do because I believe it helps to save the Union; and what I forbear, I forbear because I do not believe it would help to save the Union.

I shall do less whenever I shall believe that what I am doing hurts the cause; and I shall do more whenever I shall believe doing more will help the cause.

I shall try to correct errors where shown to be errors, and I shall adopt new views as fast as they shall appear to be true views.

I have here stated my purpose according to my views of official duty, and I intend no modification of my oft-expressed personal wish that all men everywhere could be free.

From his Reply to the Chicago Committee of United Religious Denominations. September 13, 1862

The subject presented in the memorial is one upon which I have thought much for weeks past, and I may even say for months. I am approached with the most opposite opinions and advice, and that by religious men, who are equally certain that they represent the Divine will. I am sure that either the one or the other class is mistaken in that belief, and perhaps, in some respects, both. I hope it will not be irreverent for me to say, that if it is probable that God would reveal His will to others, on a point so connected with my duty, it might be supposed that He would reveal it directly to me; for, unless I am more deceived in myself than I often am, it is my earnest desire to know the will of Providence in this matter. And if I can learn what it is, I will do it. These are not, however, the days of miracles, and I suppose it will be granted that I am not to expect a direct revelation. I must study the plain, physical facts of the case, ascertain what is possible, and learn what appears to be wise and right.

The subject is difficult, and good men do not agree. For instance, four gentlemen of standing and intelligence, from New York, called as a delegation on business connected with the war; but before leaving, two of them earnestly besought me to proclaim general emancipation, upon which the other two at once attacked them. You also know that the last session of Congress had a decided majority of anti-slavery men, yet they could not unite on this policy. And the same is true of the religious people.

Why, the rebel soldiers are praying with a great deal more earnestness, I fear, than our own troops, and expecting God to favour their side: for one of our soldiers who had been taken prisoner told Senator Wilson a few days since that he met nothing so discouraging as the evident sincerity of those he was among in their prayers. But we will talk over the merits of the case.

What good would a proclamation of emancipation from me do, especially as we are now situated? I do not want to issue a document that the whole world will see must necessarily be inoperative, like the Pope's bull against the comet! Would my word free the slaves, when I cannot even enforce the Constitution in the rebel States? Is there a single court or magistrate or individual that would be influenced by it there?

And what reason is there to think it would have any greater effect upon the slaves than the late law of Congress, which I approved, and which offers protection and freedom to the slaves of rebel masters who come within our lines? Yet I cannot learn that that law has caused a single slave to come over to us. And suppose they could be induced by a proclamation of freedom from me to throw themselves upon us, what should we do with them? How can we feed and care for such a multitude? General Butler wrote me a few days since that he was issuing more rations to the slaves who have rushed to him than to all the white troops under his command. They eat, and that is all; though it is true General Butler is feeding the whites also by the thousand, for it nearly amounts to a famine there. If now, the pressure of the war should call off our forces from New Orleans to defend some other point, what is to prevent the masters from reducing the blacks to slavery again? For I am told that whenever the rebels take any black prisoners, free or slave, they immediately auction them off! They did so with those they took from a boat that was aground in the Tennessee River a few days ago. And then I am very ungenerously attacked for it. For instance, when, after the late battles at and near Bull Run, an expedition went out from Washington under a flag of truce to bury the dead and bring in the wounded, and the rebels seized the blacks who went along to help, and sent them into slavery, Horace Greeley said in his paper 'that the government would probably do nothing about it.' What could I do?

Now, then, tell me, if you please, what possible result of good would follow the issuing of such a proclamation as you desire? Understand, I raise no objections against it on legal or constitutional grounds, for, as commander-in-chief of the army and navy, in time of war I suppose I have a right to take any measures which may best subdue the enemy; nor do I urge objections of a moral nature, in view of possible consequences of insurrection and massacre at the South. I view this matter as a practical war-measure, to be decided on according to the advantages or disadvantages it may offer to the suppression of the rebellion.

[The committee had said that emancipation would secure us the sympathy of the world, slavery being the cause of the war. To which the President replied:]

I admit that slavery is at the root of the rebellion, or at least its *sine qua non*. The ambition of politicians may have instigated them to act, but they would have been impotent without slavery as their instrument. I will also concede that emancipation would help us in Europe, and convince them that we are incited by something more than ambition. I grant further, that it would help somewhat at the North, though not so much, I fear, as you and those you represent, imagine. Still, some additional strength would be added in that way to the war — and then, unquestionably, it would weaken the rebels by drawing off their labourers, which is of great importance; but I am not so sure that we could do much with the blacks. If we were to arm them, I fear that in a few weeks the arms would be in the hands of the rebels; and indeed, thus far, we have not had arms enough to equip our white troops. I will mention another thing, though it meet only your scorn and contempt. There are fifty thousand bayonets in the Union armies from the border slave States. It would be a serious matter if, in consequence of a proclamation such as you desire, they should go over to the rebels. I do not think they all would — not so many indeed, as a year ago, nor as six months ago; not so many today as yesterday. Every day increases their Union feeling. They are also getting their pride enlisted, and want to beat the rebels. Let me say one thing more: I think you should admit that we already have an important principle to rally and unite the people, in the fact that constitutional government is at stake. This is a fundamental idea, going down about as deep as anything.

Do not misunderstand me because I have mentioned these objections. They indicate the difficulties that have thus far prevented my action in some such way as you desire. I have not decided against a proclamation of liberty to the slaves, but hold the matter under advisement. And I can assure you that the subject is on my mind by day and night, more than any other. Whatever shall appear to be God's will, I will do. I trust that in the freedom with which I have canvassed your views, I have not in any respect injured your feelings.

From the Annual Message to Congress. December 1, 1862

Since your last annual assembling, another year of health and bountiful harvests has passed; and while it has not pleased the Almighty to bless us with a return of peace, we can but press on, guided by the best light He gives us, trusting that in His own good time and wise way, all will yet be well.

The correspondence, touching foreign affairs, which has taken place during the last year, is herewith submitted, in virtual compliance with a request to that effect made by the House of Representatives near the close of the last session of Congress.

If the condition of our relations with other nations is less gratifying than it has usually been at former periods, it is certainly more satisfactory than a nation so unhappily distracted as we are, might reasonably have apprehended. In the month of June last, there were some grounds to expect that the maritime powers, which, at the beginning of our domestic difficulties, so unwisely and unnecessarily, as we think, recognized the insurgents as a belligerent, would soon recede from that position, which has proved only less injurious to themselves than to our own country. But the temporary reverses which afterward befell the national arms, and which were exaggerated by our own disloyal citizens abroad, have hitherto delayed that act of simple justice.

The Civil War, which has so radically changed for the moment the occupations and habits of the American people, has necessarily disturbed the social condition and affected very deeply the prosperity of the nations with which we have carried on a commerce that has been steadily increasing throughout a period of half a century. It has, at the same time, excited political ambitions and apprehensions which have produced a profound agitation throughout the civilized world. In this unusual agitation we have forborne from taking part in any controversy between foreign States, and between parties or factions in such States. We have attempted no propagandism and acknowledged no revolution. But we have left to every nation the exclusive conduct and management of its own affairs. Our struggle has been, of course, contemplated by foreign nations with reference less to its own merits than to its supposed and often exaggerated effects and consequences resulting to those nations themselves. Nevertheless, complaint on the part of this government, even if it were just, would certainly be unwise. . . .

There is no line, straight or crooked, suitable for a national boundary, upon which to divide. Trace through from east to west upon the line between the free and the slave country, and we shall find a little more than one-third of its length are rivers, easy to be crossed, and populated, or soon to be populated, thickly upon both sides; while nearly all its remaining length are merely surveyors' lines, over which people may walk back and forth without any consciousness of their presence. No part of this line can be made any more difficult to pass, by writing it down on paper or parchment as a national boundary. The fact of separation, if it comes, gives up, on the part of the seceding section, the fugitive-slave clause, along with all other constitutional obligations upon the section seceded from, while I should expect no treaty stipulation would be ever made to take its place.

But there is another difficulty. The great interior region bounded east by the Alleghanies, north by the British dominions, west by the Rocky Mountains, and south by the line along which the culture of corn and cotton meets, . . . already has above ten millions of people, and will have fifty millions within fifty years, if not prevented by any political folly or mistake. It contains more than one-third of the country owned by the United States – certainly more than one million of square miles. Once half as populous as Massachusetts already is, and it would have more than seventy-five millions of people. A glance at the map shows that, territorially speaking, it is the great body of the republic. The other parts are but marginal borders to it, the magnificent region sloping west from the Rocky Mountains to the Pacific being the deepest, and also the richest, in undeveloped resources. In the production of provisions, grains, grasses, and all which proceed from them, this great interior region is naturally one of the most important in the world. Ascertain from the statistics the small proportion of the region which has, as yet, been brought into cultivation, and also the large and rapidly increasing amount of its products, and we shall be overwhelmed with the magnitude of the prospect presented. And yet this region has no sea-coast, touches no ocean anywhere. As part of one nation, its people now find, and may for ever find, their way to Europe by New York, to South America and Africa by New Orleans, and to Asia by San Francisco. But separate our common country into two nations, as designed by the present rebellion, and every man of this great interior region is thereby cut off from one or more of these outlets – not perhaps by a physical barrier, but by embarrassing and onerous trade regulations.

And this is true, wherever a dividing or boundary line may be fixed. Place it between the now free and slave country, or place it south of Kentucky, or north of Ohio, and still the truth remains that none south of it can trade to any port or place north of it, except upon terms dictated by a government foreign to them. These outlets, east, west, and south, are indispensable to the well-being of the people inhabiting, and to inhabit, this vast interior region. Which of the three may be the best, is no proper question. All are better than either; and all of right belong to that people and their successors for ever. True to themselves, they will not ask where a line of separation shall be, but will vow rather that there shall be no such line. Nor are the marginal regions less interested in these communications to and through them to the great outside world. They too, and each of them, must have access to this Egypt of the west, without paying toll at the crossing of any national boundary.

Our national strife springs not from our permanent part, not from the land we inhabit, not from our national homestead. There is no possible severing of this but would multiply and not mitigate evils among us. In all its adaptations and aptitudes, it demands union and abhors separation. In fact, it would ere long force reunion, however much of blood and treasure the separation might have cost. . . .

Fellow-citizens, we cannot escape history. We of this Congress and this Administration will be remembered in spite of ourselves. No personal significance or insignificance can spare one or another of us. The fiery trial through which we pass will light us down, in honour or dishonour, to the latest generation. We say we are for the Union. The world will not forget that we say this. We know how to save the Union. The world knows we do know how to save it.

We, even we here, hold the power and bear the responsibility. In giving freedom to the slave, we assure freedom to the free – honourable alike in what we give and what we preserve. We shall nobly save or meanly lose the last, best hope of earth. Other means may succeed; this could not fail. The way is plain, peaceful, generous, just – a way which, if followed, the world will for ever applaud, and God must for ever bless.

Emancipation Proclamation. *January 1, 1863*

Whereas, on the twenty-second day of September, in the year of our Lord one thousand eight hundred and sixty-two, a proclamation was issued by the President of the United States, containing, among other things, the following, to wit:

That on the first day of January, in the year of our Lord one thousand eight hundred and sixty-three, all persons held as slaves within any State, or designated part of a State, the people whereof shall then be in rebellion against the United States, shall be then, thenceforward, and for ever free; and the Executive Government of the United States, including the military and naval authority thereof, will recognize and maintain the freedom of such persons, and will do no act or acts to repress such persons, or any of them, in any efforts they may make for their actual freedom.

That the Executive will, on the first day of January aforesaid, by proclamation, designate the States and parts of States, if any, in which the people thereof respectively shall then be in rebellion against the United States; and the fact that any State, or the people thereof, shall on that day be in good faith represented in the Congress of the United States by members chosen thereto at elections wherein a majority of the qualified voters of such State shall have participated, shall in the absence of strong countervailing testimony be deemed conclusive evidence that such State and the people thereof are not then in rebellion against the United States.

Now, therefore, I, Abraham Lincoln, President of the United States, by virtue of the power in me vested as commander-in-chief of the army and navy of the United States, in time of actual armed rebellion against the authority and government of the United States, and as a fit and necessary war measure for suppressing said rebellion, do, on this first day of January, in the year of our Lord one thousand eight hundred and sixty-three, and in accordance with my purpose so to do, publicly proclaimed for the full period of one hundred days from the day first above mentioned, order and designate as the States and parts of States wherein the people thereof, respectively, are this day in rebellion against the United States, the following, to wit:

Arkansas, Texas, Louisiana (except the parishes of St Bernard, Plaquemines, Jefferson, St John, St Charles, St James, Ascension, Assumption, Terrebonne, Lafourche, St Mary, St Martin, and Orleans, including the city of New Orleans), Mississippi, Alabama, Florida, Georgia, South Carolina, North Carolina, and Virginia (except the forty-eight counties designated as West Virginia, and also the counties of Berkeley, Accomac, Northampton, Elizabeth City, York, Princess Anne, and Norfolk, including the cities of Norfolk and Portsmouth), and which excepted parts are for the present left precisely as if this proclamation were not issued.

And by virtue of the power and for the purpose aforesaid, I do order and declare that all persons held as slaves within said designated States and parts of States are, and henceforward shall be, free; and that the Executive Government of the United States, including the military and naval authorities thereof, will recognize and maintain the freedom of said persons.'

And I hereby enjoin upon the people so declared to be free to abstain from all violence, unless in necessary self-defence; and I recommend to them that, in all cases when allowed, they labour faithfully for reasonable wages.

And I further declare and make known that such persons of suitable condition will be received into the armed service of the United States to garrison forts, positions, stations, and other places, and to man vessels of all sorts in said service.

And upon this act, sincerely believed to be an act of justice, warranted by the Constitution upon military necessity, I invoke the considerate judgment of mankind and the gracious favour of Almighty God.

In witness whereof, I have hereunto set my hand, and caused the seal of the United States to be affixed.

> Done at the city of Washington, this first day of January, in the year of our Lord one thousand eight hundred and sixty-three, and of the independence of the United States of America the eighty-seventh.

ABRAHAM LINCOLN

By the President:
WILLIAM H. SEWARD
Secretary of State

Letter to General Grant. July 13, 1863

My dear General, I do not remember that you and I ever met personally. I write this now as a grateful acknowledgment for the almost inestimable service you have done the country. I wish to say a word further. When you first reached the vicinity of Vicksburg, I thought you should do what you finally did – march the troops across the neck, run the batteries with the transports, and thus go below; and I never had any faith, except a general hope that you knew better than I, that the Yazoo Pass expedition and the like could succeed. When you got below and took Port Gibson, Grand Gulf, and vicinity, I thought you should go down the river and join General Banks, and when you turned northward, east of the Big Black, I feared it was a mistake. I now wish to make the personal acknowledgment that you were right and I was wrong.

Yours very truly,
A. LINCOLN

Letter to — Moulton. Washington. July 31, 1863

My dear Sir, There has been a good deal of complaint against you by your superior officers of the Provost-Marshal-General's Department, and your removal has been strongly urged on the ground of 'persistent disobedience of orders and neglect of duty'.

Firmly convinced, as I am, of the patriotism of your motives, I am unwilling to do anything in your case which may seem unnecessarily harsh or at variance with the feelings of personal respect and esteem with which I have always regarded you. I consider your services in your district valuable, and should be sorry to lose them. It is unnecessary for me to state, however, that when differences of opinion arise between officers of the government, the ranking officer must be obeyed. You of course recognize as clearly as I do the importance of this rule. I hope you will conclude to go on in your present position under the regulations of the department. I wish you would write to me.

Letter to Mrs Lincoln. Washington. August 8, 1863

My dear Wife, All as well as usual, and no particular trouble anyway. I put the money into the Treasury at five per cent., with the privilege of withdrawing it any time upon thirty days' notice. I suppose you are glad to learn this. Tell dear Tad poor 'Nanny Goat' is lost, and Mrs Cuthbert and I are in distress about it. The day you left Nanny was found resting herself and chewing her little cud on the middle of Tad's bed; but now she's gone! The gardener kept complaining that she destroyed the flowers, till it was concluded to bring her down to the White House. This was done, and the second day she had disappeared and has not been heard of since. This is the last we know of poor 'Nanny'.

Letter to James H. Hackett. Washington. August 17, 1863

My dear Sir, Months ago I should have acknowledged the receipt of your book and accompanying kind note; and I now have to beg your pardon for not having done so.

For one of my age I have seen very little of the drama. The first presentation of *Falstaff* I ever saw was yours here, last winter or spring. Perhaps the best compliment I can pay is to say, as I truly can, I am very anxious to see it again. Some of Shakespeare's plays I have never read; while others I have gone over perhaps as frequently as any unprofessional reader. Among the latter are *Lear*, *Richard III*, *Henry VIII*, *Hamlet*, and especially *Macbeth*. I think nothing equals *Macbeth*. It is wonderful.

Unlike you gentlemen of the profession, I think the soliloquy in *Hamlet* commencing 'Oh, my offence is rank', surpasses that commencing 'To be or not to be'. But pardon this small attempt at criticism. I should like to hear you pronounce the opening speech of *Richard III*. Will you not soon visit Washington again? If you do, please call and let me make your personal acquaintance.

Note to Secretary Stanton. Washington. November 11, 1863

Dear Sir, I personally wish Jacob Freese, of New Jersey, to be appointed Colonel of a coloured regiment, and this regardless of whether he can tell the exact shade of Julius Caesar's hair.

The Letter to James C. Conkling. August 26, 1863

Your letter inviting me to attend a mass meeting of unconditional Union men, to be held at the capital of Illinois on the third day of September, has been received. It would be very agreeable to me to thus meet my old friends at my own home, but I cannot just now be absent from here so long as a visit there would require.

The meeting is to be of all those who maintain unconditional devotion to the Union; and I am sure my old political friends will thank me for tendering, as I do, the nation's gratitude to those and other noble men whom no partisan malice or partisan hope can make false to the nation's life.

There are those who are dissatisfied with me. To such I would say: You desire peace, and you blame me that we do not have it. But how can we attain it? There are but three conceivable ways. First, to suppress the rebellion by force of arms. This I am trying to do. Are you for it? If you are, so far we are agreed. If you are not for it, a second way is to give up the Union. I am against this. Are you for it? If you are, you should say so plainly. If you are not for force, nor yet for dissolution, there only remains some imaginable compromise. I do not believe any compromise embracing the maintenance of the Union is now possible. All I learn leads to a directly opposite belief. The strength of the rebellion is its military, its army. That army dominates all the country and all the people within its range. Any offer of terms made by any man or men within that range, in opposition to that army, is simply nothing for the present, because such man or men have no power whatever to enforce their side of a compromise, if one were made with them.

To illustrate: Suppose refugees from the South and peace men of the North get together in convention, and frame and proclaim a compromise embracing a restoration of the Union. In what way can that compromise be used to keep Lee's army out of Pennsylvania? Meade's army can keep Lee's out of Pennsylvania, and, I think, can ultimately drive it out of existence. But no paper compromise, to which the controllers of Lee's army are not agreed, can at all affect that army. In an effort at such compromise we should waste time which the enemy would improve to our disadvantage; and that would be all. A compromise, to be effective, must be made either with those who control the rebel army, or with the people first liberated from the domination of that army by the success of our own army. Now, allow me to assure you that no word or intimation from that rebel army, or from any of the men controlling it, in relation to any peace compromise, has ever come to my knowledge or belief. All charges and insinuations to the contrary are deceptive and groundless. And I promise you that if any such proposition shall hereafter come, it shall not be rejected and kept a secret from you. I freely acknowledge myself the servant of the people, according to the bond of service – the United States Constitution – and that, as such, I am responsible to them.

But to be plain. You are dissatisfied with me about the negro. Quite likely there is a difference of opinion between you and myself upon that subject. I certainly wish that all men could be free, while I suppose you do not. Yet I have neither adopted nor proposed any measure which is not consistent with even your views, provided you are for the Union. I suggested compensated emancipation, to which you replied, you wished not to be taxed to buy negroes. But I had not asked you to be taxed to buy negroes, except in such way as to save you from greater taxation to save the Union exclusively by other means.

You dislike the Emancipation Proclamation, and perhaps would have it retracted. You say it is unconstitutional. I think differently. I think the Constitution invests its commander-in-chief with the law of war in time of war. The most that can be said – if so much – is that slaves are property. Is there, has there ever been, any question that, by the law of war, property, both of enemies and friends, may be taken when needed? And is it not needed whenever taking it helps us or hurts the enemy? Armies the world over destroy enemies' property when they cannot use it, and even destroy their own to keep it from the enemy. Civilized belligerents do all in their power to help themselves or hurt the enemy, except a few things regarded as barbarous or cruel. Among the exceptions are the massacre of vanquished foes and noncombatants, male and female.

But the proclamation, as law, either is valid or is not valid. If it is not valid, it needs no retraction. If it is valid, it cannot be retracted any more than the dead can be brought to life. Some of you profess to think its retraction would operate favourably for the Union. Why better after the retraction than before the issue? There was more than a year and a half of trial to suppress the rebellion before the proclamation issued, the last one hundred days of which passed under an explicit notice that it was coming, unless averted by those in revolt returning to their allegiance. The war has certainly progressed as favourably for us since the issue of the proclamation as before. I know, as fully as one can know the opinions of others, that some of the commanders of our armies in the field who have given us our most important successes, believe the emancipation policy and the use of coloured troops constitute the heaviest blow yet dealt to the rebellion, and that at least one of these important successes could not have been achieved when it was but for the aid of black soldiers. Among the commanders holding these views are some who have never had any affinity with what is called Abolitionism or with Republican party politics, but who hold them purely as military opinions. I submit these opinions as being entitled to some weight against the objections often urged, that emancipation and arming the blacks are unwise as military measures, and were not adopted as such in good faith.

You say you will not fight to free negroes. Some of them seem willing to fight for you; but no matter. Fight you, then, exclusively to save the Union. I issued the proclamation on purpose to aid you in saving the Union. Whenever you shall have conquered all resistance to the Union, if I shall urge you to continue fighting, it will be an apt time then for you to declare you will not fight to free negroes.

I thought that in your struggle for the Union, to whatever extent the negroes should cease helping the enemy, to that extent it weakened the enemy in his resistance to you. Do you think differently? I thought that whatever negroes could be got to do as soldiers leaves just so much less for white soldiers to do in saving the Union. Does it appear otherwise to you? But negroes, like other people, act upon motives. Why should they do anything for us, if we will do nothing for them? If they stake their lives for us, they must be prompted by the strongest motive, even the promise of freedom. And the promise being made, must be kept.

The signs look better. The Father of Waters again goes unvexed to the sea. Thanks to the great Northwest for it. Nor yet wholly to them. Three hundred miles up they met New England, Empire, Keystone, and Jersey hewing their way right and left. The sunny South, too, in more colours than one, also lent a hand. On the spot, their part of the history was jotted down in black and white. The job was a great national one, and let none be banned who bore an honourable part in it. And while those who cleared the great river may well be proud, even that is not all. It is hard to say that anything has been more bravely and well done than at Antietam, Murfreesboro, Gettysburg, and on many fields of lesser note. Nor must Uncle Sam's web-feet be forgotten. At all the watery margins they have been present. Not only on the deep sea, the broad bay, and the rapid river, but also up the narrow, muddy bayou, and wherever the ground was a little damp, they have been and made their tracks. Thanks to all – for the great Republic, for the principle it lives by and keeps alive, for man's vast future – thanks to all.

Peace does not appear so distant as it did. I hope it will come soon, and come to stay; and so come as to be worth the keeping in all future time. It will then have been proved that among freemen there can be no successful appeal from the ballot to the bullet, and that they who take such appeal are sure to lose their case and pay the cost. And then there will be some black men who can remember that with silent tongue, and clenched teeth, and steady eye, and well-poised bayonet, they have helped mankind on to this great consummation, while I fear there will be some white ones unable to forget that with malignant heart and deceitful speech they strove to hinder it.

Still, let us not be over-sanguine of a speedy, final triumph. Let us be quite sober. Let us diligently apply the means, never doubting that a just God, in His own good time, will give us the rightful result.

His Proclamation for a Day of Thanksgiving. October 3, 1863

The year that is drawing toward its close has been filled with the blessings of fruitful fields and healthful skies. To these bounties, which are so constantly enjoyed that we are prone to forget the source from which they come, others have been added, which are of so extraordinary a nature that they cannot fail to penetrate and soften the heart which is habitually insensible to the ever-watchful providence of Almighty God.

In the midst of a civil war of unequalled magnitude and severity, which has sometimes seemed to foreign States to invite and provoke their aggressions, peace has been preserved with all nations, order has been maintained, the laws have been respected and obeyed, and harmony has prevailed everywhere, except in the theatre of military conflict; while that theatre has been greatly contracted by the advancing armies and navies of the Union.

Needful diversions of wealth and strength from the fields of peaceful industry to the national defence have not arrested the plough, the shuttle, or the ship; the axe has enlarged the borders of our settlements, and the mines, as well of iron and coal as of the precious metals, have yielded even more abundantly than heretofore. Population has steadily increased, notwithstanding the waste that has been made in the camp, the siege, and the battlefield; and the country, rejoicing in the consciousness of augmented strength and vigour, is permitted to expect continuance of years with large increase of freedom.

No human counsel hath devised, nor hath any mortal hand worked out these great things. They are the gracious gifts of the Most High God, who, while dealing with us in anger for our sins, hath nevertheless remembered mercy.

It has seemed to me fit and proper that they should be solemnly, reverently, and gratefully acknowledged as with one heart and one voice by the whole American people. I do, therefore, invite my fellow-citizens in every part of the United States, and also those who are at sea, and those sojourning in foreign lands, to set apart and observe the last Thursday of November next as a day of thanksgiving and praise to our beneficent Father who dwelleth in the heavens. And I recommend to them that while offering up the ascriptions justly due to Him for such singular deliverances and blessings, they do also, with humble penitence for our national perverseness and disobedience, commend to His tender care all those who have become widows, orphans, mourners, or sufferers in the lamentable civil strife in which we are unavoidably engaged, and fervently implore the inter-position of the Almighty Hand to heal the wounds of the nation, and to restore it, as soon as may be consistent with the Divine purposes, to the full enjoyment of peace, harmony, tranquillity, and union.

Address at the Dedication of the National Cemetery at Gettysburg. November 19, 1863

Fourscore and seven years ago our fathers brought forth upon this continent a new nation, conceived in liberty, and dedicated to the proposition that all men are created equal.

Now we are engaged in a great civil war, testing whether that nation, or any nation so conceived and so dedicated, can long endure. We are met on a great battlefield of that war. We have come to dedicate a portion of that field as a final resting-place for those who here gave their lives that that nation might live. It is altogether fitting and proper that we should do this.

But in a larger sense we cannot dedicate, we cannot consecrate, we cannot hallow this ground. The brave men, living and dead, who struggled here, have consecrated it far above our power to add or detract. The world will little note nor long remember what we say here, but it can never forget what they did here. It is for us, the living, rather, to be dedicated here to the unfinished work which they who fought here have thus far so nobly advanced. It is rather for us to be here dedicated to the great task remaining before us; that from these honoured dead we take increased devotion to that cause for which they gave the last full measure of devotion; that we here highly resolve that these dead shall not have died in vain; that this nation, under God, shall have a new birth of freedom; and that government of the people, by the people, and for the people, shall not perish from the earth.

From the Annual Message to Congress. December 8, 1863

. . . When Congress assembled a year ago, the war had already lasted nearly twenty months, and there had been many conflicts on both land and sea, with varying results. The rebellion had been pressed back into reduced limits; yet the tone of public feeling and opinion at home and abroad was not satisfactory. With other signs, the popular elections then just past indicated uneasiness among ourselves; while, amid much that was cold and menacing, the kindest words coming from Europe were uttered in accents of pity that we were too blind to surrender a hopeless cause. Our commerce was suffering greatly from a few vessels built upon and furnished from foreign shores, and we were threatened with such additions from the same quarter as would sweep our trade from the seas and raise our blockade. We had failed to elicit from European governments anything hopeful upon this subject. The preliminary Emancipation Proclamation, issued in September, was running its assigned period to the beginning of the new year. A month later the final proclamation came, including the announcement that coloured men of suitable condition would be received into the war service. The policy of emancipation and of employing black soldiers gave to the future a new aspect, about which hope and fear and doubt contended in uncertain conflict. According to our political system, as a matter of civil administration, the general government had no lawful power to effect emancipation in any State, and for a long time it had been hoped that the rebellion could be suppressed without resorting to it as a military measure. It was all the while deemed possible that the necessity for it might come and that, if it should, the crisis of the contest would then be presented. It came, and, as was anticipated, was followed by dark and doubtful days. Eleven months having now passed, we are permitted to take another review. The rebel borders are pressed still farther back, and by the complete opening of the Mississippi, the country dominated by the rebellion is divided into distinct parts, with no practical communication between them. Tennessee and Arkansas have been substantially cleared of insurgent control, and influential citizens in each, owners of slaves and advocates of slavery at the beginning of the rebellion, now declare openly for emancipation in their respective States. Of those States not included in the Emancipation Proclamation, Maryland and Missouri, neither of which three years ago would tolerate any restraint upon the extension of slavery into new Territories, only dispute now as to the best mode of removing it within their own limits.

Of those who were slaves at the beginning of the rebellion, full one hundred thousand are now in the United States military service, about one-half of which number actually bear arms in the ranks; thus giving the double advantage of taking so much labour from the insurgent cause and supplying the places which otherwise must be filled with so many white men. So far as tested, it is difficult to say they are not as good soldiers as any. No servile insurrection or tendency to violence or cruelty has marked the measures of emancipation and arming the blacks. These measures have been much discussed in foreign countries, and contemporary with such discussion the tone of public sentiment there is much improved. At home the same measures have been fully discussed, supported, criticized, and denounced, and the annual elections following are highly encouraging to those whose official duty it is to bear the country through this great trial. Thus we have the new reckoning. The crisis which threatened to divide the friends of the Union is passed.

Letter to Secretary Stanton. Washington. March 1, 1864

My dear Sir, A poor widow, by the name of Baird, has a son in the army, that for some offence has been sentenced to serve a long time without pay, or at most with very little pay. I do not like this punishment of withholding pay – it falls so very hard upon poor families. After he had been serving in this way for several months, at the tearful appeal of the poor mother, I made a direction that he be allowed to enlist for a new term, on the same condition as others. She now comes, and says she cannot get it acted upon. Please do it.

Letter to Governor Michael Hahn. Washington. March 13, 1864

My dear Sir, I congratulate you on having fixed your name in history as the first free-State governor of Louisiana. Now you are about to have a convention, which, among other things, will probably define the elective franchise. I barely suggest for your private consideration, whether some of the coloured people may not be let in – as, for instance, the very intelligent, and especially those who have fought gallantly in our ranks. They would probably help, in some trying time to come, to keep the jewel of liberty within the family of freedom. But this is only a suggestion, not to the public, but to you alone.

An Address at a Fair for the Sanitary Commission. March 18, 1864

I appear to say but a word. This extraordinary war in which we are engaged falls heavily upon all classes of people, but the most heavily upon the soldier. For it has been said, 'all that a man hath will he give for his life'; and while all contribute of their substance, the soldier puts his life at stake, and often yields it up in his country's cause. *The highest merit, then, is due to the soldier.*

In this extraordinary war extraordinary developments have manifested themselves, such as have not been seen in former wars; and amongst these manifestations nothing has been more remarkable than these fairs for the relief of suffering soldiers and their families. And the chief agents in these fairs are the women of America.

I am not accustomed to the language of eulogy. I have never studied the art of paying compliments to women. But I must say, that if all that has been said by orators and poets since the creation of the world in praise of women were applied to the women of America, it would not do them justice for their conduct during this war. I will close by saying, God bless the women of America!

Letter to A. G. Hodges, of Kentucky. April 4, 1864

I am naturally anti-slavery. If slavery is not wrong, nothing is wrong. I cannot remember when I did not so think and feel, and yet I have never understood that the Presidency conferred upon me an unrestricted right to act officially upon this judgment and feeling. It was in the oath that I took, that I would, to the best of my ability, preserve, protect, and defend the Constitution of the United States. I could not take office without taking the oath. Nor was it my view that I might take an oath to get power, and break the oath in using the power. I understood, too, that in ordinary civil administration this oath even forbade me to practically indulge my primary abstract judgment on the moral question of slavery. I had publicly declared this many times and in many ways. And I aver that, to this day, I have done no official act in mere deference to my abstract feeling and judgment on slavery. I did understand, however, that my oath to preserve the Constitution to the best of my ability imposed upon me the duty of preserving, by every indispensable means, that government – that nation – of which that Constitution was the organic law. Was it possible to lose the nation and yet preserve the Constitution? By general law, life and limb must be protected, yet often a limb must be amputated to save a life; but a life is never wisely given to save a limb. I felt that measures, otherwise unconstitutional, might become lawful by becoming indispensable to the preservation of the Constitution through the preservation of the nation. Right or wrong, I assumed this ground; and now avow it. I could not feel that, to the best of my ability, I had even tried to preserve the Constitution, if, to save slavery or any minor matter, I should permit the wreck of government, country, and Constitution, all together. When, early in the war, General Fremont attempted military emancipation, I forbade it, because I did not then think it an indispensable necessity. When, a little later, General Cameron, then Secretary of War, suggested the arming of the blacks, I objected, because I did not think it an indispensable necessity. When, still later, General Hunter attempted military emancipation, I again forbade it, because I did not yet think the indispensable necessity had come. When, in March and May and July, 1862, I made earnest and successive appeals to the border States to favour compensated emancipation, I believed the indispensable necessity for military emancipation and arming the blacks would come, unless averted by that measure. They declined the proposition, and I was, in my best judgment, driven to the alternative of either surrendering the Union, and with it the Constitution, or laying strong hand upon the coloured element. I chose the latter. In choosing it, I hoped for greater gain than loss; but of this I was not entirely confident. More than a year of trial now shows no loss by it in our foreign relations, none in our home popular sentiment, none in our white military force – no loss by it anyhow or anywhere. On the contrary, it shows a gain of quite one hundred and thirty thousand soldiers, seamen, and labourers. These are palpable facts, about which, as facts, there can be no cavilling. We have the men, and we could not have had them without the measure.

And now let any Union man who complains of the measure, test himself by writing down in one line that he is for subduing the rebellion by force of arms; and in the next, that he is for taking these hundred and thirty thousand men from the Union side, and placing them where they would be but for the measure he condemns. If he cannot face his case so stated, it is only because he cannot face the truth.

I add a word which was not in the verbal conversation. In telling this tale, I attempt no compliment to my own sagacity. I claim not to have controlled events, but confess plainly that events have controlled me. Now, at the end of three years' struggle, the nation's condition is not what either party, or any man, devised or expected. God alone can claim it. Whither it is tending seems plain. If God now wills the removal of a great wrong, and wills also that we of the North, as well as you of the South, shall pay fairly for our complicity in that wrong, impartial history will find therein new cause to attest and revere the justice and goodness of God.

From an Address at a Sanitary Fair in Baltimore. April 18, 1864

. . . The world has never had a good definition of the word 'liberty', and the American people, just now, are much in want of one. We all declare for liberty; but in using the same word, we do not all mean the same thing. With some, the word 'liberty' may mean for each man to do as he pleases with himself and the product of his labour; while with others, the same word may mean for some men to do as they please with other men and the product of other men's labour. Here are two, not only different, but incompatible things, called by the same name – liberty. And it follows that each of the things is, by the respective parties, called by two different and incompatible names – liberty and tyranny.

The shepherd drives the wolf from the sheep's throat, for which the sheep thanks the shepherd as his liberator, while the wolf denounces him for the same act as the destroyer of liberty, especially as the sheep was a black one. Plainly, the sheep and the wolf are not agreed upon a definition of the word 'liberty'; and precisely the same difference prevails today, among us human creatures, even in the North, and all professing to love liberty. Hence we behold the process by which thousands are daily passing from under the yoke of bondage hailed by some as the advance of liberty, and bewailed by others as the destruction of all liberty. Recently, as it seems, the people of Maryland have been doing something to define liberty, and thanks to them that, in what they have done, the wolf's dictionary has been repudiated.

Letter to General Grant. April 30, 1864

Not expecting to see you again before the spring campaign opens, I wish to express in this way my entire satisfaction with what you have done up to this time, so far as I understand it. The particulars of your plans I neither know nor seek to know. You are vigilant and self-reliant; and, pleased with this, I wish not to obtrude any constraints nor restraints upon you. While I am very anxious that any great disaster or capture of our men in great numbers shall be avoided, I know these points are less likely to escape your attention than they would be mine. If there is anything wanting which is within my power to give, do not fail to let me know it. And now, with a brave army and a just cause, may God sustain you.

From an Address to the 166th Ohio Regiment. August 22, 1864

I almost always feel inclined, when I happen to say anything to soldiers, to impress upon them, in a few brief remarks, the importance of success in this contest. It is not merely for today, but for all time to come, that we should perpetuate for our children's children that great and free government which we have enjoyed all our lives. I beg you to remember this, not merely for my sake, but for yours. I happen, temporarily, to occupy this White House. I am a living witness that any one of your children may look to come here as my father's child has. It is in order that each

one of you may have, through this free government which we
have enjoyed, an open field and a fair chance for your industry,
enterprise, and intelligence; that you may all have equal privileges
in the race of life, with all its desirable human aspirations. It is for
this the struggle should be maintained, that we may not lose our
birthright – not only for one, but for two or three years. The
nation is worth fighting for, to secure such an inestimable jewel.

Reply to a Serenade. November 10, 1864

It has long been a grave question whether any government not
too strong for the liberties of its people, can be strong enough
to maintain its existence in great emergencies. On this point
the present rebellion brought our Republic to a severe test; and
a presidential election, occurring in regular course during the
rebellion, added not a little to the strain.

If the loyal people united were put to the utmost of their
strength by the rebellion, must they not fail when divided and
partially paralyzed by a political war among themselves? But the
election was a necessity. We cannot have free government without
elections; and if the rebellion could force us to forego or postpone
a national election, it might fairly claim to have already conquered
and ruined us. The strife of the election is but human nature
practically applied to the facts of the case. What has occurred in
this case must ever occur in similar cases. Human nature will not
change. In any future great national trial, compared with the men
of this, we shall have as weak and as strong, as silly and as wise, as
bad and as good. Let us, therefore, study the incidents of this as
philosophy to learn wisdom from, and none of them as wrongs
to be revenged. But the election, along with its incidental and
undesirable strife, has done good too. It has demonstrated that a
people's government can sustain a national election in the midst of
a great civil war. Gold is good in its place, but living, brave,
patriotic men are better than gold.

But the rebellion continues; and now that the election is over,
may not all having a common interest reunite in a common effort
to save our common country? For my own part, I have striven and
shall strive to avoid placing any obstacle in the way. So long as I
have been here, I have not willingly planted a thorn in any man's

bosom. While I am deeply sensible to the high compliment of a re-election, and duly grateful as I trust to Almighty God for having directed my countrymen to a right conclusion, as I think, for their own good, it adds nothing to my satisfaction that any other man may be disappointed or pained by the result.

May I ask those who have not differed with me, to join with me in this same spirit towards those who have? And now let me close by asking three hearty cheers for our brave soldiers and seamen, and their gallant and skilful commanders.

A Letter to Mrs Bixley, of Boston. November 21, 1864

Dear Madam, I have been shown in the files of the War Department a statement of the Adjutant-General of Massachusetts that you are the mother of five sons who have died gloriously on the field of battle. I feel how weak and fruitless must be any words of mine which should attempt to beguile you from the grief of a loss so overwhelming. But I cannot refrain from tendering to you the consolation that may be found in the thanks of the Republic they died to save. I pray that our heavenly Father may assuage the anguish of your bereavement, and leave you only the cherished memory of the loved and lost, and the solemn pride that must be yours to have laid so costly a sacrifice upon the altar of freedom.

Yours very sincerely and respectfully,

ABRAHAM LINCOLN

Letter to General Grant. Washington. January 19, 1865

Please read and answer this letter as though I was not President, but only a friend. My son, now in his twenty-second year, having graduated at Harvard, wishes to see something of the war before it ends. I do not wish to put him in the ranks, nor yet to give him a commission, to which those who have already served long are better entitled, and better qualified to hold. Could he, without embarrassment to you or detriment to the service, go into your military family with some nominal rank, I, and not the public, furnishing his necessary means? If no, say so without the least hesitation, because I am as anxious and as deeply interested that you shall not be encumbered as you can be yourself.

The Second Inaugural Address. March 4, 1865

Fellow-countrymen, At this second appearance to take the oath of the Presidential office, there is less occasion for an extended address than there was at the first. Then a statement, somewhat in detail, of a course to be pursued, seemed fitting and proper. Now, at the expiration of four years, during which public declarations have been constantly called forth on every point and phase of the great contest which still absorbs the attention and engrosses the energies of the nation, little that is new could be presented. The progress of our arms, upon which all else chiefly depends, is as well known to the public as to myself; and it is, I trust, reasonably satisfactory and encouraging to all. With high hope for the future, no prediction in regard to it is ventured.

On the occasion corresponding to this four years ago, all thoughts were anxiously directed to an impending civil war. All dreaded it – all sought to avert it. While the inaugural address was being delivered from this place, devoted altogether to saving the Union without war, insurgent agents were in the city seeking to destroy it without war – seeking to dissolve the Union, and divide effects, by negotiation. Both parties deprecated war; but one of them would make war rather than let the nation survive, and the other would accept war rather than let it perish. And the war came.

One-eighth of the whole population were coloured slaves, not distributed generally over the Union, but localized in the southern part of it. These slaves constituted a peculiar and powerful interest. All knew that this interest was, somehow, the cause of the war. To strengthen, perpetuate, and extend this interest was the object for which the insurgents would rend the Union, even by war; while the government claimed no right to do more than to restrict the territorial enlargement of it. . . .

With malice toward none; with charity for all; with firmness in the right, as God gives us to see the right – let us strive on to finish the work we are in: to bind up the nation's wounds; to care for him who shall have borne the battle, and for his widow and his orphan; to do all which may achieve and cherish a just and lasting peace among ourselves, and with all nations.

*A Letter to Thurlow Weed. Executive Mansion, Washington.
March 15, 1865*

Dear Mr Weed, Every one likes a compliment. Thank you for yours on my little notification speech and on the recent inaugural address. I expect the latter to wear as well as – perhaps better than – anything I have produced; but I believe it is not immediately popular. Men are not flattered by being shown that there has been a difference of purpose between the Almighty and them. To deny it, however, in this case, is to deny that there is a God governing the world. It is a truth which I thought needed to be told, and, as whatever of humiliation there is in it falls most directly on myself, I thought others might afford for me to tell it.

Truly yours,

A. LINCOLN

From an Address to an Indiana Regiment. March 17, 1865

There are but few aspects of this great war on which I have not already expressed my views by speaking or writing. There is one – the recent effort of 'Our erring brethren', sometimes so called, to employ the slaves in their armies. The great question with them has been, 'Will the negro fight for them?' They ought to know better than we, and doubtless do know better than we. I may incidentally remark, that having in my life heard many arguments – or strings of words meant to pass for arguments – intended to show that the negro ought to be a slave – if he shall now really fight to keep himself a slave, it will be a far better argument why he should remain a slave than I have ever before heard. He, perhaps, ought to be a slave if he desires it ardently enough to fight for it. Or, if one out of four will for his own freedom fight to keep the other three in slavery, he ought to be a slave for his selfish meanness. I have always thought that all men should be free; but if any should be slaves, it should be first those who desire it for themselves, and secondly those who desire it for others. Whenever I hear anyone arguing for slavery, I feel a strong impulse to see it tried on him personally.

From his Reply to a Serenade. Lincoln's Last Public Address.
April 11, 1865

Fellow-citizens, We meet this evening, not in sorrow but in glad-ness of heart. The evacuation of Richmond and Petersburg, and the surrender of the principal insurgent army, give the hope of a just and speedy peace, the joyous expression of which cannot be restrained. In all this joy, however, He from whom all blessings flow must not be forgotten. A call for a national thanksgiving is in the course of preparation, and will be duly promulgated. Nor must those whose harder part give us the cause for rejoicing be over-looked. Their honours must not be parcelled out with others. I, myself, was near the front, and had the high pleasure of trans-mitting much of the good news to you; but no part of the honour for plan or execution is mine. To General Grant, his skilful officers and brave men, all belongs. The gallant navy stood ready, but was not in reach to take an active part.

By these recent successes the reinauguration of the national authority − reconstruction − which has had a large share of thought from the first, is pressed much more closely upon our attention. It is fraught with great difficulty. Unlike a case of war between independent nations, there is no organized organ for us to treat with − no one man has authority to give up the rebellion for any other man. We simply must begin with and mould from disorganized and discordant elements. Nor is it a small additional embarrassment that we, the loyal people, differ among ourselves as to the mode, manner, and measure of reconstruction. As a general rule I abstain from reading the reports of attacks upon myself, wishing not to be provoked by that to which I cannot properly offer an answer. In spite of this precaution, however, it comes to my knowledge that I am much censured for some supposed agency in setting up and seeking to sustain the new State government of Louisiana.

In this I have done just so much as, and no more than, the public knows. In the annual message of December 1863, and in the accompanying proclamation, I presented a plan of reconstruction, as the phrase goes, which I promised, if adopted by any State, should be acceptable to and sustained by the executive govern-ment of the nation. I distinctly stated that this was not the only plan which might possibly be acceptable, and I also distinctly protested that the executive claimed no right to say when or whether members should be admitted to seats in Congress from such States. This plan was in advance submitted to the then Cabinet, and approved by every member of it. . . .

When the message of 1863, with the plan before mentioned, reached New Orleans, General Banks wrote me that he was confident that the people, with his military co-operation, would reconstruct substantially on that plan. I wrote him and some of them to try it. They tried it, and the result is known. Such has been my only agency in getting up the Louisiana government. As to sustaining it, my promise is out, as before stated. But as bad promises are better broken than kept, I shall treat this as a bad promise and break it, whenever I shall be convinced that keeping it is adverse to the public interest; but I have not yet been so convinced. I have been shown a letter on this subject, supposed to be an able one, in which the writer expresses regret that my mind has not seemed to be definitely fixed upon the question whether the seceded States, so called, are in the Union or out of it. It would perhaps add astonishment to his regret were he to learn that since I have found professed Union men endeavouring to answer that question, I have purposely forborne any public expression upon it. . . .

We all agree that the seceded States, so called, are out of their proper practical relation with the Union, and that the sole object of the government, civil and military, in regard to those States, is to again get them into that proper practical relation. I believe that it is not only possible, but in fact easier, to do this without deciding or even considering whether these States have ever been out of the Union, than with it. Finding themselves safely at home, it would be utterly immaterial whether they had ever been abroad. Let us all join in doing the acts necessary to restoring the proper practical relations between these States and the Union, and each for ever after innocently indulge his own opinion whether in doing the acts he brought the States from without into the Union, or only gave them proper assistance, they never having been out of it. The amount of constituency, so to speak, on which the new Louisiana government rests, would be more satisfactory to all if it contained forty thousand, or thirty thousand, or even twenty thousand, instead of only about twelve thousand as it does. It is also unsatisfactory to some that the elective franchise is not given to the coloured man. I would myself prefer that it were now conferred on the very intelligent, and on those who serve our cause as soldiers.

Still, the question is not whether the Louisiana government, as it stands, is quite all that is desirable. The question is, will it be wiser to take it as it is and help to improve it, or to reject and disperse it? Can Louisiana be brought into proper practical relation with the Union sooner by sustaining or by discarding her new State government? Some twelve thousand voters in the heretofore slave State of Louisiana have sworn allegiance to the Union, assumed to be the rightful political power of the State, held elections, organized a State government, adopted a free-State constitution, giving the benefit of public schools equally to black and white, and empowering the legislature to confer the elective franchise upon the coloured man. Their legislature has already voted to ratify the constitutional amendment recently passed by Congress, abolishing slavery throughout the nation. These twelve thousand persons are thus fully committed to the Union and to perpetual freedom in the State – committed to the very things, and nearly all the things, the nation wants – and they ask the nation's recognition and its assistance to make good their committal.

If we reject and spurn them, we do our utmost to disorganize and disperse them. We, in effect, say to the white man: You are worthless or worse; we will neither help you, nor be helped by you. To the blacks, we say: This cup of liberty, which these, your old masters, hold to your lips, we will dash from you, and leave you to the chances of gathering the spilled and scattered contents in some vague and undefined when, where, and how. If this course, discouraging and paralyzing both white and black, has any tendency to bring Louisiana into proper, practical relations with the Union, I have so far been unable to perceive it. If, on the contrary, we recognize and sustain the new government of Louisiana, the converse of all this is made true. We encourage the hearts and nerve the arms of twelve thousand to adhere to their work, and argue for it, and proselyte for it, and fight for it, and feed it, and grow it, and ripen it to a complete success. The coloured man, too, in seeing all united for him, is inspired with vigilance, and energy, and daring to the same end. Grant that he desires the elective franchise, will he not attain it sooner by saving the already advanced steps towards it, than by running backward over them?

. . . I repeat the question, Can Louisiana be brought into proper practical relation with the Union sooner by sustaining or by discarding her new State government?

. . . What has been said of Louisiana will apply generally to other States. And yet so great peculiarities pertain to each State, and such important and sudden changes occur in the same State, and withal so new and unprecedented is the whole case, that no exclusive and inflexible plan can safely be prescribed as to details and collaterals. Such exclusive and inflexible plan would surely become a new entanglement. Important principles may and must be inflexible. In the present situation, as the phrase goes, it may be my duty to make some new announcement to the people of the South. I am considering, and shall not fail to act when satisfied that action will be proper.

APPENDIX
Anecdotes

LINCOLN'S ENTRY INTO RICHMOND THE DAY AFTER IT WAS TAKEN
As Described at that time by a Writer in the Atlantic Monthly

They gathered around the President, ran ahead, hovered about the flanks of the little company, and hung like a dark cloud upon the rear. Men, women and children joined the constantly-increasing throng. They came from all the by-streets, running in breathless haste, shouting and hallooing, and dancing with delight. The men threw up their hats, the women waved their bonnets and handkerchiefs, clapped their hands, and sang, 'Glory to God! Glory, glory!' rendering all the praise to God, who had heard their wailings in the past, their moanings for wives, husbands, children, and friends sold out of their sight; had given them freedom, and after long years of waiting had permitted them thus unexpectedly to behold the face of their great benefactor.

'I thank you, dear Jesus, that I behold President Linkum!' was the exclamation of a woman who stood upon the threshold of her humble home, and with streaming eyes and clasped hands gave thanks aloud to the Saviour of men.

Another, more demonstrative in her joy, was jumping and striking her hands with all her might, crying, 'Bless de Lord! Bless de Lord! Bless de Lord!' as if there could be no end to her thanksgiving.

The air rang with a tumultuous chorus of voices. The street became almost impassable on account of the increasing multitude, till soldiers were summoned to clear the way. . . .

The walk was long, and the President halted a moment to rest. 'May de good Lord bless you, President Linkum!' said an old negro, removing his hat and bowing, with tears of joy rolling down his cheeks. The President removed his own hat, and bowed in silence; but it was a bow which upset the forms, laws, customs,

and ceremonies of centuries. It was a death-shock to chivalry and a
mortal wound to caste. 'Recognize a nigger! Fough!' A woman in
an adjoining house beheld it, and turned from the scene in
unspeakable disgust.

[The following nine anecdotes were related by Frank B. Carpenter, the painter, who, while executing his picture of the first
reading in cabinet council of the Emancipation Proclamation,
had the freedom of Mr Lincoln's private office and saw much of
the President while he posed, and whose relations with him
became of an intimate character.]

'YOU DON'T WEAR HOOPS – AND I WILL . . . PARDON YOUR BROTHER'

A distinguished citizen of Ohio had an appointment with the
President one evening at six o'clock. As he entered the vestibule
of the White House, his attention was attracted by a poorly-clad
young woman who was violently sobbing. He asked her the cause
of her distress. She said she had been ordered away by the servants
after vainly waiting many hours to see the President about her only
brother, who had been condemned to death. Her story was this –
She and her brother were foreigners, and orphans. They had been in
this country several years. Her brother enlisted in the army, but,
through bad influences, was induced to desert. He was captured,
tried and sentenced to be shot – the old story. The poor girl had
obtained the signatures of some persons who had formerly known
him, to a petition for a pardon, and alone had come to Washington
to lay the case before the President. Thronged as the waiting-rooms
always were, she had passed the long hours of two days trying in
vain to get an audience, and had at length been ordered away.

The gentleman's feelings were touched. He said to her that he
had come to see the President, but did not know as *he* should
succeed. He told her, however, to follow him upstairs, and he
would see what could be done for her. Just before reaching the
door, Mr Lincoln came out, and meeting his friend said good-
humouredly, 'Are you not ahead of time?' The gentleman showed
him his watch, with the hand upon the hour of six. 'Well,' returned
Mr Lincoln, 'I have been so busy today that I have not had time to
get a lunch. Go in, and sit down; I will be back directly.'

The gentleman made the young woman accompany him into the office, and, when they were seated, said to her, 'Now, my good girl, I want you to muster all the courage you have in the world. When the President comes back, he will sit down in that armchair. I shall get up to speak to him, and as I do so you must force yourself between us, and insist upon the examination of your papers, telling him it is a case of life and death, and admits of no delay.' These instructions were carried out to the letter. Mr Lincoln was at first somewhat surprised at the apparent forwardness of the young woman, but observing her distressed appearance, he ceased conversation with his friend, and commenced an examination of the document she had placed in his hands. Glancing from it to the face of the petitioner, whose tears had broken forth afresh, he studied its expression for a moment, and then his eye fell upon her scanty but neat dress. Instantly his face lighted up. 'My poor girl,' said he, 'you have come here with no governor, or senator, or member of Congress, to plead your cause. You seem honest and truthful; *and you don't wear hoops* – and I will be whipped but I will pardon your brother.'

HIS JOY IN GIVING A PARDON

One night Schuyler Colfax left all other business to ask him to respite the son of a constituent, who was sentenced to be shot, at Davenport, for desertion. He heard the story with his usual patience, though he was wearied out with incessant calls, and anxious for rest, and then replied – 'Some of our generals complain that I impair discipline and subordination in the army by my pardons and respites, but it makes me rested, after a hard day's work, if I can find some good excuse for saving a man's life, and I go to bed happy as I think how joyous the signing of my name will make him and his family and his friends.' And with a happy smile beaming over that care-furrowed face, he signed that name that saved that life.

HIS SIMPLICITY AND UNOSTENTATIOUSNESS

The simplicity and absence of all ostentation on the part of Mr Lincoln, is well illustrated by an incident which occurred on the occasion of a visit he made to Commodore Porter, at Fortress

Monroe. Noticing that the banks of the river were dotted with flowers, he said: 'Commodore, Tad (the pet name for his youngest son, who had accompanied him on the excursion) is very fond of flowers; won't you let a couple of men take a boat and go with him for an hour or two, along the banks of the river, and gather the flowers?' Look at this picture, and then endeavour to imagine the head of a European nation making a similar request, in this humble way, of one of his subordinates!

A PENITENT MAN CAN BE PARDONED

One day I took a couple of friends from New York upstairs, who wished to be introduced to the President. It was after the hour for business calls, and we found him alone, and, for *once*, at leisure. Soon after the introduction, one of my friends took occasion to indorse, very decidedly, the President's Amnesty Proclamation, which had been severely censured by many friends of the Administration. Mr S—'s approval touched Mr Lincoln. He said, with a great deal of emphasis, and with an expression of countenance I shall never forget: 'When a man is sincerely *penitent* for his misdeeds, and gives satisfactory evidence of the same, he can safely be pardoned, and there is no exception to the rule!'

'KEEP SILENCE, AND WE'LL GET YOU SAFE ACROSS'

At the White House one day some gentlemen were present from the West, excited and troubled about the commissions and omissions of the Administration. The President heard them patiently, and then replied: 'Gentlemen, suppose all the property you were worth was in gold, and you had put it in the hands of Blondin to carry across the Niagara River on a rope, would you shake the cable, or keep shouting out to him, "Blondin, stand up a little straighter – Blondin, stoop a little more – go a little faster – lean a little more to the north – lean a little more to the south?" No, you would hold your breath as well as your tongue, and keep your hands off until he was safe over. The Government are carrying an immense weight. Untold treasures are in their hands. They are doing the very best they can. Don't badger them. Keep silence, and we'll get you safe across.'

REBUFF TO A MAN WITH A SMALL CLAIM

During a public 'reception', a farmer, from one of the border counties of Virginia, told the President that the Union soldiers, in passing his farm, had helped themselves not only to hay, but his horse, and he hoped the President would urge the proper officer to consider his claim immediately.

Mr Lincoln said that this reminded him of an old acquaintance of his, 'Jack Chase', who used to be a lumberman on the Illinois, a steady, sober man, and the best raftsman on the river. It was quite a trick, twenty-five years ago, to take the logs over the rapids; but he was skilful with a raft, and always kept her straight in the channel. Finally a steamer was put on, and Jack was made captain of her. He always used to take the wheel going through the rapids. One day when the boat was plunging and wallowing along the boiling current, and Jack's utmost vigilance was being exercised to keep her in the narrow channel, a boy pulled his coat-tail, and hailed him with: 'Say, Mister Captain! I wish you would just stop your boat a minute – I've lost my apple overboard!'

THE PRESIDENT'S SILENCE OVER CRITICISMS

The President was once speaking about an attack made on him by the Committee on the Conduct of the War for a certain alleged blunder, or something worse, in the South-west – the matter involved being one which had fallen directly under the observation of the officer to whom he was talking, who possessed official evidence completely upsetting all the conclusions of the Committee.

'Might it not be well for me,' queried the officer, 'to set this matter right in a letter to some paper, stating the facts as they actually transpired?'

'Oh, no,' replied the President, 'at least, not now. If I were to try to read, much less answer, all the attacks made on me, this shop might as well be closed for any other business. I do the very best I know how – the very best I can; and I mean to keep doing so until the end. If the end brings me out all right, what is said against me won't amount to anything. If the end brings me out wrong, ten angels swearing I was right would make no difference.'

'GLAD OF IT'

On the occasion when the telegram from Cumberland Gap reached Mr Lincoln that 'firing was heard in the direction of Knoxville', he remarked that he was 'glad of it'. Some person present, who had the perils of Burnside's position uppermost in his mind, could not see *why* Mr Lincoln should be *glad* of it, and so expressed himself. 'Why, you see,' responded the President, 'it reminds me of Mistress Sallie Ward, a neighbour of mine, who had a very large family. Occasionally one of her numerous progeny would be heard crying in some out-of-the-way place, upon which Mrs Ward would exclaim, "There's one of my children that isn't dead yet!"'

HIS DEMOCRATIC BEARING

The evening before I left Washington an incident occurred, illustrating very perfectly the character of the man. For two days my large painting had been on exhibition, upon its completion, in the East Room, which had been thronged with visitors. Late in the afternoon of the second day, the 'black-horse cavalry' escort drew up as usual in front of the portico, preparatory to the President's leaving for the 'Soldiers' Home', where he spent the midsummer nights. While the carriage was waiting, I looked around for him, wishing to say a farewell word, knowing that I should have no other opportunity. Presently I saw him standing halfway between the portico and the gateway leading to the War Department, leaning against the iron fence – one arm thrown over the railing, and one foot on the stone coping which supports it, evidently having been intercepted, on his way in from the War Department, by a plain-looking man, who was giving him, very diffidently, an account of a difficulty which he had been unable to have rectified. While waiting, I walked out leisurely to the President's side. He said very little to the man, but was intently studying the expression of his face while he was narrating his trouble. When he had finished, Mr Lincoln said to him, 'Have you a blank card?' The man searched his pockets, but finding none, a gentleman standing near, who had overheard the question, came forward, and said, 'Here is one, Mr President.' Several persons had, in the meantime, gathered around. Taking the card and a pencil, Mr Lincoln sat down upon the stone coping, which is not more than five or six inches above the pavement, presenting almost the appearance of sitting upon the pavement itself, and wrote an order upon the card to the proper official to 'examine this man's case'. While writing this, I observed several persons passing down the promenade, smiling at each other, at what I presume they thought the undignified appearance of the Head of the Nation, who, however, seemed utterly unconscious, either of any impropriety in the action, or of attracting any attention. To me it was not only a touching picture of the native goodness of the man, but of innate nobility of character, exemplified not so much by a disregard of conventionalities, as in unconsciousness that there *could* be any breach of etiquette, or dignity, in the manner of an honest attempt to serve, or secure justice to a citizen of the Republic, however humble he may be.